IARIA

AA004357

SECURWARE 2025

The Nineteenth International Conference on Emerging Security Information, Systems and Technologies

October 26th - 30th, 2025

Barcelona, Spain

SECURWARE 2025 Editors

Alexander Lawall, IU International University of Applied Science, Germany

Fan Wu, Tuskegee University, USA

Printed from e-media with permission by:

Curran Associates, Inc.
57 Morehouse Lane
Red Hook, NY 12571

Some format issues inherent in the e-media version may also appear in this print version.

International Academy, Research, and Industry Association (IARIA)
412 Derby Way
Wilmington, DE 19810

Phone: (408) 893-6407
Fax: (408) 527-6351

petre@iaria.org

Additional copies of this publication are available from:

Curran Associates, Inc.
57 Morehouse Lane
Red Hook, NY 12571 USA
Phone: 845-758-0400
Fax: 845-758-2633
Email: curran@proceedings.com
Web: www.proceedings.com

Table of Contents

SECURWARE 2025

Forward

The Nineteenth International Conference on Emerging Security Information, Systems and Technologies (SECURWARE 2025), held between October 26th, 2025, and October 30th, 2025, in Barcelona, Spain, continued a series of events covering related topics on theory and practice on security, cryptography, secure protocols, trust, privacy, confidentiality, vulnerability, intrusion detection and other areas related to law enforcement, security data mining, malware models, etc.

Security, defined for ensuring protected communication among terminals and user applications across public and private networks, is the core for guaranteeing confidentiality, privacy, and data protection. Security affects business and individuals, raises the business risk, and requires a corporate and individual culture. In the open business space offered by Internet, it is a need to improve defenses against hackers, disgruntled employees, and commercial rivals. There is a required balance between the effort and resources spent on security versus security achievements. Some vulnerability can be addressed using the rule of 80:20, meaning 80% of the vulnerability can be addressed for 20% of the cost. Other technical aspects are related to the communication speed versus complex and time-consuming cryptography/security mechanisms and protocols.

A Digital Ecosystem is defined as an open decentralized information infrastructure where different networked agents, such as enterprises (especially SMEs), intermediate actors, public bodies and end users, cooperate and compete enabling the creation of new complex structures. In digital ecosystems, the actors, their products and services can be seen as different organisms and species that are able to evolve and adapt dynamically to changing market conditions.

Digital Ecosystems lie at the intersection between different disciplines and fields: industry, business, social sciences, biology, and cutting-edge ICT and its application driven research. They are supported by several underlying technologies such as semantic web and ontology-based knowledge sharing, self-organizing intelligent agents, peer-to-peer overlay networks, web services-based information platforms, and recommender systems.

To enable safe digital ecosystem functioning, security and trust mechanisms become essential components across all the technological layers. The aim is to bring together multidisciplinary research that ranges from technical aspects to socio-economic models.

We take the opportunity to warmly thank all the members of the SECURWARE 2025 technical program committee, as well as all the reviewers. The creation of such a high-quality conference program would not have been possible without their involvement. We also kindly thank all the authors who dedicated much of their time and effort to contribute to SECURWARE 2025. We truly believe that, thanks to all these efforts, the final conference program consisted of top-quality contributions. We also thank the members of the SECURWARE 2025 organizing committee for their help in handling the logistics of this event.

We hope that SECURWARE 2025 was a successful international forum for the exchange of ideas and results between academia and industry for the promotion of progress in the field of security information, systems, and technologies.

SECURWARE 2025 Chairs

SECURWARE 2025 Steering Committee
Steffen Fries, Siemens, Germany
Rainer Falk, Siemens AG, Corporate Technology, Germany
George O. M. Yee, Aptusinnova Inc. / Carleton University, Ottawa, Canada
Hans-Joachim Hof, INSicherheit - Ingolstadt Research Group Applied IT Security, CARISSMA – Center of Automotive Research on Integrated Safety Syst, Germany
Ki-Woong Park, Sejong University, South Korea
Alexander Lawall, IU International University of Applied Science, Germany

SECURWARE 2025 Publicity Chairs
Lorena Parra Boronat, Universidad Politécnica de Madrid, Spain
Laura Garcia, Universidad Politécnica de Cartagena, Spain

SECURWARE 2025
Committee

SECURWARE 2025 Steering Committee

Steffen Fries, Siemens, Germany
Rainer Falk, Siemens AG, Corporate Technology, Germany
George O. M. Yee, Aptusinnova Inc. / Carleton University, Ottawa, Canada
Hans-Joachim Hof, INSicherheit - Ingolstadt Research Group Applied IT Security, CARISSMA – Center of Automotive Research on Integrated Safety Syst, Germany
Ki-Woong Park, Sejong University, South Korea
Alexander Lawall, IU International University of Applied Science, Germany

SECURWARE 2025 Publicity Chairs

Lorena Parra Boronat, Universidad Politécnica de Madrid, Spain
Laura Garcia, Universidad Politécnica de Cartagena, Spain

SECURWARE 2025 Technical Program Committee

Aysajan Abidin, imec-COSIC KU Leuven, Belgium
Abbas Acar, Florida International University, Miami, USA
Afrand Agah, West Chester University of Pennsylvania, USA
Chuadhry Mujeeb Ahmed, University of Strathclyde, UK
Md Mojibur Rahman Redoy Akanda, Texas A&M University, College Station, USA
Sedat Akleylek, University of Tartu, Estonia
Oum-El-Kheir Aktouf, Greboble INP | LCIS Lab, France
Mamoun Alazab, Charles Darwin University, Australia
Asif Ali laghari, SMIU, Karachi, Pakistan
Luca Allodi, Eindhoven University of Technology, Netherlands
Robert Altschaffel, Institut für Technische und Betriebliche Informationssysteme | Otto-von-Guericke-Universität Magdeburg, Germany
Eric Amankwa, Presbyterian University College, Ghana
Prashant Anantharaman, Dartmouth College, USA
Mohammadreza Ashouri, Virginia Tech, USA
Alexandre Augusto Giron, Federal University of Technology - Parana, Brazil
Ilija Basicevic, University of Novi Sad, Serbia
Luke A. Bauer, University of Florida, USA
Malek Ben Salem, Accenture, USA
Smriti Bhatt, Purdue University, USA
Catalin Bîrjoveanu, "Al. I. Cuza" University of Iasi, Romania
Malte Breuer, RWTH Aachen University, Germany
Robert Brotzman, Pennsylvania State University, USA
Francesco Buccafurri, University Mediterranea of Reggio Calabria, Italy
Arun Balaji Buduru, IIIT-Delhi, India
Enrico Cambiaso, Consiglio Nazionale delle Ricerche (CNR) - IEIIT Institute, Italy

Hugo Jonker, Open Universiteit, Netherlands
Taeho Jung, University of Notre Dame, USA
Kaushal Kafle, William & Mary, USA
Sarang Kahvazadeh, Centre Tecnològic de Telecomunicacions de Catalunya (CTTC), Spain
Harsha K. Kalutarage, Robert Gordon University, UK
Georgios Kambourakis, University of the Aegean, Greece
Mehdi Karimi, The University of British Columbia, Vancouver, Canada
Georgios Karopoulos, European Commission JRC, Italy
Sokratis K. Katsikas, Norwegian University of Science and Technology, Norway
Basel Katt, Norwegian University of Science and Technology, Norway
Joakim Kävrestad, University of Skövde, Sweden
Hyunsung Kim, Kyungil University, Korea
Paris Kitsos, University of the Peloponnese, Greece
Meret Kristen, OTH Regensburg, Germany
Harsha Kumara, Robert Gordon University, UK
Hiroki Kuzuno, SECOM Co. Ltd., Japan
Hyun Kwon, Korea Military Academy, Korea
Romain Laborde, University Paul Sabatier Toulouse III, France
Cecilia Labrini, University of Reggio Calabria, Italy
Nada Lahjouji, University of California, Irvine, USA
Yosra Lakhdhar, SUP'COM / Digital Research Centre of Sfax, Tunisia
Vianney Lapôtre, Université Bretagne Sud, France
Martin Latzenhofer, AIT Austrian Institute of Technology | Center for Digital Safety and Security, Vienna, Austria
Alexander Lawall, IU International University of Applied Science, Germany
Wen-Chuan Lee, Apple Inc., USA
Ferenc Leitold, University of Dunaújváros, Hungary
Albert Levi, Sabanci University, Istanbul, Turkey
Shimin Li, Winona State University, USA
Wenjuan Li, The Hong Kong Polytechnic University, China
Zhihao Li, Meta Platform Inc., USA
Stefan Lindskog, SINTEF Digital, Norway / Karlstad University, Sweden
Shaohui Liu, School of Computer Science and Technology | Harbin Institute of Technology, China
Shen Liu, NVIDIA, USA
Yi Liu, University of Massachusetts Dartmouth, USA
Giovanni Livraga, Universita' degli Studi di Milano, Italy
George Lord, University of Chicago, USA
Jakob Löw, Technische Hochschule Ingolstadt, Germany
Giuseppe Loseto, LUM "Giuseppe Degennaro" University, Italy
Flaminia Luccio, University Ca' Foscari of Venice, Italy
Duohe Ma, Institute of Information Engineering | Chinese Academy of Sciences, China
Rabi N. Mahapatra, Texas A&M University, USA
Mahdi Manavi, Mirdamad Institute of Higher Education, Iran
Anuradha Mandal, University of Arizona, USA
Michele Mastroianni, University of Salerno, Italy
Wojciech Mazurczyk, Warsaw University of Technology, Poland
Weizhi Meng, Lancaster University, UK
Ulrike Meyer, RWTH Aachen University, Germany

Amit Kumar Sikder, Georgia Institute of Technology, USA
Christian Skalka, University of Vermont, USA
Rocky Slavin, University of Texas at San Antonio, USA
Christoph Stach, University of Stuttgart, Germany
Dean Sullivan, University of New Hampshire, USA
Shi-Feng Sun, Shanghai Jiao Tong University, China
Zhibo Sun, Drexel University, USA
Sheng Tan, Trinity University, USA
Kunsheng Tang, University of Science and Technology of China, China
Michael Tempelmeier, Giesecke+Devrient, Germany
Scott Trent, IBM Research - Tokyo, Japan
Yazhou Tu, University of Louisiana at Lafayette, USA
Vincent Urias, Sandia National Labs, USA
Sokratis Vavilis, Inlecom Innovation, Greece
Andreas Veneris, University of Toronto, Canada
Andrea Visconti, Università degli Studi di Milano, Italy
Qi Wang, University of Illinois Urbana-Champaign / Stellar Cyber Inc., USA
Shu Wang, George Mason University, USA
Wenhao Wang, Institute of Information Engineering | Chinese Academy of Sciences, China
Wenqi Wei, Georgia Institute of Technology, USA
Ian Welch, Victoria University of Wellington, New Zealand
Zhonghao Wu, Shanghai Jiao Tong University, China
Ehsan Yaghoubi, University of Beira Interior, Portugal
Muhammet Anıl Yağız, Kırıkkale University, Türkiye
Limin Yang, University of Illinois at Urbana-Champaign, USA
Ping Yang, Binghamton University, USA
Wun-She Yap, Universiti Tunku Abdul Rahman, Malaysia
Qussai M. Yaseen, Jordan University of Science and Technology, Irbid, Jordan
George O. M. Yee, Aptusinnova Inc. / Carleton University, Ottawa, Canada
Amr Youssef, Concordia University, Montreal, Canada
Chia-Mu Yu, National Yang Ming Chiao Tung University, Taiwan
Wei Yu, Institute of Information Engineering | Chinese Academy of Sciences, China
Thomas Zefferer, Secure Information Technology Center Austria (A-SIT), Austria
Dongrui Zeng, Palo Alto Networks, Santa Clara, USA
Penghui Zhang, Meta Platforms Inc., USA
Tianwei Zhang, Nanyang Technological University, Singapore
Yubao Zhang, Palo Alto Networks, USA
Yue Zheng, Nanyang Technological University, Singapore
Huadi Zhu, Georgia State University, USA
Tommaso Zoppi, University of Florence, Italy

Copyright Information

Optimizing Certificate Validation in OT Environments

Steffen Fries*, Rainer Falk*, Andreas Guettinger+
Foundational Technologies*; Smart Infrastructure+
Siemens AG, Germany
e-mail: { steffen.fries | rainer.falk | andreas.guettinger }@siemens.com

Abstract—**User authentication based on digital certificates is becoming more and more common in industrial environments, also known as Operational Technology (OT). Users may be both human users, as well as technical users like devices or applications. Common to all types of certificate-based authentication is that a certificate must be validated before trusting it. This poses a significant effort on the involved devices concerning compute power, memory, and the complexity of the required validation logic. Different approaches already exist to offload certificate validation from specifically constrained end entities. To increase overall efficiency even more, this paper proposes an optimization for infrastructures supporting offloading certificate validation.**

Keywords–cybersecurity; credential; digital certificate; public-key infrastructure; device authentication, industrial security; power system automation.

I. INTRODUCTION

User authentication in Operational Technology (OT), including critical infrastructures is increasingly achieved involving X.509 [1] certificates and corresponding private keys as authentication and authorization credentials. Users in this context may be human users, but also technical users like devices or applications. Examples for critical infrastructures are power system automation systems, spanning from centralized power generation up to increasingly deployed Distributed Energy Resources (DER). Further examples are industrial automation or intelligent traffic systems. Utilized credentials are typically managed by a so-called Public-key Infrastructure (PKI) following well-defined operational processes involving Identity and Access Management (IAM) to ensure proper authorization of certificate issuance.

X.509 certificates are prominently used in several security protocols to support secure communication between different entities. Most commonly, Transport Layer Security (TLS, version 1.2 [2] is still widely used, version 1.3 [3] application is increasing) is applied to protect TCP/IP-based communication, or the complementary Datagram Transport Layer Security (DTLS) [4] for the protection of UDP/IP communication. They employ certificates in the handshake for peer authentication and to negotiate security parameters of the intended communication session. Specifically, TLS is used in different industrial environments to protect domain-specific communication protocols. An example from power system automation is to secure IEC 61850 [5], specified in the IEC 62351 series [6]. A further example from the industrial automation domain is OPC-UA [7], which supports TLS as underlying security protocol.

Even though certificates are issued by Certification Authorities (CA), part of a PKI following procedural security requirements and policies, they need to be validated by a relying party, before accepting the certificates to establish trusted communication, or before accepting signed information received from a sender. Certificate validation can be a time and performance consuming process, as it includes the verification of the certificate itself but also the verification along the certification path up to a common trust anchor (root certificate). This effort becomes amplified when Post-Quantum Cryptography (PQC) is used for X.509 certificates (see also [8]). This is caused by the much larger key sizes for public-keys for some of the post-quantum cryptographic algorithms, which may turn out to be a problem when employed on constrained devices. The certification validation policies may become complex and even operator-specific during the transition phase towards PQC if classical and PQC algorithms are used in combination.

This paper provides insight into typically used certificate validation approaches and proposes a novel approach to keep the effort for the validation of the relying party certificate overall as low as possible. This optimization targets operational infrastructures using constrained devices, which may either not have enough processing power or memory to perform the validation locally or devices in environments, or which do not have access to information from other sources required in the validation procedure. It utilizes available technology but provides an enhancement to also limit the burden on the infrastructure.

The remainder of this industrial research paper is structured as follows. Section II introduces certificates and already known approaches for their validation. Section III introduces an optimization concept of certificate validation services, to allow a relying party to determine trustworthiness in the received certificate more efficiently. Section IV concludes the paper and gives an outlook towards future work.

II. RELATED TECHNOLOGY

This section provides an overview of X.509 certificates, their structure and validation options. Specifically discussed is the potential offloading of certificate validation tasks (partially or completely) from an end entity to a supporting infrastructure or communication peer to save memory, time, and processing power. Moreover, local caching of revocation information is further considered, as it is already applied in today's communication infrastructures.

A. *Public-key Certificates – Structure and Validation*

As stated before, ITU-T X.509 [1] certificates are used for different purposes like entity authentication, e.g., in the context of key establishment in security protocols like TLS or DTLS, or to provide authenticity and integrity-protection of data, e.g., for firmware or software updates. Figure 1 shows the general concept of a public-key certificate, the binding of the user identity to the corresponding public-key. The user possesses also the corresponding private key, which is kept secret and is used to provide proof-of-possession, which can be verified by the relying party based on the certificate.

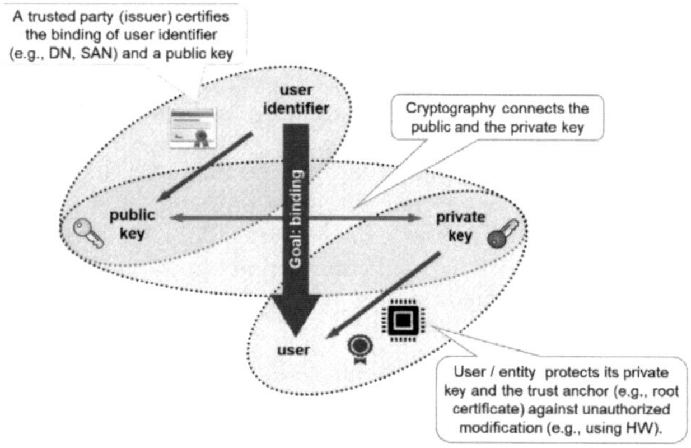

Figure 1. Concept of Binding Public-keys to User Identities [8]

The certificate itself is issued by a trusted third party, a CA of a PKI that digitally signs the certificate during certificate issuing. When the certificate is used by the user to authenticate, the certificate signature is verified by the relying party as part of certificate validation, similar for all certificates in the path up to a trust anchor (sometimes also called root certificate). Also, further attributes included in the certificate are validated.

In addition to public-key certificates, attribute certificates are also defined in X.509, which can be seen as temporary enhancement of public-key certificates. They do not contain public keys but additional attributes that are typically connected to the holder of the public-key certificate [8]. Regarding the certificate validation, which is the focus of this paper, they are handled in a similar way. For simplicity, the paper will therefore concentrate on public-key certificates for the description of the validation optimization, as this is the most broadly used form of X.509 certificates.

```
Certificate ::= SIGNED{TBSCertificate}

TBSCertificate ::= SEQUENCE {
  version                    [0]  Version DEFAULT v1,
  serialNumber                    CertificateSerialNumber,
  signature                       AlgorithmIdentifier{{SupportedAlgorithms}},
  issuer                          Name,
  validity                        Validity,
  subject                         Name,
  subjectPublicKeyInfo            SubjectPublicKeyInfo,
  issuerUniqueIdentifier     [1] IMPLICIT UniqueIdentifier OPTIONAL,
  ...,
  [[2:  -- if present, version shall be v2 or v3
  subjectUniqueIdentifier   [2] IMPLICIT UniqueIdentifier OPTIONAL]],
  [[3:  -- if present, version shall be v2 or v3
  extensions                [3]  Extensions OPTIONAL ]]
  -- If present, version shall be v3]]
 } (CONSTRAINED BY { -- shall be DER encoded -- } )
```

Figure 2. Public-key Certificate structure (see [1])

ITU-T X.509 [1] defines the structure and content of public-key certificates, as well as the verification of the components. As shown in Figure 2, the certificate is a structure signed by the CA, containing the `subject` as the name of the entity (user) and the `subjectPublicKeyInfo` structure with further information about cryptographic algorithm and the contained public-key. The signature is created typically using traditional asymmetric cryptographic signature algorithms like Rivest Shamir, Adleman (RSA) or Elliptic Curve Digital Signature Algorithm (ECDSA). Different key sizes are supported by these signature algorithms. As outlined in [8], PQC algorithms are increasingly demanded to address potential threats in the advent of a cryptographically relevant quantum computer. A PQC algorithm considered as replacement is for instance Module-Lattice-Based Digital Signature Algorithm (ML-DSA), formerly known as CRYSTALS-Dilithium [9], which has a much larger key size compared to traditional cryptographic algorithms.

During the certificate validation, several components of the certificate are verified. Depending on an organization's security policy, the minimum set of components of an X.509 certificate to be verified comprises the

- expected identity (typically contained in the subject or subject alternative name),
- validity period,
- signature of issuing certificate authority.

In addition, the certificate revocation state is checked. This information is commonly provided by the issuing CA and indicates if the certificate has been revoked before the validity end has been reached. The revocation information can be fetched from the CA in different ways (see subsections II.B.1) and II.B.2) below). Revocation may be done if the certificate or the corresponding key has been compromised, or the certificate was superseded.

As stated before, the verification must be done not only for the end entity certificate, but for all certificates in the certificate chain up to the trust anchor, including the verification of their revocation state, which also requires communication with different issuing CAs.

B. *Certificate Validation Support Approaches*

1) *Online Certificate Validation Protocol*

CAs typically provide Certificate Revocation Lists (CRLs), containing information about revoked certificates, signed by the CA. These lists may grow and may be difficult to handle, specifically on constrained devices. CRLs are generally distributed by a CRL distribution point to which at least temporary access is necessary. An alternative is the use of the Online Certificate Status Protocol (OCSP, IETF RFC 6960, [10]). It enables clients to query the revocation state of single or set of certificates via an OCSP responder. This lifts the handling of complete CRLs from the clients. OCSP support needs an online connection to the OCSP responder. OCSP responder URL and CRL-DP URL are included in issued certificates.

2) *Server Certificate Validation Protocol*

Applying OCSP, as shown in the previous subsection, still requires validation of certificate components locally on the verifying device. A further approach exists, which delegates the certificate validation to a central authority. It is specified as Server Certificate Validation Protocol (SCVP, IETF RFC 5055, [11]) and allows a client to send the certificate in question and a validation policy to the SCVP server, which takes over end entity certificate validation, certificate path construction, and certificate path validation. This increases efficiency on the client side, but still poses load to the server side, specifically in networks with a high number of clients employing certificates more frequently. The approach proposed in Section III kicks in here to optimize server-side processing.

3) *Certificate Authorization Validation Lists*

The complete opposite way to certificate revocation is the explicit authorization of certificates using so called Certificate Authorization Validation Lists (CertAVL, see ITU-T X.509, [1]). They constitute allow lists, which explicitly provide the information, which certificates are considered trustworthy. This allows to offload revocation handling to the central point creating the CertAVL. X.509 also defines critical extensions to mandate the validation of an CertAVL before accepting it. In contrast to CRLs or OCSP responses, CertAVLs are managed by the system operator, not by the issuing CA.

4) *DNS-based Authentication of Named Entities (DANE)*

A further approach is known as Domain Name Service-based Authentication of Named Entities, (DANE, IETF RFC 6698, [12]), which is protected by DNSSEC (IETF RFC 9364, [13]). It enables domain administrators to specify the keys or certificates used by TLS servers as DANE TLSA resource record. The DNS administrator for a domain name is typically authorized to specify identifying information about the zone. Supporting DANE, he also makes an authoritative binding between the domain name and a certificate used by a TLS server in that domain. Thus, a TLS client trusts the certificate information received via DNSSEC, after validation of the DNSSEC signature. It avoids certificate validation, as it got the authoritative information from the DNS server.

5) *OCSP Stapling*

A further approach is known as OCSP stapling, specifically in the context of TLS. Using OSCP stapling a constraint device can request an OCSP response from the remote site and thus avoid separate communication with an OCSP responder. This may be adventurous in situations when the requesting peer has either communication restrictions and may not reach the OCSP responder or if the OCSP communication protocol is not implemented.

For TLSv1.2 [2], this feature is specified in IETF RFC 6066 [14] as a certificate status request (`status_request`) and response extension allowing TLSv1.2 to provide an OSCP response for the server certificate along with its certificate. As this extension only allows to provide a single OCSP response, a further extension is defined in IETF RFC 6961 [15] for multi-stapling, allowing to request (`status_requestv2`) and staple OCSP responses also for intermediate CA certificates contained in the certificate list of the server certificate message. TLSv1.3 [3] provides support for requesting and stapling OCSP responses as described in IETF RFC 6066 for all certificates in the certificate list provided by the client or the server side. As it works in both directions it can accommodate situations in which the server is the constraint device, and the client is more capable peer. An example scenario would be web-based access to communication controllers.

C. *Caching of Revocation Information*

A common practice to avoid fetching fresh CRLs whenever a certificate is received and validated, is the usage of CRL caching (see also [1]). CRLs contain information about CRL issue time and when the next update will be provided. This allows a local implementation to cache the CRL for the period until the next update. Caching avoids additional communication and decreases the processing time for certificate validation. The downside of caching until the next update is that emergency updates during the validity period of the CRL may not be recognized. Caching of revocation information is also the base for the proposed optimization described in Section III.

III. PROPOSED OPTIMIZATION OF CERTIFICATE VALIDATION SERVICE

As discussed in Section II, different approaches are already available to offload certificate validation from a client. Not all of them are equally suited for OT networks. For instance, DNS is not always available, which limits the possibility to utilize the DANE approach outlined in Section II.B.4) For OT networks, specifically the use of allow lists as in Section II.B.3) or the complete offload of certificate validation as in Section II.B.2) becomes more interesting. While the use of SCVP optimizes the client-side operation, the handling of the SCVP response server can be optimized, too. This is the focus of the novel approach in this section.

As specified in IETF RFC 5055 [11], an SCVP client sends a request containing the certificate to be validated including specific verifications to be done, like the construction and validation of the certification path, key usages, etc. The validation result will be provided to the requesting client, which in turn only needs to verify the server's signed response. To optimize the SCVP server handling, it is proposed that the result of a certificate validation or certificate chain validation is provided on an SCVP Response Collector (SRC in Figure 3). This information can be used to reduce the response time for client queries for the same certificate or certificate chain, as it is no longer necessary to perform all validations separately. The SRC can be realized via different mechanisms, like:

1. publishing the result of the validation of the certificate and/or the certificate chain in a public directory (e.g., LDAP, HTTP, FTP, ...),
2. publishing the result of the validation of the certificate and/or the certificate chain using in hash chain-based ledger technology (e.g., Ethereum, Hyperledger).

Note that the choice of realization of the SRC specifically for a chosen ledger technology may have an influence on the validation effort. This counts for both the infrastructure for the SRC, but also on the client side for the interaction to query and process a SCVP response.

In addition, the security policy of the organization may need to consider that caching of validation results provides an optimization but also requires further consideration in an organization's security policy. An example storage duration of validation results to ensure it matches freshness requirements.

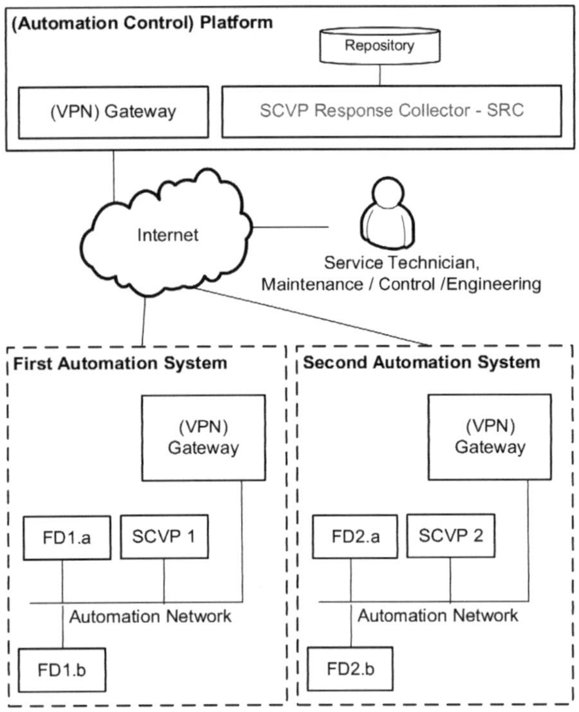

Figure 3. Example Setup for SRC operation

Figure 3 shows two automation environments (e.g., production environment, substation, etc., described as First and Second Automation System), in which SCVP server (SCVP 1 and 2) exist, which work locally as proxy for certificate validation and certificate chain validation. In both automation environments, local communication and communication with outside the domains (e.g., for remote maintenance, access to information in other networks) takes place. As soon as a Field Device (FD) of the automation environment 1 makes a certificate validation request, this is processed by the local SCVP 1 server. If a client (e.g., FD1.a) is allowed to process cached responses, SCVP 1 can first ask the SCVP Response Collector (SRC), which may be public or part of the control center, whether a corresponding validation already exists. If not, it carries out the validation and makes the response available to the field device FD. At the same time, it publishes the result of its validation in a repository as a signed data structure (signed with the private key of the SCVP 1) and thus makes the information available to the SRC for subsequent requests.

The connection to a repository can be realized either via LDAP or via ledger technology. The described interaction and abstract message flow is shown in Figure 4.

The described approach addresses the design goal to benefit the delegation of certificate validation on (constrained) clients to a more powerful centralized service and to optimize the backend service operation. A locally cached certificate validation result supports the availability of the automation system even if the central validation service should temporarily not be available.

IV. Conclusion and Future Work

This paper provides an introduction to the use of certificates and certificate validation in OT. Focus is placed on an optimization to offload efforts for certificate validation, including the validation of the certification path and revocation state of involved certificates to device external services. The proposed solution simplifies the implementation on constrained devices, e.g., by avoiding additional communication protocol stacks to be supported, and it enhances availability of the automation system if the functionality of a central CRL or OCSP responder in the infrastructure is temporarily not available or connectivity to these remote peers cannot be guaranteed from the OT environment.

The novel approach proposed to optimize the operation of a certificate validation infrastructure in an automaton environment utilizes SCVP as a standardized protocol and combines it with caching of certificate validation information. With this approach an OT system, like an automation system, is enhanced with a (local) caching functionality for certificate validation information. As caching directly relates to the freshness of validation information, the caching time is a parameter to be considered in an organization's security policy. The caching time will typically be determined based on a risk-based approach and may vary between installations.

At the time being, only the concept has been developed. The next consequent step is a practical evaluation of the proposed solution regarding the impact to the overall system, based on implementation to proof its efficiency and effectiveness. Specific points for the evaluation besides the provisioning of cached certificate validation information may comprise the analysis of the

- performance impact on the client site when using cached validation response instead of local calculation. This may be considered specifically with different certificate path length,
- impact on code size for the client side as communication protocol stacks for selected protocols may be omitted,
- impact on the infrastructure site, e.g., depending on the chosen approach for the publishing of validation results as outlined in Section III.

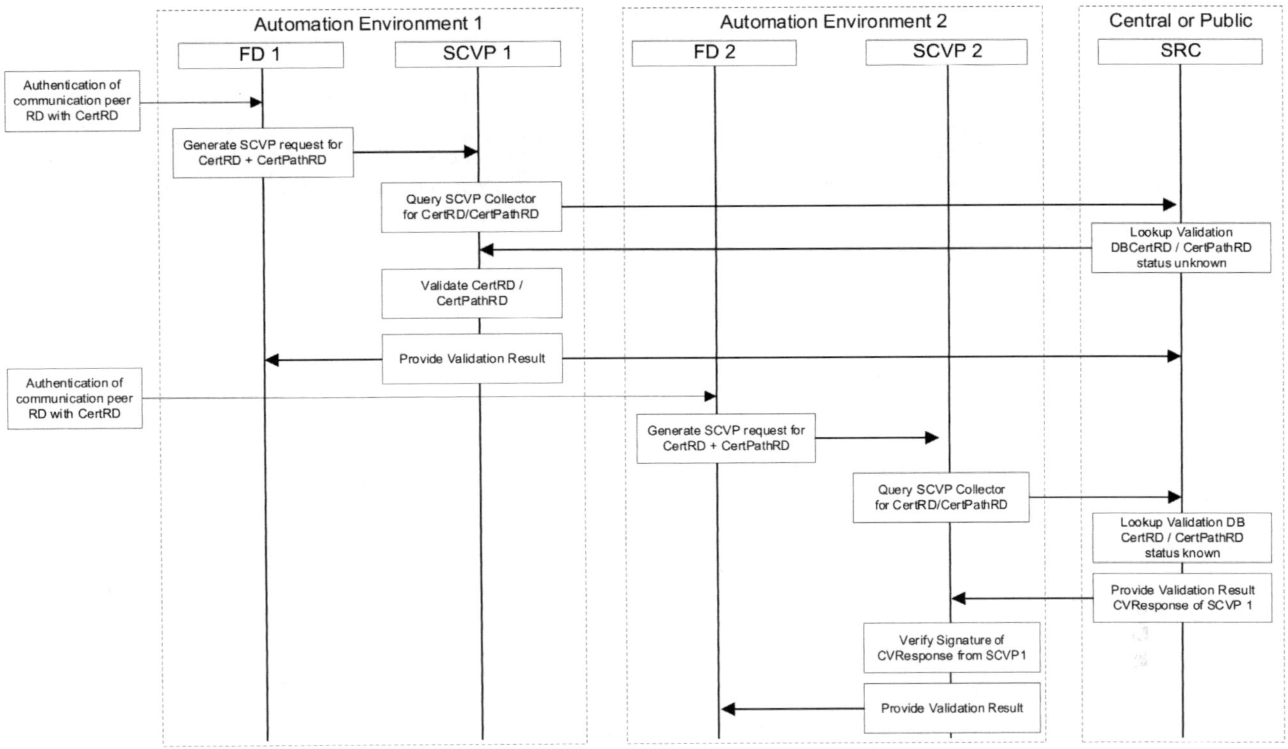

Figure 4. Example Call Flow

REFERENCES

[1] ITU-T X.509 ISO/IEC 9594-8:2020, „ITU-T X.509 Information technology – Open systems interconnection – The Directory: Public-key and attribute certificate frameworks", 2019, [Online]. Available from: https://www.itu.int/rec/T-REC-X.509-201910-I/en, [retrieved: August 2025]

[2] T. Dierks and E. Rescorla, IETF RFC 5246, "Transport Layer Security (TLS) Protocol v1.2", August 2008, [Online]. Available from https://tools.ietf.org/html/rfc5246, [retrieved: August 2025]

[3] E. Rescorla, IETF RFC 8446, "Transport Layer Security (TLS) Protocol v1.3", August 2018, [Online]. Available from https://tools.ietf.org/html/rfc8446, [retrieved: August 2025]

[4] E. Rescorla, H. Tschofenig, and N. Modadugu, IETF RFC 9147, "The Datagram Transport Layer Security (DTLS) Protocol Version 1.3", April 2022, [Online]. Available from https://datatracker.ietf.org/doc/html/rfc9147, [retrieved: August 2025]

[5] IEC 61850-x, "Power systems management and associated information exchange", [Online]. Available from: https://webstore.iec.ch/en/publication/6028, [retrieved: August 2025]

[6] IEC 62351-x, "Power systems management and associated information exchange – Data and communication security", [Online]. Available from: https://webstore.iec.ch/en/publication/6912, [retrieved: August 2025]

[7] OPC-UA, "Open Platform Communications Unified Architecture", [Online]. Available from https://reference.opcfoundation.org/, [retrieved: August 2025]

[8] S. Fries and R. Falk, "Supporting Cryptographic Algorithm Agility with Attribute Certificates", IARIA International Journal of Advances in Security, 2025 vol 17 nr. 1&2, pg. 92-98. [Online], Available from https://www.iariajournals.org/security/sec_v17_n12_2024_paged.pdf, [retrieved: August 2025]

[9] L. Ducas et al., "CRYSTALS-Dilithium: A Lattice-Based Digital Signature Scheme", 2017, [Online]. Available from https://eprint.iacr.org/2017/633.pdf, [retrieved: August 2025]

[10] S. Santesson et al., IETF RFC 6960, "X.509 PKI Online Certificate Status Protocol - OCSP", June 2013, [Online]. Available from https://datatracker.ietf.org/doc/html/rfc6960, [retrieved: August 2025]

[11] T. Freeman, R. Housley, A. Malpani, D. Cooper, and W. Polk, IETF RFC 5055, "Server-Based Certificate Validation Protocol (SCVP)", December 2007, [Online]. Available from https://datatracker.ietf.org/doc/html/rfc5055, [retrieved: August 2025]

[12] P. Hoffman and J. Schlyter, IETF RFC 6698, "The DNS-Based Authentication of Named Entities (DANE) Transport Layer Security (TLS) Protocol: TLSA", August 2012, [Online]. Available from https://datatracker.ietf.org/doc/html/rfc6698, [retrieved: August 2025]

[13] P. Hoffmann, IETF RFC 9364, "DNS Security Extensions (DNSSEC)", February 2023, [Online]. Available from https://datatracker.ietf.org/doc/html/rfc9364, [retrieved August 2025]

[14] D. Eastlake 3rd, IETF RFC 6066, "Transport Layer Security (TLS) Extensions: Extension Definitions", January 2011, [Online]. Available from https://datatracker.ietf.org/doc/html/rfc6066, [retrieved: August 2025]

[15] Y. Petterson, IETF RFC 6961, "The Transport Layer Security (TLS) Multiple Certificate Status Request Extension", June 2013, [Online]. Available from https://datatracker.ietf.org/doc/html/rfc6961, [retrieved: August 2025]

Threat-Based Vulnerability Management: Mapping CVEs to the MITRE ATT&CK Framework

Logan McMahon
School of Electronics, Electrical Engineering and Computer Science
Queen's University Belfast, United Kingdom
e-mail: lmcmahon25@qub.ac.uk

Oluwafemi Olukoya
School of Electronics, Electrical Engineering and Computer Science
Queen's University Belfast,, United Kingdom
e-mail: o.olukoya@qub.ac.uk

***Abstract*—Mapping Common Vulnerabilities and Exposures (CVEs) to the MITRE Adversarial Tactics, Techniques, and Common Knowledge (ATT&CK) framework plays a crucial role in cybersecurity, particularly in threat mitigation and risk management. Accurate and automated CVE-to-ATT&CK mapping enables defenders to better assess the risks posed by emerging vulnerabilities. Prior work has relied primarily on CVE descriptions to establish links to relevant tactics and techniques. However, these approaches struggle when descriptions are incomplete or poorly written. This research proposes that enriching CVE descriptions with extended features, such as exploitability scores, software weaknesses, system and software identifiers, attack patterns, and classification data, substantially improves mapping accuracy. In unsupervised evaluations, this enrichment increased correct mappings by 42 % to 66.7% and reduced misclassifications by 6%. In supervised experiments, the proposed SecRoBERTa model significantly outperformed prior work. While baseline models achieved a weighted F1 score of 78.88%, the fully extended and *Optuna*-tuned version reached 93.47%, marking a 14.6% improvement. These results demonstrate the effectiveness of combining structured feature enrichment with hyperparameter optimization to enhance the accuracy and reliability of CVE-to-ATT&CK mappings.**

Keywords-MITRE ATT&CK; CVE; Vulnerability; Machine Learning; Data Augmentation; Threat Intelligence.

I. INTRODUCTION

In 2024, 40,077 Common Vulnerabilities and Exposures (CVEs) were published, a 39% increase from 2023, underscoring the growing challenge organizations face in managing vulnerabilities at scale [1]. Studies show that most organizations are only able to remediate 10% to 15% of open vulnerabilities each month, leaving a persistent backlog [2]. While only an estimated 1% to 6% of CVEs are actively exploited, these few can have severe consequences [3][4]. According to the Mandiant M-Trends 2025 Report [5], vulnerability exploitation was the most common initial attack vector observed in incident response investigations, emphasizing the importance of effective vulnerability prioritization.

Since it is neither feasible nor necessary to remediate every vulnerability, organizations are shifting toward risk-based vulnerability prioritization. This approach focuses on addressing vulnerabilities that pose the greatest risk, incorporating threat intelligence to enable a threat-informed defense [6]. Central to this approach is the MITRE ATT&CK framework, a widely adopted knowledge base of adversary tactics and techniques derived from real-world observations [7][8]. Within this framework, tactics represent high-level attacker goals (such as *Initial Access* or *Persistence*), while techniques describe how those goals are achieved (e.g., *exploiting a public-facing application or executing a script*).

Mapping CVEs to MITRE ATT&CK tactics and techniques allows defenders to better understand the potential impact of unpatched vulnerabilities, prioritize them based on adversary behavior, and align vulnerability management with real threat scenarios [9]. For example, prioritizing CVEs linked to tactics like *privilege escalation* or *lateral movement* can help security teams mitigate high-impact risks more effectively. However, given the rapid growth of CVEs, manually labeling each with ATT&CK mappings is infeasible. This highlights the urgent need for automated solutions to support scalable, threat-informed vulnerability management.

Recent research [10]–[16] has increasingly focused on automating the mapping of CVEs to MITRE ATT&CK techniques. Most existing methods rely heavily on CVE descriptions, with some efforts incorporating additional data, such as Common Vulnerability Scoring System (CVSS) vectors and Common Weakness Enumeration (CWE) identifiers [17][18]. However, prior studies have shown that patterns derived from CWE and CVSS can be unreliable, and vulnerability descriptions themselves are often inconsistent, incomplete, outdated, or inaccurate [17][19]–[22].

A major challenge remains in accurately mapping CVEs with poor-quality descriptions, as these often lack sufficient detail about exploitation methods or impact. To address these limitations, recent approaches have explored using Large Language Models (LLMs) to infer missing or unclear information, though gaps in domain knowledge constrain these methods and the complexity of vulnerability language [23].

This research proposes a comprehensive, automated approach to mapping CVEs to MITRE ATT&CK tactics, formulated as a multilabel classification problem that integrates structured data to enhance accuracy, particularly when descriptive fields are limited or ambiguous. The primary contributions of this research are as follows:

- **Extended Unsupervised Mapping Pipeline:** We adapt and expand the SMET framework [13] to operate on a larger, feature-enriched CVE dataset, using mappings from the Centre for Threat-Informed Defence [24]. By integrating pre-processed CVSS, CWE, and Common Platform Enumeration (CPE) data, the modified pipeline achieves measurable improvements in full and partial mappings without requiring labelled data.

- **Creation of an Enriched Dataset for Supervised Learning:** We compile an extended dataset by incorporating structured data from the National Vulnerability Database (NVD), Common Attack Pattern Enumeration and Classification (CAPEC), and Exploit Prediction Scoring System (EPSS). This dataset enables systematic evaluation of the contribution of each feature to the CVE-to-ATT&CK mapping process.
- **Systematic Feature Evaluation:** We perform a detailed feature importance analysis to assess the impact of each added feature on model performance. This includes tactic-level analysis, particularly focusing on historically difficult-to-predict classes, such as *Initial Access*, *Impact*, *Collection* and *Reconnaissance* [14].
- **Hyperparameter Optimization with Optuna:** We apply *Optuna* [25] to fine-tune model hyperparameters, resulting in notable performance gains on the extended dataset and highlighting the importance of optimization in supervised models.
- **Public Release of Resources:** All datasets, code, and supplementary materials are made publicly available via the project's GitHub repository to support reproducibility. We present and release an extended dataset comprising 7,328 CVE entries, each enriched with CWE, CPE, and CVSS information, and optionally annotated with CAPEC and EPSS data.

The rest of the paper is structured as follows: Section II reviews related work on supervised and unsupervised approaches for mapping CVEs to MITRE ATT&CK tactics and techniques. Section III outlines the methodology, including data collection, preprocessing, model development, and evaluation. Section IV presents the research objectives and hypotheses, and the experimental results. In Section V, we interpret the research findings and the implications. Section VI discusses the limitations of the study, and Section VII concludes with a summary and directions for future work.

II. Related Work

A. Supervised Mapping

Existing approaches to mapping CVEs to the MITRE ATT&CK framework predominantly rely on supervised learning. Branescu et al. [14] modelled this as a multi-label classification task using CVE descriptions for ATT&CK tactics mappings. Ampel et al. [15] employed self-distillation to capture long-term textual dependencies. Vulcan Cyber [17] proposed enriching input features with CWE and CVSS Version 3.x data. BERT-based models, such as CVE2ATT&CK [11], showed promise using only CVE descriptions for mapping 31 of 92 ATT&CK techniques. Mendsaikhan et al. [16] expanded coverage to 52 techniques using textual features from CVE descriptions, though performance declined with label expansion due to limited training data. Adam et al. [18] introduced a two-step mapping via CWEs, but their method is constrained by incomplete CWE annotations in CVEs and the lack of comprehensive CWE-to-ATT&CK mappings.

B. Unsupervised Mapping

The SMET framework [13] employs semantic role labelling to rank ATT&CK techniques based on CVE descriptions, without requiring labelled data. Kuppa et al. [12] demonstrated an unsupervised approach that maps CVEs to 37 ATT&CK techniques by extracting relevant phrases from both threat reports and ATT&CK descriptions. However, they observed that many CVE entries contain minimal textual content, resulting in incomplete or failed mappings.

Since SMET does not leverage structured NVD attributes (e.g., CVSS, CWE, CPE) or EPSS probability scores, it struggles with sparse or ambiguous descriptions. Furthermore, as a fully unsupervised pipeline with no learnable parameters, SMET lacks adaptability to evolving CVE patterns or domain-specific requirements. Its logistic regression classifier and embedding model are trained on ATT&CK descriptions, not CVE text, rendering the system insensitive to changes in vulnerability language, emerging exploit types, or shifts in reporting conventions.

The MITRE ATT&CK Enterprise framework comprises 14 tactics, 211 techniques, and 468 sub-techniques, making comprehensive CVE-to-technique mapping a complex task. Due to limited annotated data for many techniques, prior work has focused on a subset of them. In this study, we shift the focus to mapping CVEs to ATT&CK tactics, emphasizing higher-level adversary objectives, such as *Reconnaissance, Initial Access, Collection*, and *Impact*, all of which have been historically difficult for state-of-the-art (SOTA) methods [14].

Mapping at the tactic level offers practical benefits for vulnerability prioritization, attacker path modeling, and risk propagation [26]. To address the challenges of sparse textual descriptions and limited adaptability, we enhance both supervised and unsupervised approaches by incorporating structured NVD data (CVSS, CWE, CAPEC, CPE) and EPSS scores, going beyond CVE descriptions alone.

While our long-term goal remains mapping to techniques, we argue that tactic-level mapping can be substantially improved with richer input features. This work lays a scalable foundation for future expansion to technique-level mappings with broader dataset coverage.

III. Methodology

The proposed methodology for automatically mapping CVEs to MITRE ATT&CK tactics comprises four main phases: dataset collection, dataset processing, mapping using both unsupervised and supervised approaches, and performance evaluation. The overall architecture is shown in Figure 1, with each phase described in detail below.

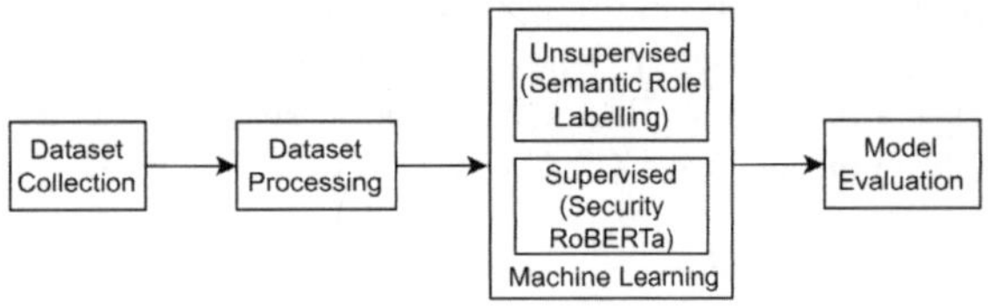

Figure 1. An overview of the proposed framework for automated mapping of CVEs to MITRE ATT&CK Tactics

A. Dataset Collection

The phase begins with the collection of an initial dataset to support both unsupervised and supervised approaches. We use datasets from SMET [13] and Branescu et al.[14], representing state-of-the-art methods in each category. These datasets include CVE IDs and their corresponding descriptions as primary features. To enrich this initial dataset, we incorporated five additional sources from the NVD and related repositories:

- CVE Descriptions (baseline): Textual descriptions of vulnerabilities from CVE entries. For instance, the CVE description for CVE-2025-49163 is "*Arris VIP1113 devices through 2025-05-30 with KreaTV SDK allow booting an arbitrary image via a crafted /usr/bin/gunzip file.*"
- Common Weakness Enumeration (CWE) [27]: Standardized identifiers for software weaknesses (e.g., CWE-79 Improper Neutralization of Input During Web Page Generation ('Cross-site Scripting')).
- Common Vulnerability Scoring System (CVSS) [28]: Quantitative scores (0–10) reflecting exploitability and impact.
- Common Platform Enumeration (CPE) [29]: Machine-readable identifiers for vulnerable software/hardware (e.g., `cpe:2.3:a:microsoft:edge:`)
- Exploit Prediction Scoring System (EPSS)[30]: Probabilities (0–1) estimating the likelihood of a CVE being exploited in the wild.
- Common Attack Pattern Enumeration and Classification (CAPEC) [31]: Titles describing adversary tactics (e.g., CAPEC-209: XSS Using MIME Type Mismatch).

NVD data was retrieved using the official API [32], EPSS scores via the EPSS API [33], and CAPEC titles were obtained through web scraping and HTML parsing of the CAPEC website.

Following enrichment, the unsupervised dataset retains its original size but is enhanced with additional features, including CWE, CPE, and CVSS data. The supervised dataset initially comprises 9,986 CVEs from prior work [14], but is reduced to 7,328 entries after filtering out CVEs lacking sufficient NVD attributes (CWE, CPE, CVSS). Features with missing values across any dataset entries are removed to prevent negative impacts on machine learning performance. This preprocessing step of filtering out rows with null values to improve system effectiveness is consistent with established machine-learning approaches for automated CVE-to-MITRE ATT&CK tactic mapping [34].

For supervised learning, we adopt an 80/20 train-test split as recommended by [14], using 80% of the 7,328 CVEs for training and 20% for testing. The *extended* dataset is enriched with EPSS scores, processed CVSS (v2/v3), CWE, CPE, and later CAPEC features. A comparative summary between the initial dataset [14] and the enriched version used in this work is provided in Table I.

TABLE I. COMPARISON BETWEEN THE INITIAL DATASET INTRODUCED BY BRANESCU ET AL.[14] AND OUR FULLY ENRICHED DATASET

ATT&CK Tactic Class	CVE Record Count	
	Initial Dataset[14]	**Our Dataset**
Reconnaissance	170	141
Resource Development	170	117
Initial Access	722	573
Execution	2642	1183
Persistence	3016	1591
Privilege Escalation	3218	1731
Defense Evasion	7552	5354
Credential Access	614	534
Discovery	2369	1959
Lateral Movement	1932	620
Collection	663	576
Command & Control	427	382
Exfiltration	171	126
Impact	349	286
Total	**9,986 CVEs**	**7,328 CVEs**

The unsupervised dataset comprises 827 CVEs distributed over 120 ATT&CK techniques, selected from publicly available CVE-to-ATT&CK mappings provided by the Center for Threat-Informed Defense [24], allowing for direct evaluation against verified mappings. This differs from the dataset used in SMET [13], which lacked consistent NVD feature coverage. Accordingly, the SMET baseline was re-evaluated on our 827-entry *description-only* dataset, compared to the original 303 entries used in SMET distributed over 41 techniques from the ATT&CK matrix.

Two primary datasets are created for the unsupervised and supervised mappings: (1) the *Description-Only* dataset, containing CVE IDs and textual descriptions, and (2) the *Extended* dataset, which builds upon the former by incorporating pre-processed CWE, CVSS, CPE, EPSS scores, and optionally CAPEC data.

B. Dataset Processing

A key design decision in this research was to enrich the original CVE dataset with additional structured fields, CWE, CVSS, CPE, and optionally EPSS and CAPEC, to improve the accuracy of CVE-to-ATT&CK tactic mappings. This enrichment supports both the unsupervised (SMET) and supervised (SecRoBERTa) approaches by enhancing the semantic and contextual representation of each CVE. To ensure consistency across data types, all extended features (except EPSS scores, which are numeric) were pre-processed into natural language format. This was necessary due to the inconsistent quality of CVE descriptions and the structured, non-linguistic format of most added fields.

1) CVSS Pre-Processing: CVSS Version 2.0 and CVSS Version 3.x vector strings were transformed into natural language using mappings from the NVD CVSS calculators [35][36]. For example, the CVSS v3.1 vector `CVSS:3.1/AV:N/AC:L/PR:N/UI:N/S:U/C:H/I:H/A:H` of CVE-2023-23333 is pre-processed into:

- *"The CVE is Exploited by the Network Attack Vector. The CVE has Low Attack Complexity. The CVE Requires No Privileges. The CVE Does Not Require User Interaction. The CVE scope is Unchanged. The CVE has a High Confidentiality Impact. The CVE has High Integrity Impact. The CVE has High Availability Impact."*

2) CWE Pre-Processing: CWEs were converted into natural language by combining their titles and descriptions. For instance, CWE-78 is rendered as:

- *"The CVE is affected by Improper Neutralization of Special Elements used in an OS Command ('OS Command Injection'): The product constructs all or part of an OS command using externally-influenced input from an upstream component, but it does not neutralize or incorrectly neutralizes special elements that could modify the intended OS command when it is sent to a downstream component."*

For multiple CWEs associated with a single CVE ID, the processed CWE strings will be concatenated to create a longer sentence.

3) CAPEC Pre-processing: CAPEC titles were processed similarly to CWEs. However, due to limited API support and outdated data (last reviewed in 2023), CAPEC enrichment was used selectively. A pilot study indicated that the inclusion of CAPEC features did not improve mapping accuracy.

4) CPE Pre-Processing: CPE strings were parsed to extract three key attributes: component type (application, Operating System, or hardware), vendor, and product. These were reformatted into natural language. For example: `cpe:2.3:o:contec:solarview_compact_firmware:*:*:*:*:*:*:*:*` was converted to: *The "CVE affects Contec Solarview_compact_firmware Operating System."*.

To reduce noise from highly variable product names, a standardization step was applied. Generic terms, such as "Product", were substituted when the product name was not essential. In contrast, critical operating system identifiers (e.g., Windows, Linux, Mac_os_x and Linux_kernel) were preserved. For instance: `cpe:2.3:a:microsoft:365_apps:-:*:*:*:enterprise:*:*:*` was converted to: *"The CVE affects Microsoft Product Application."*. This generalization improves model robustness by minimizing irrelevant variance while preserving key distinctions necessary for accurate CVE-to-ATT&CK tactic mapping.

C. Machine Learning

This research addresses the challenge of automatically mapping CVEs to the MITRE ATT&CK framework using both unsupervised and supervised machine learning techniques.

For the unsupervised approach, we employ the SMET framework [13], a state-of-the-art method that does not require labelled data. SMET extracts semantically meaningful attack vectors from CVE textual descriptions by leveraging semantic role labelling and other semantic similarity techniques. We extend the original SMET implementation, designed for *description-only* inputs, to incorporate structured features from the NVD, including CVE ID, CWE, CVSS, and CPE. We hypothesise that even in the absence of labelled data, incorporating this extended feature set enhances the quality of semantic mappings.

For the supervised approach, we utilize SecRoBERTa [37], a transformer-based model derived from RoBERTa [38], which is an optimized version of BERT (Bidirectional Encoder Representations from Transformers), and has been fine-tuned on cybersecurity-specific corpora. Prior work has shown that SecRoBERTa achieves state-of-the-art performance in mapping CVEs to ATT&CK techniques [14]. Castano et al. [39] trained five BERT-based models and found SecRoBERTa to be the most effective at linking CTI sources via external references, resulting in more complete datasets and improved threat intelligence.. We further fine-tune a pre-trained ATT&CK-BERT model from *Hugging Face* [37] using our extended dataset, which includes NVD features, EPSS probability scores, and CAPEC identifiers. Tokenization and model management are performed using the *Hugging Face* Transformers library [40]. While we maintain the default settings for batch size and number of epochs, we adjust the learning rate to `3.884755049077609e-05` and the dropout rate to `0.4864913766068174` to optimize model performance.

The dual-method study aims to investigate whether both unsupervised and supervised models can benefit from enhanced CVE representations, which could improve automated mappings to adversarial tactics in ATT&CK.

D. Model Evaluation

We evaluated the machine learning models using *accuracy, validation loss*, and both *macro* and *weighted F1 scores*. *Validation loss* serves as an indicator of generalization performance, with lower values suggesting reduced overfitting or underfitting. *Accuracy* reflects the overall proportion of correctly predicted tactic labels. The *macro F1 score*, as the unweighted average of per-tactic F1 scores, emphasizes performance on less frequent classes. The *weighted F1 score*, our primary metric, accounts for class imbalance by weighting each tactic's F1 score by its frequency.

IV. EVALUATION

To support a comprehensive evaluation of our system, we define specific hypotheses for validation:

- **H1**: An *extended* dataset improves overall mapping accuracy compared to the commonly used *description-only* datasets [11][13][14][16].
- **H2**: Tactics that are typically harder to classify, such as *Reconnaissance, Initial Access, Collection*, and *Impact*,

as identified by Branescu et al. [14], will show improvements in their F1-scores.

- **H3**: Hyperparameter tuning leads to additional gains in mapping accuracy.

A. Unsupervised Mapping Validation

Given that SMET is an unsupervised methodology that ranks mappings based on semantic similarity. In the proposed solution, rankings greater than 0.1 are considered potentially correct mappings. When an entry is labelled as *Completely Accurate*, it indicates a 1:1 match with the testing data provided for a CVE. If the entry is designated as *Semi-Accurate*, it means that while the accepted mappings included correct ones, they also incorporated some incorrect mappings that exceeded the threshold. Conversely, if the entry is marked as *Inaccurate*, it signifies that no correct mappings were obtained that met the threshold (>0.1). We compared the SMET results from a *Description Only* dataset with an *extended* dataset, verifying an increase in mapping accuracy. As shown in Table II, the enriched unsupervised dataset with CVSS vectors, CWE and CPE summaries outperformed the baseline *description only* in every metric.

TABLE II. COMPARISON OF UNSUPERVISED MAPPING ACCURACY ON 828 CVES, *Description Only* VS. *Enriched* DATASET

	Description Only	Enriched (+CVE, CVSS & CPE)	Impact (%)
Completely Accurate	6	10	+66.7
Semi Accurate	88	125	+42.0
Inaccurate	733	692	-5.6

Despite notable improvements in mapping accuracy, over 80% of CVEs remain incorrectly mapped without supervised learning, demonstrating that feature enrichment alone is insufficient. While enriched features capture semantically meaningful attack vectors, they do not match the performance of supervised models. Results show that mapping CVEs to ATT&CK Techniques suffers from low accuracy due to limited labelled data.

For example, SMET, a state-of-the-art unsupervised method, uses text similarity between CVEs and ATT&CK technique descriptions, enabling semantic mapping of 303 CVEs to 41 techniques. In contrast, our improved unsupervised dataset includes 828 CVEs mapped to 120 techniques, with both datasets averaging 7 CVEs per technique. Meanwhile, the leading supervised dataset includes 9,985 CVEs across 14 tactics, with each tactic supported by a minimum of 170 samples and an average of 713 entries (see Table I). This data imbalance leads to better performance when mapping to ATT&CK Tactics rather than Techniques.

Given the limited performance of unsupervised methods, this research adopts a supervised approach. Nonetheless, the unsupervised results confirm that *enriched* datasets are more effective than *description-only* inputs for offensive technique mapping.

B. Supervised Mapping Validation

This section presents the results of the supervised learning experiments. First, we analyze performance across dataset variants to assess the impact of added features, including comparisons with and without CAPEC. Second, we report per-tactic F1 scores for MITRE ATT&CK tactics. Finally, we benchmark our approach against the state-of-the-art method by Branescu et al. [14].

Table III presents the overall performance across the supervised dataset variants, enabling a detailed comparison of feature-specific contributions. Incorporating the EPSS feature alone consistently improves all four performance metrics: validation loss, accuracy, macro F1 score, and weighted F1 score, relative to the *description-only*baseline. Similar improvements are observed when CWE, CPE, and CVSS features are added, each contributing to increased model performance. In contrast, the inclusion of the CAPEC feature results in a decline across all four metrics, with the CAPEC Title-only extension causing a particularly notable degradation. As a result, CAPEC was excluded from the fully extended feature set. All other feature combinations outperform the description-only baseline, thereby supporting Hypothesis **H1**. Additionally, hyperparameter tuning yields a consistent performance boost over the enriched but untuned models, with gains of approximately 2% to 3% in mapping accuracy and macro F1 score, thereby supporting Hypothesis **H3**.

TABLE III. OVERALL PERFORMANCE ACROSS SUPERVISED DATASET VARIANTS.

Supervised Dataset Variant	Validation Loss	Accuracy	Macro F1 Score	Weighted F1 Score
Description Only	0.0747	0.8286	0.7948	0.9232
Description + EPSS	0.0729	0.8335	0.8138	0.9277
Description + CWE	0.0724	0.8407	0.7979	0.9248
Description + CVSS	0.0815	0.8229	0.8024	0.9163
Description + CPE	0.0746	0.8286	0.8050	0.9244
Description + CAPEC	0.0870	0.8179	0.7119	0.9011
Fully Extended (Description + EPSS + CVSS + CPE)	0.0743	0.8383	0.8144	0.9245
Fully Extended + Tuned	**0.0658**	**0.8538**	**0.8401**	**0.9347**

Table IV presents F1 scores for the *description-only* baseline, the fully enriched dataset (with and without tuning), and the Branescu et al. [14] SecRoBERTa model. The most notable improvements were observed for hard-to-predict tactics: *Initial Access* improved from 65.27% to 67.44%, *Collection* from 79.44% to 84.34%, *Impact* from 67.57% to 72.00%, and *Reconnaissance* from 37.33% to 46.15%, confirming Hypothesis **H2**. Medium-difficulty tactics, such as *Credential Access* and *Command & Control*, saw moderate gains of 1%–7%. Well-predicted tactics, such as *Defense Evasion, Discovery, Privilege Escalation, Persistence, Lateral Movement*, and *Execution* began above 90% and saw only marginal improvements (1%–2%), with fine-tuning contributing an additional 0.5%–1%. The final model achieved a 93.5% weighted F1 score.

TABLE IV. PLOTS PER-CLASS F1 SCORES FOR THE SUPERVISED DATASET VARIANT AND COMPARISON BETWEEN THE SECROBERTA PER-CLASS ON DESCRIPTION ONLY REPORTED IN [14]

Tactics	Description only (Benchmark)	Full Extended Dataset (+EPSS+CWE +CVSS+CPE)	+ Optuna Fine-Tuning	SOTA [14]
Reconnaissance	37.33%	36.73%	**46.15%**	53.84%
Resource Development	51.47%	65.81%	**65.79%**	79.13%
Initial Access	65.27%	61.52%	**67.44%**	37.18%
Execution	89.56%	89.25%	**89.95%**	74.43%
Persistence	94.42%	94.52%	**94.87%**	80.78%
Privilege Escalation	94.66%	94.90%	**95.11%**	80.46%
Defense Evasion	98.67%	98.00%	**98.41%**	91.96%
Credential Access	84.82%	89.39%	**91.81%**	67.27%
Discovery	97.24%	97.29%	**97.92%**	81.55%
Lateral Movement	92.87%	94.59%	**94.97%**	81.37%
Collection	79.44%	81.82%	**84.34%**	51.47%
Command & Control	95.21%	95.81%	**96.43%**	61.79%
Exfiltration	64.23%	74.83%	**81.01%**	88.88%
Impact	67.57%	65.73%	**72.00%**	31.11%

Compared to *Branescu et al.'s*[14] model trained on 9,986 CVEs (weighted F1: 78.88%), our approach, applied to 7,786 CVEs, achieves 93.45%. This performance gain is attributed to structured feature enrichment from NVD (CWE, CVSS, CPE) and the addition of EPSS, coupled with effective hyperparameter tuning. The results demonstrate that enriched features and tuning significantly enhance CVE-to-ATT&CK tactic mapping accuracy, especially for previously underperforming tactics.

To ensure a fair comparison with Branescu et al. [14], we grouped predicted MITRE ATT&CK tactics into three difficulty levels based on F1 scores: *hard* (<60%), *medium* (60%–80%), and *easy* (>80%). As shown in Table V, Branescu et al. [14] identified *four* hard, *four* medium, and *six* easy tactics. Using our enriched dataset and improved processing pipeline, our method reduced the number of hard tactics to *one*, with *three* medium and *ten* easy-to-predict tactics. Notably, *three* tactics previously classified as hard in [14] were reclassified as two medium and one easy, while three of the four medium tactics shifted to the easy category in our mapping methodology. The *six* easy tactics remained unchanged. These results support Hypothesis **H2**, demonstrating that dataset enrichment and enhanced modelling reduce classification difficulty for previously challenging tactics.

TABLE V. COMPARISON BETWEEN THE PREDICTED ATT&CK TACTICS BY BRANESCU ET AL. [14] AND OUR PROPOSED APPROACH

Difficulty Level	ATT& CK Tactics in Branescu et al. [14]	ATT&CK Tactics in our proposed approach
Hard	Reconnaissance, Collection, Initial Access, Impact	Reconnaissance
Medium	Resource Development, Credential Access, Execution, Command & Control	Resource Development, Initial Access, Impact
Easy	Privilege Escalation, Discovery, Persistence, Exfiltration, Defense Evasion, Lateral Movement	Privilege Escalation, Discovery, Persistence, Exfiltration, Defense Evasion, Lateral Movement, Execution, Credential Access, Collection, Command & Control

V. DISCUSSION

According to the CVE Key Details Phrasing Guidelines by MITRE [41], a comprehensive CVE description should articulate several key aspects, including the vulnerability type or root cause, attack vector, impact, attacker type, component identification, affected product(s) and version(s), and product vendor(s). However, despite the importance of these details, many CVE descriptions and their associated references suffer from inconsistencies, a lack of structure, or insufficient information [17][22][42], which poses a significant challenge for downstream tasks such as mapping vulnerabilities to offensive tactics and techniques, particularly within the MITRE ATT&CK framework.

This research demonstrates that supplementing CVE descriptions with structured data, such as software weaknesses (CWE), platform identifiers (CPE), exploit prediction scores (EPSS), attack patterns (CAPEC), and vulnerability scoring metrics (CVSS vector strings), can significantly enhance the completeness and utility of CVE records. By enriching the original textual descriptions with these standardized attributes, the proposed approach improves the effectiveness of both supervised and unsupervised models for mapping CVEs to ATT&CK techniques.

Vulnerability descriptions serve as a critical foundation in the identification and communication of security weaknesses in software, systems, and hardware. High-quality descriptions not only support threat assessment and mitigation but are also essential for enabling automated systems to aid in vulnerability prioritization and response. This study contributes to the growing body of work aimed at automating the mapping of CVEs to adversary behavior models, thereby advancing vulnerability analysis and threat-informed defense.

VI. LIMITATION

A key limitation of this research is the dynamic nature of the MITRE ATT&CK framework and the fast-paced evolution of the cyber threat landscape, which may lead to misalignment between the framework and the most current adversary tactics, techniques, and procedures (TTPs). Despite the enhanced approach, the *Reconnaissance* tactic remains difficult to predict. While this could be attributed to its underrepresentation in the dataset, this explanation is insufficient, as *Exfiltration*, similarly sized (see Table I), achieves significantly better performance and falls into the more predictable category. Another limitation stems from the exclusion of CVEs that lack extended fields, which introduces bias toward well-documented vulnerabilities and excludes zero-day threats. These cannot be included until evaluated by the NVD and assigned relevant attributes, such as CPE. To address this, future work may explore partial feature selection to enable broader coverage until a fully extended dataset becomes available. Furthermore, LLMs can enhance textual vulnerability descriptions by utilising historical data, enabling the system to comprehend new vulnerabilities without requiring retraining of the LLM. Additionally, the CAPEC feature was poorly represented due to incomplete web scraping, which extracted only CAPEC Titles. This limited the utility of the CAPEC data and negatively impacted performance.

VII. Conclusion and Future Work

This research demonstrates that augmenting CVE descriptions with extended features, including EPSS, CWE, CVSS, CPE, and CAPEC, significantly improves mapping accuracy to MITRE ATT&CK tactics. In unsupervised experiments, enrichment increased the number of correct mappings and reduced misclassifications. In supervised experiments, the proposed SecRoBERTa-based model outperformed the current state-of-the-art models. Accurate CVE-to-ATT&CK mapping enables Security Operations Centers (SOCs) to prioritize and mitigate unpatched vulnerabilities more effectively. As CVE descriptions often lack consistency and technical detail, enriching them with well-processed structured features leads to more reliable mapping outcomes.

Future work will focus on developing a CAPEC API to streamline the integration of CAPEC features. Building on the high mapping accuracy to ATT&CK tactics, the next phase will extend this approach to ATT&CK techniques, using a supervised methodology while constraining predictions to the relevant parent tactic. Beyond enriching textual vulnerability descriptions with structured information such as EPSS, CWE, CAPEC, CVSS vector strings, and CPE configurations, future work will explore methods for detecting and augmenting missing key aspects of CVE entries. This can be approached through machine learning techniques that predict the labels of absent attributes based on known vulnerability characteristics or through software feature inference. Such enhancements have the potential to improve downstream applications that rely on CVE data, including vulnerability severity prediction, automated alignment with adversary tactics and techniques, the development of exploitation prediction models, and automated vulnerability classification.

Acknowledgments

This work was supported by the NICYBER2025 programme funded by Innovate UK.

References

[1] The MITRE Corporation, "Metrics," Retrieved: July 2025, 2025, [Online]. Available: https://www.cve.org/about/Metrics.

[2] W. Baker, "The pithy p2p: 5 years of vulnerability remediation & exploitation research," Retrieved: July 2025, 2025, [Online]. Available: https://www.cyentia.com/pithy-p2p/.

[3] P. Garrity, "State of exploitation - a peek into the last decade of vulnerability exploitation," Retrieved: July 2025, 2024, [Online]. Available: https://vulncheck.com/blog/state-of-exploitation-a-decade.

[4] Cyentia Institute, "A visual exploration of exploitation in the wild: The inaugural study of epss data and performance," Retrieved: July 2025, 2024, [Online]. Available: https://www.cyentia.com/wp-content/uploads/2024/07/EPSS-Exploration-Of-Exploits.pdf.

[5] Google Cloud Security, "Mandiant m-trends 2025 report," Retrieved: September 2025, 2025, [Online]. Available: https://services.google.com/fh/files/misc/m-trends-2025-en.pdf.

[6] J. Baker, "2023 r&d roadmap to advance threat-informed defense," Retrieved: July 2025, 2023, [Online]. Available: https://medium.com/mitre-engenuity/2023-r-d-roadmap-to-advance-threat-informed-defense-cf726d30e583.

[7] B. E. Strom, A. Applebaum, D. P. Miller, K. C. Nickels, A. G. Pennington, and C. B. Thomas, "Mitre att&ck: Design and philosophy," in *Technical report*, The MITRE Corporation, 2018.

[8] The MITRE Corporation., "Att&ck®," Retrieved: August 2025, 2025, [Online]. Available: https://attack.mitre.org/.

[9] J. Baker, "Cve + mitre att&ck® to understand vulnerability impact," Retrieved: July 2025, 2021, [Online]. Available: https://medium.com/mitre-engenuity/cve-mitre-att-ck-to-understand-vulnerability-impact-c40165111bf7.

[10] D.-Y. Kim, S.-S. Yoon, and I.-C. Euom, "V2tsa: Analysis of vulnerability to attack techniques using a semantic approach," *IEEE Access*, 2024.

[11] O. Grigorescu, A. Nica, M. Dascalu, and R. Rughinis, "Cve2att&ck: Bert-based mapping of cves to mitre att&ck techniques," *Algorithms*, vol. 15, no. 9, p. 314, 2022.

[12] A. Kuppa, L. Aouad, and N.-A. Le-Khac, "Linking cve's to mitre att&ck techniques," in *Proceedings of the 16th International Conference on Availability, Reliability and Security*, 2021, pp. 1–12.

[13] B. Abdeen, E. Al-Shaer, A. Singhal, L. Khan, and K. Hamlen, "Smet: Semantic mapping of cve to att&ck and its application to cybersecurity," in *IFIP annual conference on data and applications security and privacy*, Springer, 2023, pp. 243–260.

[14] I. Branescu, O. Grigorescu, and M. Dascalu, "Automated mapping of common vulnerabilities and exposures to mitre att&ck tactics," *Information*, vol. 15, no. 4, p. 214, 2024.

[15] B. Ampel, S. Samtani, S. Ullman, and H. Chen, "Linking common vulnerabilities and exposures to the mitre att&ck framework: A self-distillation approach," *arXiv preprint arXiv:2108.01696*, 2021.

[16] O. Mendsaikhan, H. Hasegawa, Y. Yamaguchi, and H. Shimada, "Automatic mapping of vulnerability information to adversary techniques," in *The Fourteenth International Conference on Emerging Security Information, Systems and Technologies SECUREWARE2020*, 2020, pp. 53–59.

[17] Vulcan Cyber, "Cve to t&ts: Using cve attributes for mitre att&ck mapping," Retrieved: July 2025, 2023, [Online]. Available: https://web.archive.org/web/20240429155732/https://l.vulcan.io/hubfs/Ebooks-and-White-Papers/Vulcan-Cyber-Mapping-CVEs-to-MITRE.pdf.

[18] C. Adam, M. F. Bulut, D. Sow, S. Ocepek, C. Bedell, and L. Ngweta, "Attack techniques and threat identification for vulnerabilities," *arXiv preprint arXiv:2206.11171*, 2022.

[19] Q. Li, W. Tang, X. Chen, and H. Ren, "Vuldifffinder: Discovering inconsistencies in unstructured vulnerability information," *Computers & Security*, p. 104 447, 2025.

[20] Y. Dong, W. Guo, Y. Chen, X. Xing, Y. Zhang, and G. Wang, "Towards the detection of inconsistencies in public security vulnerability reports," in *28th USENIX security symposium (USENIX Security 19)*, 2019, pp. 869–885.

[21] Y. Chen, A. E. Santosa, A. Sharma, and D. Lo, "Automated identification of libraries from vulnerability data," in *Proceedings of the ACM/IEEE 42nd International Conference on Software Engineering: Software Engineering in Practice*, 2020, pp. 90–99.

[22] H. Guo, S. Chen, Z. Xing, X. Li, Y. Bai, and J. Sun, "Detecting and augmenting missing key aspects in vulnerability descriptions," *ACM Transactions on Software Engineering and*

Methodology (TOSEM), vol. 31, no. 3, pp. 1–27, 2022. DOI: 10.1145/3498537.
[23] T. Chen *et al.*, "Vullibgen: Identifying vulnerable third-party libraries via generative pre-trained model," *CoRR*, 2023.
[24] Center for Threat-Informed Defense, "Mapping mitre att&ck® to cves for impact," Retrieved: July 2025, 2021, [Online]. Available: https://github.com/center-for-threat-informed-defense/attack_to_cve.
[25] T. Akiba, S. Sano, T. Yanase, T. Ohta, and M. Koyama, "Optuna: A next-generation hyperparameter optimization framework," in *Proceedings of the 25th ACM SIGKDD international conference on knowledge discovery & data mining*, 2019, pp. 2623–2631.
[26] P. Bhosale, W. Kastner, and T. Sauter, "Mapping ics vulnerabilities: Prioritization and risk propagation analysis with mitre att&ck framework and bayesian belief networks," in *2024 IEEE 29th International Conference on Emerging Technologies and Factory Automation (ETFA)*, IEEE, 2024, pp. 1–8.
[27] The MITRE Corporation (MITRE), "Common weakness enumeration," Retrieved: September 2025, 2025, [Online]. Available: https://cwe.mitre.org/.
[28] Forum of Incident Response and Security Teams, "Common vulnerability scoring system," Retrieved: July 2025, 2025, [Online]. Available: https://www.first.org/cvss/.
[29] NIST, "Official common platform enumeration (cpe) dictionary," Retrieved: July 2025, 2025, [Online]. Available: https://nvd.nist.gov/products/cpe.
[30] J. Jacobs, S. Romanosky, B. Edwards, I. Adjerid, and M. Roytman, "Exploit prediction scoring system (epss)," *Digital Threats: Research and Practice*, vol. 2, no. 3, pp. 1–17, 2021.
[31] The MITRE Corporation, "Common attack pattern enumeration and classification," Retrieved: July 2025, 2023, [Online]. Available: https://capec.mitre.org/.
[32] NIST, "Vulnerabilities: Cve api," Retrieved: July 2025, 2025, [Online]. Available: https://nvd.nist.gov/developers/vulnerabilities.
[33] Forum of Incident Response and Security Teams, "Epss api," Retrieved: July 2025, 2025, [Online]. Available: https://www.first.org/epss/api.
[34] Y. Lakhdhar and S. Rekhis, "Machine learning based approach for the automated mapping of discovered vulnerabilities to adversial tactics," in *2021 IEEE Security and Privacy Workshops (SPW)*, IEEE, 2021, pp. 309–317.
[35] NIST, "Common vulnerability scoring system calculator - cvss version 2.0," Retrieved: July 2025, 2025, [Online]. Available: https://nvd.nist.gov/vuln-metrics/cvss/v2-calculator.
[36] NIST, "Common vulnerability scoring system calculator - cvss version 3.0, cvss version 3.1," Retrieved: July 2025, 2025, [Online]. Available: https://nvd.nist.gov/vuln-metrics/cvss/v3-calculator.
[37] Kun jackaduma, "Secroberta," Retrieved: July 2025, 2023, [Online]. Available: https://huggingface.co/jackaduma/SecRoBERTa.
[38] Y. Liu *et al.*, "Roberta: A robustly optimized bert pretraining approach," *arXiv preprint arXiv:1907.11692*, 2019.
[39] F. Castaño, A. Gil-Lerchundi, R. Orduna-Urrutia, E. F. Fernandez, and R. Alaiz-Rodríguez, "Wave-27k: Bringing together cti sources to enhance threat intelligence models," in *Proceedings of the First International Conference on Natural Language Processing and Artificial Intelligence for Cyber Security*, 2024, pp. 119–126.
[40] T. Wolf *et al.*, "Transformers: State-of-the-art natural language processing," in *Proceedings of the 2020 Conference on Empirical Methods in Natural Language Processing: System Demonstrations*, Online: Association for Computational Linguistics, 2020, pp. 38–45. DOI: 10.18653/v1/2020.emnlp-demos.6.
[41] J. Evans, "Mitre key details phrasing," Retrieved: September 2025, 2020, [Online]. Available: https://cveproject.github.io/docs/content/key-details-phrasing.pdf.
[42] C. Madden, "Vulnerability description quality checks and data analysis," Retrieved: September 2025, 2025, [Online]. Available: https://github.com/CyberSecAI/VulnerabilityDescriptionQualityChecker.

Secure Software Brownfield Engineering – Sequence Diagram Identification

Aspen Olmsted
School of Computer Science and Data Science
Wentworth Institute of Technology
Boston, MA 02115
email: olmsteda@wit.edu

Abstract— **The process of securing existing "brownfield" software systems becomes challenging when trying to identify and mitigate vulnerabilities in complex and often undocumented codebases. The paper investigates the essential requirement for improved program execution flow comprehension in legacy PHP applications to support secure software development. The proposed solution utilizes the trace functionality of program execution tracing through the PHP extension to obtain detailed execution paths dynamically. The methodology generates complete UML Sequence Diagrams through automated processing of program execution trace logs. These diagrams present object and function interactions through visual representations, which developers and security analysts use as essential tools. The sequence diagrams provide a straightforward, high-level view of runtime operations, which enhances code understanding and reveals concealed dependencies and security-critical control paths. The automated visualization system helps security professionals detect potential attack vectors, verify the implementation of security controls, and identify insecure data handling practices. The research demonstrates how a debugging tool can be leveraged as a security enhancement tool for brownfield environments, enabling developers to identify vulnerabilities more efficiently without relying on manual code reviews or architectural documentation. This method offers a practical solution to enhance the security posture of legacy PHP applications.**

Keywords- cyber-security; software engineering; secure software development.

I. INTRODUCTION

In the realm of software development, there is a distinction between developing greenfield systems and maintaining and advancing existing "brownfield " applications. When it comes to greenfield projects, there's the advantage of integrating up-to-date security measures from the start. However, brownfield systems, which comprise the majority of deployed software, pose a significant challenge. These older applications, developed over years or even decades, often lack security protocols, have inadequate documentation, and carry a burden of technical debt. Businesses depend on them for their operations, but their nature and lack of clarity make them vulnerable to security risks. The process of managing and addressing these vulnerabilities in established settings proves to be quite challenging because it needs strategies that combine traditional practices with modern security needs.

The primary challenge in securing software lies in its inherently black-box nature - a term used to describe its complex and opaque structure that is difficult to comprehend from the outside perspective alone. Developers and security analysts tasked with ensuring the security of these systems often face obstacles due to the lack of up-to-date information about how the software operates. The original developers may have moved on to other projects or roles, and the design documents might have also changed. Even when missing altogether, the sheer size of the codebase can be overwhelming to navigate efficiently. The system's lack of transparency creates significant difficulties for users in detecting control pathways within the codebase and tracking data movement across software components. The system's lack of transparency creates problems for both identifying vulnerabilities that allow harmful input to enter the system and detecting accidental mishandling of sensitive information.

Traditional tools for analysis may highlight problems but often yield numerous incorrect alerts or struggle to understand the intricate context of older code bases. On the one hand, manual code inspections are comprehensive. It can be too time-consuming and costly for established applications. Dynamic analysis—observing how a system behaves during operation—provides an approach to grasping real-time attributes. However, it frequently lacks a deep understanding of function calls and object interactions, which is necessary for accurately pinpointing vulnerabilities.

This article explores the world of existing PHP applications that have been around for a while and have undergone numerous changes and updates over time, often without prioritizing security from the outset. Due to PHP's flexibility and popularity in the online world, these applications have frequently lacked a security-first approach. An immediate requirement arises for widely applicable strategies to enhance the security posture of these yet vulnerable programs.

In our study, we propose a practical method to enhance software development methods in existing PHP environments by automatically generating UML Sequence Diagrams from XDebug trace logs. XDebug is an open-source tool used by developers for debugging and profiling PHP code. The robust tracing capability of XDebug primarily serves for debugging and performance evaluation, but it also provides an opportunity for security assessment. XDebug enables the capture of runtime information about function calls, method invocations, and variable assignments, which provides visibility into program execution behavior.

Our goal is to repurpose this known developer tool to offer an approach for comprehending intricate legacy code with minimal overhead and maximum effectiveness.

Our approach includes a series of steps to achieve our goal efficiently. Firstly, we start by activating an XDebug trace for scenarios or attack situations in the existing PHP system under consideration, creating logs of the exact sequence of actions taken. Secondly, we programmatically process these logs to extract essential details, such as, function names, class methods, arguments, return values, and execution order. We transform the extracted data into a format that works for creating UML Sequence Diagrams. The visual representations illustrate how individual objects and functions interact with each other over time, demonstrating the control flow and data movement within the software application.

There are many benefits of utilizing reverse-engineered UML Sequence Diagrams in the realm of software engineering. These diagrams play a role in enhancing the understanding of code structures. This becomes especially valuable for developers or security experts who face deciphering intricate legacy codebases, as the sequence diagram provides a holistic overview of how various components collaborate to accomplish specific functionalities. This visual representation simplifies comprehension compared to sifting through lines of undocumented code. Furthermore, the utility of diagrams extends to revealing concealed dependencies and unforeseen interactions within the system. In systems that have undergone development or modifications (brownfield systems), functions could interact with each other in unexpected ways, or data could pass through unforeseen middle steps or components not easily recognizable at first glance. Sequence diagrams bring clarity to these hidden connections by spelling out the relationships, for a deeper examination of possible repercussions or unintentional data disclosures.

Essentially, from a security standpoint, these diagrams point out control pathways. By showing the order of actions, analysts can easily identify areas of attack, such as, points where user inputs are handled, where outside data is used, or where essential tasks are performed. They can assist in tracking how unreliable data moves, from where it enters to processing steps, exposing spots for injections or flaws, in deserialization security. Additionally, sequence diagrams help confirm that security measures are properly implemented. For example, a person can visually verify whether authentication checks are executed in real-time, if input validation processes are regularly utilized, or if authorization determinations are made before accessing resources. This automated display enables security teams to conduct efficient security evaluations, reducing the need for tedious manual techniques.

The primary objective of this study is to demonstrate that utilizing debugging tools for security analysis is not only feasible but also highly beneficial. By converting execution data into a visual display format, we create a valuable tool that can be integrated into the secure development process of legacy applications. This strategy provides a solution for companies facing security issues in their systems, enabling them to identify and resolve vulnerabilities more efficiently without incurring significant costs for re-documentation or re-engineering efforts. Our research suggests that this method offers a reliable way to enhance the security of PHP programs, ultimately contributing to a safer online environment. The paper is organized as follows. Section II describes the related work and the limitations of current methods. Section III describes a motivating example for our work. Section IV discusses the implementation of our parser. Section V discusses the creation of sequence diagrams. We conclude and discuss future work in Section VI.

II. RELATED WORK

Secure software engineering has made substantial progress through greenfield development, which enables security integration at the beginning of software development. The distinctive obstacles of brownfield systems require separate attention. This section examines relevant literature on secure software development, with special attention to research that addresses security integration in existing codebases and the application of dynamic analysis and visualization techniques.

A foundational aspect of secure software engineering is the proactive integration of security considerations throughout the software development lifecycle. Aspen Olmsted's seminal work, "Security Driven Software Development" [1], provides a comprehensive framework for embedding security into every phase of development, from requirements gathering to deployment and maintenance. This book emphasizes the importance of a security-first mindset and offers strategies for identifying and mitigating risks early. While primarily focused on new development, the principles outlined by Olmsted, such as threat modeling and secure coding practices, are equally relevant to brownfield remediation efforts. Our proposed methodology, which aims to improve understanding of existing brownfield code, directly supports the application of such security principles by making the implicit explicit.

The paper by Olmsted titled "Secure software development through non-functional requirements modeling" [2] expands on the significance of early security integration by demonstrating how Non-Functional Requirements (NFRs) serve as essential elements for software security. The paper indicates that security requirements should be treated as an NFR, which should be explicitly modeled during the initial development phase.

The precision and verifiability of security requirements can be enhanced through the use of formal specification languages such as, Object Constraint Language (OCL) and UML stereotypes in this context [3]. For brownfield systems, where NFRs may not have been formally captured during initial development, our approach of generating UML Sequence Diagrams helps in reverse-engineering the system's behavior. By visualizing execution flows, it becomes possible to infer how security-related NFRs (e.g., access control, input validation) are currently being handled, or where they are conspicuously absent. The analysis results will guide the redefinition of security NFRs and direct the remediation process.

The paper "Secure Software Development–Models, Tools, Architectures and Algorithms" by Olmsted [3] presents a comprehensive overview of the various elements necessary for developing secure software systems. This paper discusses multiple models for security, the tools that aid in analysis, architectural considerations for building secure systems, and the algorithms underlying security mechanisms. Our research aligns with this broader vision by introducing a practical tool-based approach (leveraging XDebug) to generate a specific model (UML Sequence Diagrams) that aids in understanding the architecture and behavior of brownfield PHP applications. The generated diagrams serve as essential inputs for security models and algorithm applications, helping analysts detect hidden vulnerabilities in complex legacy code by tracing data and control flow.

While existing literature extensively covers secure software development, a gap remains in practical, low-overhead methods tailored explicitly for thoroughly understanding the runtime behavior of brownfield applications for security purposes. Static analysis tools (e.g., SAST solutions) are effective at identifying patterns of vulnerabilities but often struggle with context and produce false positives in complex legacy code. The interaction of Dynamic Application Security Testing (DAST) tools with running applications reveals vulnerabilities, but it operates at a higher abstraction level than XDebug traces provide function-level details. Our solution enhances existing tools by creating detailed visual execution flow maps, which aid in manual security auditing, threat modeling, and vulnerability impact assessment for complex brownfield PHP applications. The re-purposing of XDebug for this task provides a unique advantage because it uses a widely available and familiar developer tool, which reduces the learning curve and integration overhead for teams working with legacy PHP systems.

III. MOTIVATING EXAMPLE

Our proposed methodology demonstrates practical utility through an example that focuses on SuiteCRM, an open-source Customer Relationship Management (CRM) system widely used by many organizations. The open-source PHP application SuiteCRM represents an excellent brownfield example, as it contains extensive complexity from multiple years of development, without complete modern architectural documentation. The complex nature of SuiteCRM's functionalities makes it challenging for new developers and security auditors to understand its security aspects. Our method of creating UML Sequence Diagrams from XDebug traces enables effective business process reverse-engineering, which improves code understanding and security analysis capabilities.

The following common user scenarios in SuiteCRM demonstrate how program traces reveal their execution flows:

1. Scenario 1: User Creates Contact

- User Action: A sales representative navigates to the "Contacts" module, fills in various contact details (e.g., name, email, phone number, address), and submits the form to save the new contact record.
- Trace Insight and Security Relevance: When XDebug tracing is enabled during this operation, the generated trace log meticulously records every function call, method invocation, and file inclusion that occurs from the moment the form submission is processed. This includes the initial handling of the HTTP POST request, validation routines, and, critically, the data persistence logic. The trace would capture calls to files such as, modules/Contacts/Save.php, revealing the sequence of operations involved in taking the submitted data and committing it to the database.
- A detailed analysis of the sequence diagram derived from this trace shows:
- Input Handling: How the raw form data is received and sanitized (or not) before processing. This is crucial for identifying potential Cross-Site Scripting (XSS) or SQL Injection vulnerabilities if input validation is insufficient or bypassed.
- Data Flow: The path of sensitive contact information (e.g., email addresses, personal details) as it moves from the web form, through various PHP functions, and ultimately to the database. This helps in understanding where data might be exposed or mishandled.
- Database Interaction: The specific functions responsible for constructing and executing SQL queries for insertion into the contacts table. Insecure practices like direct string concatenation for SQL queries would be immediately apparent, highlighting SQL injection risks.
- Workflow Triggers: If the creation of a contact triggers other business logic (e.g., sending a welcome email, updating related accounts, or initiating a workflow), the trace would show the invocation of these subsequent functions. This helps in understanding the full impact of a contact creation operation and identifying any security implications of these cascading actions (e.g., unauthorized email sending).
- Access Control: The diagram could reveal where authorization checks are performed (or omitted) before data is saved, indicating potential Insecure Direct Object Reference (IDOR) or unauthorized data modification vulnerabilities if a user can manipulate data they shouldn't.

2. Scenario 2: User Schedules a Meeting

- User Action: A user accesses the "Meetings" module, enters details such as the meeting subject, time, date, duration, and invites participants (e.g., other users, contacts, leads), then saves the meeting record.
- Trace Insight and Security Relevance: Tracing this scenario would provide a rich sequence of interactions involving the logical meeting module and its dependencies. The trace illustrates how meeting details are processed, how participants are associated, and how notifications may be generated.
- The resulting sequence diagram would be invaluable for:
- Participant Management: Understanding how participants are linked to the meeting. This is critical for assessing potential information leakage (e.g., if a user can view participants they shouldn't) or unauthorized access to meeting details.
- Cross-Module Interactions: Visualizing the calls to linked modules, such as, Users and Contacts, to retrieve participant information. This helps identify potential privilege escalation paths if the

system implicitly trusts data retrieved from these modules without proper revalidation.

- Calendar Integration: If the meeting scheduling integrates with an internal calendar or external service, the trace would expose the functions responsible for these interactions. This enables security analysis of data exchanged with external systems.
- Notification Mechanisms: Tracing the functions responsible for sending meeting invitations or reminders. This can reveal vulnerabilities related to email spoofing, content injections in notifications, or denial-of-service if the notification system can be abused.
- Time and Date Handling: How time and date inputs are processed and stored. Incorrect handling of time zones or date formats can lead to logical flaws or even a denial-of-service attack if parsing errors are not handled gracefully.

3. Scenario 3: User Creates an Invoice

- User Action: An accountant generates a new invoice through the "Invoices" module, associating it with a specific client (Account), adding various products or services, specifying quantities and prices, and saving the invoice.
- Trace Insight and Security Relevance: This scenario is particularly sensitive due to its financial implications. The XDebug trace would capture the complex interactions involved in creating invoice entries, calculating totals, and establishing relationships between Accounts, Products, and Invoices modules.
- The sequence diagram would reveal:
- Financial Calculation Logic: The precise functions involved in calculating line item totals, taxes, and the grand total of the invoice. This is paramount for identifying potential manipulation vulnerabilities (e.g., rounding errors, incorrect tax calculations, or unauthorized price modifications) that could lead to financial discrepancies.
- Relationship Management: How the invoice is linked to an Account (client) and Products. This helps in understanding access control mechanisms for financial data and preventing unauthorized association of invoices with incorrect clients or products.
- Data Integrity: Tracing the flow of product quantities, prices, and client details into the invoice. Any points where these values are not adequately validated or where they could be tampered with before persistence would be highlighted.
- State Transitions: If an invoice goes through different states (e.g., Draft, Pending, Paid), the trace shows the functions responsible for these state changes, allowing for analysis of potential unauthorized state transitions.
- Reporting and Export: If invoice creation triggers the generation of a PDF or an export to an accounting system, the trace would expose the functions handling this, allowing for security review of data serialization and external communication.

In each of these scenarios, the automatically generated UML Sequence Diagrams provide a visual roadmap of the application's runtime behavior. This "living documentation" is far more accurate and up-to-date than static, manually created diagrams, which often become obsolete as the codebase evolves. For brownfield applications like SuiteCRM, these diagrams transform opaque execution paths into transparent, analyzable flows, significantly reducing the time and effort required for security auditing, vulnerability discovery, and targeted remediation. They empower security professionals and developers to ask precise questions about data handling, access control, and business logic, ultimately leading to a more secure and resilient system.

IV. PARSER IMPLEMENTATION

The core of our methodology lies in the ability to accurately parse and interpret the detailed trace logs generated by XDebug. This section describes the implementation of our parser developed in Java, designed to transform the raw, verbose XDebug output into a structured, actionable format suitable for subsequent UML Sequence Diagram generation.

XDebug trace files, typically in the .xt format, contain a chronological record of every function call, method invocation, file inclusion, and variable assignment during a PHP script's execution. While incredibly rich in detail, their raw format is not directly consumable by UML diagramming tools. Our Java parser addresses this by extracting salient information and organizing it into a programmatic representation that captures the essential elements of a sequence diagram: lifelines (objects/functions), messages (method calls), and their temporal order.

1. XDebug Trace File Format Overview

Before detailing the parser's design, it's essential to understand the structure of XDebug trace files. XDebug offers several trace formats, but the most common and detailed is the "computer readable" format (format 1). Each line in this format represents an event (e.g., function entry, function exit, include, require, eval) and contains a series of tab-separated fields. Key fields include:

- Level: The nesting level of the function call.
- Function Number: A unique identifier for the function call instance.
- Type: Indicates the event type (e.g., 0 for function call, 1 for function return, 2 for include, 3 for require, 4 for eval).
- Function Name: The name of the function or method being called.
- File Name: The PHP file where the function call originated.
- Line Number: The line number within the file.

- Time: Timestamp of the event.
- Memory: Memory usage at the time of the event.
- Arguments: A representation of the arguments passed to the function (if configured to be included).

2. Parser Design and Architecture

Our Java parser is designed as a modular component, following a typical parsing pipeline: reading, lexical analysis, syntactic analysis, and data model construction.

3. File Reading and Line-by-Line Processing:

The parser begins by reading the XDebug trace file line by line. Given that trace files can be very large (hundreds of megabytes for complex operations), an efficient line-by-line reading mechanism is crucial to avoid excessive memory consumption. Java's BufferedReader is employed for this purpose.

4. Lexical Analysis (Tokenization):

Each line read from the trace file undergoes lexical analysis. Since the fields are tab-separated, a simple String.split("\t") operation is sufficient to break down each line into its constituent tokens. Robust error handling is incorporated to manage malformed lines or unexpected field counts, preventing parser crashes due to corrupted trace data.

5. Syntactic Analysis and Event Interpretation:

After tokenization, the parser performs syntactic analysis by interpreting the meaning of each token based on its position and the event Type field. A switch statement or a strategy pattern can be used to handle different event types (0 for call, 1 for return, etc.).

Function/Method Calls (Type 0): When a function call event is encountered, the parser extracts the function name, the originating file and line number, and the call level. This information is used to identify the "caller" and "callee" in the sequence. The Function Number is critical for matching function calls with their corresponding returns.

Function/Method Returns (Type 1): Upon encountering a function return event, the parser uses the Function Number to locate the corresponding outstanding function call. This pairing is essential for determining the duration of a call and for correctly nesting messages in the sequence diagram.

Includes/Requires (Type 2, 3): These events indicate file inclusions. While not direct messages in a UML Sequence Diagram, they are important for understanding the context and dependencies within the PHP application. The parser can record these events to provide additional context or to help in identifying the "lifeline" associated with the executed code.

6. Data Model Construction:

The most critical phase is the construction of an in-memory data model that represents the sequence of interactions. We define several Java classes to represent the elements of a UML Sequence Diagram:

7. SequenceDiagram: The top-level class representing the entire diagram, containing a list of lifelines and messages.

Lifeline: Represents an object or function participating in the sequence. For PHP, this typically maps to a class name, an object instance, or a global function. The parser dynamically creates lifelines as new, unique function or method owners are encountered.

Message: Represents a communication between two lifelines. Key attributes include:

- sender: The Lifeline initiating the message.
- receiver: The Lifeline receiving the message.
- methodName: The name of the function/method being called.
- callLevel: The nesting depth of the call.
- startTime: Timestamp of the call.
- endTime: Timestamp of the return.
- arguments: (Optional) Parsed arguments.
- returnValue: (Optional) Parsed return value.
- messageType: (e.g., synchronous call, return).

The parser maintains a stack-like structure (e.g., a Deque or Stack in Java) to keep track of current active function calls. When a Type 0 event (call) occurs, a new Message object is created and pushed onto the stack. When a Type 1 event (return) occurs, the corresponding Message is popped, its endTime is set, and it is added to the Sequence Diagram's list of messages. This stack-based approach correctly handles nested function calls and ensures the proper temporal ordering of messages.

V. UML SEQUENCE DIAGRAM GENERATION

Once the XDebug trace data has been successfully parsed into our structured Java data model (comprising Sequence Diagram, Lifeline, and Message objects), the next step is to translate this model into a visual UML Sequence Diagram. For this purpose, we leverage PlantUML, a powerful open-source tool that allows users to create UML diagrams using a simple, human-readable text description.

The choice of PlantUML offers several significant advantages:

- Text-Based Definition: Diagrams are defined in plain text, making them easy to generate programmatically, version-controlled, and collaboratively worked on. This aligns well with automated generation from trace files, as our Java parser can directly output the PlantUML syntax.
- Ease of Integration: PlantUML can be integrated into various environments and workflows. The generated text file can be rendered into images (PNG, SVG) or other formats using the PlantUML command-line tool, a dedicated server, or IDE plugins.
- Flexibility and Expressiveness: PlantUML supports a wide range of UML diagram types, including Sequence Diagrams, with rich features for actors, participants, messages, activation bars, loops, conditionals, and notes, allowing for detailed and expressive visualizations.

Our Java parser, after constructing the Sequence Diagram object, includes a component responsible for generating the PlantUML syntax. This component iterates through the Lifeline and Message objects in the data model and translates them into PlantUML's specific syntax.

- Participants/Lifelines: Each unique Lifeline object identified during parsing (e.g., a class name like

ContactService, DatabaseHandler, or a generic Application for global functions) is declared as a participant in PlantUML using keywords like participant, actor, or boundary.

- Messages: Each Message object is translated into a PlantUML message arrow. The sender and receiver lifelines determine the source and target of the arrow, and the methodName becomes the message label. Activation bars are automatically handled by PlantUML when -> (call) and <- (return) messages are used.
- Nesting and Call Levels: The callLevel attribute of our Message objects is crucial for correctly representing nested calls and activation bars. PlantUML inherently handles nesting through the sequence of -> and <- messages, but explicit activate and deactivate keywords can be used for finer control.
- Conditional Logic and Loops: While XDebug traces capture the executed path, they don't directly provide information about if conditions or for loops that weren't taken. However, for executed loops or branches, the repeated messages or specific sequences can be grouped using PlantUML's loop or alt/else constructs, which can be inferred from patterns in the trace or added manually for clarity.

The output of this component is a plain text file (e.g., diagram.puml) containing the PlantUML definition. This file can then be fed into a PlantUML renderer to produce the final visual sequence diagram, providing an intuitive and accurate representation of the brownfield application's runtime behavior. This automated generation significantly reduces the manual effort traditionally associated with creating and maintaining such diagrams, making them a practical tool for security analysis and code comprehension.

VI. CONCLUSION AND FUTURE WORK

Future work should address multiple challenges starting with the issue of large file sizes according to our research findings. XDebug trace files tend to expand their size when complex operations or scripts run for extended periods. The parser needs both memory efficiency and the ability to handle files which exceed RAM capacity.

The trace data produced by XDebug includes all function arguments in its output. The process of interpreting complex PHP data structures (arrays, objects) in Java requires advanced logic to convert them into meaningful representations. The initial development should begin with basic data types before moving on to raw string logging of arguments.

The performance speed becomes vital when handling massive trace files. String manipulation using StringBuilder alongside data structure efficiency and object creation minimization will substantially boost performance.

Real-world trace files may contain corrupted lines or unexpected formats because of system crashes or misconfigurations. The parser needs to maintain robustness by either skipping malformed entries or logging warnings so it can prevent crashes.

Converting PHP dynamic elements like global functions and anonymous functions and closures into standard UML lifelines and messages requires thorough analysis. The system should treat global tasks as part of a basic "Application" lifeline and each object should receive its own lifeline based on its class name.

Our solution transforms XDebug trace data through Java parsing followed by PlantUML diagram generation to create structured programmatic models which become visual sequence diagrams. The generated model functions as the direct input source for any UML diagramming library or tool which produces valuable visual sequence diagrams to analyze and secure brownfield PHP applications. The parser architecture allows future extensions for new XDebug features while providing flexibility for processing various trace formats.

REFERENCES

[1] A. Olmsted, Security-Driven Software Development: Learn to analyze and mitigate risks in your software projects, Birmingham, UK: Packt Publishing, 2024.

[2] A. Olmsted, "Secure software development through non-functional requirements modeling," in *Proceedings of the 2010 International Conference on Software Engineering Research and Practice (SERP)*, 2010.

[3] A. Olmsted, "Secure Software Development–Models, Tools, Architectures and Algorithms," *Journal of Software Engineering and Applications*, pp. 743-750, 2012.

Measurability: Toward Integrating Metrics into Ratings for Scalable Proactive Cybersecurity Management

William Yurcik[†]
Centers for Medicare & Medicaid Services (CMS)
Baltimore, MD USA
william.yurcik@cms.hhs.gov

Stephen North
Infovisible
Oldwick, NJ USA
scnorth@gmail.com

Rhonda O'Kane
BitSight Technologies
Boston, MA USA
rhonda.okane@bitsighttech.com

O. Sami Saydjari
Dartmouth College
Hanover, NH USA
sami.saydjari@dartmouth.edu

Fabio Roberto de Miranda
Rodolfo da Silva Avelino
Insper Institute of Education and Research
São Paulo, Brazil
{fabiomiranda, rodolfosa1}@insper.edu.br

Gregory Pluta
University of Illinois
Urbana-Champaign, IL USA
gpluta@illinois.edu

***Abstract*— We share our experience implementing cybersecurity metric-based algorithmic ratings to proactively manage the cybersecurity of a large critical national infrastructure - U.S. healthcare. We describe the cybersecurity metrics we use, how cybersecurity ratings are algorithmically produced from these metrics, and empirical evidence for the value of cybersecurity ratings to both benchmark and make comparisons. Specifically, we share examples of how cybersecurity ratings can be used to baseline the cybersecurity posture of large hospital systems and how cybersecurity ratings can be used to calculate Return-On-Investment (ROI).**

Keywords - cybersecurity risk quantification; cybersecurity risk management; cybersecurity investment; cybersecurity metrics.

I. INTRODUCTION

Cybersecurity ratings based on empirical metrics are an attempt to characterize overall cybersecurity posture by integrating multiple cybersecurity aspects that can be measured. Ideally, we would like to derive one number that provides intuitive information about an enterprise cybersecurity posture at a point in time, as well as trends over longer time periods. However, cybersecurity ratings also raise challenges such as:

- *Are cybersecurity ratings measuring the right things?*
- *Are important cybersecurity aspects unmeasurable and/or unquantifiable?*
- *Is an overall cybersecurity rating meaningful, a false sense of cybersecurity, or a mischaracterization of effective cybersecurity practices?*
- *Can cybersecurity ratings be covertly gamed by adversaries to misrepresent results?*

As Anderson and Moore stated emphatically in 2006 – "*Risks cannot be managed better until they can be measured better"* [1]. In this paper, we report that nineteen years later that understanding of cybersecurity metrics have matured to the point where risks are now being measured, albeit imperfectly, such that enterprises are able to make decisions based on cybersecurity metrics, processed algorithmically into the form of cybersecurity rating, for improved cybersecurity operations and accountable cybersecurity investments.

The remainder of this paper is structured as follows. In Section II, we make the case for enterprise cybersecurity posture information as vital to enterprise cybersecurity operations. In Section III, we provide background on security metric research. In Section IV, we describe how we derive cybersecurity ratings from empirical security metric measurements. In Section V, we use cybersecurity ratings to perform cybersecurity posture analysis of a large national infrastructure – U.S. healthcare. We end with a summary and conclusions in Section VI.

II. CYBERSECURITY OPERATIONS

Cybersecurity operations encompass a range of functions aimed at protecting an organization's information and systems from cyber threats. These functions include monitoring, detecting, responding to, and recovering from cybersecurity incidents, as well as implementing preventative measures and ensuring compliance. Key areas include maintaining network defense, deploying new cybersecurity solutions, and managing Security Operations Centers (SOCs).

Figure 1 graphically depicts cybersecurity operations in multiple dimensions – we would like to highlight that the "evaluate" stages are reactive and the "direct and monitor" stages are proactive – which is where a cybersecurity operations team should strive to be positioned in order to prevent successful cybersecurity attacks.

In order to operate at the proactive cybersecurity operation stages, information is needed to focus efforts.

[†] Corresponding Author; Official Organizational Disclaimer: "The views presented herein do not represent the views of the Federal Government."

Cybersecurity operations leverage information from an organization's enterprise attack surface to improve cybersecurity posture and minimize risk – with the attack surface consisting of all IT assets that are potentially exposed to attackers (public-facing assets), including both known and unknown assets. To do this cybersecurity operations teams probe attack surface assets for vulnerabilities, misconfigurations, and other weaknesses that attackers could exploit, typically using vulnerability scanning and penetration testing. Threat modeling also helps to identify potential attack paths and impacts on business operations.

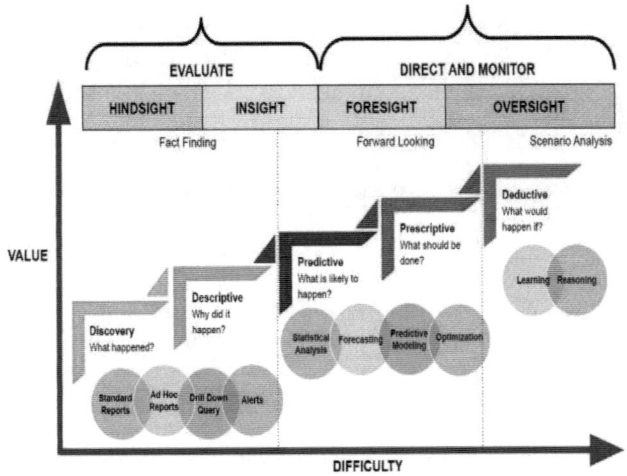

Figure 1. Overview of the Cybersecurity Operations Process.

Figure 2 shows a graphic depiction of the cybersecurity vulnerability cycle - a continuous cyclical process that includes identifying, assessing, prioritizing, remediating, and monitoring vulnerabilities before they can be exploited. Since addressing the number of vulnerabilities and attacks paths to be remediated is a continuous cyclical process, protective actions need to be prioritized based on risk.

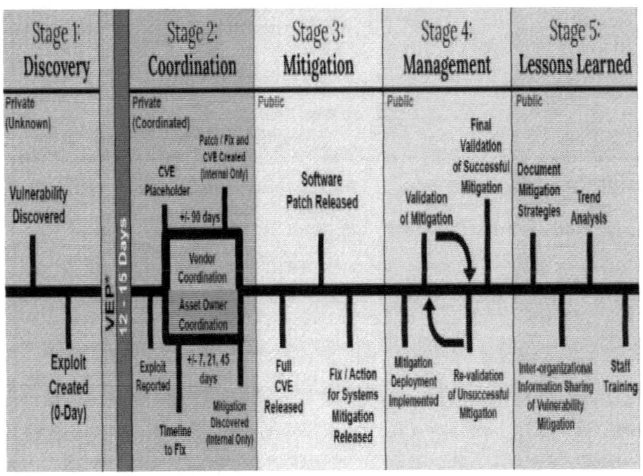

Figure 2. Lifecycle of a Cybersecurity Software Vulnerability.

Figure 3 shows a knowledge gap resulting from two other worrisome effects, the number of undetected attack surface threats is significant and growing over time.

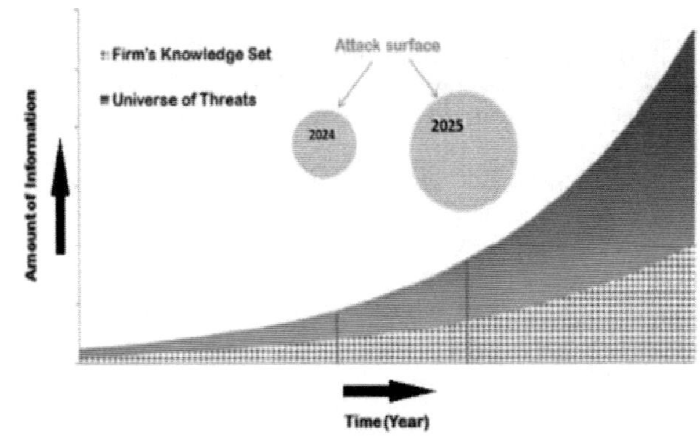

Figure 3. Knowledge Gap with Attack Surface Growth Over Time.

III. CYBERSECURITY METRICS

One of the most frustrating and ultimately dangerous things about cybersecurity is that it can *almost* be measured [2]. Creating an overall cybersecurity posture by measuring various components is complex and currently unsolved [3]. While security metrics can quantify aspects of security, they cannot definitively determine if a system is secure in absolute or relative terms [4].

There continues to be an essential requirement for organizations and engineers to more accurately evaluate overall security posture beyond subjective qualitative assessments. Unfortunately, misinformation and snakeoil are also filling this space. This work aims to quantitatively assess the overall cybersecurity posture, recognizing that it is an approximation. It is our stance that insistence on perfection in the form of a mathematical proof should not prevent implementation of "good enough" improvements over the status quo, especially when a vital need exists.

The U.S. National Institute of Standards and Technology (NIST) defines a metric as a measurement tool that supports human decision-making to enhance cybersecurity performance [5]. Cybersecurity metrics lack a standard best practice, as they are shaped by individual enterprise environments and the staff responsible for implementing cybersecurity operations.

The challenge of identifying cybersecurity metrics persists despite significant efforts over the past two decades. Since June 2000, numerous dedicated forums have addressed this topic, starting with NIST. Below, we present a partial list of major cybersecurity metric forums and highlight key contributions outside these forums [6] - [32].

- NIST Computer System Security and Privacy Advisory Board (CSSPAB) *"Approaches to Measuring Security"*, June 2000.
- *Workshop on Security Metrics (MetriCon)* 2006-2019.

- *International Workshop on Security Measurements and Metrics (MetriSec)* 2010-2012.
- *International Workshop on Quantitative Aspects in Security (QASA)* 2012-2017.

Possible security metrics include quantitative discrete and/or continuous data sources. In Figure 4, we show *proactive* cybersecurity metrics we have used in experimentation. Note these metrics look forward beyond reactive dashboard tracking the remediation of Known Exploited Vulnerabilities (KEVs) and Common Vulnerabilities and Exposures (CVEs) [33][34]. The objective for these cybersecurity metrics is to provide an indication what may happen next, beyond what has already happened in the past.

The cybersecurity metrics in Figure 4 can all be measured and quantified in different ways from *numerical-native* metrics such as incident-response-times and number-of-tested-systems-with-assessments to *categorical string-native* metrics that can be quantified in rankings (different levels of reported exposed credentials) or binary (existence of unapproved applications or not).

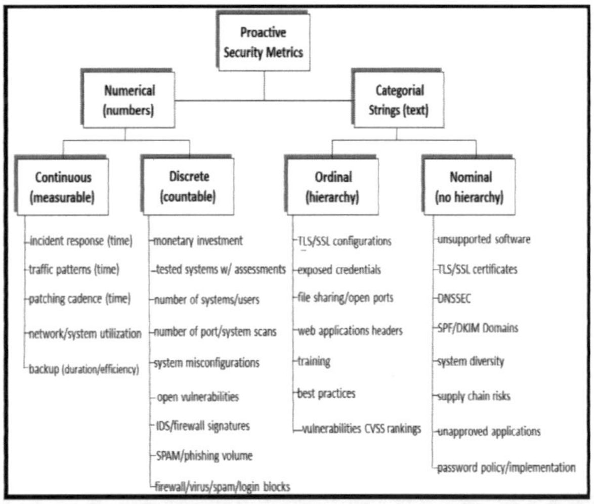

Figure 4. Selected Proactive Cybersecurity Metrics.

For example, about the proactive nature of just two of these cybersecurity metrics, a shorter patching cadence has been documented to be correlated with less risk since it reduces the window of time that a system is vulnerable to a known exploit [35] and implementation of any or all of the following email-related protocols – the Sender Policy Framework (SPF) protocol, the DomainKeys Identified Mail (DKIM) protocol, and the Domain-based Message Authentication, Reporting & Conformance (DMARC) protocol - have proven effective at preventing email spoofing, reducing spam and potential for phishing attacks by verifying legitimacy of email senders [36].

IV. CYBERSECURITY RATINGS

A Cybersecurity Rating is a data-driven dynamic measurement of an organization's cybersecurity performance used to manage enterprise and third-party cyber risk.

In everyday life, assessment ratings systems based on underlying metrics are in ubiquitous use to assess complex systems. Three examples include (1) human physical health, (2) national economies, and (3) financial instruments.

To assess human physical health, doctors use a variety of metrics such as age, weight, sex, heart rate, breathing rate, blood pressure, temperature, waist size, and blood test scores including cholesterol and blood sugar levels. To assess national economies, economists use metrics such as inflation rate, unemployment rates, gross domestic product growth, consumer spending, and gross national income per capita. For financial instruments such as a stock, analysts use price-to-earnings ratio, price-to-sales ratio, earnings per share, debt-to-equity ratio, return on equity, free cash flow, and enterprise value. For each of these examples, the underlying metrics can be combined to provide an overall assessment of physical health, national economic health, and stock price valuation respectively.

Cybersecurity ratings measure security effectiveness and have been validated against actual cybersecurity attacks. One such study positively matched cyberinsurance claims data with cybersecurity ratings showing lower ratings indicate the higher probability of a successful cybersecurity attack [37].

A. *Selecting Cybersecurity Metrics*

In this same way as these intuitive real-world examples, cybersecurity ratings combine security metrics to a single data point indication of overall cybersecurity assessment. Figure 5 shows 13 cybersecurity metrics that we have utilized as workable inputs to a cybersecurity ratings algorithm.

01	Bitsight Security Rating	08	Web Application Headers
02	Patching Cadence	09	User Behavior
03	Desktop Software	10	TLS/SSL Configurations
04	Potentially Exploited Systems	11	Open Ports
05	Mobile Software	12	TLS/SSL Certificates
06	Botnet Infections	13	Spam Propagation
07	Insecure Systems	14	Unsolicited Communications

Figure 5. Selected Metrics for Cybersecurity Ratings Algorithm.

B. *Weighting Cybersecurity Metrics in a Linear Algorithm*

The largest weight (70.5%) measures 11 different underlying submetrics for best practice implementation [patching cadence, web application headers, TLS/SSL certificates/configurations]. The next largest weight is an indication of compromised systems (27%) which measures evidence of preventing (or lacking to prevent) malicious or unwanted software [unsupported software, potentially exploited systems, botnet infection, insecure systems, spam]. The smallest weight is user behavior (2.5%), which measures three different activity metrics [open ports, password re-use, and file sharing traffic].

C. *Longitudinal Analysis*

A cybersecurity rating is a single data point in time, but its trend over time is more important. Analysts in securities, credit, and insurance industries prioritize these trends to better assess risk. For this reason, we use longitudinal "sparklines" to show the cybersecurity rating varying over a one-year time period. Figure 6 shows a cybersecurity rating sparkline varying over a year with a shaded rectangle indicating the expected "technology industry range" where organizations of the same type should be operating.

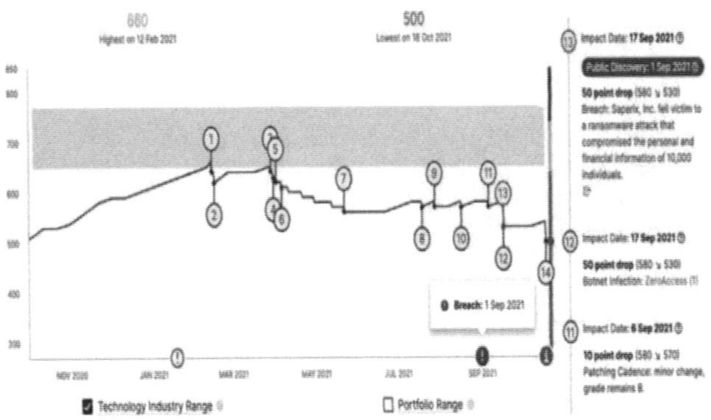

Figure 6. Cybersecurity Rating Sparkline Over a One Year Time Period.

V. CYBERSECURITY RATING RESULTS

We applied cybersecurity ratings to tangibly assess the cybersecurity posture of USA healthcare. We converged on hospitals as a central point touching every part of healthcare – most providers have hospital privileges and hospitals are typically the parent organization of subsidiary activity such as associated out-patient services/facilities. We used multiple open-source authorities to assemble a database of 7,490 USA hospitals hosted at the University of Illinois which has been vetted multiple times. Figure 7 shows all USA hospitals mapped to their geographical continental coordinates.

Hospitals have a broad network attack surface due to their public interactions. Their IT systems manage medical, administrative, financial, and record-keeping operations. Each application and device on the hospital network is a potential entry point for cyberattacks. Therefore, assessing hospital cybersecurity is crucial.

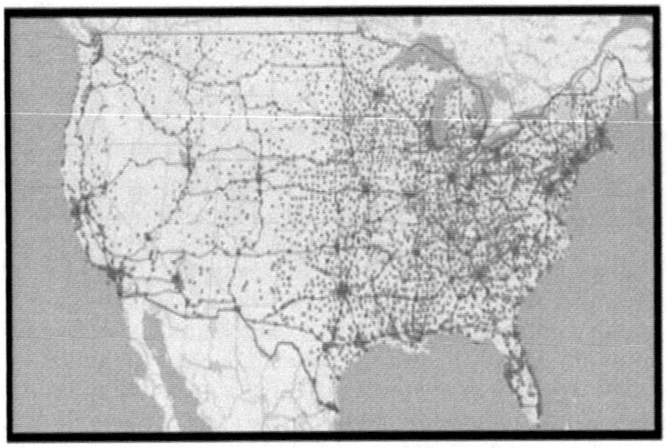

Figure 7. USA Hospitals Mapped to Geographical Coordinates.

Given the critical nature of hospitals, cybercriminals have realized that if they can successfully compromise a hospital enterprise environment using ransomware, then there is a high probability of payment. Hospitals handle Personally Identifiable Information (PII) (including financial data) and Personal Health Information (PHI) that can be monetized in dark web marketplaces. With financial viability at stake and healthcare-related investments being a cost center, hospital investments in cybersecurity protection in terms of staff and equipment are far below other industry levels [38]. Despite this below average investment, hospitals have cybersecurity ratings consistent with other industries, as shown in Figure 8.

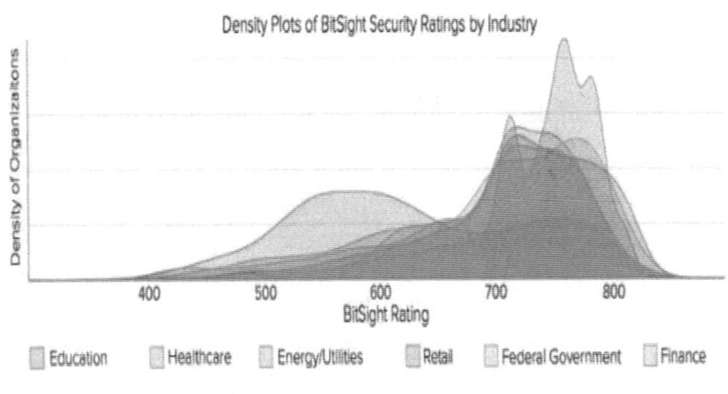

Figure 8. Industry Density Plot of Cybersecurity Ratings (provided by BitSight).

A. *Cybersecurity Ratings for Baselines*

Baselines provide a starting point for measuring continuous improvement as reflected in higher cybersecurity rating scores. Achieving higher cybersecurity ratings will not happen on its own but requires strategic cybersecurity investments in order to maintain and improve. Without strategic cybersecurity investments over long periods of time, decreased cybersecurity ratings will result as technology advances and existing cybersecurity protection techniques degrade and become obsolete.

Table I provides a comparison of the cybersecurity rating baselines for each of the hospital systems we analyzed. The baselines of the Indian Health Service (IHS) and Veterans Health Administration (VHA) hospital systems are statistically significantly different from each other and statistically significantly different from both Interstate/Intrastate Hospital Systems since their 95% confidence intervals for their means do not overlap. However, the baselines of Interstate/Intrastate Hospital Systems are not statistically significantly different from each other since their 95% confidence intervals for their means do overlap. This makes intuitive sense since both the IHS and VHA Hospital Systems have their own unique centralized IT coordination while Interstate/Intrastate Hospital Systems each consist of many different independent hospital systems, with each hospital system acting independently with little IT coordination between hospital systems.

TABLE I. CYBERSECURITY RATINGS FOR FOUR HOSPITAL SSTEMS.

Security Rating Stats	**IHS**	**VHA**	**INTERSTATE SYSTEMS**	**INTRA-STATE SYSTEMS**
Mean	719.8	753.8	682.7	699.3
95% CI	+/- 7.25	+/- 2.96	+/- 12.00	+/- 5.62
Median	730	760	690	710
Range	650-760 (110)	690-780 (90)	500-800 (300)	460-800 (340)
Skew	-1.23	-2.27	-0.52	-0.89
Targets	12	25	50	29

B. *Cybersecurity Ratings for Identifying Interventions*

Interventions in cybersecurity protection can be measured with changes in cybersecurity ratings in order to quantify the impact of managing strategic cybersecurity investments. It would be expected that an investment in cybersecurity protection would move the mean cybersecurity rating higher. To claim a positive change from the baseline (with statistical significance) confidence intervals should not overlap.

Larger enterprises typically have lower cybersecurity ratings than smaller enterprises since having more IT assets/systems creates a larger attack surface which is harder to protect. In order to ensure ratings are calculated in a way that does not unfairly bias results based on size, we need to normalize cybersecurity ratings based on organizational size using employee count as a surrogate for size. We acknowledge that this normalization approach of using employee count as an approximation for organizational size may be problematic since organizations vary greatly in their IT complexity.

Even with normalization for size, comparison using a mean cybersecurity rating still treats all hospitals in a hospital system as being equal. We know all hospitals in a hospital system are not equal; when a hospital outage occurs due to a successful ransomware attack some hospitals treat more patients than others (as measured in admittance levels and in-patient beds) and other hospitals are more likely to suffer adverse patient impacts (as measured in mortality). Thus, selecting investments for cybersecurity protection in order to improve the cybersecurity posture of a hospital system becomes a multidimensional optimization problem.

While deriving a multidimensional optimization problem as expressed in a weighted linear equation is beyond the scope of this paper, we can visually illustrate this optimization problem limited to two dimensions, cybersecurity ratings and hospital beds, using the hospital systems we have analyzed.

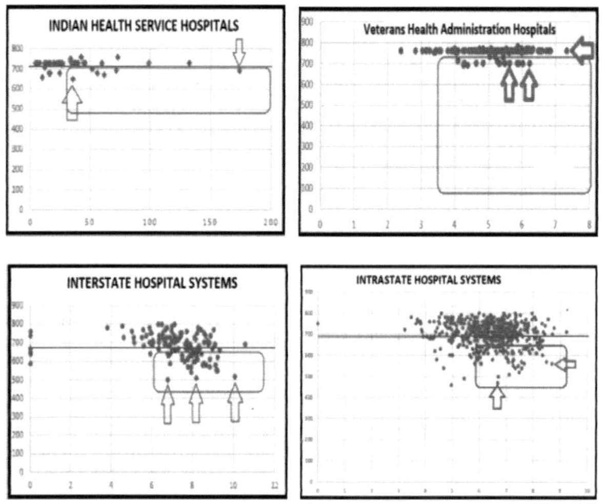

Figure 9. Hospital Targets for Cybersecurity Protection Investment.

Figure 9 shows scatterplots of hospital systems we have analyzed with each scatterplot mapping cybersecurity ratings versus hospital size as measured by in-patient hospital beds. We consider two dimensions for selecting hospitals for investment in cybersecurity protection resulting in the largest beneficial patient outcome and the largest increase in cybersecurity rating score, the largest hospitals with the lowest cybersecurity rating, basically the lower right quadrant. The last row in Table I indicates the number of potential target hospitals/systems which would be the best candidates for cybersecurity protection investment within each hospital system, resulting in a statistically significant increase in cybersecurity rating.

We would like to demonstrate the utility of this new paradigm approach by calculating results for two hypothetical cybersecurity investment intervention scenarios.

C. *Return-On-Investment (ROI) Scenarios*

Scenario One *(broad & shallow)* is a small ratings impact but broad intervention across a large number of hospitals based on three low-weighted vectors in the cybersecurity ratings algorithm which are approximately binary: SPF protocol implementation (1%), Desktop Software (3%), and Mobile Software (1%). Correctly configuring the SPF protocol to prevent email spoofing and having supported software on enterprise desktops/mobile devices are both binary observations. A strategic intervention to satisfy these three vectors simultaneously (all three vectors originally unsatisfied) may result in an estimated modest cybersecurity ratings score increase of 20 points. This is a low intensity effort in resources at each hospital but treating more hospitals. Depending on the low-level treatment required at each hospital, it may be possible to accomplish treatment remotely via conferencing and shipment of equipment as needed.

Scenario Two *(focused & deep)* is a large ratings impact but focused intervention involving a small number of hospitals performing poorly in cybersecurity management. Prioritizing hospitals starting with the lowest cybersecurity rating and working upward intervening to bring each treated hospital up to the highest system rating prior to intervention. This is an intensive effort in resources at each hospital but treating less hospitals and less travel. Since this is a high level of treatment at each hospital, it cannot be accomplished remotely and will demand more time at each hospital.

TABLE II. SCENARIOS ONE/TWO STRATEGIC INTERVENTION RESULTS.

	IHS	VHA	INTERSTATE	STATE
SCENARIO ONE	YES-31	NO–21	NO-41	NO-85
SCENARIO TWO	YES-7	YES-9	YES-12	YES-18

Table II shows results from the two scenarios. The Scenario One intervention (a broad and shallow intervention consisting of a small treatment across a large number of hospitals) results in only one hospital system (IHS) increasing its mean ratings with statistical significance (after interventions at 31 hospitals). The Scenario Two intervention (a focused and deep intervention treatment consisting of a large treatment across a small number of hospitals) results in all four hospital systems increasing their mean ratings with statistical significance.

For these two scenarios, and an infinite number of other scenarios, ROI can be measured in cybersecurity ratings changes. Intervention investments can then be optimized, under a budget constraint, for evidence-driven strategic ROI cybersecurity management decisions.

V. Conclusion And Future Work

In summary, we have introduced the use of cybersecurity ratings, based on cybersecurity metrics, to assess enterprise cybersecurity posture. Experimental results were demonstrated on large national infrastructures (U.S. hospital systems) where we empirically compared cybersecurity rating baselines for different large U.S. hospital systems. Lastly, we showed how interventions with cybersecurity investments can be strategically designed to improve cybersecurity and quantitatively measured for their ROI.

In the introduction, we raised challenges about the use of cybersecurity ratings which we address now. Cybersecurity ratings are a process, an algorithm with weighted cybersecurity metrics, thus if different metrics are proven to be more effective, then these new metrics can be easily substituted within the same process. Any qualitative or subjective cybersecurity aspect found to be important that may not be directly quantified, can be made measurable with analysis. We have shown multiple examples where cybersecurity ratings are meaningfully providing valuable baseline information for comparison and for calculating ROI. Unlike reputational rating systems, cybersecurity ratings are direct empirical measurements which cannot be gamed by adversaries without an adversary either having a successful man-in-the-middle spoofing capability or covert compromised control of the enterprise system being assessed to be able to manipulate metrics being measured.

For transparency, future work will provide more details on these algorithmic calculations including sensitivity of ratings to different weighting schemes and/or metric selections. We are also exploring dataset sharing options.

Acknowledgments

This research was enabled through a cooperative agreement between the University of Illinois at Urbana-Champaign and BitSight. BitSight provided no financial support to this research. Cybersecurity ratings for hospitals presented in this research were processed by BitSight engineers led by Rhonda O'Kane and supported by Tadd Hopkins, Tim Jackson, Tom Linehan, and Will Ricardi. Geocoding was provided by GeoCoder.ca who provided public service access to their geography mapping scripts. GeoCoder.ca provided no financial support to this research. Authors Miranda and Avelino were supported by a joint funding support agreement between the Insper Institute of Education & Research and the Computer Science Department at the University of Illinois at Urbana-Champaign.

References

[1] R. Anderson and T. Moore, "The Economics of Information Security," Science, Nov 2006.<doi: 10.1126/science.1130992>

[2] M. Blaze, "Afterword" within "Applied Cryptography 2nd Edition." by Bruce Schneier, 1996.

[3] INFOSEC Research Council, "Hard Problem List," Nov 2005.

[4] N. Mansourzadeh and A. Somayaji, "Towards Foundational Security Metrics," ACM New Security Paradigms Workshop, 2024.

[5] National Institute of Standards and Technology (NIST), "Measurement Guide for Information Security: Volume 1 – Identifying and Selecting Measures," NIST SP 800-55, vol. 1, January 17, 2024.

[6] N. Bartol, B. Bates, K. M. Goertzel, and T. Winograd, "Measuring Cybersecurity and Information Assurance," DoD Information Assurance SOAR Technology Analysis Center (IATAC), May 8, 2009.

[7] S. M. Bellovin, "On the Brittleness of Software and the Infeasibility of Security Metrics," IEEE Security & Privacy, 4(4) July/August 2006.

[8] D. J. Bodeau, R. D. Graubart, R. M. McQuaid, and J. Woodill, "Cyber Resiliency Metrics, Measures of Effectiveness, and Scoring," MITRE Technical Report. Release Case No 18-2579, 2018.

[9] D. Chapin and S. Akridge, "How Can Security Be Measured?" Information Systems Control Journal, vol. 2 2005.

[10] J-H. Cho, P. Hurley, and S. Xu, "Metrics and Measurements of Trustworthy Systems," IEEE Mil Comm Conf (MILCOM), 2016.

[11] L. F. DeKoven et al., "Measuring Security Practices," Comm of the ACM, 65(9), 93-102, Sept 2022. <doi:10.1145/3547133>

[12] D. Flater, "Bad Security Metrics – Part 1: Problems," IEEE IT Professional, Jan/Feb 2018.

[13] D. Flater, "Bad Security Metrics – Part 2: Solutions," IEEE IT Professional, March/April 2018.

[14] F. Innerhofer–Oberperfler and R. Breu, "Potential Rating Indicators for Cyberinsurance: An Exploratory Qualitative Study," Workshop on the Economics of Information Security (WEIS), 2009.

[15] W. Jansen, "Directions in Security Metrics Research," NIST Internal Report 7564, April 2009.

[16] G. Jelen, "SSE-CMM Security Metrics," NIST and CSSPAB Workshop, Washington DC. 2000.

[17] R. Khudhair and A. Ahmed, "Overview of Security Metrics," Software Engineering, 4(4): 2016. <doi:10.11648/j.se.20160404.11>

[18] P. Manadhata and J. M. Wing, "An Attack Surface Metric," CMUCS-05-155, Carnegie Mellon University, 2005.

[19] M. Pendleton, R. Garcia-Lebron, J-H. Cho, and S. Xu, "A Survey on Systems Security Metrics," ACM Computing Surveys, 49(4), Dec 2016.

[20] S. L. Pfleeger, "Useful Cybersecurity Metrics," IEEE IT Professional, May/June 2009.

[21] S. L. Pfleeger and R. K. Cunningham, "Why Measuring Security is Hard," IEEE Security & Privacy, July/Aug 2010.

[22] A. S. Pope, R. Morning, D. R. Tauritz, and A. D. Kent, "Automated Design of Network Security Metrics," ACM Genetic and Evolutionary Computation Conference (GECCO), 2018.

[23] W. H. Sanders, "Quantitative Security Metrics: Unattainable Holy Grail or a Vital Breakthrough within Our Reach?" IEEE Security & Privacy, 12(2), March/April 2014. <doi:10.1109/MSP.2014.31>

[24] R. M. Savola, "Towards a Taxonomy for Information Security Metrics," Intl Conf on Software Engineering Advances (ICSEA), 2007.

[25] S. Schechter, "Quantitatively Differentiating System Security," Workshop on the Economics of Information Security (WEIS), 2002.

[26] D. Snyder et al., "Measuring Cybersecurity and Cyber Resiliency," RAND Corporation 2020. <doi:10.7249/RR2703>

[27] S. Stolfo, S. M. Bellovin, and D. Evans, "Measuring Security," IEEE Security & Privacy, 9(3) May/June 2011. <doi:10.1109/MSP.2011.56>

[28] M. Torgerson, "Security Metrics," 12th Intl Command and Control Research and Technology Symposium, 2007.

[29] R. B. Vaughn, A. Siraj, and D. A. Dampier, "Information Security System Rating and Ranking," CrossTalk: J of Defense Software Engineering, May 2002.

[30] R. B. Vaughn, A. Siraj, and R. Henning, "Information Assurance Measures and Metrics—State of Practice and Proposed Taxonomy," 36th Hawaii Intl Conf on System Sciences (HICSS-36), Jan 2003.

[31] G. O. M. Yee., "Designing Good Security Metrics," IEEE Annual Intl. Computer Software and Applications Conference (COMPSAC), 2019.

[32] J. Zalewski, S. Drager. W. McKeever, and A .J. Kornecki, "Measuring Security: A Challenge for the Generation," Fed Conf on Computer Science and Information Systems, 2014. <doi:10.15439/2014F490>

[33] National Institute of Standards and Technology (NIST), "National Vulnerability Database (NVD)/Known Exploited Vulnerabilities," Retrieved 3/24/24 from <https://nvd.nist.gov/general/news/cisa-exploit-catalog>

[34] MITRE, "CVE Program Mission," retrieved 3/29/24 from <https://www.cve.org/>

[35] National Institute of Standards and Technology (NIST), "Guide to Enterprise Patch Management Planning: Preventive Maintenance for Technology," NIST SP 800-40 Rev. 4, April 2022.

[36] M. S. Ragheb, W. Elmedany, and M. S. Sharif, "The Effectiveness of DKIM and SPF in Strengthening Email Security," 10th International Conference on Future Internet of Things and Cloud (FiCloud), 2023.

[37] S. J. Choi and M. E. Johnson, "The Relationship Between Cybersecurity Ratings and the Risk of Hospital Data Breaches," J of the American Med Informatics Assoc., 28(10), 2021.

[38] T. Hwang, S. J. Choi, and J. Lee, "The Impact of Data Breach on IT Investment at Neighboring Hospitals: Evidence from California Hospitals," Digital Health, 2025. <doi: 10.1177/20552076251375930>

Identification of Dual Processes Using Power Side-channels

Jakob Sternby, Niklas Lindskog & Håkan Englund
Ericsson Research
Lund, Sweden
e-mail: {jakob.sternby | niklas.lindskog | hakan.englund}@ericsson.com

***Abstract*—Malware is one of the main threats against electronic devices, as malicious software can damage the device, disrupt network communications and provide an entry point for additional attacks. While software-based countermeasures such as antivirus can be effective, they require presence on the device and can furthermore be disabled or fooled by advanced malware. Monitoring of physical side-channels, on the other hand, provides a non-invasive and hard-to-spoof method to detect unauthorized software being executed on a device. However, in a modern device, several processes may execute at once, making detection of alterations difficult, especially in the case where more than one process is security sensitive and should be monitored. In this paper, we present a solution for enabling granular side-channel monitoring for complex, multi-core devices. We apply new machine-learning enhanced methodology, focused on efficiently representing the measurements in latent space, to enable classification of two simultaneously executing processes. The classification training is based on labeled power side-channel traces of dual-core measurements. Our results show that it is feasible to classify two processes on separate cores having observed a single power trace obtained from a single probe.**

Keywords-Security; Side-channel Monitoring; Dual-core.

I. INTRODUCTION

Physical side-channel monitoring observes unintended information leakage from electronic devices, e.g., such as changes in the power consumption, alterations in electromagnetic fields or temperature fluctuations [1]. An important distinction, compared to classical cryptographic side-channel analysis, is that primarily data-independent architectural process leakage is observed. This approach provides a promising field for non-invasive monitoring of software processes executing on an electronic device. By analyzing these physical side-channels, an external monitor can determine which software processes are executing on a device, even without logical access to it. Figure 1 for a high level illustration of how a machine learning model is trained, and later used for inference on monitored data from a target.

However, there is still a large gap between academic literature and real world settings, preventing large scale deployments of side-channel monitors. One of the primary obstacles is the lack of research for more complex monitored environments, e.g., devices where multiple processes execute simultaneously on more than one processor or processor cores; and processor optimizations that cause non-determinism in the execution patterns. Most prior art [1][2] assumes single threaded targets. This is a reasonable assumption for low-cost embedded devices and for microcontrollers where the primary objective is to perform a very specific task. Alternatively, the assumption is made that only a single process is of interest and the rest of the processes executing should be treated as noise to filter out [3–5]. To make side-channel monitoring viable also in settings where several processes of interest execute simultaneously on different processors or processor cores it is important to overcome these hurdles. In this paper, we investigate the possibility of classifying two simultaneously executing processes, on two separate CPU cores, by measuring the power consumption of the entire device. Further, we perform the classification using a one-shot classification, i.e., the classification is done using a single power trace, without the need of repeated executions of the software. Our contribution is three-fold:

1) A multi-model machine-learning solution that improves feasibility of multiprocess side-channel monitoring.
2) An evaluation of side-channel monitoring-based classification of multiple, simultaneously executing, software processes.
3) A machine learning-based approach to classify a single side-channel measurement trace as two classes from a set of predefined processes.

The remainder of the paper is organized as follows: We describe the relevant background in Section II and discuss previous work in Section III. In Section IV, we describe the setup and properties of our solution followed by an evaluation of the effectiveness of our approach in Section V. We provide discussion of our results, as well as future work in Section VI and conclude our findings in Section VII.

II. BACKGROUND

A. Side-channel emissions

Side-channel emissions refer to unintended information leaks from a physical device that occur as byproducts of its operation. These emissions can include power consumption, electromagnetic (EM) radiation, timing variations, thermal signatures, acoustic signals, and optical signals. Electronic components such as processors, memories, and data buses emit distinct side-channel data based on their current state, the instruction being executed, and the data being processed. Side-channel leakage originates from variations in power from charging and discharging transistors in hardware. The variation may both be data dependent but also depend on the set of active logic gates at the specific time. For example, power consumption can be correlated to the Hamming weight (the number of binary '1´s) of the current state; another common leakage mode is to consider the Hamming distance between current and previous states of the device. Historically, side-channel emissions of a device have been regarded primarily as

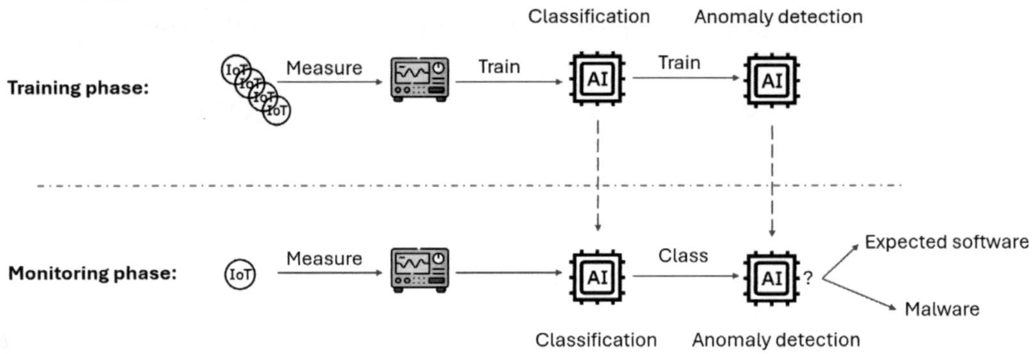

Figure 1. Overview of side-channel monitoring. Usually there is a profiling phase where e.g. a machine learning model is trained on measurements from potentially a large set of devices and varying code; and the monitoring phase where the model is used to for inference on monitored targets.

vulnerabilities that attackers could exploit to extract sensitive information [6]. An attacker can exploit the leakages to infer sensitive information in a device, e.g., to extract a cryptographic key used to encrypt data. Side-channel attacks are effective because there is a measurable correlation between the physical measurements (power consumption, EM emissions, timing, etc.) taken at various points during computation with both the data and the set of active gates of the processing device.

B. Side-channel monitoring

There is a growing interest in using side-channel monitoring as a method to detect malicious software. In this approach, a monitor records the device's side-channel emissions and determines whether its behavior aligns with predefined expected criteria. For this type of usage, called side-channel monitoring, leakage originating from data is of less relevance. Instead, the activation of components, such as different execution units and registers in a CPUs, contributes to the side-channel profile which can be used to determine the executing process. Activation patterns present in the side-channel measurements can indicate if a given process is executing on a device.

External monitoring comes with the additional advantage of not having to solely rely on information originating from processes in the device, which is a common case for system control and monitoring. A security monitoring scheme that relies on a device to itself detect deviations and non-compliances, incorporates the risk that an attacker may remain undetected, especially if he is able to mimic normality towards the control system. In this aspect, side-channel monitoring provides a compelling property of air-gapped monitoring; as the device is usually not aware if and when it is being monitored externally, stealthy malware can be detected. This is due to the fact that any unexpected process running on a device will cause an abnormal side-channel leakage.

C. Machine Learning (ML) for side-channel monitoring

Physical side-channel data, such as power consumption, can be captured as a time-series of floating point values. Depending on what is monitored, as well as the sampling rate such a time-series typically contain thousands, if not millions, of values and it would be very challenging to analyze such data without data-driven methods. In the past decade machine learning models trained on such data has surpassed prior statistically based methods when it comes to side-channel attacks [7]. Machine learning has also been an enabler for side-channel monitoring. The monitoring can include different tasks such as determining which process(es) is running as well as determining if a known process is running as expected. For determining which of a number of executing programs is running, a classification model can be trained to perform this classification based on the obtained side-channel patterns. Although a classification model produces likelihoods for their respective classes, these are not reliable to use for determining anomalies since classification models are often over-confident [8]. Training a specialized binary classifier to distinguish attacks from normal execution may be a more straightforward approach for this problem but in practice attack data is dynamic to its nature and such a model risks quickly becoming obsolete and failing to classify new attacks correctly. In anomaly or novelty detection, a model is instead trained exclusively on side-channel data from normal program executions with the aim of being able to detect anything not part of the training distribution.

Side-channel traces, or measurements, are discrete amplitude samples at regular time intervals, i.e., the data is serial. Hence, an ML-architecture with the capacity to learn correlations between different elements of sequences, such as Long-Short Term Memory (LSTM) or Recurrent Neural Networks (RNN) has been the architecture of choice for most published work on using side-channels to monitor processes [9][10]. In recent years, the Transformer architecture - a key component in the breakthrough of large language models - has shown success in a wide range of sequential ML tasks and has recently also been used with power side-channel data [11].

III. Previous Work

Side-channel monitoring using physical side-channels is well established in the literature [1]-[4][9][12]. However, to our knowledge, there is no previous attempt at dual process classification. In [5], a process is classified amid other processes executing on the device but the authors do not attempt to classify the other processes. In [3] instruction-level disassembly is performed on a process executing on a dual core ARM Cortex-A9 CPU, however, they schedule the process on a specific core and surround the payload code with No Operation (NOP) instructions [3].

Early work on machine learning-based side-channel monitoring used a LSTM-network to classify legitimate Programmable Logic Controller (PLC) control sequences and used a threshold on the calculated softmax as an indicator of malicious code [9]. Vidal et al. use a Dynamic Time Warping with a nearest neighbor approach to align and match different power side-channel traces to classify execution blocks [2]. Classification models on power measurements have also been used to identify intrusion attacks on IoT devices. In [12], power measurements on external devices were taken every 0.2 seconds and then grouped into various feature sets. A last window of features was used to train a range of simpler models that could run on resource scarce Internet-of-Things (IoT) systems.

IV. Solution Overview

We present a solution to enable side-channel monitoring of devices with multiple processors or processors with multiple cores. We denote the monitored device as Device-under-Monitoring (DuM) for the remainder of the paper. The DuM can run several different benign processes, either distinct programs or different threads of the same program. Hence, allowing the software executing on the respective processors to be simultaneously monitored is desirable.

In the proposed solution, two processor cores execute distinct software components simultaneously on the DuM. While it would be possible to monitor the power consumption of these cores individually, it would require invasive monitoring, probing power lines to individual processors, and hardware changes. Instead, the side-channel monitor observes a physical side-channel using a single probe, e.g., monitoring the main power line of the device. One of the advantages with such side-channel monitoring is that it can be retrofitted and be entirely external to the DuM.

The monitor scans for a start trigger pattern to start measuring, e.g., a power reset indicating a boot sequence. Once the trigger is detected, the monitor collects samples until a pattern indicating an end trigger is found or a pre-defined number of samples has been collected. From the collected samples, the monitor must decide whether the measurement indicates normal behaviour or not. The solution must be able to extract this information from a set of measurements obtained during a single execution as repetition of the processes is infeasible in real-world scenarios. E.g., a boot procedure only occurs at startup and classification of processes cannot rely on obtaining measurements from multiple executions. To facilitate this, the monitor uses a machine learning-enhanced two-step approach to detect whether the processes execute as expected, as shown in Figure 1. In a first step, the monitor classifies which set of processes have been executed by the processors. In a second step, given the classified set of processes, the monitor

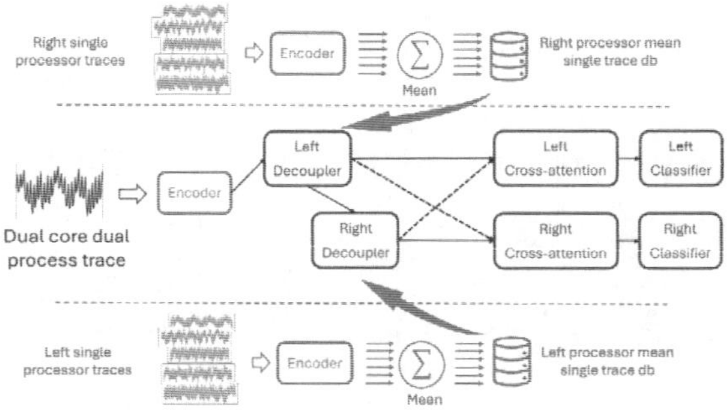

Figure 2. Overview of the ML-architecture used for dual trace classification in Section V.

selects a model trained for said combination and determines whether the execution was as expected.

In this paper, we focus on evaluating the first step, as this is a prerequisite for the second step to function. For multi-core processors which can execute several different allowed processes, effective anomaly detection cannot be performed before the monitor has determined what process it is monitoring. As it has been proven that one can monitor a known process in the presence of noise sources in a dual-core processor [3], indicating the feasibility of the second step, we aim to prove that we can identify which processes are executing. That is, the goal of our method is to use an obtained set of side-channel measurements to classify the processing class of both processors.

A. ML model architecture

The machine learning architecture used in the experiments consists of four distinct blocks: pretrained encoder, decoupler, cross-attention and classifier. A schematic overview is shown in Figure 2. Each component is based on blocks with multi-head attention, also known as transformers [13]. The purpose of the separately trained encoder is to produce a contextual representation of the side-channel traces well-suited for the classification and that this can use more and varied data without necessary labeling. The encoder is used both to convert the trace with two parallel processes running on a dual-core, as well as to convert prototype examples of a single process running on each of the cores. The encoded single process traces are used to produce static input to the decoupler modules as information of what the respective classes running on the other core could look like. Cross-attention blocks are used to mix in attention of the right and left decoupled representations to each other and finally the separated parallel classifier blocks serve to produce logits (the unnormalized probability scores) for each of the process classes of the right and left cores.

1) Pretraining a side-channel encoder with data2vec2: The encoder is trained using the data2vec2 framework [14] with a slightly modified feature encoder for side-channel measurements. Although data2vec supports multiple modalities each modality requires a specific feature encoder. As power side-channel measurements are 1D time-series similar to those of audio data, we reuse the audio encoder from data2vec with a

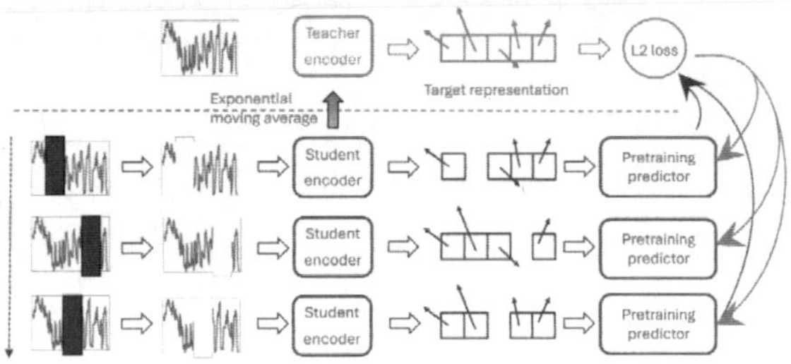

Figure 3. Overview of the pretraining process for learning side-channel latent representations.

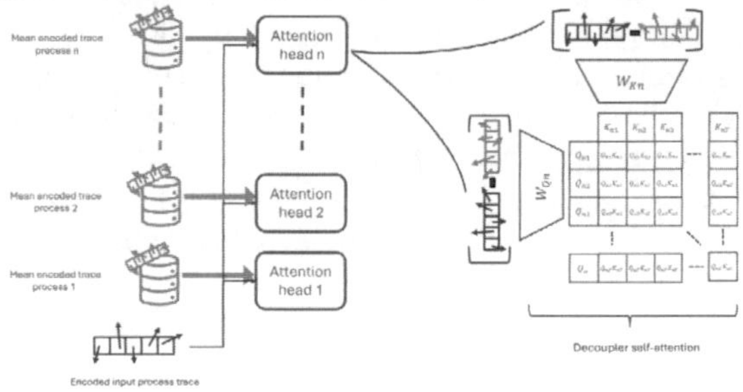

Figure 4. Overview of the self-attention mechanism in the decoupler block, incorporating the a priori knowledge of processor classes running on single cores through separate attention heads with the difference to the encoded dual trace.

stack of convolutional filters but alter the dimensions to adjust to the sampling frequency. The large share of parameters in the encoder is, however, resulting from the stack of transformer layers after these convolutional filters. The transformer layers enable the model to encode contextual information of the surrounding into each time step of the encoded sequence and the output of the encoder is commonly referred to as a contextual latent representation.

Data2vec implements a self-supervised learning paradigm where the learning task is to predict masked portions of the input sample. As depicted in Figure 3, data2vec2 employs a teacher-student configuration where the task of the student is to predict masked parts of a sample based on targets produced by the teacher. The teacher on the other hand is an exponential moving average of the student encoder. In order to enable prediction of the masked parts, the student network has an additional prediction network component which in this implementation is a stack of 1D convolutional layers. Each target representation is reused for multiple maskings of one sample for efficiency as shown in the figure. Note that the pretraining prediction network is only used during the pretraining of the encoder and is discarded afterwards.

2) Training a dual-trace classifier with single process representations: The neural network architecture presented in this paper has two major differences from a conventional transformer-based sequence classifier. Firstly, the dual-core classifier presented here has two output blocks - one for each core - to enable classifying two processes simultaneously, as seen in Figure 2. Secondly, with the aim of incorporating knowledge of the side-channel measurements of single core processes, it contains novel decoupler blocks that mix in knowledge of these encodings into separate attention heads.

The idea is that a neural network could learn to separate two processes in a combined dual-core trace if given the difference of each process in the encoded representation. To accomplish this, the decoupler block has been designed as a multi-head attention block where each attention head takes class-specific input, as seen in Figure 4. The class-specific input of a processor are the mean encoded representations of measurements for each process running on a single core. Each attention head then performs normal self-attention on the difference between the class-specific input of that head and its encoded input. By placing two decouplers, first one left with class-specific inputs from single processes running on the left processor followed by one on the right taking the output of the first decoupler and class-specific input from single processes running on the right processor, the model could learn to successively separate the processes present in the dual-core measurements.

The final output from all attention heads in one decoupler is concatenated and projected back to the input dimension. After the decouplers, the respective left and right outputs are separated and continue with cross-attention blocks which add another possibility to adjust the right and left outputs with respect to each other. The cross-attention blocks are identical to the cross-attention blocks in a typical decoder of a encoder-decoder network [13], where the key and query inputs are the separated left and right outputs from the decouplers, respectively. The two parallel classification blocks consist of multi-headed attention followed by a projection from the concatenation of the sequence to the number of classes and ending with a softmax outputting the class probabilities. All of the components after the encoder contain two identical serial blocks and the cross-attention and classification blocks have four attention-heads each in the multi-headed attention.

V. EVALUATION

Our experimental setup comprised a ChipWhisperer Husky measuring power consumption on targets implemented on a DuM embodied by a NAE-CW305-04-7A100 FPGA. The FPGA was configured with two soft-core realizations of Cortex-M3 cores [15] with 32 kB instruction memory and 32 kB data memory, both implemented in block RAM. The respective cores have a three-stage instruction pipeline, which has branch prediction, and do not have a cache. Moreover, the first Cortex-M3 (denoted $\mathcal{C}_{\mathcal{A}}$) has a trigger signal for informing the Husky of process start. The first and second Cortex-M3 (denoted $\mathcal{C}_{\mathcal{B}}$) share a reset signal, and therefore start to execute their respective software programs simultaneously. The cores are executing at a clock speed of 20 MHz and the monitor samples at a rate of 80 MS/s. 4x oversampling was selected as it is sufficient to identify the patterns of the programs executed on the respective CPU core, but still low enough to generate reasonable amounts of data. The evaluation utilized programs from the BEEBS [16] suite and we selected 10

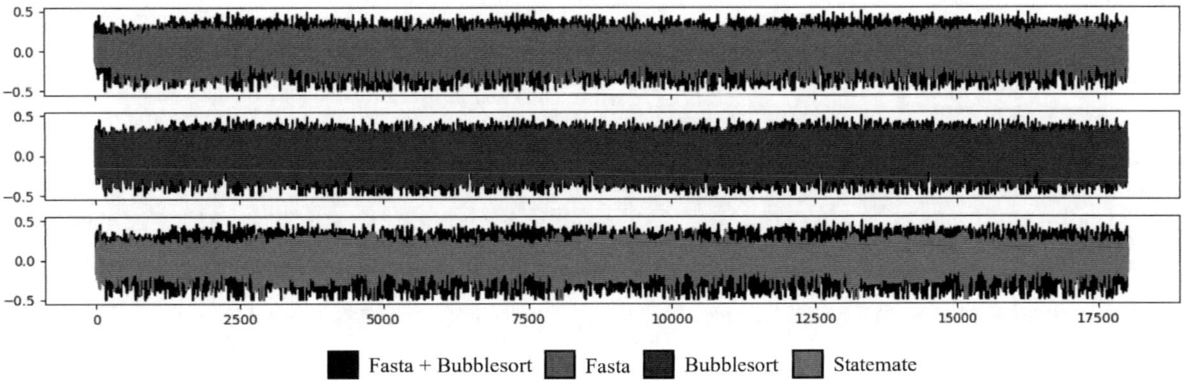

Figure 5. An example of the contribution of each process to a joint side-channel trace. Each measurement trace indicates the relative power consumption of the device during 4500 clock cycles. The black trace is a measurement of the FASTA program executing on $\mathcal{C}_{\mathcal{A}}$ and the BUBBLESORT program on $\mathcal{C}_{\mathcal{B}}$. In the green trace, the FASTA program is executing by itself on $\mathcal{C}_{\mathcal{A}}$, i.e., $\mathcal{C}_{\mathcal{B}}$ is idle. In the blue example, the BUBBLESORT program is executing by itself on $\mathcal{C}_{\mathcal{B}}$. In the red example, a program not present in the black trace, STATEMATE, is executing on $\mathcal{C}_{\mathcal{B}}$.

programs $P = \{P_i \mid 0 \leq i \leq 9\}$ of suitable execution length. The selected programs have deterministic execution e.g. without non-deterministic branch conditions. We measured each program for 18000 samples, i.e., during 4500 clock cycles. For programs shorter than 4500 clock cycles, the program was restarted. An example of the collected samples can be seen in Figure 5.

Let $P^{\mathcal{A}}$ ($P^{\mathcal{A}} \in P$) denote a program running on $\mathcal{C}_{\mathcal{A}}$, and $P^{\mathcal{B}}$ a program on $\mathcal{C}_{\mathcal{B}}$ respectively.

During the measurement collection phase, we collected 1000 measurements from each combination of programs ($\{[P^{\mathcal{A}}, P^{\mathcal{B}}] \mid \forall P^{\mathcal{A}}, P^{\mathcal{B}} \in P\}$), as well as each program running alone on respective processor. 70% of these were fed to the evaluation model during training 10% was used as a validation set and the rest as a held-out independent test set.

A. Training the ML model

The pretraining of the encoder was conducted with the data2vec framework [14] in an unsupervised manner with side-channel measurements from 10 different programs on a single-core, as well as some measurements from two processes running on a dual-core processors. For the first convolution layers of the encoder we used four layers of dimensions `(256, 256, 128, 128)`. Corresponding kernel sizes and strides of the layers were: `(32, 12, 4, 4)` and `(12, 8, 3, 2)`. The encoder dimension was 48 and in total the encoder produced 29 time steps for each trace-segment of length 18,000. The disposable 1D convolutional decoder only used in the pretraining had 4 layers with 64 dimensions, 8 groups and kernel size 7. In total, the pretraining with a total of 120120 traces ran for 120000 steps using the Adam optimizer with a learning rate of 0.0001 and weight decay of 0.01.

The dual classification model is trained without changing the pretrained model. It starts by calculating the mean of the encoder output of the single process training traces for each right and left class, these are then added as static elements in the right and left decoupler blocks seen in Figure 2. The training then proceeds with two parallel cross-entropy loss calculations of the corresponding labels for left and right processor, each contributing to updating the specific and common weights of the network. The model was trained for 140 epochs with the Adam optimizer with a starting learning rate of 0.0002 and a weight decay of 0.00003. The best model as evaluated by the loss on the validation set was chosen as the final model of each run. The seed was changed for each of 5 runs included in Table I to get a different split of the collected data into training / validation / test.

B. Classification results

The classification model is evaluated with two accuracy metrics as seen in Table I. The accuracy listed is the percentage of test traces where the complete dual label is correct whereas the *single acc.* is calculated as the percentage of single labels being correct. *Single acc.* is consequently at least as high as accuracy but usually higher since accuracy will classify an output as incorrect even when one of the two labels is correct. The results show the mean and the standard deviation of five runs with different seeds causing differing splits into training / validation and test sets. To compress the table only the aggregation of results for all processes running on the $\mathcal{C}_{\mathcal{A}}$ is shown $\mathcal{C}_{\mathcal{B}}$ in Table I.

VI. Discussion

In this paper, we have allowed the simplification of having synchronous executions by using a single reset signal to both processors. A natural next step would be to determine how well the presented solution works for programs which are slightly displaced in time, as the assumption of deterministic process start is only viable in very specific situations.

The Cortex-M3 processors does not have any cache and thus no shared state. The co-varience of processes with shared caches should be studied further.

Furthermore, we have only considered simple processes with deterministic execution, without branching. Combining

TABLE I. DUAL-CORE CLASSIFICATION ACCURACY LISTED BY THE CLASS OF THE PROCESS RUNNING ON $\mathcal{C}_{\mathcal{A}}$.

$\mathcal{C}_{\mathcal{A}}$ class	Accuracy	Single acc.	# Test	# Valid	# Train
cnt	96.1% ± 0.9	98.0% ± 0.5	2200	1100	7700
fasta	91.1% ± 1.1	95.6% ± 0.5	2000	1000	7000
prime	97.5% ± 0.4	98.8% ± 0.2	2200	1100	7700
ahacompress	95.8% ± 4.8	97.9% ± 2.4	2200	1100	7700
bubblesort	97.3% ± 4.2	98.6% ± 2.1	2200	1100	7700
cover	98.2% ± 4.1	99.1% ± 2.0	2200	1100	7700
tarai	91.9% ± 2.0	95.9% ± 1.0	2200	1100	7700
lcdnum	96.3% ± 3.6	98.2% ± 1.8	2200	1100	7700
crc32	85.4% ± 3.6	92.7% ± 1.8	2200	1100	7700
statemate	96.4% ± 5.0	98.2% ± 2.5	2200	1100	7700
idle[a]	88.5% ± 5.0	94.2% ± 2.5	2200	1100	7700
Total	94.1% ± 2.2	97.0% ± 1.1	24000	12000	84000

[a]No process currently executing on $\mathcal{C}_{\mathcal{A}}$.

our multi-process work with control flow graphs has potential to enable monitoring of the current internal state of multiple processes simultaneously.

In this paper, we have performed our tests on an FPGA implementation of the two CPUs. This has enabled us to make simplifications in order to fine-tune the methodology. How additional complexity impacts the results, in the form of executing the software on hard processors, with or without out-of-order execution and processor optimizations, should be researched further.

VII. Conclusion and Future Work

We showed that two distinct processes execution on two separate ARM Cortex M3 processors can be correctly classified with an average accuracy of 94.1%. This indicates that the side-channel monitoring can adapt to more complex devices and that monitoring can be viable also for use cases going beyond to single-process CPUs and FPGAs implementations.

References

[1] Y. Han, I. Christoudis, K. I. Diamantaras, S. Zonouz, and A. Petropulu, "Side-channel-based code-execution monitoring systems: A survey", *IEEE Signal Processing Magazine*, vol. 36, no. 2, pp. 22–35, 2019.

[2] B. Vidal, C. Moreno, S. Fischmeister, and G. Carvajal, "Monitoring software execution flow through power consumption and dynamic time warping", *IEEE Embedded Systems Letters*, vol. 15, no. 2, pp. 101–104, 2022.

[3] J. Maillard, T. Hiscock, M. Lecomte, and C. Clavier, "Side-channel disassembly on a system-on-chip: A practical feasibility study", *Microprocessors and Microsystems*, vol. 101, p. 104 904, 2023.

[4] A. Nazari, N. Sehatbakhsh, M. Alam, A. Zajic, and M. Prvulovic, "Eddie: Em-based detection of deviations in program execution", in *Proceedings of the 44th Annual International Symposium on Computer Architecture*, 2017, pp. 333–346.

[5] Y. Chen, X. Jin, J. Sun, R. Zhang, and Y. Zhang, "Powerful: Mobile app fingerprinting via power analysis", in *IEEE INFOCOM 2017-IEEE Conference on Computer Communications*, IEEE, 2017, pp. 1–9.

[6] P. Kocher, J. Jaffe, and B. Jun, "Differential power analysis", in *Advances in Cryptology — CRYPTO' 99*, Springer Berlin Heidelberg, 1999, pp. 388–397, ISBN: 978-3-540-48405-9.

[7] E. Bursztein *et al.*, "Generalized power attacks against crypto hardware using long-range deep learning", *CHES*, 2024.

[8] J. Grabinski, P. Gavrikov, J. Keuper, and M. Keuper, "Robust models are less over-confident", in *Advances in Neural Information Processing Systems*, S. Koyejo *et al.*, Eds., vol. 35, Curran Associates, Inc., 2022, pp. 39 059–39 075.

[9] Y. Han, S. Etigowni, H. Liu, S. Zonouz, and A. Petropulu, "Watch me, but don't touch me! contactless control flow monitoring via electromagnetic emanations", in *Proceedings of the 2017 ACM SIGSAC Conference on Computer and Communications Security*, ser. CCS '17, Dallas, Texas, USA: Association for Computing Machinery, 2017, pp. 1095–1108, ISBN: 9781450349468. DOI: 10.1145/3133956.3134081.

[10] Y. Han, M. Chan, Z. Aref, N. O. Tippenhauer, and S. Zonouz, "Hiding in plain sight? on the efficacy of power side channel-based control flow monitoring", in *31st USENIX Security Symposium (USENIX Security 22)*, 2022, pp. 661–678.

[11] N. Lindskog, H. Englund, J. Sternby, and E. Dubrova, "Machine learning-assisted side-channel analysis for software integrity verification", in *2025 IEEE European Test Symposium (ETS)*, 2025, pp. 1–6. DOI: 10.1109/ETS63895.2025.11049653.

[12] A. D. Campos, F. Lemus-Prieto, J.-L. González-Sánchez, and A. C. Lindo, "Intrusion detection for iot environments through side-channel and machine learning techniques", *IEEE Access*, vol. 12, pp. 98 450–98 465, 2024. DOI: 10.1109/ACCESS.2024.3362670.

[13] A. Vaswani *et al.*, "Attention is all you need", in *Proceedings of the 31st International Conference on Neural Information Processing Systems*, ser. NIPS'17, Long Beach, California, USA: Curran Associates Inc., 2017, pp. 6000–6010, ISBN: 9781510860964.

[14] A. Baevski, A. Babu, W.-N. Hsu, and M. Auli, "Efficient self-supervised learning with contextualized target representations for vision, speech and language", in *Int. Conf. on Mach. Learn.*, PMLR, 2023, pp. 1416–1429.

[15] New AE, CW305 DesignStart, [Online]. Available: https://github.com/newaetech/CW305-Arm-DesignStart (visited on 09/01/2025).

[16] J. Pallister, S. Hollis, and J. Bennett, "Beebs: Open benchmarks for energy measurements on embedded platforms", *arXiv preprint arXiv:1308.5174*, 2013.

General Conversion Scheme of Card-based Protocols for Two-colored Cards to Updown Cards

Takumi Sakurai
Nagoya University
Nagoya, Japan
email: sakurai.takumi.j1@s.mail.nagoya-u.ac.jp

Yuichi Kaji
Nagoya University
Nagoya, Japan
email: kaji.yuichi.a0@f.mail.nagoya-u.ac.jp

Abstract—**Besides the majorly investigated two-colored cards, there are studies of card-based protocols that use updown cards printed with rotationally asymmetric symbols. A card-based protocol for updown cards is advantageous in making the protocol simple and efficient, but not so much effort has been made to develop updown card protocols, and not so much is known about the relation between protocols for two-colored cards and updown cards. In fact, the number of cards for computing an arbitrary function is not known. This study discusses the sufficient condition of two-colored cards protocols under which the protocol can be converted for updown cards, and describes the actual conversion procedure. With the conversion, it is clarified that there are updown card protocols that compute an arbitrary Boolean function with three additional cards, and protocols that compute a symmetric Boolean function with only one additional card.**

Keywords-Card-based cryptography; Secure multi-party computation; Updown cards.

I. INTRODUCTION

Card-based cryptography is a technique for secure multi-party computation using physical cards [5][6][7][8][10][12]. Participants in a computation encode their input bits by using cards with symbols, such as those on playing cards. The cards are placed with their faces down so that the input bits are kept secret. The cards are shuffled, permuted, and flipped according to a specific rule. At the end, the participants learn only the information corresponding to the computation's output from the cards.

Card-based cryptography enables secure multi-party computation without specialized knowledge or equipment, such as a computer. Therefore, card-based cryptography is regarded as an appealing material for the lectures of security and zero-knowledge proof for puzzles [1][13]. On the other hand, the procedure should be as simple as possible because all operations must be performed manually by human operators. Therefore, reducing the number of cards is an important issue, and research has been conducted on the minimum number of cards that are required to compute meaningful functions and to solve other problems.

In card-based cryptography, we often consider using two-colored cards (hereafter called *TC cards*) that are printed with either "♣" or "♡" on their front and "?" on their back. A single bit is encoded by a pair of cards placed so that

$$\boxed{\clubsuit}\boxed{\heartsuit} = 0, \boxed{\heartsuit}\boxed{\clubsuit} = 1.$$

A *commitment* is a pair of face-down cards that encodes a single bit according to the above encoding rule. In this paper, the commitment to $x \in \{0,1\}$ is denoted as

$$\underbrace{\boxed{?}\,\boxed{?}}_{x}$$

which represents nobody can see the faces of the cards. If a bit value x is represented as a commitment, then its negation $\bar{x}$ is easily obtained by swapping the places of the two cards of the commitment.

We call a *protocol* the entire procedure of taking an input in the form of a commitment, performing operations, such as permutation, flip, and shuffle, and finally determining the output from a sequence of cards. A protocol for TC cards in this paper follows the Mizuki-Shizuya model [4], which allows only these operations: *permutation* that rearranges the position of the cards, *flip* that faces down or up the cards, and *shuffle* that secretly and probabilistically applies the permutation.

Protocols in which the output is obtained in the form of a commitment are called *committed-format protocols*. Committed-format protocols are important because they allow us to construct complicated protocols from simpler ones. For example, if we have committed-format protocols for basic logical operations, such as AND, OR, and NOT and for copying a Boolean value, then we can construct a committed-format protocol for an arbitrary Boolean function. The result of the function is obtained by opening the commitment of the final result, and no information leaks out about the inputs and the intermediate values that are used in the computation.

In addition to commonly studied TC cards, there is a direction of studies of card-based cryptography that uses cards of a single type. Such cards are called updown cards (hereafter called *UD cards*) and assumed to have "↑" on the front and "(blank)" on the back [5]. Let

$$\boxed{\downarrow} = 0, \boxed{\uparrow} = 1$$

be the encoding of a single bit on these cards. For UD cards, a commitment is defined as a single card representing a single bit but its face down, and protocols are realized by performing operations, such as the permutation, flip, shuffle (that applies the permutations and rotations), and *rotation* that rotates a card by 180 degrees and reverses the upside and the downside of a card. The protocol for the logical NOT is realized by simply rotating the commitment (a single card) of the input.

Generally speaking, protocols for UD cards require fewer cards than protocols for TC cards. This is especially important because cards are operated by a human. Besides the advantage in efficiency, a smaller number of cards is favorable in discussing the computational capabilities of the card-based protocol. Since two TC cards are expressed by one UD card, the number of possible combinations of cards can be reduced, though the operation on UD cards are more complex than those on TC cards. However, not so many investigations have been made for protocols with UD cards, while TC cards are eagerly studied. For example, there are TC protocols that can safely compute arbitrary n-variable Boolean functions with $2n + 6$ cards ($2n$ cards for the commitments of n bits and six additional cards for "working memory"), and symmetric functions with $2n + 2$ cards [7]. On the other hand, no such general protocol is known for UD cards. To promote the study of UD protocols, it is convenient if we can transform a TC protocol to a corresponding UD protocol. However, it is likely that not all TC protocols can be transformed to UD protocols.

In this study, we illustrate a general method for converting a TC protocol that satisfies certain constraints into an UD protocol, where the latter uses half the number of cards of the former. It is demonstrated that the TC protocols in [7] fulfill the constraint described above. Consequently, our conversion method brings UD protocols that compute arbitrary n-variable Boolean function with $n + 3$ cards and any n-variable symmetric function with $n + 1$ cards. To avoid possible misunderstanding, we remark that this study is a compilation of many known results and protocols, rather than a proposal of a novel protocol that is based on a new idea. The compilation, however, indicates a strong relationship between TC protocols and UD protocols, which has not been recognized explicitly.

This paper is organized as follows. In Section II, we introduce AND and XOR protocols with TC cards. In Section III, we show the basic idea of converting TC protocols to UD protocols. In Section IV, we introduce AND and XOR protocols with UD cards, discussing equivalency to TC cards. In Section V, using converting constraints, we show the example of convertible TC protocols. In Section VI, this paper is concluded.

II. TC Cards Protocols

This section reviews committed-format TC protocols that realize computing AND and XOR of input bits.

A. TC Cards AND Protocol with Six Cards

For a pair of bits (x, y) and a bit value i, we define the functions "get" and "shift" as

$$\mathrm{get}^i(x,y) = \begin{cases} x & (i = 0), \\ y & (i = 1), \end{cases}$$

$$\mathrm{shift}^i(x,y) = \begin{cases} (x,y) & (i = 0), \\ (y,x) & (i = 1). \end{cases}$$

For an input bit $a, b \in \{0,1\}$, the logical conjunction $a \wedge b$ can be written as

$$a \wedge b = \mathrm{get}^a(0,b) = \mathrm{get}^{a\oplus r}\left(\mathrm{shift}^r(0,b)\right)$$

with any bit $r \in \{0,1\}$ [8]. This principle describes committed-format protocols for AND computation.

Mizuki and Sone's AND protocol is realized with six TC cards, including four cards for the commitments of two input bits [6]. The protocol consists of the following five steps. (Hereafter, card positions are given address numbers from left to right for clarity.)

1. The cards are arranged as follows, with input $a, b \in \{0,1\}$ as the commitments placed at positions 1 and 3. The additional two cards encode 0 and are placed face down at position 2.

   ① ② ③

   ?? ?? ??

   a 0 b
2. Permute the cards as follows.

   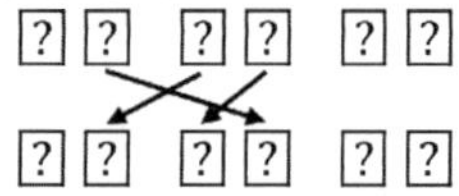
3. Shuffle the cards in such a way that the left and right halves of the cards are each bundled and randomly swapped, which is called a *random bisection cut* and denoted by $[\cdot \mid \cdot]$. In practice, we can use card sleeves or clips and throw them to realize this shuffle.

   [?? ?|? ??]
4. Permute the cards as follows.

   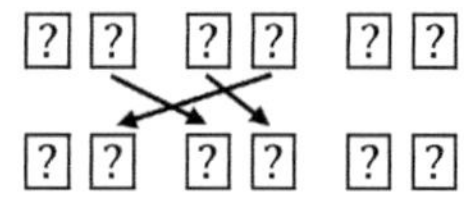

   If the random bisection cut in Step 3 does not change the order of the cards, then this permutation cancels the permutation in Step 2, resulting the commitments to a, 0, and b placed in this order from the left. If the random bisection cut in the previous Step 3 changes the order of the cards, then this permutation brings the commitment to the negation of a, which is written as $a \oplus 1$, in position 1. We can also confirm that the commitment to b moves to position 2 and the commitment to 0 moves to position 3, and hence they swap their positions in the original order. Summarizing the two cases, we have the commitments to $a \oplus r$ and $\mathrm{shift}^r(0, b)$ after the permutation of this step, where $r = 0$ and 1 represent the two different cases of the random bisection cut in Step 3. The results is therefore illustrated as

   ① ② ③

   ?? ?? ??.

   $a \oplus r$ $\mathrm{shift}^r(0, b)$
5. Flip the cards at position 1 and open the commitment to $a \oplus r$ over. If $a \oplus r = 0$, then the cards at positions 2 and 3 are the commitments to $a \wedge b$ and $\bar{a} \wedge b$, respectively. If $a \oplus r = 1$, then the cards at positions 2 and 3 are the commitments to $\bar{a} \wedge b$ and $a \wedge b$, respectively. Therefore, the commitment to $a \wedge b$ is obtained at position 2 if $a \oplus r = 0$, and at 3 if $a \oplus r = 1$. Remark that opening $a \oplus r$ does not reveal the value of a because r is unknown.

   ① ② ③ ① ② ③

   ♣♡ ?? ?? or ♡♣ ?? ??

   0 $a \wedge b$ $\bar{a} \wedge b$ 1 $\bar{a} \wedge b$ $a \wedge b$

Given the commitments to a, 0, and b, this protocol computes $a \wedge b = \text{get}^a(0, b)$. If the commitments to $x, y, z \in \{0,1\}$ are provided instead of a, 0, and b, then this same protocol computes $\text{get}^x(y, z)$.

B. TC Cards XOR Protocol with Four Cards

Here, we introduce committed-format protocols that compute exclusive-or $a \oplus b$ for bits $a, b \in \{0,1\}$. Mizuki and Sone's XOR protocol is realized with only four input TC cards, thus using no additional cards [6].

1. The cards are arranged as follows, with input $a, b \in \{0,1\}$ as the commitments.

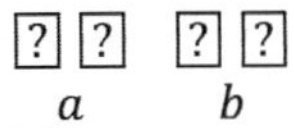

2. Permute the cards as follows.

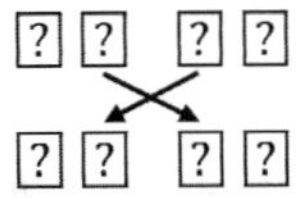

3. Make a random bisection cut.

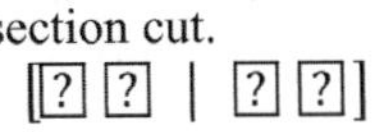

4. Permute the cards as follows. The commitment after this permutation is represented by a bit r that represents the result of the bisection cut in the previous step.

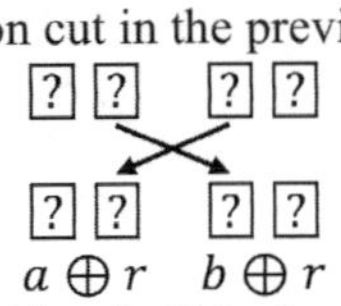

5. Flip the cards at position 1. This does not reveal the value of a because r has been chosen randomly. If the cards at position 1 were the commitment to 0, then the cards at position 2 are the commitment to $a \oplus b$. If the cards at position 1 were the commitment to 1, then the cards at position 2 are the commitment to the complement to $a \oplus b$. In this latter case, swap the cards at position 2, and we obtain the commitment to $a \oplus b$.

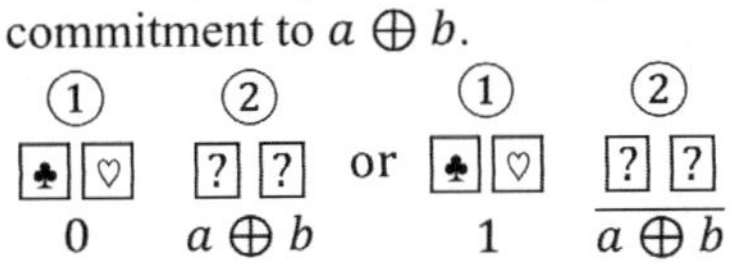

The protocol extracts one card from each commitment, combines them into one, makes a random bisection cut and returns them to their original placement (Steps 2-4). This operation adds a common random bit r to the two input bits. This principle can be easily extended to the case where the input is more than two bits. For example, let $a, b, c \in \{0,1\}$ be the input bits and arrange the cards to represent the commitments of the three input bits. All commitments can be shuffled by dividing them into left and right bundles of cards to give them the random bit as well. Finally, the value of $a \oplus r$ is checked, yielding the commitments to $a \oplus b$ and $a \oplus c$. If the value of b and c are 0, then $a \oplus b = a$ and $a \oplus c = a$. Therefore, two copies of the commitments to a can be obtained while keeping the value of a secret.

III. Conversion to UD Protocols

Given an arbitrary UD protocol, it is clearly possible to construct a TC card protocol that is computationally equivalent to the given UD protocol [11]. Specifically, the commitment represented by one UD card is replaced by a pair of two TC cards representing the same commitment. Though there are some differences between the operations on the UD cards and those on the TC cards, a permutation on the UD cards can be converted to a permutation on the commitment of the TC cards, a rotate operation of a UD card can be converted to a swap operation of the two cards that constitute a commitment in the TC cards, and so on.

If we were able to reverse the conversion from the UD protocol to the TC protocol, we could obtain an UD protocol that can be executed based on the same principles as the TC protocol with exactly half the number of cards. It is always possible to replace one card in the UD protocol with two cards in the TC protocol, while the converse is not always true. For example, in the TC protocol, it is possible for the shuffle or other operations to separate the two cards of a commitment that represent one bit. Obviously, such operations cannot be simulated with UD cards. It is strongly conjectured that the TC protocols can be converted to the UD protocol only if the TC protocols satisfy certain conditions.

We name a TC protocol *commitment-preserving* if the protocol uses only the following four types of operations.

1. Permutation that does not destroy the commitment
2. Shuffle that does not destroy the commitment
3. Flip operation that turns a card face up or face down
4. NOT operation that exchanges the cards of the commitment

Note that destroying the commitment means separating the two cards that are used to constitute a commitment of a single bit. For example, all the permutations in previous section's protocols destroy the commitments, and reversing the order of even cards is one of the operations that do not destroy the commitments, tracing with UD cards. The permutation 1. Prohibits this kind of permutations, and the permutations that fulfill this condition 1. can be converted to a permutation and a rotation in the UD protocol. The shuffle of 2. can be converted to a shuffle that applies a permutation and a rotation in the UD protocol. The flip of 3. can face up one of two cards that constitute a commitment of a TC protocol. Another card of the commitment may not be opened, but the operation of opening a single card completely reveals the value of the commitment. Therefore, the flip of 3. brings the same effect as flipping two cards of a commitment of a TC protocol, which is simulated by a simple flip of a UD card representing the corresponding commitment. The NOT operation in 4. can be converted to a rotation of the cards in the UD protocol.

For TC protocols, we can make use of KWH-tree developed by Koch, Walzer, and Härtel for verifying the security and the correctness [3]. However, the security and correctness of the converted UD protocol depend on the original TC protocol because this conversion only traces the original.

IV. UD Cards Protocols

A commitment-preserving protocol with TC cards can be converted to a protocol with half the number of UD cards, but many TC protocols do not satisfy those conditions. We can see that AND and XOR protocols, illustrated in Section II, break the commitments by permutations and shuffles, and they cannot be converted to UD protocols in a naive manner. Fortunately, for the two protocols of AND and XOR, there are UD protocols that realize the same computation as the TC protocols with half the number of cards [5][12]. These UD protocols can lead to commitment-preserving AND and XOR protocols with TC cards. This implies that there are non-commitment-preserving protocols that perform equivalent computations of commitment-preserving protocols. Therefore, we add these non-commitment-preserving protocols to the convertible operations. This section briefly introduces the UD cards AND and XOR protocols in [5][12].

A. UD cards AND Protocols with Three Cards

Mizuki and Shizuya's AND protocol [5] with UD cards is designed based on the same principle as the TC protocol in the previous section. The only difference is that a commitment consists of a single card, and we need just three cards to complete the computation.

1. The cards are arranged as follows, with input $a, b \in \{0,1\}$ as the commitments. The additional cards are also placed face down.

   □ □ □
   a b 0

2. Repeat a shuffle operation for an arbitrary time, where one shuffle operation consists of a rotation of the card at position 1 and a swapping of the cards at position 2 and 3. The commitments after shuffle are represented by a random bit $r \in \{0,1\}$ corresponding to this shuffle as follows.

   ① ② ③
   □ □ □
   $a \oplus r$ $\mathrm{shift}^r(0, b)$

3. Flip the cards at position 1. The output position can be determined by $a \oplus r$ while keeping the value of a secret.

   ① ② ③ ① ② ③
   [↓] □ □ or [↑] □ □
   0 $a \wedge b$ 1 $a \wedge b$

Since the shuffle in Step 2 is difficult to perform, there is another protocol that is easy to implement [12].

1. The cards are arranged as follows, with input $a, b \in \{0,1\}$ as the commitments. The additional cards are also placed face down.

   □ □ □
   1 a b

2. Shuffle the entire row of cards in a rotation, which is called a *tornado shuffle*. The value of each commitment is either of the following two results. In practice, we can use a device something like a turn-table to realize this suffle.

   □ □ □ or □ □ □
   1 a b $\bar{b}$ $\bar{a}$ 0

3. Flip the card at position 2, which was a commitment to either of a or $\bar{a}$. If the opened value is 0, then take the card at position 1 and rotate it. If the opened value is 1, then take the card at position 3.

   ① ② ③ ① ② ③
   □ [↓] □ or □ [↑] □
   $\overline{a \wedge b}$ 0 1 $a \wedge b$

The TC cards AND protocol in Section II creates commitments $a \wedge b$ and $\bar{a} \wedge b$ with six cards for the input bits $a, b \in \{0,1\}$. The UD cards AND protocol in this section, which uses the less realistic shuffle, is based on the same principle as the TC cards AND protocol, and it is obviously equivalent to the TC cards AND protocol. For the second protocol that uses a tornado shuffle in this section, we can confirm that the cards are arranged as

□ [↓] □ or □ [↑] □
$\overline{a \wedge b}$ 0 $\bar{a} \wedge b$ $\overline{\bar{a} \wedge b}$ 1 $a \wedge b$

after the protocol. Therefore, the equivalent computation to the TC protocol is realized. It can be said that the commitments to $a \wedge b$ and $\bar{a} \wedge b$ can be obtained with three cards together with the input for input bits $a, b \in \{0,1\}$. It can also be confirmed that $\mathrm{get}^x(y, z)$ can be computed for both UD protocols. Therefore, the AND protocols with TC cards in Section II can be added to the convertible operations of commitment-preserving protocols in Section III.

B. UD cards XOR Protocol with Two Cards

Mizuki and Shizuya's XOR protocol with UD cards can be constructed according to the same principle as the TC cards case [5]. The protocol uses only two input cards, and no additional card is required.

1. The cards are arranged as follows, with input $a, b \in \{0,1\}$ as the commitments.

   □ □
   a b

2. The cards are shuffled by bundling them and rotating them. The commitment after this shuffle is represented by a random bit $r \in \{0,1\}$ as follows.

   □ □
   $a \oplus r$ $b \oplus r$

3. Flip the cards at position 1. If it is 0, then the card at position 2 is the commitment to $a \oplus b$. If the opened card is 1, then the card at position 2 is the commitment to $\overline{a \oplus b}$. In the latter case, rotate the card at position 2 and we obtain the commitment to $a \oplus b$.

   ① ② ① ②
   [↓] □ or [↑] □
   0 $a \oplus b$ 1 $\overline{a \oplus b}$

This protocol can be extended for three or more input bits and used to obtain multiple copies of an input commitment as in the TC cards case.

The UD cards XOR protocol in this section follows the same principle as the TC protocol. Then, it clearly achieves an equivalent computation with half the number of cards. Therefore, the XOR protocols with TC cards in Section II can be added to the convertible operations of commitment-preserving protocols in Section III.

V. EXAMPLE OF APPLICATIONS OF THE CONVERSION METHOD

The conversion method described in the previous section can be applied to any commitment-preserving protocol. In this section, we demonstrate that TC card protocols for computing arbitrary Boolean function and symmetric functions are commitment-preserving, namely, they use only the operations that are listed in the previous section. This means that the TC protocols can be converted to protocols for UD cards, which brings efficient protocols for computing arbitrary Boolean functions and symmetric functions by using UD cards.

Note that all the permutations of the TC protocols discussed in this section are the operations of commitment-conserving protocols.

A. Preparation

To efficiently compute the arbitrary Boolean function and the symmetric functions, an *improved AND* protocol and a half adder protocol have been developed [7].

The improved AND protocol produces two commitments, one for $a \wedge b$ and one for b, for given three commitments to a, b, and 0. The protocol is composed of the AND and XOR protocols in Section II.

1. For input bits $a, b \in \{0,1\}$, use the AND protocol to the commitments to a, b, and 0, which yields the commitments to $a \wedge b$ and $\bar{a} \wedge b$.

   ? ? ? ? ♣ ♡ → ♣ ♡ ? ? ? ?
   a b 0 → 0 (or 1) $a \wedge b$ $\bar{a} \wedge b$

2. Use the XOR protocol to the commitments to $a \wedge b, \bar{a} \wedge b$ and 0, which yields the commitments to $(a \wedge b) \oplus (\bar{a} \wedge b) = b$ and $(a \wedge b) \oplus 0 = a \wedge b$.

   ? ? ? ? ♣ ♡ → ♣ ♡ ? ? ? ?
   $a \wedge b$ $\bar{a} \wedge b$ 0 → 0 (or 1) $a \wedge b$ b

Notice that the two cards that were used as the commitment to 0 (or 1) after Step 1 can be used to encode 0 in this second step, and hence the improved AND protocol is realized with six cards. Notice also that the AND and XOR protocols are used here. Thus, the improved AND protocol can be converted to an UD protocol.

The half-adder protocol is composed of the XOR, NOT, and improved AND protocols.

1. For input bits $a, b \in \{0,1\}$, use the XOR protocol to the commitments to a, b, and 0, which yields the commitments to $a \oplus b$ and a.

   ? ? ? ? ♣ ♡ → ♣ ♡ ? ? ? ?
   a b 0 → 0 (or 1) $a \oplus b$ a

2. The NOT protocol yields the commitment to $\overline{a \oplus b}$.
3. The improved AND protocol yields the commitments to $a \wedge (\overline{a \oplus b}) = a \wedge b$ and $\overline{a \oplus b}$, where the two opened cards of Step 1 is reused to realize the improved AND protocol.

   ? ? ? ? ♣ ♡ → ♣ ♡ ? ? ? ?
   $\overline{a \oplus b}$ a 0 → 0 (or 1) $a \wedge b$ $\overline{a \oplus b}$

4. The NOT protocol yields the commitments to $a \oplus b$. We now have the commitments to $a \wedge b$ and $a \oplus b$.

Notice that the protocol uses six cards, and that the half adder protocol is also the commitment-preserving protocol and can be converted to an UD protocol.

B. Arbitrary n-variable Boolean Function

A protocol for computing arbitrary n-variable Boolean functions with $2n + 6$ two-color cards is proposed by Nishida et al. [7]. The Boolean function, say $f(x_1, x_2, \ldots, x_n)$, is expressed as

$$\begin{aligned} f(x_1, x_2, \ldots, x_n) &= x_1 x_2 \cdots x_n f(1,1,\ldots,1) \\ &\oplus \overline{x_1} x_2 \cdots x_n f(0,1,\ldots,1) \\ &\vdots \\ &\oplus \overline{x_1}\,\overline{x_2} \cdots \overline{x_n} f(0,0,\ldots,0) \end{aligned}$$

from the Shannon expansion [9]. Remark that the values of the function f in the right-hand side are either of 0 or 1. Terms with $f(\cdot) = 0$ dismisses from the expression while terms with $f(\cdot) = 1$ brings the AND value of literals of $x_1, \ldots, x_n$. The entire function is therefore obtained as the XOR of the AND values of the literals that make the value of $f(\cdot) = 1$. The protocol for computing $f(x_1, x_2, \ldots, x_n)$ is described as follows. Use $2n$ cards to represent $x_1, x_2, \ldots, x_n$ as commitments, and additional six cards to represent three commitments to 0. Among the three commitments to 0, two are used as a working memory to compute an AND value of literals of $x_1, x_2, \ldots, x_n$. The remaining one commitment to 0 is used to record an intermediate value of the XOR of AND values. In the following description, only relevant commitments are shown in the explanation.

1. Assume that $f(1,1,\ldots,1) = 1$. In this case, for input bits $x_1, x_2, \ldots, x_n \in \{0,1\}$, the commitment to $x_1 x_2 \cdots x_n$ is created as follows while keeping the input commitments unchanged.
   a. Perform the XOR protocol for the commitments to x_1 and the two commitments of the working memory. The protocol yields the two commitments to x_1 and two free cards.

      ? ? ♣ ♡ ♣ ♡ → ♣ ♡ ? ? ? ?
      x_1 0 0 → 0 (or 1) x_1 x_1

      Open the two free cards and reformat the cards as a commitment to 0. This brings $2n$ cards for the commitments to $x_1, x_2, \ldots, x_n$, a pair of cards for the commitment to a copy of x_1, a pair of cards for the commitment to 0 for the working memory and a pair of cards (0 at this moment) to record the intermediate value.

b. The improved AND protocol for the commitments to x_1, x_2 and 0 yields the commitments to x_1x_2, x_2 and two free cards.

??	??	♣♡	→	♣♡	??	??
x_1	x_2	0		0 (or 1)	x_1x_2	x_2

Similarly to the previous step, we have a commitment to x_1x_2, to 0 for a working memory, and 0 for an intermediate value.

c. Repeatedly use the improved AND protocols like b. operations, which yields the commitment to $x_1x_2 \cdots x_n$. These whole operations use four additional cards. Regard this commitment as an intermediate value, and we still have four free cards for two commitments to 0 for working memory.

2. Similarly, create a commitment to $\overline{x_1}x_2 \cdots x_n$ if $f(0,1,\dots,1) = 1$. This operation uses four cards for the working memory.
3. The XOR protocol yields the commitment to $x_1x_2 \cdots x_n \oplus \overline{x_1}x_2 \cdots x_n$, which is regarded as an intermediate value.
4. In the same way, create the commitment to the term that makes the value of $f(\cdot) = 1$ while the input commitments are maintained, and the XOR protocol is repeated. Finally, the commitment to $f(x_1, x_2, \dots, x_n)$ is obtained at the commitment of the result of the XOR protocols.

From the above, the protocol with $2n + 6$ TC cards for any n-variable Boolean function is commitment-preserving and can thus be converted to a protocol with $n + 3$ UD cards.

C. Arbitrary n-variable Symmetric Boolean Function

A Boolean function is said to be symmetric if its function value is invariant to the permutation of inputs, that is, $f(x_1, \dots, x_n) = f(x_{\pi(1)}, \dots, x_{\pi(n)})$ holds for an arbitrary permutation π. For a symmetric Boolean function, we have a TC protocol that uses only two extra cards rather than six [7][8].

The value of a symmetric Boolean function is irrelevant to the order of inputs. This implies that the function value is determined by the number of 1's contained in the input. Consequently, a symmetric Boolean function f is characterized as

$$f(x_1, \dots, x_n) = g\left(\sum_{i=1}^{n} x_i\right)$$

where g is a mapping from $\{0, 1, \dots, n\}$ to $\{0, 1\}$. Such a mapping g is further characterized by $X \subseteq \{0, 1, \dots, n\}$ where X is defined as $X = \{s | 0 \leq s \leq n, g(s) = 1\}$. The number of subsets of $\{0, 1, \dots, n\}$ is 2^{n+1}, and it is understood that the number of symmetric Boolean functions with n inputs is 2^{n+1}. However, it is not necessary to consider all symmetric Boolean functions, since the negation of commitments can be easily performed. We will use NPN equivalence classes based on input-output negation and input reordering for the discussion that follows [9].

For $n \leq 2$, symmetric functions are obviously computed by a combination of the AND, XOR, and NOT protocols. These protocols use at most two additional cards.

For $n = 3$, symmetric function f for input bits $a, b, c \in \{0,1\}$ is characterized by

$$S_X^3(a,b,c) = \begin{cases} 1 & (a + b + c \in X) \\ 0 & \text{(otherwise)} \end{cases}.$$

where $X \subseteq \{0,1,2,3\}$. From the NPN equivalence class, the symmetric functions are limited to six patterns as follows [8][9]. For example, $S_{\{0,1,2,3\}}^3$ can be computed by using the negation output of $S_\emptyset^3$.

- $S_\emptyset^3(a,b,c) = 0$
- $S_{\{3\}}^3(a,b,c) = a \wedge b \wedge c$
- $S_{\{1,2\}}^3(a,b,c) = \mathrm{get}^{a \oplus b}(a \oplus c, 1)$
- $S_{\{1,3\}}^3(a,b,c) = a \oplus b \oplus c$
- $S_{\{2,3\}}^3(a,b,c) = \mathrm{get}^{a \oplus b}(a, c)$
- $S_{\{0,2,3\}}^3(a,b,c) = \mathrm{get}^{a \oplus b \oplus c}(1, a \wedge c)$

Each of them is constructed by XOR and AND protocols in TC cards. These patterns use at most two additional cards.

When $n = 4$, the value of $\sum_{i=1}^{4} x_i$ can be encoded in terms of $2(\lfloor \log_2 4 \rfloor + 1) = 6$ cards by using the half adder protocol repeatedly. It uses two additional cards and yields four free cards. The function g is defined as

$$g\left(\sum_{i=1}^{4} x_i\right) = \begin{cases} g(4) & (s_1 = 1) \\ g'(s_2, s_3) & (s_1 = 0) \end{cases}$$

where (s_1, s_2, s_3) is the bits of $\sum_{i=1}^{4} x_i$. The function $g'(s_2, s_3)$ is a Boolean function with the lower two bits of $\sum_{i=1}^{4} x_i$ as inputs. This function can be computed with two additional cards (using free cards above). Then, it can be expressed as $g(\sum_{i=1}^{4} x_i) = \mathrm{get}^{s_1}(g'(s_2, s_3), g(4))$, which is computed by the AND protocol. Thus, the whole protocol uses two additional cards.

When $n \geq 5$, we define a function g similarly. By the half adder protocol, the value of $\sum_{i=1}^{n} x_i$ can be encoded by $2(\lfloor \log_2 n \rfloor + 1)$ cards. Since the total number of cards used in the protocol is $2n + 2$, the number of cards not used to represent the value of $\sum_{i=1}^{n} x_i$ is $(2n + 2) - 2(\lfloor \log_2 n \rfloor + 1) = 2(n - \lfloor \log_2 n \rfloor)$. From $n \geq 5$, $2(n - \lfloor \log_2 n \rfloor) \geq 6$, which is more than 6 cards, can be used freely. Then, by using these six cards as additional cards, g can be computed using the protocol of this section.

From the above, the protocol with $2n + 2$ TC cards for any n-variable symmetric Boolean function is commitment-preserving and can thus be converted to a protocol with $n + 1$ UD cards.

VI. Conclusion and Future Work

In this paper, we proposed a general method to convert a TC protocol to an UD protocol by restricting the operations of the TC protocol. It is also shown that the TC protocols, which allow multi-party computation of arbitrary n-variable Boolean function with $2n + 6$ cards and n-variable symmetric functions with $2n + 2$ cards, can be converted to an UD protocol with half the number of cards.

We focused on the fact that the AND and XOR protocols on the UD cards can perform calculations equivalent to those on the TC protocols. Since UD protocols can be converted to TC protocols [11], there are the AND and XOR TC protocols not destroying commitments, which ignore the ease of operations. On the other hand, we did not mention anything about the possibility of converting other TC protocols that are not commitment-preserving. In fact, a TC protocol [10] that computes symmetric functions of 8 or more variables with only input cards, i.e., with no additional cards, has been proposed, but it has also been shown that AND computation is not possible on UD cards without additional cards [2]. Thus, the calculation cannot be converted to an UD protocol unless it has the commitment-preserving protocol. This gap between the two classes is being clarified. In addition, the minimum number of cards required for Boolean functions and symmetric functions as a computational capability of the TC protocols is still unresolved. Such studies are expected to contribute to the clear computational capability of TC protocols in the future.

REFERENCES

[1] R. Gradwohl, M. Naor, B. Pinkas, and G. N. Rothblum, "Cryptographic and physical zero-knowledge proof systems for solutions of sudoku puzzles," Internatinal Conference on Fun with Algorithms, pp. 166–182, 2007.

[2] S. Iino, Y. Li, K. Sakiyama, and D. Miyahara, "On the impossibility of n-card and protocols," 42nd Symposium on Cryptography and Information Security, 4D2-3, 2025 (in Japanese).

[3] A. Koch, S. Walzer, and K. Härtel, "Card-based cryptographic protocols using a minimal number of cards," International Conference on the Theory and Application of Cryptology and Information Security, pp. 783–807, 2015.

[4] T. Mizuki and H. Shizuya, "A formalization of card-based cryptographic protocols via abstract machine," International Journal of Information Security, 13, pp. 15–23, 2014.

[5] T. Mizuki and H. Shizuya, "Practical card-based cryptography," International Conference on Fun with Algorithms, pp. 313–324, 2014.

[6] T. Mizuki and H. Sone, "Six-card secure and and four-card secure xor," International Workshop on Frontiers in Algorithmics, pp. 358–369, 2009.

[7] T. Nishida, Y. Hayashi, T. Mizuki, and H. Sone, "Card-based protocols for any boolean function," 12th Annual Conference on Theory and Applications of Models of Computation, pp. 110–121, 2015.

[8] T. Nishida, T. Mizuki, and H. Sone, "Securely computing the three-input majority function with eight cards," Second International Conference on Theory and Practice of Natural Computing, pp. 193–204, 2013.

[9] T. Sasao, "Switching theory for logic synthesis," Kluwer Academic Publishers, 1999.

[10] H. Shikata, K. Toyoda, D. Miyahara, and T. Mizuki, "Card-minimal protocols for symmetric boolean functions of more than seven inputs," International Colloquium on Theoretical Aspect of Computing, pp. 388–406, 2022 (in Japanese).

[11] K. Shinagawa, "Card types and encodings of card-based cryptography," presentation slide, Organizing Mathematical Unsolved and New Problems in Card-based Cryptography through Industry-academia Collaboration. [Online]. Available from: https://joint.imi.kyushu-u.ac.jp/wp-content/uploads/2023/06/IMI_shinagawa.pdf (accessed 2025-07-03) (in Japanese)

[12] K. Shinagawa, K. Nuida, T. Nishide, G. Hanaoka, and E. Okamoto, "Committed AND protocol using three cards with more handy shuffle," 2016 International Symposium on Information Theory and Its Applications, pp. 700–702, 2016.

[13] K. Shinagawa, "A report on a lecture for elementary and junior high school using card-based cryptography," 39th Symposium on Cryptography and Information Security, 2F4-4, 2022 (in Japanese).

From ECU to VSOC: UDS Security Monitoring Strategies

Ali Recai Yekta*, Nicolas Loza†, Jens Gramm†, Michael Peter Schneider†, Stefan Katzenbeisser‡
*Yekta IT GmbH, Dortmund, Germany
†ETAS GmbH, Stuttgart, Germany
‡University of Passau, Passau, Germany
EMails: ali@yekta-it.de, {nicolas.loza | jens.gramm | michaelpeter.schneider}@etas.com,
stefan.katzenbeisser@uni-passau.de

***Abstract*—Increasing complexity and connectivity of modern vehicles have heightened their vulnerability to cyberattacks. This paper addresses security challenges associated with the Unified Diagnostic Services (UDS) protocol, a critical communication framework for vehicle diagnostics in the automotive industry. We present security monitoring strategies for the UDS protocol that leverage in-vehicle logging and remote analysis through a Vehicle Security Operations Center (VSOC). Our approach involves specifying security event logging requirements, contextual data collection, and the development of detection strategies aimed at identifying UDS attack scenarios. By applying these strategies to a comprehensive taxonomy of UDS attack techniques, we demonstrate that our detection methods cover a wide range of potential attack vectors. Furthermore, we assess the adequacy of current AUTOSAR standardized security events in supporting UDS attack detection, identifying gaps in the current standard. This work enhances the understanding of vehicle security monitoring and provides an example for developing robust cybersecurity measures in automotive communication protocols.**

***Keywords*-Automotive Networks, Automotive Security, UDS, Security Monitoring, VSOC, UN R155, IDS.**

I. Introduction

The growing complexity and interconnectivity of modern vehicles have created notable security challenges. Vehicles are increasingly susceptible to cyberattacks, which poses serious risks to both vehicle integrity and safety. This issue is tackled by the recent UN R155 regulation [1], which emphasizes the urgent requirement for strong cybersecurity management systems and protective measures. One essential layer of defense involves implementing effective security monitoring systems.

Cybersecurity challenges are particularly relevant for the Unified Diagnostic Services (UDS) protocol [2], which is the most commonly used diagnostic protocol in the automotive sector. UDS facilitates communication between vehicle Electronic Control Unit (ECU)s and diagnostic testers — either external to the vehicle or vehicle-internal units. The services provided by UDS encompass a broad range of fundamental functionalities that the automotive industry utilizes throughout all phases of an ECU's lifecycle, including development, testing, operation, maintenance, and decommissioning. Consequently, these services are of significant interest to attackers, as they enable a high degree of control over the ECU. While the security of the UDS protocol has been explored in various studies [3]–[6], security monitoring for UDS has not been studied systematically before.

This paper presents security monitoring strategies for the UDS protocol, wherein detection is based on in-vehicle logging and on processing log events in a remote Vehicle Security Operations Center (VSOC) [7]. The VSOC collects security events from the vehicle fleet and puts them in context with other data sources, e.g., vehicle records including maintenance plans, and threat intelligence digests. More concretely, firstly, we present log strategies specifying which security events are to be logged in vehicles. Secondly, we describe context data to be logged with security events. Finally, we describe detection strategies to analyze logged vehicle security events, with the goal to detect UDS attack scenarios. Strategies are formulated for the specific case of UDS but have the potential to generalize to the security monitoring of vehicle security events in general.

We underline the relevance of the presented monitoring strategies by applying them to a comprehensive taxonomy of UDS attack techniques [8]. This taxonomy is based on Tactics, Techniques, and Procedures (TTP) and is structured along the automotive-specific 'Vehicle Adversarial Tactics, Techniques, and Expert Knowledge' (VATT&EK) [9] and the more general MITRE 'Adversarial Tactics, Techniques, and Common Knowledge' (ATT&CK) [10] frameworks. Our results show that presented detection strategies cover almost all of the attack techniques in this taxonomy. Among others. Moreover, our results show which attack techniques can be detected already on the vehicle side and which techniques require correlation of data sources in a fleet backend. We also show to which extent the security events standardized by a current industry standard, AUTOSAR, are already suited to support the detection of UDS attack techniques, and we identify corresponding gaps in the standard.

In summary, we give an overview on detection strategies for attack techniques misusing the UDS protocol. In this way, our approach gives an example for developing security monitoring strategies for an automotive communication protocol. While VSOC infrastructures have been established in recent years by vehicle manufacturers, it is still a challenge how to detect the occurrence of higher-level attack techniques based on low-level security events. The presented end-to-end monitoring strategies address this challenge. They can be used to implement UDS security monitoring, by deriving vehicle-side logging requirements and by guiding backend-side log processing in a VSOC.

The paper is structured as follows. Section II provides background and related work. Section III lays down the methodology used in this work and Section IV presents the evaluation of the results. In Section V, we conclude our discussion and refer to possible future work.

II. Background and Related Work

Background. Cybersecurity attacks have become a highly relevant threat for modern cars. First standards and regulations on security have already been created in the automotive industry. Examples are the ISO/SAE 21434 standard on vehicle cybersecurity [11] and the United Nations (UN) R155 regulation [1] providing cybersecurity provisions for vehicle type approval. The latter requests automotive manufacturers to be able to detect and respond to security attacks in their vehicles. For this goal, automotive manufacturers introduce security monitoring solutions for their vehicle fleets.

UDS. In this work, we specifically consider security monitoring targeting to detect threat scenarios for the UDS protocol. The UDS protocol, standardized in [2], is the most widely used protocol for vehicle diagnostics. It allows diagnostic tools to contact the ECU installed in a vehicle which has UDS services enabled. Diagnostic services cover, among others, testing, calibration, or software updates. Table I provides an overview on UDS services. More details about the services can be found in [2].

UDS Security. There are a number of reported vehicle vulnerabilities based on UDS services, e.g., [12]–[14], which underlines the relevance to study security aspects of UDS. A focus of recent research on UDS security has been on implementation weaknesses of the UDS Security Access Service [15]–[17]. For first systematic evaluations of the attack surface of automotive diagnostic protocols, see [4][6].

TABLE I. UDS Services overview.

SID	Service	Short
0x10	DiagnosticSessionControl	DSC
0x11	ECUReset	ER
0x14	ClearDiagnosticInformation	CDTCI
0x19	ReadDTCInformation	RDTCI
0x22	ReadDataByIdentifier	RDBI
0x23	ReadMemoryByAddress	RMBA
0x24	ReadScalingDataByIdentifier	RSDBI
0x27	SecurityAccess	SA
0x28	CommunicationControl	CC
0x29	Authentication	AUTH
0x2A	ReadDataByPeriodicIdentifier	RDBPI
0x2C	DynamicallyDefineDataIdentifier	DDDID
0x2E	WriteDataByIdentifier	WDBI
0x2F	InputOutputControlByIdentifier	IOCBI
0x31	RoutineControl	RC
0x34	RequestDownload	RD
0x35	RequestUpload	RU
0x36	TransferData	TD
0x37	RequestTransferExit	RTE
0x38	RequestFileTransfer	RFT
0x3D	WriteMemoryByAddress	WMBA
0x3E	TesterPresent	TP
0x83	AccessTimingParameters	ATP
0x84	SecuredDataTransmission	SDT
0x85	ControlDTCSetting	CDTCS
0x86	ResponseOnEvent	ROE
0x87	LinkControl	LC

A comprehensive analysis of attack techniques for UDS has been provided in [8]. The derived taxonomy categorizes 53 UDS attack techniques along 9 tactics of known attack frameworks. Concretely, the used tactics are *Resource Development (RD)*, *Persistence (PS)*, *Privilege Escalation (PE)*, *Defense Evasion (DE)*, *Credential Access (CA)*, *Discovery (DS)*, *Lateral Movement (LM)*, *Collection (CL)*, and *Affect Vehicle Function (AF)*. The attack techniques are used in the evaluation of detection strategies in Section IV (Table III).

Security Monitoring. As part of security monitoring solutions, in-vehicle software sensors are used to monitor automotive systems for security anomalies. Also research has so far focused on these on-board Intrusion Detection Systems (IDSs), for an overview see [18]. Network IDS (NIDS) monitors in-vehicle networks, e.g., Controller Area Network (CAN) busses or Ethernet networks. Host IDS (HIDS) monitors in-vehicle electronic control units, e.g., on the operating system level or on their interfaces. The setup of VSOC, i.e., backend infrastructures for fleet security monitoring, has been described in [7][19][20].

AUTOSAR Security Events. AUTOSAR is a firmware specification that is widely used in the automotive industry. AUTOSAR supports a set of Security Events (SEvs) for different technologies [21], as well as modules to qualify SEvs [22] and distribute them on the network [23]. Within this work, we will compare our results with what has been standardized in AUTOSAR, to determine which functionality can be used off-the-shelf and where extensions are needed.

III. Methodology

In this section, a systematic strategy for UDS security monitoring is developed. First, in Section III-A, a set of logging strategies is defined that allows the generation of appropriate security-related logs in the vehicle components running UDS. Then, in Section III-B, we provide a context data strategy, specifiying context data to be captured with vehicle security logs. Finally, in Section III-C, we define *detection strategies* allowing to identify higher-level attack scenarios with high certainty. In general, detection can be executed both on the vehicle side as well as on the backend side in a VSOC. However, in many cases, detection relies on the VSOC receiving the data from the vehicle and validating it against information only available in offboard systems, in order to differentiate attacks from false positives.

A. Logging Strategies

This section defines the logging strategies that a vehicle and its subcomponents can implement to detect attacks on the UDS protocol. Due to constraints in the vehicle – runtime, storage, connectivity limitations – it is not possible to just record and send all data generated by the vehicle for analysis to a remote VSOC. Therefore, we need to rely on an appropriate logging concept, defining which events are to be logged. In the following, we present a set of three logging strategies.

a) Invalid Request (IR): Logs are generated whenever a UDS request is recognized as invalid due to one of the following reasons.

- A UDS request is observed which does not satisfy input validation checks due to unexpected formats, parameters out of range, or invalid payloads.
- A UDS request is observed under unexpected or non-permitted circumstances, at ECU or vehicle level, e.g., while the vehicle is driving at high speed or without required authorizations.

b) Function Execution (FE): Log the execution of selected SIDs, due to their criticality for the security of the ECU. This can be used by VSOC to validate if the operation makes sense in the context the vehicle is in. Examples are given by memory modifications or the execution of critical routines.

c) Message Flow Inconsistency (MFI): Logs are generated whenever a UDS SID is recognized as inconsistently routed due to one of the following reasons.

- A message is observed with unexpected source.
- A routed message is different from the original message.
- A routed message appears without first seeing the original message.
- Messages are observed in an unexpected sequence, e.g., multiple 0x27 seed requests are observed without a subsequent key response.

These logging strategies can then be activated or deactivated for each single UDS SID, according to the needs of the identified threats. Note that *Invalid Request* and *Function Execution* are both logging mechanisms that can be implemented by a HIDS or a NIDS, whereas implementing *Message Flow Inconsistency* is more feasible as part of a NIDS, since an overview of the different vehicle networks is needed.

B. Log Context Data Strategy

Whenever one of the previously introduced logging strategies is activated, it generates a log. In order to enrich a log, to make it more useful for further analysis, it must be complemented with appropriate *context data*.

For the strategy *Message Flow Inconsistency*, the context data strategy is always the same: the observed UDS SID, the targeted ECU, the observed request origin, and the expected request origin.

For the strategies *Invalid Request* and *Function Execution*, context data depend on the associated UDS SID. Table II specifies context data to be logged for these two logging strategies.

The column *AR support* indicates whether AUTOSAR already provides security events for this UDS service, based on the logging strategies outlined before. The AUTOSAR security events define context data that is very well aligned with the proposal from Table II. The only differences are that AUTOSAR does not provide hashes over data for SIDs WriteDataByIdentifier (WDBI (0x2E)) and WriteMemoryByAddress (WMBA (0x3D)), but it does provide the logical client source address for all UDS security events.

TABLE II. CONTEXT DATA TO BE LOGGED FOR EACH UDS SERVICE WITH STRATEGIES INVALID REQUESTS (IR) AND FUNCTION EXECUTION (FE).

SID	Context data to be logged for logging strategies **Invalid Requests** (1) and **Function Execution** (2)	**AR support**
0x10	SID$^{(1,2)}$, SF$^{(1,2)}$, NRC$^{(1)}$	-
0x11	SID$^{(1,2)}$, SF$^{(1,2)}$, NRC$^{(1)}$	IR, FE
0x14	SID$^{(1,2)}$, groupOfDTC$^{(1,2)}$, MemorySelection $^{(1,2)}$, NRC$^{(1)}$	IR, FE
0x19	SID$^{(1,2)}$, SF$^{(1,2)}$, NRC$^{(1)}$	-
0x22	SID$^{(1,2)}$, DID1$^{(1,2)}$, ..., DIDn$^{(1,2)}$, NRC$^{(1)}$	-
0x23	SID$^{(1,2)}$, memAddr$^{(1,2)}$, memSize$^{(1,2)}$, NRC$^{(1}$	-
0x24	SID$^{(1,2)}$, DID$^{(1,2)}$, NRC$^{(1)}$	-
0x27	SID$^{(1,2)}$, SF$^{(1,2)}$, NRC$^{(1)}$	IR, FE
0x28	SID$^{(1,2)}$, SF$^{(1,2)}$, NRC$^{(1)}$	IR, FE
0x29	SID$^{(1,2)}$, SF$^{(1,2)}$, NRC$^{(1)}$	IR, FE
0x2A	SID$^{(1,2)}$, transmissionMode$^{(1,2)}$, periodicDID#1$^{(1,2)}$, ..., periodicDID#n$^{(1,2)}$, NRC$^{(1)}$	-
0x2C	SID$^{(1,2)}$, SF$^{(1,2)}$, dynamicallyDefinedDID$^{(1,2)}$, sourceDID#1$^{(1,2)}$, ..., sourceDID#n$^{(1,2)}$, memAddr$^{(1,2)}$, memSize$^{(1,2)}$, NRC$^{(1)}$	-
0x2E	SID$^{(1,2)}$, DID$^{(1,2)}$, hash over dataRecord$^{(1,2)}$, NRC$^{(1)}$	IR, FE
0x2F	SID$^{(1,2)}$, DID$^{(1,2)}$, I/O controlParameter$^{(1,2)}$, NRC$^{(1)}$	IR, FE
0x31	SID$^{(1,2)}$, SF$^{(1,2)}$, RID$^{(1,2)}$, NRC$^{(1)}$	IR, FE
0x34	SID$^{(1,2)}$, memAddr$^{(1,2)}$, memSize$^{(1,2)}$, NRC$^{(1)}$	IR, FE
0x35	SID$^{(1,2)}$, memAddr$^{(1,2)}$, memSize$^{(1,2)}$, NRC$^{(1)}$	IR, FE
0x36	SID$^{(1)}$, blockSequenceCounter$^{(1)}$, NRC$^{(1)}$	-
0x37	SID$^{(1,2)}$, NRC$^{(1)}$, hash over transferred data$^{(2)}$	-
0x38	SID$^{(1,2)}$, modeOfOperation$^{(1,2)}$, filePathAndName$^{(1,2)}$, NRC$^{(1)}$	IR, FE
0x3D	SID$^{(1,2)}$, memAddr$^{(1,2)}$, memSize$^{(1,2)}$, NRC$^{(1)}$, hash over transferred data$^{(2)}$	IR, FE
0x3E	n/a	-
0x84	SID$^{(1,2)}$, Apar$^{(1,2)}$, Signature/Encryption Calculation$^{(1,2)}$, req. SID$^{(1,2)}$, NRC$^{(1)}$	-
0x85	SID$^{(1,2)}$, SF$^{(1,2)}$, NRC$^{(1)}$	IR, FE
0x86	SID$^{(1,2)}$, SF$^{(1,2)}$, SID for response$^{(1,2)}$, NRC$^{(1)}$	-
0x87	SID$^{(1,2)}$, SF$^{(1,2)}$, NRC$^{(1)}$	-

SID = service ID, SF = subfunction, NRC = negative response code, DID = data identifier, other context data fields refer to parameters defined in [2].

The proposed context data from Table IIcombines data from the UDS request and response and provides hence the security-relevant information in a compact form. Using the raw UDS requests/responses as context data is not recommended due to (1) possibly large messages (up to several hundred bytes e.g. for Authentication (Auth29 (0x29)), TransferData (TD (0x36)) or WMBA (0x3D)) which could exhaust the resources of deeply embedded ECUs, (2) risk of information disclosure when sending UDS payload data in clear text to the VSOC and (3) separate SEvs for UDS requests and responses, which would need to be mapped in the VSOC and would prohibit the configuration of IR SEvs without FE SEvs.

Note that the presented logging strategies together with the context data strategy described in this subsection can generate a lot of false positives if applied indiscriminately, e.g., when activating *Function Execution* for ReadDataByIdentifier (RDBI (0x22)) without any additional conditions. Therefore, on top of the logging strategies, additional detection strategies must be defined, to differentiate between true attacks and false positives.

C. Detection Strategies

This section defines *detection strategies* allowing to identify higher-level attack scenarios. Detection strategies are needed for two reasons. Firstly, many of the logs proposed in Section III-A will also be generated under regular vehicle operations. Advanced checks and validations are needed to avoid false positive alerts. Secondly, there are attack scenarios which cannot be detected by vehicle-side logs alone. We introduce three detection strategies as follows.

a) Suspicious Log Patterns (SLP): This detection strategy monitors for the occurrence of suspicious patterns in logs collected in the vehicle. They refer to failed, rejected or inconsistent UDS operations in the vehicle. This strategy includes pattern matching rules with counting. Counting is required to implement checks against thresholds, since, during regular vehicle operation, occasional failed UDS operations are to be expected. Therefore, for each SID service, a threshold defines how many failed operations are to be observed within a time interval before an alert is triggered. Detection of this category can be executed on the vehicle side.

b) Contextualized Log Checks (CLC): This detection strategy assesses the (successful or failed) execution of UDS services in context of additional information. Context information includes the vehicle state, vehicle records with maintenance and service plans, as well as summaries of preceding and succeeding logs. Vehicle records are usually maintained in a backend but not in a single vehicle. Concrete checks to be executed as part of this strategy are given as follows:

- Service calls are inconsistent with the vehicle status, e.g., workshop session, development/production mode.
- Service call uses unexpected permissions.
- Service call is inconsistent with vehicle configurations.
- Service call is inconsistent with other logs, also from backend systems.
- In a service call, memory hashes do not match hashes of authentic software releases.
- In a service call, DIDs or memory ranges rated as sensitive are referenced, e.g., when files or memory are to be read out or modified.

Detection of this category can be executed on the vehicle side only if required context data is available, otherwise it needs to be done in the backend.

c) Product Threat Intelligence (PTI): This detection strategy uses threat intelligence information about the vehicle and its components to identify attack patterns. Sources for this can span from publicly available information, e.g., entries in public vulnerability databases, forums, or research papers, to confidentially disclosed information. Examples for the latter are supplier vulnerability disclosures, responsible vulnerability disclosures by white-hat-hackers, or internal penetration tests. For concrete cases, tags can be defined, including vehicle model, ECU type and attack patterns, to filter information feeds and to link them to concrete attack techniques. Alerts are then triggered whenever, based on this filtering, relevant information is identified.

In the implementation of detection strategies a)-c), a baseline of rules and their configuration is initially derived from the service specification of a vehicle model, and is finetuned based on evaluating false positive logs collected from test vehicles.

IV. Evaluation

This section evaluates the effectiveness of the logging and detection strategies presented in Section III. To this end, we applied the logging and detection strategies to a comprehensive taxonomy of attack techniques [8]. For each attack technique of this taxonomy, we evaluated which strategies can be applied to detect the respective attack technique. The resulting mapping table is presented in Table III. The table lists all attack techniques of this taxonomy, with their ID, name and affected UDS SIDs. Attack techniques are grouped by attack tactics. Columns "Logging Strategies" and "Detection Strategies" specify which strategies from Section III can be used to detect an occurrence of the respective attack technique. Moreover, column "AUTOSAR support" indicates that logging requirements of strategies IR and FE are already covered by the current AUTOSAR standardization.

Our evaluation focuses on three major topics. In Section IV-A, we focus on the logging aspects and compare our proposed logging strategies with the AUTOSAR-provided security events to identify gaps that need to be addressed in implementation projects. In Section IV-B, we discuss how to actually detect UDS attacks based on illustrative examples. Finally, in Section IV-C we draw conclusions and formulate take-away messages based on our analysis.

A. AUTOSAR Logging Coverage

Efficient intrusion detection is relying on standardized logging strategies that are available off-the-shelf and hence easy to deploy and use. AUTOSAR lends itself as a basis for such an approach, due to its good acceptance in the automotive domain and native support for security events.

As shown in Table II and discussed in Section III-B, AUTOSAR defines Security Events for 50% of the UDS services (13 of 26). The coverage analysis for the UDS attacks shown in Table III is a bit more complex, since AUTOSAR does not provide support for all SIDs and can hence log certain attacks only partially. Out of the 53 attacks, AUTOSAR supports full logging for 20 and partial logging for an additional 10 attacks, rendering the overall logging support to 38-56%.

While AUTOSAR provides a good basis for UDS attack logging, it fails at providing complete coverage. It is hence advised to introduce additional security events based on the context data proposal in Table II. This can be done by automotive manufacturers for their respective products, or directly in AUTOSAR by extending the available Security Events.

In addition, please note that AUTOSAR supports only the logging strategies IR and FE. MFI is not supported by AUTOSAR, since it is typically implemented as part of an NIDS. Automotive manufacturers should take care that their NIDS specification supports the MFI security event proposed in Section III-B.

TABLE III. UDS ATTACK TECHNIQUES AND THEIR DETECTION STRATEGIES.

Attack ID	Attack Name	SIDs	Logging Strategies	AUTOSAR Support	Detection Strategies
AT-RD-1	Firmware Reverse-Engineering	-	NA	No	PTI
AT-RD-2	Leak Secrets		NA	No	PTI
AT-PS-1	Download Custom Package	0x34, 0x36, 0x37	IR, FE	Only 0x34	SLP, CLC, PTI
AT-PE-1	Change to Privileged Session	0x10	FE, MFI	No	CLC
AT-PE-2	Valid Credentials	0x27, 0x29	FE	✓	CLC, PTI
AT-PE-3	Replay Attack SA	0x27	IR, FE, MFI	✓	SLP, CLC, PTI
AT-PE-4	Brute-Force SA	0x27	IR, FE	✓	SLP, CLC
AT-PE-5	Weak Auth29 configurations	0x29	IR, FE	✓	CLC
AT-DE-1	Block DTCs Generation	0x85	FE	✓	CLC
AT-DE-2	Remove Attack Traces in DTCs	0x14	FE	✓	CLC
AT-DE-3	Replay Download	0x34, 0x36, 0x37	FE	Only 0x34	CLC
AT-DE-4	Bypass Checks	Multiple	Various	No	CLC, PTI
AT-DE-5	Bypass Read Protections using DDDID	0x2C, 0x22	FE	No	CLC, PTI
AT-CA-1	Extract Secrets	0x22, 0x23, 0x31	FE	Only 0x31	CLC
AT-DS-1	Service Discovery	Multiple	IR, FE	(✓)	SLP, CLC
AT-DS-2	Subfunction Discovery	Multiple	IR, FE	(✓)	SLP, CLC
AT-DS-3	Diagnostic Sessions Discovery	0x10	IR, FE	No	SLP, CLC
AT-DS-4	UDS Fuzzing	Multiple	IR, FE	(✓)	SLP, CLC
AT-DS-5	Check seed entropy in SA	0x27	IR, MFI	No	SLP
AT-DS-6	Reverse-engineer SA algorithm	0x27	FE	✓	CLC, PTI
AT-DS-7	Identify Auth29 configuration	0x29	FE	No	CLC, PTI
AT-DS-8	Enumerate algorithms, Auth29	0x29	FE	No	CLC, PTI
AT-DS-9	Check challenge entropy, Auth29	0x29	IR, MFI	No	SLP
AT-DS-10	Identify Configurations for SDT	0x84	FE	No	CLC, PTI
AT-DS-11	DID Enumeration	0x22	IR, FE	No	CLC, SLP
AT-DS-12	Routine Enumeration	0x31	IR, FE	✓	CLC, SLP
AT-DS-13	File System Discovery	0x38	IR, FE	✓	CLC, SLP
AT-DS-14	Eavesdropping	Multiple	NA	No	NA
AT-LM-1	Man-in-the-Middle	Multiple	IR, FE, MFI	(✓)	SLP, CLC, PTI
AT-CL-1	Event-Based Data Extraction	0x86	IR, FE	No	SLP, CLC
AT-CL-2	Periodic Data Extraction	0x2A	IR, FE	No	SLP, CLC
AT-CL-3	DID Data Extraction	0x22	IR, FE	No	CLC
AT-CL-4	Memory Extraction	0x23, 0x35	IR, FE	Only 0x35	CLC
AT-CL-5	File Extraction	0x38	IR, FE	✓	CLC
AT-CL-6	Read DTCs	0x19	IR, FE	No	SLP, CLC
AT-AF-1	Request Flooding	Multiple	IR, FE	(✓)	SLP, CLC, PTI
AT-AF-2	Request Blocking	Multiple	IR, FE, MFI	(✓)	PTI, SLP
AT-AF-3	Interrupt Operations, DSC	0x10	IR, FE, MFI	No	SLP
AT-AF-4	Impede Usage of SA	0x27	IR	✓	SLP
AT-AF-5.1	Resource Overload via ROE	0x86	IR, FE	No	SLP, CLC
AT-AF-5.2	Resource Overload via RDBPI	0x2A	IR, FE, MFI	No	SLP, CLC
AT-AF-6	Interrupt Periodic Data Readout	0x2A	IR, FE	No	SLP, CLC
AT-AF-7	Change IO Configuration	0x2F	IR, FE, MFI	✓	SLP, CLC
AT-AF-8	Routine Misuse	0x31	FE	✓	CLC
AT-AF-9	Early Transfer Termination	0x37	IR, FE, MFI	No	SLP, CLC
AT-AF-10	Interrupt Routine	0x31	IR, FE, MFI	✓	SLP, CLC
AT-AF-11	Keep Session Open	0x10, 0x3E	FE, MFI	No	CLC
AT-AF-12	I/O Control	0x2F	IR, FE	✓	CLC
AT-AF-13	Disrupt ECU Communication	0x28	IR, FE, MFI	✓	CLC
AT-AF-14	Reset ECU	0x11	IR, FE, MFI	✓	SLP, CLC
AT-AF-15	DID Manipulation	0x2E	IR, FE	✓	SLP, CLC
AT-AF-16	File Manipulation	0x38	IR, FE	✓	SLP, CLC
AT-AF-17	Memory Manipulation	0x3D, 0x34	IR, FE	✓	SLP, CLC

— Attack IDs refer to UDS attack techniques derived in [**Anonymous2025uds**], where IDs have the format AT-<TT>-<NO> where <TT> refers to the attack tactic and <NO> to the number of the attack technique in the respective category.

— (✓) refers to logging for supported SIDs only.

B. UDS attack detection - examples

Detection of UDS attacks is very individual and strongly depending on the actual attack technique. Space restrictions do not allow to describe detection for every attack technique in detail. Instead, we illustrate the detection capabilities of our approach through three representative attack techniques, each demonstrating different aspects of our multi-layered security monitoring approach. Figure 1 shows the general detection process, highlighting the detection possibilities in the vehicle and in the VSOC, while locating the detection of the following examples.

(1) AT-PE-4 Brute-Force SA Attack: In this attack technique, an attacker tries to brute-force all possible response ("key") values for SA (0x27). Applying logging strategy IR, Security Access brute-force attacks can be detected using existing AUTOSAR security events for SID 0x27, namely this is AUTOSAR security event 103 (SEV_UDS_SECURITY_ACCESS_ FAILED) [21]. By application of detection strategy SLP, multiple occurrences of this event within a short timeframe indicate a brute-force attempt against the Security Access service. This demonstrates effective detection using established AUTOSAR events with simple rate-based analysis. Additionally, detection strategy CLC may identify when authorizations are not consistent with the vehicle status.

(2) AT-CL-3 DID Data Extraction: In this attack technique, an attacker uses UDS service RDBI (0x22) to extract the information stored behind the DIDs, which may contain confidential data, e.g., keys. Detection of unauthorized RDBI operations is not possible through existing AUTOSAR security events, as no events are specified for this service. By application of logging strategies IR (logging unsuccessful access attempts) and FE (logging successful access), security events can address this gap by logging all accesses to sensitive DIDs, e.g., accessing cryptographic material. Context-data strategies ensure that DIDs are available as context data, and, for unsuccessful access attempts, the reason for rejection is available as Negative Response Code (NRC). Using strategy CLC, it can be ensured that only critical data identifier access attempts are captured, enabling detection of attacks targeting sensitive ECU information.

(3) AT-PS-1 Download Custom Package: In this attack technique, an attacker uses UDS services RD (0x34, request download), TD (0x36, transfer data), and RTE (0x37, request transfer exit) to download their own data into the ECU. Detection is possible by using logging strategies FE and IR, logging successful and unsuccessful invocation of relevant services (0x34, 0x36, 0x37). Context-data strategies ensure that firmware hashes are captured when completing download operations (0x37). By application of logging strategy CLC, these hashes are transmitted from the vehicle to the VSOC, where they are correlated with authorized firmware databases to detect downgrade attacks and unauthorized firmware installations. Logging strategies SLP and PTI can additionally be used to raise reliability of the detection, e.g., by detecting failed attempts in the operation, or by looking for known exploit patterns to install firmware. This attack cannot be detected by AUTOSAR security events alone, due to two fundamental limitations:

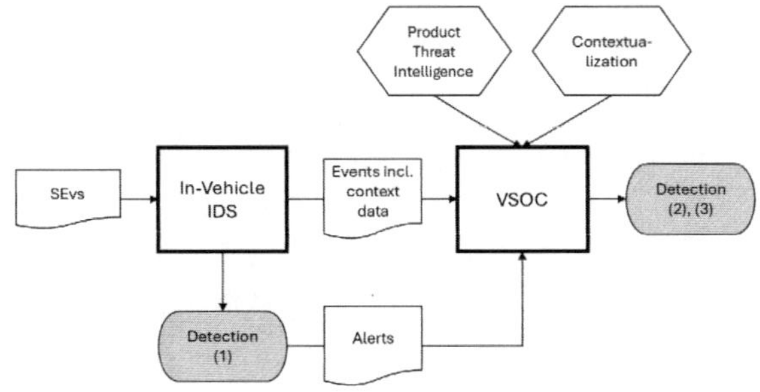

Figure 1. Detection process, including in-vehicle detection and VSOC-based detection. The numbers refer to the examples from Section IV-B

1) Attack detection requires firmware hash validation, which is not included in standard AUTOSAR security events.
2) Determining whether older or modified firmware is being installed requires backend knowledge of authorized firmware versions, which cannot be maintained locally in each vehicle.

C. UDS attack detection - take-aways

Based on our analysis from Section IV-B, we can compile the following take-away messages for detecting UDS attacks:

Vehicle-side detection can only cover a subset of UDS attack techniques. Some attack techniques can be reliably detected on the vehicle-side. Examples are given by techniques of the Discovery tactic, e.g., service discovery or UDS Fuzzing, which can be detected by observing a large number of certain requests in a short time window. However, for the majority of attacks, the additional information and contextualization possibilities of a VSOC are needed for reliable detection, as described by the following two points.

Product Threat Intelligence is needed as part of a VSOC infrastructure. For attack techniques of the attack tactic Resource Development, detection is possible using strategy PTI (Product Threat Intelligence) alone. Reverse engineering of firmware and leakage of secrets is usually done offline and can neither be detected by sensors in the vehicle nor by consistency analysis of logs in the backend. It can only be detected by observing reports of leakage of ECU firmware or UDS cryptographic material, e.g., in forums or news feeds.

A *combination* of detection strategies as well as backend processing in a VSOC are needed for a maximum coverage and reliable detection of UDS attack techniques. For many attack techniques, single detection strategies alone cannot provide sufficient evidence on the occurrence of an attack technique. However, the combination of detection strategies allows to reach a higher confidence by elimination of false positives. For example, consider AT-PE-1 "Change to Privileged Session" - an attacker using DSC (0x10) to change to a privileged session. In this case, the vehicle-side can log that DSC was called but needs additional data to distinguish whether this happened in context of a valid scenario, e.g., in context of a planned car service session.

V. Conclusion and Future Work

This paper presents multi-layered detection strategies for UDS-based attack techniques — combining vehicle-level intrusion detection sensors with VSOC-level processing and threat intelligence. It is shown that strategies are suited to cover almost all elements from a comprehensive taxonomy of UDS techniques. Security monitoring strategies presented in this paper can be used as a guide to implement the detection of UDS attack techniques in a VSOC infrastructure:

Logging requirements. Logging and context data strategies can be used as requirements for on-board intrusion detection components. The analysis from Table III also shows in which cases we can refer to AUTOSAR standardized security events.

Automated processing rules. Detection strategies of the Suspicious Log Pattern and Contextualized Log Check categories can be used to define automated processing rules in a processing pipeline for aggregated onboard logs. Depending on system architecture, resources, and availability of context data, log processing may be done on the onboard side as well as on the backend side. Automated processing results in alerts to be handled in an incident management system.

Threat intelligence triggers. Detection strategies of the Product Threat Intelligence category can be used to define trigger criteria for the evaluation of threat intelligence information. Depending on the trigger critria, news feeds will be filtered down towards notifications relevant for the UDS monitoring use cases, and can be linked to alerts.

Playbooks. On a higher level, detection scenarios can be implemented in playbooks, guiding the validation of alerts in an incident management system, also including manual analysis steps. Each UDS security attack technique can be covered by a playbook, while alerts with similar processing steps can be bundled in a joint playbook.

In this way, this paper gives concrete guidelines on building VSOC detection scenarios based on the UDS protocol, and our accepted follow-up describes a VSOC for automotive and rail, specifying formats for vehicle security events and alerts, as well as detection and response capabilities [24].

While this paper gives a qualitative assessment of detection strategies, their experimental evaluation with real vehicles remains a topic for future work.

Acknowledgment

This research is accomplished within the project "FINESSE" (FKZ 16KIS1584K). We acknowledge the financial support for the project by the Federal Ministry of Research, Technology and Space (BMFTR).

References

[1] UNECE, "UN Regulation No. 155 - Cyber security and cyber security management system," United Nations Economic Commission for Europe (UNECE), Geneva, CH, Standard UN R155, 2021. [Online]. Available: https://unece.org/transport/documents/2021/03/standards/un-regulation-no-155-cyber-security-and-cyber-security (visited on 09/05/2025).

[2] ISO, "Road Vehicles — Unified Diagnostic Services (UDS) Part 1: Application Layer," International Organization for Standardization, Geneva, CH, Standard ISO 14229:2020, 2020. [Online]. Available: https://www.iso.org/standard/72439.html.

[3] S. Kulandaivel, S. Jain, J. Guajardo, and V. Sekar, "CANdid: A stealthy stepping-stone attack to bypass authentication on ECUs," *Journal on Autonomous Transportation Systems*, pp. 1–17, 2024.

[4] T. Lauser and C. Krauß, "Formal security analysis of vehicle diagnostic protocols," in *Proceedings of the 18th International Conference on Availability, Reliability and Security (ARES)*, ACM, 2023, pp. 1–11. DOI: 10.1145/3600160.3600184.

[5] M. Matsubayashi *et al.*, "Attacks against UDS on DoIP by exploiting diagnostic communications and their countermeasures," in *Proceedings of the 93rd IEEE Vehicular Technology Conference (VTC2021-Spring)*, IEEE, 2021, pp. 1–6.

[6] N. Weiss, S. Renner, J. Mottok, and V. Matoušek, "Automated threat evaluation of automotive diagnostic protocols," in *ESCAR USA*, 2021, pp. 1–16.

[7] K. Mayer, T. Volkersdorfer, J. Hofbauer, P. Heinl, and H.-J. Hof, "Vehicle security operations center for cooperative, connected and automated mobility," in *Proceedings of the 18th International Conference on Emerging Security Information, Systems and Technologies (SECURWARE 2024)*, IARIA, 2024, pp. 156–164.

[8] A. R. Yekta, N. Loza, J. Gramm, M. P. Schneider, and S. Katzenbeisser, "Uds attack taxonomy: Systematic classification of vehicle diagnostic threats," in *2025 IEEE Conference on Communications and Network Security (CNS)*, 2025, pp. 1–8. DOI: 10.1109/CNS66487.2025.11195020.

[9] A. R. Yekta, D. Spychalski, E. Yekta, C. Yekta, and S. Katzenbeisser, "VATT&EK: Formalization of cyber attacks on intelligent transport systems - a TTP based approach for automotive and rail," in *Proceedings of the 7th ACM Computer Science in Cars Symposium (CSCS)*, ACM, 2023, pp. 1–17. [Online]. Available: https://doi.org/10.1145/3631204.3631867.

[10] T. M. Corporation, *MITRE ATT&CK*, 2024. [Online]. Available: https://attack.mitre.org/ (visited on 09/05/2025).

[11] ISO/SAE, "Road Vehicles — Cybersecurity Engineering," International Organization for Standardization, Geneva, CH, Standard ISO/SAE 21434:2021, 2021. [Online]. Available: https://www.iso.org/standard/70918.html (visited on 09/05/2025).

[12] ASRG, *CVE-2024-6348 - Predictable seed generation in the security access mechanism of UDS in the Blind Spot Protection Sensor ECU in Nissan Altima.* 2024. [Online]. Available: https://nvd.nist.gov/vuln/detail/CVE-2024-6348 (visited on 09/05/2025).

[13] N. Ronge, S. Zari, and A. Yadav, *KIA-SELTOS-Vehicle-Cluster-Vulnerabilities*, 2024. [Online]. Available: https://github.com/nitinronge91/KIA-SELTOS-Cluster-Vulnerabilities (visited on 09/05/2025).

[14] P. Pełechaty and Ł. Konieczny, "Analysis of security vulnerabilities in vehicle on-board diagnostic systems," *Diagnostyka*, vol. 25, no. 3, pp. 1–8, 2024. DOI: 10.29354/diag/192162.

[15] J. Dürrwang, J. Braun, M. Rumez, and R. Kriesten, "Security evaluation of an airbag ECU by reusing threat modeling artefacts," in *2017 International Conference on Computational*

Science and Computational Intelligence (CSCI), IEEE, 2017, pp. 37–43.

[16] J. Van den Herrewegen and F. D. Garcia, "Beneath the bonnet: A breakdown of diagnostic security," in *Proceedings of the 23rd European Symposium on Research in Computer Security (ESORICS 2018)*, Springer, 2018, pp. 305–324. DOI: 10.1007/978-3-319-99073-6_15.

[17] M. Ring, T. Rensen, and R. Kriesten, "Evaluation of vehicle diagnostics security–implementation of a reproducible security access," in *Proceedings of the 8th International Conference on Emerging Security Information, Systems and Technologies (SECURWARE 2014)*, IARIA, 2014, pp. 214–219.

[18] B. Lampe and W. Meng, "Intrusion detection in the automotive domain: A comprehensive review," *IEEE Communications Surveys Tutorials*, vol. 25, no. 4, pp. 2356–2426, 2023.

[19] F. Langer, F. Schüppel, and L. Stahlbock, "Establishing an automotive cyber defense center," in *Proceedings of the 17th Embedded Security in Cars Conference (ESCAR Europe 2019)*, 2019, pp. 1–14. DOI: 10.13154/294-6652.

[20] D. Grimm, M. Zink, M. Schindewolf, and E. Sax, "Cyber situational awareness in vehicle security operations: Holistic monitoring and a data model," in *Proceedings of the 20th International Conference on Network and Service Management (CNSM)*, IEEE, 2024, pp. 1–7.

[21] AUTOSAR, "Technical Report on Security Events Specification," AUTOSAR R24-11, 2024.

[22] AUTOSAR, "Specification of Intrusion Detection System Manager," AUTOSAR R24-11, 2024.

[23] AUTOSAR, "Specification of Intrusion Detection System Protocol," AUTOSAR R24-11, 2024.

[24] A. R. Yekta *et al.*, "Towards a holistic and multi-modal vehicle security monitoring," in *Proceedings of the 20th International Conference on Critical Information Infrastructures Security (CRITIS 2025)*, Jönköping, Sweden: Springer, 2025.

DeepAuthVerify—A Modular Framework for Deepfake Detection in Facial Authentication Systems

Domenico Di Palma, Alexander Lawall, Kristina Schaaff
IU International University of Applied Sciences
Erfurt, Germany
{alexander.lawall | kristina.schaaff}@iu.org

***Abstract*—The rise of deepfake technologies poses a significant threat to biometric authentication systems, especially those based on facial recognition. In our study, we investigate the reliability of commercial facial recognition systems when exposed to deepfake attacks and propose a modular authentication solution (*DeepAuthVerify*) that integrates deepfake detection into the verification process. We developed *DeepAuthVerify* as a two-layered system combining deep learning-based face recognition and feature extraction with the semantic interpretability of a Large Language Model (LLM) for decision-making. Despite achieving lower accuracy (66.89%) compared to commercial solutions (OpenCV: 91.43%, Amazon Rekognition: 93.80%), *DeepAuthVerify* demonstrates the potential as a complementary layer for deepfake detection, enhancing transparency and modularity. The results indicate that commercial systems, when properly configured, offer robust protection against deepfake attacks. However, their black-box nature limits adaptability and auditability. Our proposed system provides a novel, extensible architecture that fosters explainability and integration into existing authentication environments. In addition to the evaluation, we publicly release the evaluation pipeline to allow reproducibility and comparability of future research.**

Keywords-Deepfake Detection; Facial Recognition; Authentication Systems; Large Language Models.

I. INTRODUCTION

The rise of deepfake technologies, synthetically generated or manipulated images and videos created using deep learning techniques, poses a growing threat to biometric authentication systems [1], particularly those based on facial recognition. While these systems are increasingly adopted in Multi-Factor Authentication (MFA) due to their convenience and user acceptance [2], their vulnerability to sophisticated impersonation attacks remains a critical security concern.

Recent advancements in generative models, such as Generative Adversarial Networks (GANs) [3] and Variational Autoencoders (VAEs) [4], have enabled the realistic creation of fake identities that can evade the detection by recognition algorithms. Simultaneously, user-friendly deepfake tools like Reface [5] and DeepFaceLab [6] have reduced the technical barrier for attackers. As reported by the Entrust Cybersecurity Institute, deepfake attacks in identity verification contexts are increasing significantly, with one attempt occurring approximately every five minutes as of 2024 [7].

In our study, we propose *DeepAuthVerify*, a novel, modular authentication framework that augments traditional recognition with a deepfake detection layer using deep learning and semantic analysis through a Large Language Model (LLM). Moreover, we systematically evaluate the resilience of facial recognition systems against deepfake attacks using a data corpus created based on the *Celeb-DF* dataset [8].

Our key contributions are:

1) A hybrid system combining deep learning-based face recognition, facial feature extraction, and LLM-based decision logic.
2) An approach that enhances modularity, interpretability, and integrability in authentication contexts.
3) A novel integration of structured semantic explanations to support transparent deepfake classification and human oversight.
4) Public release of implementation code and test setup to foster reproducibility and future research [9].

The remainder of the paper is structured as follows. Section II outlines the theoretical background of biometric authentication, deepfake generation, and detection technologies, with emphasis on LLM-based reasoning. Section III reviews related work on deepfake detection methods, highlighting their limitations in transparency and integration. Section IV introduces the design of the DeepAuthVerify framework, detailing its requirements, modular architecture, and two-phase verification process. Section V presents the evaluation methodology, datasets, and empirical results compared to commercial systems. Section VI explores system integration options, including standalone, parallel, and pre-filtering deployment modes. Section VII concludes with key findings, limitations, and directions for future research on explainable and adaptive authentication systems.

II. THEORETICAL BACKGROUND

This section outlines the (i) biometric authentication and the technologies that enable facial recognition, and (ii) machine learning foundations underlying deepfake generation and detection, including recent advances in LLMs.

A. Biometric Authentication and Facial Recognition

MFA enhances system security by combining independent factors: knowledge (e.g., passwords), possession (e.g., smartphones, tokens), and biometrics (e.g., fingerprints or facial features) [2]. Among these, facial recognition has emerged as one of the most widely adopted due to its usability and low user friction [10]. However, it introduces new attack vectors, such as presentation attacks and digital identity forgery, especially in remote settings.

Facial recognition systems typically follow a pipeline with face detection, feature extraction, and identity verification [11]. Early approaches include feature-based and template-matching methods [12], as well as holistic techniques like the Eigenfaces algorithm [13]. Recent advances use three-dimensional face modeling like in Apple's Face ID [14] and Google's Face Mesh [15]. Despite high accuracy, commercial Application Programming Interfaces (APIs), such as Amazon Rekognition and OpenCV, are typically closed-source and provide limited interpretability, making them hard to audit in sensitive applications.

B. Generative AI, Deepfake Detection, and LLM Reasoning

Modern face recognition and manipulation systems rely on deep learning. Convolutional Neural Networks (CNNs) are particularly effective at extracting facial features and achieving high classification performance under varying conditions [16]. Models like FaceNet [17] have demonstrated their strength in person identification and clustering tasks.

In parallel, generative models, such as GANs and VAEs, have enabled the creation of highly realistic synthetic face images, known as deepfakes. Techniques include face swapping, reenactment, and full-face synthesis [18], often implemented in publicly available tools, such as DeepFaceLab or StyleGAN [19]. The accessibility of such tools raises security concerns, as even low-skilled attackers can generate high-quality forgeries.

Detection models have been proposed, mostly using CNN-based binary classifiers trained on labeled datasets, such as *Celeb-DF*, to counteract these threats. While effective, these systems often operate as non-transparent detectors with limited reasoning capacity.

LLMs, such as GPT [20] and BERT [21], have shown promising results in bridging this gap by offering contextual understanding and semantic interpretation. Built on transformer architectures [22], LLMs can synthesize structured input into human-readable justifications. Their applications in anomaly detection, adversarial reasoning, and decision support have triggered increasing interest in the cybersecurity domain [23], where transparency and interpretability are relevant.

C. Implications for Authentication Systems

The convergence of these technologies enables both advanced biometric verification and new attack vectors. While commercial systems achieve high accuracy under ideal conditions, their susceptibility to deepfake manipulation and lack of interpretability raise critical concerns [24]. Integrating deepfake detection components into authentication pipelines, particularly those combining deep learning with LLM reasoning, offers a possibility for enhanced robustness and transparency.

III. Related Work

The detection of deepfakes has become an active research area due to their increasing misuse in identity fraud, misinformation, and biometric spoofing. Numerous approaches have emerged that influence advances in computer vision, signal analysis, and adversarial learning to distinguish manipulated content from authentic input.

Deepfake detectors often use CNNs to capture subtle spatial or temporal inconsistencies in face-swapped or synthesized videos. MesoNet [25], XceptionNet [26], and Capsule Networks [27] are among the architectures that have shown promising results on benchmark datasets, such as FaceForensics++ [26], ForgeryNet [28], and Celeb-DF [8]. These models often achieve better performance when trained on large-scale datasets that include both authentic and manipulated samples.

The vulnerability of facial recognition systems to presentation attacks and deepfakes has been widely studied [29], [30]. Even state-of-the-art face recognition APIs can be deceived by high-quality synthetic content [24]. As a countermeasure, ensemble classifiers [31] and temporal analysis models [32] have been proposed to improve robustness in real-time verification systems. Nevertheless, these methods often suffer from lack of transparency and limited interoperability with commercial authentication workflows.

Recent work has explored combining deep learning-based feature extraction with interpretable or modular architectures. For example, [33] discuss the integration of transformer-based language models in security incident response systems, highlighting the role of contextual reasoning. These approaches point toward a new generation of hybrid systems that prioritize transparency and human-aligned decision-making; yet their application in biometric authentication remains limited.

While prior research has explored detection accuracy and network architectures, our work contributes a novel perspective by integrating a deepfake detection module with a semantic reasoning layer into a facial authentication pipeline. Unlike black-box detectors, our system emphasizes modularity, transparency, and interpretability. We aim to bridge the gap between detection research and deployable security systems.

IV. System Design

In this paper, we propose *DeepAuthVerify*, a modular, two-layered authentication system that integrates deepfake detection and explainable decision-making into the verification process to address the increasing threat posed by deepfakes in facial recognition-based authentication. This section details the functional and non-functional requirements of the system, followed by an architectural overview of its layered design and operational flow.

A. Design Requirements

The design of *DeepAuthVerify* is driven by several core requirements, which reflect both practical integration and current research challenges in biometric security:

- **(R1) Compatibility:** The system must be compatible with existing biometric MFA infrastructures, particularly those using commercial face recognition APIs (e.g., Amazon Rekognition, OpenCV).
- **(R2) Robustness against Deepfakes:** The system must reliably detect synthetic facial images generated through deep learning methods (GANs, VAEs, etc.).

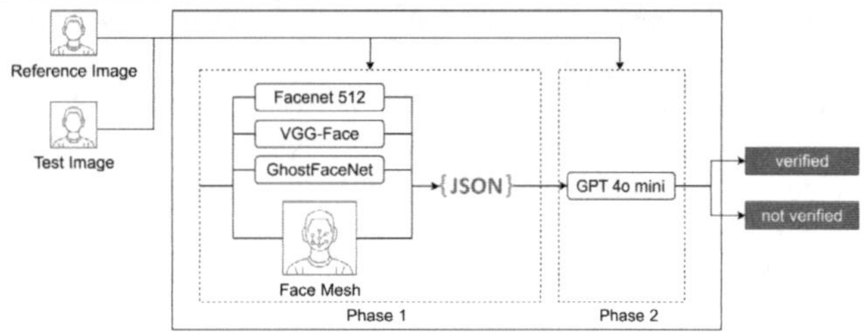

Figure 1. High-level Architecture of *DeepAuthVerify*

- **(R3) Explainability:** Decisions should be transparent and accompanied by interpretable reasoning to improve auditability and trust, especially in ambiguous or borderline cases. This is especially important in regulatory-sensitive environments to improve auditability and trust.
- **(R4) Modularity and Extensibility:** System components (e.g., detection modules, APIs, reasoning layer) must be loosely coupled to support individual updates and enhancements.

B. Design Rationale & Advantages

The modular architecture of *DeepAuthVerify* ensures the separation of concerns and simplifies both testing and future extension. For instance, the deepfake detection layer can be updated with new deep learning models without affecting the face verification logic. Similarly, the LLM layer can be replaced by task-specific models or rule-based systems, depending on deployment requirements and privacy constraints.

A key innovation lies in the semantic reasoning layer. Rather than producing a binary decision alone, the system generates an explanatory narrative that enables human reviewers to understand the rationale behind the verdict. This supports informed escalation in edge cases and fulfills demands for AI transparency in critical identity verification workflows.

Additionally, the architecture supports deployment flexibility. Components can be containerized and orchestrated via microservices, making the system suitable for both cloud-based and on-premise environments.

C. Architectural Overview

DeepAuthVerify follows a modular and multi-phase architecture that integrates deep learning-based face recognition and facial feature extraction with an LLM to verify the authenticity of facial input data. This section outlines the design and implementation of each architectural phase in detail.

Figure 1 illustrates the system's high-level architecture. The input to the system are two facial images, which are processed through each stage sequentially. Each module is independently operable and can be adapted or replaced based on specific authentication requirements. This means the system exposes methods that manage facial image input, feature extraction, and classification. The modular structure allows for reusability and supports the replacement of individual modules, such as the landmark extraction pipeline or the classification algorithm.

The verification process follows two phases: The classification by a deep learning model with facial embedding extraction and the semantic validation.

1) Phase 1—Classification and Embedding Extraction: In the first phase, facial landmarks are extracted using the Face Mesh technology from the MediaPipe framework [15]. This technique identifies three-dimensional facial landmarks, which are then normalized to ensure scale and pose invariance. These normalized landmarks serve as the basis for constructing embedding vectors used in similarity comparisons.

The system integrates three pretrained deep learning models for facial feature extraction to enhance representational power and robustness:

- FaceNet 512 [17]: generates compact embeddings using triplet loss
- VGG-Face [34]: CNN model trained on a large-scale face dataset
- GhostFaceNets [35]: lightweight model optimized for fast and efficient inference. Each model produces feature vectors that are compared to reference embeddings using cosine similarity.

Each model produces feature vectors that are compared to reference embeddings using cosine similarity. Additionally, key facial landmarks are extracted using the Face Mesh library and included in the result. The final output is returned as a structured JSON object containing the model name, verification result, threshold, cosine distance, detector backend, and the extracted facial landmarks. The system architecture allows for flexible integration, enabling these models to be exchanged or extended at any time without major adjustments.

2) Phase 2—Semantic Validation via LLM: The extracted facial features and metadata are analyzed using an LLM. We implemented the LLM integration using OpenAI's GPT API with custom prompting logic. The prompt is designed to guide the LLM in semantically interpreting the context, such as inconsistencies in facial symmetry, unnatural artifacts, or landmark misalignments. The transmitted JSON serves as support. The LLM acts as a semantic validator, assessing the likelihood that a given image is synthetically generated. Additionally, the output includes a detailed explanation of the classification result. For example, in the case of an input image classified as manipulated, the explanatory output may look as follows:

> "Discrepancies detected in left jawline contour and reflection inconsistency in the left eye region. Landmarks appear overly symmetric compared to the reference face, suggesting GAN-based synthesis."

This explanation enables reviewers to understand the rationale behind a rejection, rather than relying solely on a similarity score or binary decision. Such interpretability is crucial in edge cases or escalated verification workflows.

3) Integration Challenges: While each building block of *DeepAuthVerify*, such as face embeddings, landmark extraction, and the LLM-based semantic validator, has been studied in isolation, their combination introduces non-trivial challenges. These include synchronizing heterogeneous outputs across modules, preventing error propagation between the embedding similarity layer and the LLM interpretation, managing additional latency overhead, and maintaining consistent thresholds across components. We emphasize these integration issues as part of the motivation for adopting a modular design that allows individual components to be improved or replaced without destabilizing the overall framework.

V. System Evaluation

This section presents the evaluation of *DeepAuthVerify* and the comparison with commercial systems.

A. Evaluation Setup

We conducted a structured evaluation to assess the effectiveness and robustness of *DeepAuthVerify*. In total, we used a set of 1,178 image pairs based on the *Celeb-DF* data set [8]. As the *Celeb-DF* data set contains videos only, for our tests, we generated image pairs from the video data. The image pairs are distributed across the following test variants:

- Test set 0—Control group (342 image pairs): two unaltered images of the same person, variations in facial expression, lighting, or angle.
- Test set 1—Deepfake with preserved context (218 image pairs): One of the two images has been manipulated using deepfake techniques to replace the face, while background, pose, and clothing remain unchanged. Only the face is synthetic; the rest of the image context is identical.
- Test set 2—Deepfake with altered context (618 image pairs): The manipulated image includes both a deepfaked face and altered context (e.g., background, pose, facial expression). Both the face and the surrounding scene are synthetically modified.

The test cases consist of image comparisons distributed across four different gender categories. The dataset is composed of male (54.92%) and female (41.94%) subjects, with non-binary (1.87%) and unknown (1.27%) gender entries. A test is successful if, in test set 0, the system correctly identifies the images as matching, and in test sets 1 and 2, it correctly identifies the images as non-matching.

B. Evaluation Results

We tested our final system using the three test variants presented in Section V-A. The aim was to assess the accuracy and robustness of the optimized system under identical conditions. To determine the most suitable threshold for the selected test dataset, we performed a Receiver Operating Characteristic (ROC) analysis, allowing us to identify the optimal decision threshold that balances sensitivity and specificity.

After optimization, we were able to achieve an accuracy of 66.89%, showing a general classification performance despite the complexity of the task. The F1-score of 47.68%, shows a balance between detection sensitivity and false positive control. Our system achieved a precision of 44.09%, indicating that nearly half of the images identified as manipulated were correctly classified. Moreover, the system yielded a recall of 52.34%, which reflects its ability to detect more than half of all correct images correctly.

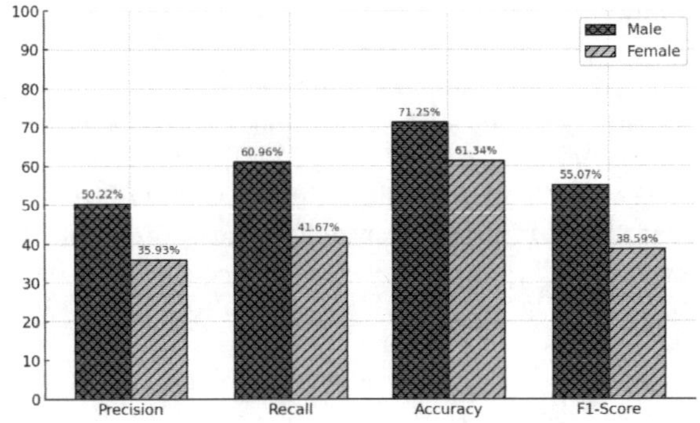

Figure 2. Gender-Specific Performance of *DeepAuthVerify*

In addition to the overall evaluation, we analyzed the performance of the optimized system with respect to gender-specific differences (cf. Figure 2). The test dataset was approximately balanced across male and female subjects to ensure a fair comparison. The results revealed a discrepancy in detection performance between the two groups.

For male subjects, the system achieved consistently higher scores across all metrics, including precision (50.22%), recall (60.96%), accuracy (71.25%), and F1-score (55.07%). In contrast, the performance for female subjects was substantially lower, particularly in recall (41.67%) and F1-score (38.59%), indicating that the system was less effective at detecting manipulated images in this group. The lower precision and accuracy for female subjects suggest a higher rate of false positives and an increased overall classification error. These findings point to a gender-related performance disparity in the optimized model.

This performance gap may be attributed to differences in facial structure, image variability, or bias introduced during the model's training phase. It emphasizes the importance of addressing demographic fairness in biometric verification systems.

C. Comparison with Commercial Systems

To assess the effectiveness of *DeepAuthVerify*, we conducted a comparative evaluation against two established commercial facial recognition solutions: Amazon Rekognition and OpenCV. All three systems were tested using the same balanced dataset, which included both authentic and manipulated facial images. This ensured a consistent evaluation environment across all systems. We focused on four key performance metrics: precision, recall, accuracy, and F1-score, providing the system's strengths and limitations in detecting manipulated identities.

DeepAuthVerify shows lower performance across all core classification metrics compared to the commercial systems Amazon Rekognition and OpenCV. *DeepAuthVerify* achieves a precision of 44.09%, whereas Amazon Rekognition reaches 85.87% and OpenCV 80.82%, indicating that *DeepAuthVerify* generates significantly more false positives when identifying manipulated images. The difference in recall is even more pronounced: *DeepAuthVerify* identifies only 52.34% of all manipulated samples correctly, while Amazon Rekognition and OpenCV reach 94.15% and 92.40%, respectively. This gap reveals a limited sensitivity of *DeepAuthVerify* to actual deepfakes. In terms of overall accuracy, *DeepAuthVerify* achieves 66.89%, which is lower than Amazon Rekognition (93.80%) and OpenCV (91.43%). This also reflects the combined weaknesses in both precision and recall. The F1-score, which balances precision and recall, further illustrates the disparity: 47.68% for *DeepAuthVerify* versus 89.82% for Amazon Rekognition and 86.22% for OpenCV. This confirms that *DeepAuthVerify* currently lacks robustness and reliability under real-world conditions, though it demonstrates the conceptual feasibility of a hybrid LLM-integrated verification pipeline.

Although *DeepAuthVerify* underperforms in accuracy due to limited data and complexity, it adds interpretable semantics and decision reasoning that are absent in commercial APIs. Moreover, the evaluation highlights that hybrid systems combining visual detection with semantic interpretation can support human decision-making in ambiguous or adversarial input scenarios.

D. Discussion

The evaluation results reveal a trade-off between raw detection accuracy and system transparency. While Amazon Rekognition and OpenCV achieve higher recognition rates, they operate as black-box models with no interpretability or context-aware feedback. While our evaluation demonstrates that commercial services provide higher accuracy in controlled settings, these are limited in terms of transparency and interpretability. Our approach trades a portion of accuracy for improved explainability and modular design. This trade-off is particularly relevant in high-risk identity verification contexts, such as remote onboarding or digital voting, where system outputs must be auditable and justifiable. This raises concerns in domains where traceability, user trust, and regulatory compliance (e.g., General Data Protection Regulation, AI Act) are essential.

DeepAuthVerify prioritizes explainability through a layered architecture that incorporates a semantic reasoning component. Nevertheless, qualitative analysis indicates that the added interpretability can enhance human-in-the-loop decision making, especially in edge cases. Another strength of *DeepAuthVerify* lies in its modularity. Each layer (face verification, detection, reasoning) can be independently updated or replaced without altering the core logic. This design enables quick adaptation to emerging deepfake techniques or new recognition APIs and supports potential integration with other biometric modalities, such as voice or gait.

VI. System Integration Options

DeepAuthVerify is designed for seamless integration into existing authentication systems. In our evaluation, we assessed the system as a stand-alone module, fully replacing the traditional facial recognition pipeline. This allowed for an isolated analysis of its detection capabilities and semantic reasoning logic.

However, one of the core strengths of *DeepAuthVerify* lies in its modular architecture, which supports flexible deployment strategies beyond full replacement. Therefore, we propose the following integration variants, which are illustrated in Figure 3. In particular, integration variants 2 and 3 offer promising options for real-world use cases:

- **Variant 1: Full Replacement**—*DeepAuthVerify* replaces the system layer entirely as in our evaluation.
- **Variant 2: Parallel Evaluation (Veto Layer)**—The system operates alongside commercial recognition APIs. Its classification output or explanation can override or verify existing decisions, enabling more transparent decision pipelines.
- **Variant 3: Pre-filtering Stage**—*DeepAuthVerify* works as a deepfake screening layer prior to conventional recognition, filtering out manipulated inputs before further processing.

These hybrid integration modes highlight a major advantage of our approach: commercial systems can be extended with a semantic explanation component without altering their internal architecture. This enables organizations to enhance the auditability and trustworthiness of their authentication workflows by adding explainable, AI-assisted reasoning without reducing the performance benefits of mature commercial solutions.

VII. Conclusion & Future Work

In our paper, we presented *DeepAuthVerify*, a novel, modular authentication system that augments commercial face recognition with deepfake detection and semantic reasoning. It was systematically evaluated on a subset of the *Celeb-DF* dataset that commercial APIs remain effective under clean conditions. Under default threshold settings, they detect deepfakes reasonably well. However, such optimizations are often tailored to the specific test dataset and may not generalize well to unseen data.

Our approach addresses this gap by using deep learning models for robust facial feature extraction, combined with an LLM to enable transparent and interpretable decision-making. This architecture provides a solid foundation for future authentication systems that are explainable, secure, and adaptive, even in adversarial settings, while the system's performance can be enhanced. *DeepAuthVerify* introduces an explainability-first design. The inclusion of LLM-driven semantic feedback empowers system operators to trace, understand, and document decisions in high-stakes environments, offering an advantage over commercial black-box solutions. As regulatory frameworks (e.g., European Union AI Act) increasingly require transparent AI reasoning, our system is positioned as a compliant and auditable alternative.

Valuable insights aside, our study has its limitations. The evaluation was conducted under controlled conditions using a predefined test dataset, which may limit the extent to which

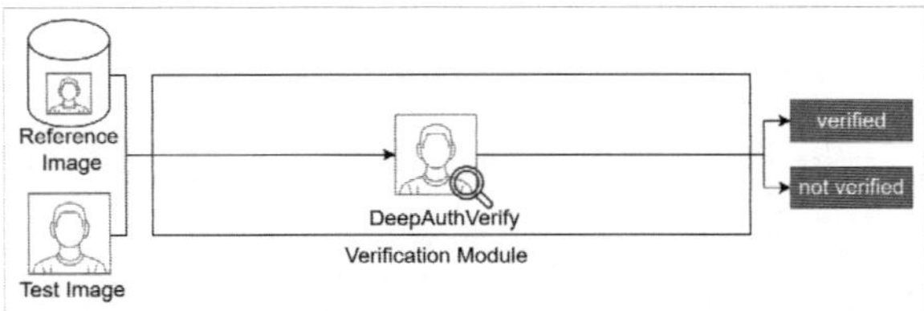

(a) Variant 1: Full Replacement

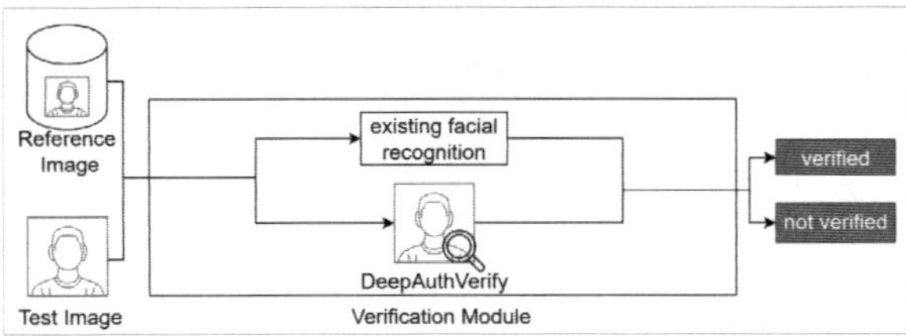

(b) Variant 2: Parallel Evaluation (Veto Layer)

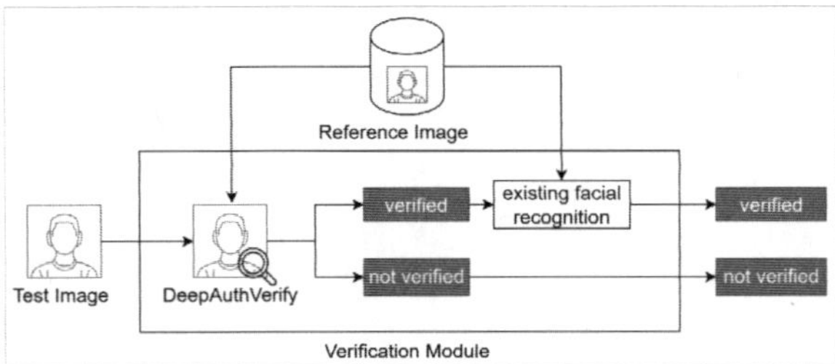

(c) Variant 3: Pre-filtering Stage

Figure 3. System Integration Options of *DeepAuthVerify*

findings can be generalized to real-world scenarios. The deep learning models in the first phase and the configuration of the large language model were based on standard parameters, providing a solid baseline but leaving room for further optimization. The similarity score generated by the LLM is based on internal mechanisms that are not fully transparent, which may pose challenges for interpretability in specific cases. Additionally, aspects, such as potential bias effects, e.g., related to gender, were explored and would benefit from a more comprehensive analysis in future research.

Future research includes advancements in prompt engineering for the LLM, the adoption of newer, higher-performing GPT architectures, and the calibration of model-specific threshold values. Moreover, the fine-tuning or selection of more effective deep learning models for the initial processing phase could yield further improvements. In the long term, extending the system architecture to support video-based analysis represents a promising direction. The integration of traditional image processing methods with explainable AI techniques may also contribute to the development of transparent and reliable security solutions for practical deployment scenarios.

Continuous advancement of deepfake detection remains necessary, as generative models are constantly evolving. Without regular updates to the detectors, their effectiveness against new types of manipulation may decline, potentially impairing the reliability of facial recognition [36]. Additionally, the system's design as an API-compatible component facilitates its integration into existing authentication workflows. Deployment on cloud platforms, such as Amazon Web Services, would enable modular connectivity with diverse systems, thereby enhancing scalability and adaptability.

References

[1] A. Lawall and P. Beenken, "Subject-and Process-Oriented Comparison of Multi-factor Authentication Methods," in *Subject-Oriented Business Process Management. Models for Designing Digital Transformations*, M. Elstermann and M. Lederer, Eds., Springer. Cham: Springer Nature Switzerland, 2024, pp. 153–159.

[2] Bundesamt für Sicherheit in der Informationstechnik, "Technische Richtlinie TR-03107: Multi-Faktor-Authentifizierung [Technical Guideline TR-03107: Multi-Factor Authentication]," BSI, Tech. Rep., 2023, [retrieved: September 2025].

[3] I. Goodfellow *et al.*, "Generative adversarial networks," in *Advances in Neural Information Processing Systems (NeurIPS)*, vol. 27, 2014, pp. 2672–2680.

[4] D. P. Kingma and M. Welling, "Auto-Encoding Variational Bayes," *arXiv preprint arXiv:1312.6114*, 2013, presented at ICLR 2014.

[5] Inc. NeoCortext, "Reface: Face Swap AI Generator," https://apps.apple.com/us/app/reface-face-swap-ai-generator/id1488782587, 2025, [retrieved: September 2025].

[6] I. Perov *et al.*, "DeepFaceLab: A Simple, Flexible and Extensive Face Swapping Framework," https://github.com/iperov/DeepFaceLab, 2020, [retrieved: May 2025].

[7] Entrust Cybersecurity Institute, "2025 identity fraud report," Entrust Corporation, Tech. Rep., 2025, available from https://www.entrust.com, [retrieved: September 2025].

[8] Y. Li, X. Yang, P. Sun, H. Qi, and S. Lyu, "Celeb-DF: A large-scale challenging dataset for deepfake forensics," in *Proceedings of the IEEE/CVF Conference on Computer Vision and Pattern Recognition (CVPR)*, 2020, pp. 3207–3216.

[9] D. D. Palma, "Face Recognition With Deepfake Detection," https://github.com/domdipa/FaceRecognitionWithDeepFakeDetection, 2025, [retrieved: June 2025].

[10] M. Liao, D. Agnihotri, and X. Zhong, ""paying with my face"–understanding users' adoption and privacy concerns of facial recognition payment," in *Proceedings of the Human Factors and Ergonomics Society Annual Meeting*, vol. 66, no. 1. SAGE Publications Sage CA: Los Angeles, CA, 2022, pp. 731–735.

[11] W. Zhao, R. Chellappa, P. J. Phillips, and A. Rosenfeld, "Face recognition: A literature survey," *ACM Computing Surveys (CSUR)*, vol. 35, no. 4, pp. 399–458, Dec. 2003.

[12] R. Brunelli and T. Poggio, "Face recognition: Features versus templates," *IEEE Transactions on Pattern Analysis and Machine Intelligence*, vol. 15, no. 10, pp. 1042–1052, Oct. 1993.

[13] M. Turk and A. Pentland, "Eigenfaces for Recognition," *Journal of Cognitive Neuroscience*, vol. 3, no. 1, pp. 71–86, Jan. 1991.

[14] Apple Inc., "Informationen zur fortschrittlichen Technologie von Face ID [Information about the advanced technology of Face ID]," https://support.apple.com/de-de/102381, Dec. 2024, [retrieved: September 2025].

[15] google-ai-edge, "MediaPipe Face Mesh," Nov. 2024, [retrieved: September 2025]. [Online]. Available: https://github.com/google-ai-edge/mediapipe/blob/master/docs/solutions/face_mesh.md#face-landmark-model

[16] C. M. Bishop and H. Bishop, *Deep Learning: Foundations and Concepts*. Cham: Springer International Publishing, 2024.

[17] F. Schroff, D. Kalenichenko, and J. Philbin, "FaceNet: A unified embedding for face recognition and clustering," in *2015 IEEE Conference on Computer Vision and Pattern Recognition (CVPR)*. Boston, MA, USA: IEEE, Jun. 2015, pp. 815–823.

[18] Z. Akhtar, "Deepfakes Generation and Detection: A Short Survey," *Journal of Imaging*, vol. 9, no. 1, p. 18, Jan. 2023.

[19] T. Karras, S. Laine, M. Aittala, J. Hellsten, J. Lehtinen, and T. Aila, "Analyzing and Improving the Image Quality of StyleGAN," in *2020 IEEE/CVF Conference on Computer Vision and Pattern Recognition (CVPR)*. Seattle, WA, USA: IEEE, Jun. 2020, pp. 8107–8116.

[20] A. Radford, K. Narasimhan, T. Salimans, and I. Sutskever, "Improving language understanding by generative pre-training," OpenAI, Technical Report, Jun. 2018, preprint. [Online]. Available: https://cdn.openai.com/research-covers/language-unsupervised/language_understanding_paper.pdf
[21] J. Devlin, M.-W. Chang, K. Lee, and K. Toutanova, "BERT: Pre-training of Deep Bidirectional Transformers for Language Understanding," in *Proceedings of NAACL-HLT*, 2019, pp. 4171–4186.
[22] A. Vaswani *et al.*, "Attention is all you need," *Advances in Neural Information Processing Systems*, vol. 30, 2017.
[23] M. Hasan, E. Rundensteiner, and E. Agu, "Emotex: Detecting Emotions in Twitter Messages," *Academy of Science and Engineering (ASE), USA,© ASE 2014*, 2014.
[24] S. Tariq, S. Jeon, and S. S. Woo, "Am I a Real or Fake Celebrity? Measuring Commercial Face Recognition Web APIs under Deepfake Impersonation Attack," 2021.
[25] D. Afchar, V. Nozick, J. Yamagishi, and I. Echizen, "MesoNet: a Compact Facial Video Forgery Detection Network," in *Proceedings of the IEEE Workshop on Information Forensics and Security (WIFS)*, Sep. 2018, presented at WIFS 2018.
[26] A. Rössler, D. Cozzolino, L. Verdoliva, C. Riess, J. Thies, and M. Nießner, "FaceForensics++: Learning to Detect Manipulated Facial Images," in *International Conference on Computer Vision (ICCV)*, 2019.
[27] H. H. Nguyen, J. Yamagishi, and I. Echizen, "Capsule-forensics: Using capsule networks to detect forged images and videos," in *ICASSP 2019 - 2019 IEEE International Conference on Acoustics, Speech and Signal Processing (ICASSP)*, 2019, pp. 2307–2311.
[28] Y. He *et al.*, "ForgeryNet: A Versatile Benchmark for Comprehensive Forgery Analysis," *arXiv preprint arXiv:2103.05630*, 2021.
[29] R. Tolosana, R. Vera-Rodriguez, J. Fierrez, A. Morales, and J. Ortega-Garcia, "Deepfakes and beyond: A survey of face manipulation and fake detection," *Information Fusion*, vol. 64, pp. 131–148, 2020. [Online]. Available: https://www.sciencedirect.com/science/article/pii/S1566253520303110
[30] S. Agarwal, H. Farid, Y. Gu, M. He, K. Nagano, and H. Li, "Protecting world leaders against deep fakes," in *Proceedings of the IEEE/CVF Conference on Computer Vision and Pattern Recognition (CVPR) Workshops*, June 2019.
[31] H. Dang, F. Liu, J. Stehouwer, X. Liu, and A. Jain, "On the detection of digital face manipulation," 06 2020, pp. 5780–5789.
[32] D. Guera and E. Delp, "Deepfake video detection using recurrent neural networks," 11 2018, pp. 1–6.
[33] I. Hasanov, S. Virtanen, A. Hakkala, and J. Isoaho, "Application of Large Language Models in Cybersecurity: A Systematic Literature Review," *IEEE Access*, vol. 12, pp. 176 751–176 778, Jan. 2024.
[34] O. M. Parkhi, A. Vedaldi, and A. Zisserman, "Deep face recognition," in *British Machine Vision Conference*, 2015.
[35] M. Alansari, O. A. Hay, S. Javed, A. Shoufan, Y. Zweiri, and N. Werghi, "GhostFaceNets: Lightweight Face Recognition Model From Cheap Operations," *IEEE Access*, vol. 11, pp. 35 429–35 446, 2023.
[36] F. Tassone, L. Maiano, and I. Amerini, "Continuous fake media detection: Adapting deepfake detectors to new generative techniques," *Computer Vision and Image Understanding*, vol. 249, p. 104143, Dec. 2024.

Comparison of Password-Authenticated Key Exchange Schemes on Android

Jörn-Marc Schmidt
IU International University of Applied Sciences
Erfurt, Thüringen, Germany
email: joern-marc.schmidt@iu.org

Alexander Lawall
IU International University of Applied Sciences
Erfurt, Thüringen, Germany
email: alexander.lawall@iu.org

Abstract—**Password-Authenticated Key Exchange (PAKE) protocols are critical for secure password-based authentication in various applications, including wireless networking, cloud services, secure messaging, and Internet of Things (IoT) ecosystems. This paper presents a systematic performance evaluation of classical and post-quantum PAKE protocols on a mobile platform, using a Google Pixel 7 Pro running Android 16. We implement a representative set of balanced PAKEs as well as augmented PAKEs. All schemes are implemented in Kotlin/Java using the Bouncy Castle cryptographic provider and evaluated using the Android Jetpack Benchmarking suite under controlled conditions. Our analysis reveals that post-quantum schemes, such as One-Way Key Encapsulation Method to PAKE (OCAKE) and an augmented PAKE scheme based on OCAKE, offer competitive or superior computational performance compared to their classical counterparts, while incurring significantly larger message sizes. We further identify mapping functions, cryptographic primitives, and protocol types as key factors influencing execution time. These results highlight the feasibility of deploying post-quantum PAKEs on constrained mobile devices and provide a benchmark for future optimizations. Future work will examine the impact of hardware acceleration and energy efficiency trade-offs for real-world deployment.**

Keywords-PAKE; post-quantum cryptography; Android; password-based authentication; mobile security.

I. Introduction

Typical credentials for authentication are passwords. They can be remembered and typed in by humans on various input devices. In terms of security, however, they are commonly easier to guess or to brute-force than cryptographic keys. Password-Authenticated Key Exchange (PAKE) schemes address this issue. They are interactive protocols for two or more parties to generate a joint session key based on a shared password. An adversary eavesdropping on the connection cannot discover the password. Active attacks are, in the best case, limited to one possible password guess per protocol run.

Hence, PAKE schemes can improve security in various cases of password use. For example, a PAKE is employed for password-based authentication in Wireless Fidelity (Wi-Fi) networks [1] and the Matter protocol [2]. Different applications, including 1Password [3] and messengers, such as WhatsApp [4] and Facebook Messenger [5] make use of such schemes. Furthermore, Apple relies on PAKE protocols for HomeKit device enrollment [6], iCloud Keychain escrow [7], and in the Car Key pairing process [8].

However, the PAKE schemes that are used in practical applications rely on the discrete logarithm problem, its elliptic-curve variant, or similar problems. As these problems cannot be considered secure in the presence of cryptographically relevant quantum computers, new protocols are required in this regard. Potential solutions are generic ways to transfer primitives, such as Key Encapsulation Mechanisms (KEMs) into secure PAKE protocols [9]. The resulting OCAKE scheme was recently implemented by Alnahawi et al. on SmartMX3 P71D600 smart card [10]. Lyu et al. published a method to transfer such schemes in asymmetric or augmented PAKE schemes to transfer a balanced PAKE scheme, where both parties know the password, in a client-server setting [11]. The authors also applied their method to lattice-based schemes, yielding lattice-based post-quantum-secure protocols.

In general, the design and analysis of PAKE schemes is an ongoing effort. The work of Alnahawi et al. lists 30 balanced schemes and 19 augmented schemes that have been published since 2015 [12]. They come with different security proofs and various levels of analysis by other researchers. Several also provide benchmark figures for their specific implementations.

In this paper, PAKES with known real-world applications are implemented for Android devices and their performance is measured and compared. In particular, we selected Dragonfly as a balanced PAKE scheme for its use in Wi-Fi Protected Access 3 (WPA3), Password-Authenticated Connection Establishment (PACE) as implemented in travel documents, and CPACE as it is used by Facebook Messenger. We implemented the One-Way Key Encapsulation Method to PAKE (OCAKE) scheme, using Module-Lattice Key Encapsulation Mechanism (ML-KEM) and, for comparison, One-Way Key Encapsulation Method (OEKE) to also include post-quantum-secure schemes.

For augmented schemes, the Secure Remote Password (SRP) protocol was chosen due to the possibility of integration with Transport Layer Security (TLS) [13] and its use with 1Password. In addition, SPAKE2+, together with its balanced version SPAKE2, was selected as it is used by Apple Homekit, Apple Car Key, and the Matter protocol. We also applied the transformation of Lyu et al. to OCAKE, to evaluate a post-quantum-secure augmented PAKE scheme.

The remainder of the paper is organized as follows. Section II gives a brief overview of the implemented PAKE schemes and their properties. The details of the test setup are given in Section III, before the results, together with implementation-specific choices, are presented in Section IV. Conclusions are drawn in Section V.

II. PAKE Schemes

Details on how a PAKE achieves its objective of agreeing on a strong cryptographic key based on a shared password

Client		Server
$x \in_R [1, q-1]$		$y \in_R [1, q-1]$
$X = xP$	$\xrightarrow{X}$	$Y = yP$
		$Y' = Enc_{pwd}(Y)$
	$\xleftarrow{Y'}$	
$Y = Dec_{pwd}(Y')$		
$K = xY$		$K = yX$

Derive Key Material

$\xrightarrow{\hspace{2em}}$

Send Authentication Message

Figure 1. Simplified version of OEKE [17], using a shared password *pwd* and a generator P of order q of an additive group

Client		Server
$p_c \in_R [1, q-1]$		$p_s \in_R [1, q-1]$
$m_c \in_R [1, q-1]$		$m_s \in_R [1, q-1]$
$s_c = (p_c + m_c)\%q$		$s_s = (p_s + m_s)\%q$
$E_c = (m_c P_{pwd})^{-1}$	$\xrightarrow{s_c, E_c}$	$E_s = (m_s P_{pwd})^{-1}$
	$\xleftarrow{s_s, E_s}$	
$K = p_c(E_s + s_s P_{pwd})$		$K = p_s(E_c + s_c P_{pwd})$

Derive Key Material

$\longleftrightarrow$

Send Authentication Messages

Figure 2. Simplified version of Dragonfly [18], using a shared password element P_{pwd} in an additive group of order q

differ from scheme to scheme. In general, it is possible to distinguish between balanced schemes, where both parties know the password, and augmented schemes, where one party, often called prover, knows the password and the other party, often called verifier, possesses a verification value but not the password itself. This prevents the verifier from impersonating the prover towards another third party. A discussion of the properties of PAKE schemes and related security considerations can be found in [14].

The following notations will be used in the remainder of the paper. Let $Enc_{key}(\cdot)$ and $Dec_{key}(\cdot)$ denote encryption and decryption of a message with a symmetric cipher using a shared key. A hash function is denoted as $H(\cdot)$. The simplified protocols show only the agreement of a shared secret – in order to derive key material, further steps, like applying key derivations, are required. In addition, every protocol requires a verification phase to ensure that both parties followed the protocol and agreed on the same key material. This can be achieved by exchanging hash or message authentication code (MAC) values over protocol data.

In 1992, Bellovin and Merritt published the first PAKE called *Encrypted Key Exchange (EKE)* [15]. It is a balanced scheme. Following different security analysis, including [16], the variant *One-Encryption Key Exchange (OEKE)* was proposed [17]. The underlying idea of those schemes is to derive a secret key from the password and use it to encrypt a public key that is used for key agreement. Hence, the receiver requires the password to decrypt the public key and continue with the protocol. Figure 1 gives a simplified version of the scheme. EKE and OEKE are the inspiration for various post-quantum (PQ) PAKE schemes, including OCAKE [9]. Instead of encrypting a key for a (Elliptic Curve) Diffie-Hellman key agreement method with the password, it uses a KEM and encrypts the related public key with the password.

Another approach is followed by the protocol Dragonfly, defined in RFC 7664 [18]. It maps the password to a group element and uses a random mask to blind it. This blinded value is exchanged and can be used for the next steps towards key agreement. The mapping into the group element requires a specific process. RFC 7664 defines an algorithm called *Hunting and Pecking*, which searches for such an element. In order to ensure a time-constant behavior to prevent side-channel leakage, a constant number of attempts is made. In addition, critical checks are masked using random values. A Dragonfly sample run is shown in Figure 2.

Another PAKE that relies on mapping the password to a group element is the PACE protocol used in travel documents [19]. PACE relies on a random value that is encrypted using the shared password. After mapping the value to the group, a key agreement is performed. For mapping the point to the group, the standard mandates support of at least two mechanisms, a) the *Generic Mapping* based on an (Elliptic Curve (EC)) Diffie-Hellman key agreement, and b) the *Integrated Mapping*, which directly maps a value into the group. A third version, called *Chip Authentication Mapping* is optional.

A similar approach is followed by the Composable Password Authenticated Connection Establishment (CPACE) [20] scheme. Both parties share group parameters and a password. For the mapping, a function specified in RFC 9380 [21] should be used, which corresponds to the algorithm used for the Integrated Mapping. Its first step at both ends is to derive a group element from the password, instead of choosing a random value as input for the mapping as in the PACE protocol. The mapped element is then used for key agreement using a (EC) Diffie-Hellman protocol.

SPAKE2 follows a different approach [22]. It does not require such a mapping function but allows one to create two elements of the used group beforehand. They are defined for the set of parameters used and are independent of the password. The password is mapped to a scalar using a memory-hard hash function (e.g., scrypt or PBKDF2). This scalar is blinded using random values and the pre-defined elements on both ends. The results are exchanged, allowing to agree on a shared element. Its flow is shown in Figure 3.

In applications with a clear client-server relationship, an asymmetric or augmented PAKE can be beneficial. Those schemes provide the server or verifier with the possibility to ensure that the client or prover knows the password, without being able to impersonate the client. This requires a registration

Client		Server
$x \in_R [1, q-1]$		$y \in_R [1, q-1]$
$X = xP$		$Y = yP$
$p_A = wM + X$	$\xrightarrow{p_A}$	$p_B = wN + Y$
	$\xleftarrow{p_B}$	
$K = x(p_B - wN)$		$K = y(p_A - wM)$

Derive Key Material
$\longleftrightarrow$
Send Authentication Messages

Figure 3. Simplified version of SPAKE2 [22], using a password element w, a generator P of order q of an additive group G and fixed elements M, N

step where a record that is stored by the verifier is generated.

An example of such an augmented PAKE is SRP. The registration phase of the SRP scheme consists of hashing the password together with a salt value and generating a password verifier in a prime field, using the hashed value as exponent of a group generator. The verifier knows only the verification value; the prover can generate it using the password and the salt. This allows the parties to perform a key agreement based on the password. The flow of the process is shown in Figure 4. Note that SRP relies on multiplying group elements and exponentiating elements in a finite field, which does not map straightforwardly onto elliptic curve groups. Hence, the protocol does not have a simple elliptic curve analogue.

Registration

$s \in_R [1, 2^{64}]$

$x = H(s|H(U|\text{“:”}|p))$

$v = g^x$

Store(s, v)

Authentication

Client		Server
$a \in_R [1, q-1]$		$b \in_R [1, q-1]$
$A = g^a$	$\xrightarrow{A}$	$B = v + g^b$
	$\xleftarrow{s, B}$	
$u = H(A, B)$		$u = H(A, B)$ $x = H(s\|pwd))$
$e = (a + u * x)$		
$K = (B - g^x)^e$		$K = (A * v^u)^b$

Derive Key Material
$\longleftrightarrow$
Send Authentication Messages

Figure 4. Simplified version of SRP [23], using a finite field G with a generator g of order q

SPAKE2+[24] is an augmented version of SPAKE2. The authentication flow is similar to SPAKE2. The augmented part is achieved via a registration step, producing a registration record. This record is used in the protocol by the verifier that does not know the password itself.

In order to transform a balanced post-quantum PAKE into an augmented post-quantum PAKE, the transformation of Lyu et al. can be applied [11]. In addition to the balanced PAKE scheme, it uses a KEM and authenticated encryption. During the registration phase, the password is hashed and used to generate a key pair for the KEM scheme, while only the hash and public key are stored. During the authentication phase, the hashed password is used as input to the balanced PAKE to agree on a key. This is followed by an authentication process where the client derives the KEM key pair from the password by following the steps of the registration procedure. Hence, the client now has the private key to the public key contained in the registration record. This enables finalization of the protocol by ensuring that the client knows the password. Using a quantum-secure balanced PAKE and a post-quantum KEM, the protocol provides quantum security.

III. TESTING SETUP

All benchmarks were performed on a Google Pixel 7 Pro smartphone, that is, the physical device, not the emulator. This device features a Google Tensor G2 SoC, 12GB RAM, and runs the Android 16 operating system. Its hardware and up-to-date system software ensure that performance measurements are representative of modern Android platforms. The Pixel 7 Pro device was connected to a Windows test PC via USB with developer options enabled, airplane mode turned on, and all connectivity (Wi-Fi, Bluetooth, mobile data) disabled to reduce interference. The battery saver mode and adaptive battery features were kept off. Using the developer options, the limit for background processes was set to zero. The implementations are written in Kotlin/JAVA and use, in addition to native libraries, a Bouncy Castle provider in version 1.81. Their build target was Android API 34 and ProGuard/R8 minification was enabled.

For performance measurements, microbenchmarking using the Android Jetpack Benchmark Library (version 1.3.4) was used [25]. The library orchestrates test runs, performs warm-up iterations, and leverages the platform's trace-based timing mechanism to reliably capture execution durations. The benchmark process pins the test process to a foreground priority and requests sustained performance mode to reduce CPU/GPU thermal throttling. During this process, 50 measurement runs are conducted. The whole measurement was repeated 100 times, leading to 5000 data points per test. However, it turned out that the measurements contained some outliers, as it was not possible to prevent all side effects during the measurement process. In order to cope with those, measurements that took more than 10 times the mean of the current set are removed. After this procedure, every set contains between 4,974 and 5,000 data points, on average 4,993 data points. The following results are the mean values and the 95% confidence interval of these measurements.

Energy consumption is measured using test functions that cover the whole scheme, that is, client and server operations. For every microbenchmark of a test function, which involves

50 runs of that function, a Perfetto trace [26] is created and analyzed. In particular, the power rail data for the large central processing unit (CPU) core is used. The data points associated with a function run are extracted, yielding an accumulated energy consumption value. Hence, the delta between the first and last measurement run a datapoint is available, gives the number of measurements that are conducted using the energy given by the value difference of those data points. Note that not every power trace contains two values that can be associated with measurement runs. In such cases, the whole run, i.e., this microbenchmark of all PAKE schemes, is discarded. Otherwise, this procedure gives an energy consumption datapoint for every test function, each covering a complete PAKE scheme. In order to prevent thermal effects on the power consumption, the order of the tests within a microbenchmark is randomized. Overall, 250 measurements were conducted, 38 of them were discarded due to missing data points, resulting in 222 energy consumption results per function to be evaluated.

IV. Implementation and Results

In order to allow a fair comparison of the different implementations, all underlying primitives were chosen with parameters for a 128 bit security level. In particular, Advanced Encryption Standard (AES) with 128 bit keys for encryption, Secure Hash Algorithm (SHA) 256 as hash function, a discrete logarithm group with 3072 bits [27], secp256r1 [28] as 256 bit elliptic curve and ML-KEM512 [29]. For modular operations, the native BigInteger library is used. For cryptographic algorithms, native implementations like javax.crypto.Cipher for AES and java.security.MessageDigest for SHA are employed. For all others, including HMAC, HKDR, PBKDF2, scrypt, ML-KEM, and ECC operations, implementations provided by Bouncy Castle are used. In this context, Bouncy Castle uses a Window Non-Adjacent Form (WNAF) multiplier for EC scalar multipication. For the implementations, the client and server components were tested on the same device. All elements that require transfer between the parties were encoded as byte array; compression was used for elliptic curve points.

As described in Section II, several schemes, especially those based on Elliptic Curve Cryptography (ECC), require a mapping from a random string to a point in the group used. Hence, different mapping functions were implemented. In particular, *Hunting and Pecking* as specified in RFC 7664 [18], *Generic Mapping*, and *Integrated Mapping* as specified in [19]. A performance comparison can be found in Table I. Note that the Generic Mapping requires a message exchange between two parties to agree on a common result of the mapping. The figures in the table only reflect the computational effort and not the potential network latency for exchanging those messages. The Hunting and Pecking was configured with a minimum of 40 iterations as suggested in the respective RFC. If the iteration ends as soon as a suitable element is found, the result is obtained on an average of $645 \pm 0.9\mu s$; however, this approach does not ensure constant-time execution. As the integrated mapping computes the result directly–without iterative steps like Hunting and Pecking or key generation and exchange as in Generic Mapping–it is, as expected, the most efficient among the evaluated methods.

TABLE I
Performance of different mapping functions from a random value to secp256r1.

Mapping	Time in μs
Hunting and Pecking	4352 ± 4.1
Generic Mapping	700 ± 0.5
Integrated Mapping	62 ± 0.0

Note that potential overhead for the generic mapping for exchanging messages is not reflected in this number.

In order to compare the performance of balanced PAKEs that provide quantum security and those relying on *traditional* asymmetric primitives, OEKE was implemented and tested using a discrete logarithm group and an elliptic curve. OCAKE was tested using ML-KEM. The implementation of OEKE follows the definition in [17]. Instances using a discrete logarithm group with 3072 bits as defined in RFC 3526[27], and using secp256r1 [28] are evaluated. Both use AES with Cipher Block Chaining (CBC) for the encryption of the public key with the password and SHA256 for computing the authentication tags. The realization of OCAKE is based on the design of Beguinet et al. [9]. A secret key is derived from the shared password using Password-Based Key Derivation Function 2 (PBKDF2) with Hash-based Message Authentication Code (HMAC) SHA256. This key is used to encrypt and transfer a ML-KEM512 public key. Again, SHA256 is used to compute the authentication tags, ensuring that both parties derive the same key material. Using elliptic curves has a notable performance advantage compared to a discrete logarithm group, whereas the OCAKE implementation is even faster. As the client in the OCAKE protocol needs to generate a key pair, it requires more computational effort than the server. In detail, OEKE required $4948 \pm 1.1\mu s$/$4,955 \pm 1.5\mu s$ on the client/server compared to $535 \pm 0.7\mu s$/$507 \pm 0.6\mu s$ when using an elliptic curve. The OCAKE scheme completed in $242 \pm 0.2\mu s$/$151 \pm 0.2\mu s$. However, this speedup comes at the cost of larger messages, as OCAKE requires exchanging the encrypted KEM public key and the ciphertext of 16+816+768 bytes in addition to two 32-byte authentication tags. In contrast, OEKE(ECC)/OEKE exchanges one public key of 33/384 bytes, one encrypted public key of 16+48/16+400 bytes in addition to a 32-byte authentication tag.

Dragonfly was implemented according to RFC [18] using secp256r1. It uses the Hunting and Pecking mapping with at least 40 iterations. For derivation of the secret from the negotiated point, HMAC-based Key Derivation Function (HKDF) SHA256 is used. In order to blind specific checks of the protocol, specific elements need to be found. This can be done once during an initialization phase that took $20 \pm 0.0\mu s$. As client and server perform the same operations, they require the same time. If blinding is omitted and a non-constant-time mapping is used, the agreement process could be reduced from $5,062 \pm 6.8\mu s$ to $1,327 \pm 1.5\mu s$. In terms of message size, Dragonfly exchanges a message containing a scalar and an

TABLE II
OVERVIEW OF USED PARAMETERS FOR IMPLEMENTED SCHEMES

Scheme	Group	Cipher	Hash	Mapping	Others
Balanced Schemes					
OEKE	3072-bit MODP Group	AES-CBC	SHA256	-	-
OEKE (ECC)	secp256r1	AES-CBC	SHA256	-	-
OCAKE	ML-KEM512	AES-CBC	SHA256	-	PBKDF2-HMAC-SHA256
Dragonfly	secp256r1	-	SHA256	Hunting and Pecking	HKDF-SHA256
SPAKE2	secp256r1	-	SHA256	-	HKDF-SHA256
PACE (IM)	secp256r1	AES-CBC	SHA256	Integrated Mapping	PBKDF2-HMAC-SHA256
PACE (GM)	secp256r1	AES-CBC	SHA256	Generic Mapping	PBKDF2-HMAC-SHA256
CPACE	secp256r1	-	SHA256	Integrated Mapping	-
Augmented Schemes					
SRP	3072-bit MODP Group	-	SHA1/SHA256	-	
SPAKE2+	secp256r1	-	SHA256	-	HKDF-SHA256/scrypt
aPAKE-PQC	ML-KEM512	AES-GCM	SHA256	-	-

ECC point from server to client and the other way round, i.e., $2 \times (33 + 33)$ bytes in addition to two authentication tags of 32 bytes each.

The implementation of SPAKE2 follows RFC 9382 [22]. It uses secp256r1 together with the points M,N as defined in the RFC. As hash SHA256 is used. The required computation time is $1,241 \pm 1,6\mu s/1,271 \pm 1.7\mu s$ for client/server, that is, around one-fourth of the time required for Dragonfly. SPAKE2 mutually exchanges 33-byte ECC points and 16-byte authentication tags.

PACE [19] was implemented with the Generic Mapping as well as the Integrated Mapping. It uses AES-CBC and PBKDF2-HMAC-SHA256 to derive an AES key from the password. For the confirmation tag of the agreed key material, SHA256 was used. The performance difference from the different mappings, see Table I, translates to the difference in the execution time of PACE. The runtime of the protocol using the Generic Mapping was $1,463 \pm 1.9\mu s/1,504 \pm 2.0\mu s$ on the client/server, compared to $797 \pm 1.0\mu s/856 \pm 1.1\mu s$ using the Integrated Mapping. In addition, the Generic Mapping requires exchanging the related public keys, which is not required for the Integrated Mapping. Both versions send an encrypted random of size 16+48 bytes from the client to the server and mutually exchange an EC Diffie-Hellmann (ECDH) key of 33 bytes. If the Generic Mapping is used, another ECDH key is mutually exchanged. Note that our implementation exchanges a serialized SubjectPublicKeyInfo object instead of the raw points, which increases the message size from 33 to 335 bytes. For the implementation of CPACE [20], the integrated mapping was used. This scheme performs the same operations on both parties and outputs a hashed transcript and a shared point. Hence, no dedicated verification step is performed in the implementation. Avoiding the exchange of an encrypted value, as is done in the PACE protocol, reduces the computation time to $715 \mp 0.7\mu s$ and the size of the exchanged messages to two times 33 bytes. For the implementation of CPACE [20], the integrated mapping was used. This scheme performs the same operations on both parties and outputs a hashed transcript and a shared point. Hence, no dedicated verification step is performed in the implementation. Avoiding the exchange of an encrypted value, as is done in the PACE protocol, reduces the computation time to $715 \mp 0.7\mu s$ and the size of the exchanged messages to two times 33 bytes.

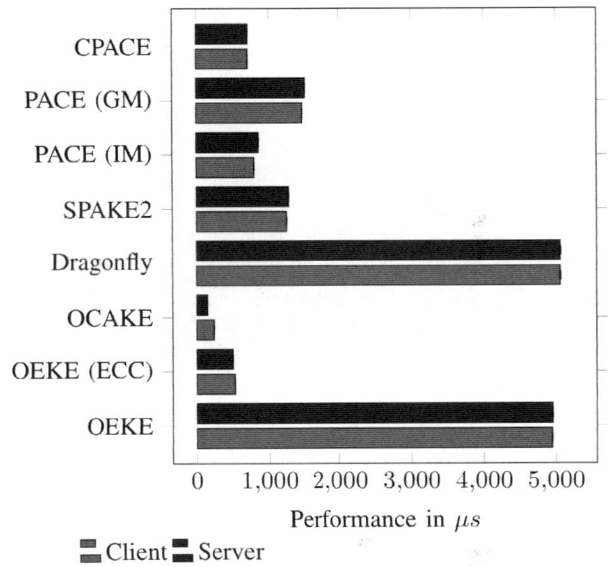

Figure 5. Performance Comparison of the balanced PAKE Schemes

A comparison of the performance of the different balanced schemes is shown in Figure 5. Due to their balanced nature, the computational effort for both parties is comparable. It should be noted that the OCAKE post-quantum scheme that uses KEM is very fast compared to the other schemes at the cost of larger exchanged messages.

In contrast to balanced schemes, where both parties use the password, augmented schemes require a registration phase to construct a verification value that is stored on the server side.

The implementation of the augmented PAKE scheme SRP uses the 3072-bit MODP Group defined in RFC 3526 [27], since a direct translation to elliptic curves is not possible. The measured implementation follows the specification of RFC 2945 [23]. The RFC specifies the use of SHA-1. In order to a) follow the specification and b) allow for a comparable result,

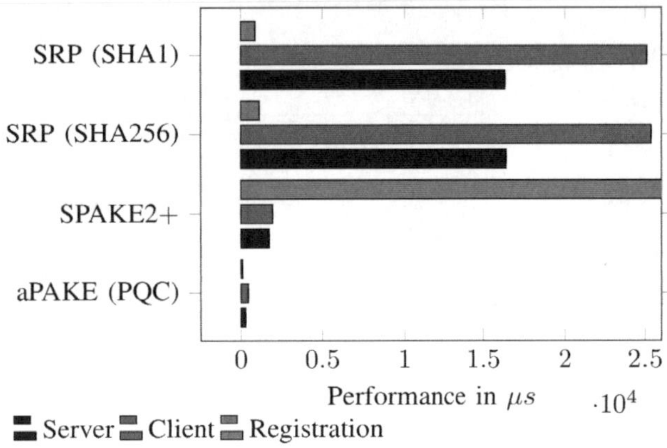

Figure 6. Performance comparison of the augmented PAKE schemes.

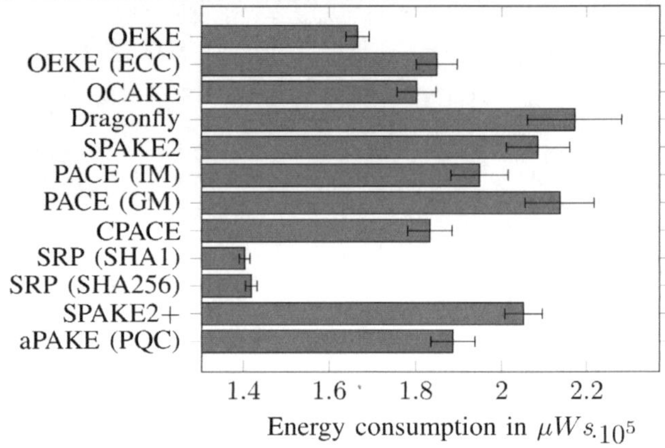

Figure 7. Energy consumption of the implemented schemes on the big CPU power rail with a 95% confidence interval

an instance using SHA1 and an instance using SHA256 were considered. The result shows that the registration process for the SHA256 variant takes about a third longer, $885 \pm 1.3 \mu s$ compared to $1,148 \pm 1.4 \mu s$, while during the authentication phase, there is only a slight difference, $25,117 \pm 9.3 \mu s$/$16,369 \pm 4.4 \mu s$ for SHA1 compared to $25,376 \pm 9.1 \mu s$/$16,438 \pm 3.8 \mu s$ for SHA256 on the client/server. In terms of message sizes, SRP requires the storage of a salt value, in our implementation 9 bytes and a group element of 385 bytes. The parties mutually exchange group 385-byte elements. In addition, the server shares the salt value with the client. In the verification step, every party creates a 20-byte challenge value that is confirmed by the other party with a 20-byte response. When switching from SHA-1 to SHA256, the size of the messages in the verification step increases from 20 to 32 byte.

The implementation of SPAKE2+ makes use of secp256r1, together with SHA256 and an HMAC key derivation function. The registration phase uses the memory-hard hash function scrypt with parameters $(32768, 8, 1)$ as recommended in the RFC. This protects against offline dictionary attacks, but also leads to a significant effort during registration ($115,966 \pm 87.2 \mu s$). Hence, Figure 6 does not show the full bar of the registration phase. The scrypt parameters have a direct impact on the performance of this first phase. Since the implementation relies on elliptic curves, it is, with $1,953 \pm 6.1 \mu s$/$1,740 \pm 6.5 \mu s$ on the client/server, faster than SRP. Note that the client measurement does not include the application of the scrypt function, which could be done during a preparation phase/the registration. Its execution would add an effort comparable to the server registration phase. The value that is stored on the server side for verification consists of a 33-byte compressed ECC point and a 32-byte value that is computed modulo the order of the base point. For the key agreement, ECC points are mutually exchanged, 33 bytes each, while verification uses 32-byte HMAC values on the client and on the server side.

The transformation published by Lyu et al. [11] was applied to the implemented OCAKE to compare augmented PAKE schemes with a quantum-secure scheme. In addition to ML-KEM512, AES-Galois/Counter Mode (GCM) was used for the additional implementations, while the OCAKE protocol still employs AES-CBC. The implemented scheme outperforms the others, requiring $103 \pm 0.1 \mu s$ for registration, $461 \pm 0.6 \mu s$ on the client, and $292 \pm 0.5 \mu s$ on the server. As it employs the balanced PQC PAKE scheme OCAKE, the message sizes are larger compared to the other schemes. The stored record requires a 32-byte hash value and an 800-byte public key. The exchanged messages include those required for OCAKE (16+816+768) plus an encrypted key encapsulation of 16+784 bytes. The verification message uses a 32-byte hash value. It is called *aPAKE (PQC)* in Figure 6, where the performance figures of the different augmented schemes are shown.

The energy consumption of the big CPU powerrail is given in Figure 7. It shows that, when considering a whole run of a scheme, OCAKE and its transformation into an augmented version require the same order of magnitude of energy as the other schemes. An outlier in this regard is SRP, which does not use ECC and hence does not require the Bouncy Castle library, but only native JAVA implementations. The powerrails of the other CPUs, i.e., mid and little, show significantly smaller consumption, but the distribution is comparable, e.g., on the mid CPU, Dragonfly consumes with $12,669 \pm 1107$ μWs the most energy amoung the schemes.

V. Conclusion and Future Work

This study provides an implementation-based comparison of classical and post-quantum PAKE schemes on a modern Android device, highlighting how protocol structure, mapping functions, and cryptographic primitives influence performance. Elliptic curve–based schemes consistently outperform those based on modular arithmetic, while integrated mapping techniques significantly reduce overhead compared to iterative or interactive mappings.

Among the evaluated protocols, post-quantum candidates, such as OCAKE and aPAKE demonstrate strong computational efficiency, achieving sub-millisecond runtimes even without hardware acceleration. Although these schemes incur higher communication overhead, they show that quantum-secure PAKEs are practical for mobile environments. In the augmented setting, the results also emphasize the trade-offs introduced by memory-hard hash functions and the potential for optimization through parameter tuning.

Our current dataset is limited to a single flagship device using the Bouncy Castle library. Generalizing absolute runtimes across the Android ecosystem requires care, because SoCs differ substantially. For example, in CPU microarchitecture, the available instruction set extensions and memory hierarchy. Future work will explore the impact of different SoCs, hardware-accelerated cryptographic instructions, energy profiling under typical usage scenarios, and integration into complete authentication stacks. In addition, a comprehensive security and side-channel resilience evaluation will complement the performance perspective established here.

REFERENCES

[1] "IEEE Standard for Information Technology–Telecommunications and Information Exchange between Systems Local and Metropolitan Area Networks–Specific Requirements Part 11: Wireless LAN Medium Access Control (MAC) and Physical Layer (PHY) Specifications", *IEEE Std 802.11-2024 (Revision of IEEE Std 802.11-2020)*, pp. 1–5956, 2025. DOI: 10.1109/IEEESTD.2025.10979691.

[2] Connectivity Standards Alliance, *Matter Specification - Version 1.4*, Nov. 2004.

[3] R. Fillion, *Secure Remote Password (SRP): How 1Password uses it*, https://blog.1password.com/developers-how-we-use-srp-and-you-can-too/, retrieved: September, 2025.

[4] G. T. Davies *et al.*, "Security analysis of the whatsapp end-to-end encrypted backup protocol", in *Advances in Cryptology – CRYPTO 2023*, H. Handschuh and A. Lysyanskaya, Eds., Cham: Springer Nature Switzerland, 2023, pp. 330–361, ISBN: 978-3-031-38551-3.

[5] Meta, *The labyrinth encrypted message storage protocol*, https://engineering.fb.com/wp-content/uploads/2023/12/TheLabyrinthEncryptedMessageStorageProtocol_12-6-2023.pdf, retrieved: September, 2025.

[6] Apple, *Apple Platform Security - HomeKit communication security*, https://support.apple.com/en-gb/guide/security/sec3a881ccb1/web, retrieved: September, 2025.

[7] Apple, *Apple Platform Security - Escrow security for iCloud Keychain*, https://support.apple.com/en-gb/guide/security/sec3e341e75d/web, retrieved: September, 2025.

[8] Apple, *Apple Platform Security - Car key security in iOS*, https://support.apple.com/en-gb/guide/security/secf64471c16/web, retrieved: September, 2025.

[9] H. Beguinet, C. Chevalier, D. Pointcheval, T. Ricosset, and M. Rossi, "Get a cake: Generic transformations from key encaspulation mechanisms to password authenticated key exchanges", in *Applied Cryptography and Network Security*, M. Tibouchi and X. Wang, Eds., Cham: Springer Nature Switzerland, 2023, pp. 516–538, ISBN: 978-3-031-33491-7.

[10] N. Alnahawi *et al.*, *Post-quantum cryptography in eMRTDs: Evaluating PAKE and PKI for travel documents*, Cryptology ePrint Archive, Paper 2025/812, 2025.

[11] Y. Lyu, S. Liu, and S. Han, "Efficient Asymmetric PAKE Compiler from KEM and AE", in *Advances in Cryptology – ASIACRYPT 2024: 30th International Conference on the Theory and Application of Cryptology and Information Security, Kolkata, India, December 9–13, 2024, Proceedings. Part V*, Kolkata, India: Springer-Verlag, 2024, pp. 34–65. DOI: 10.1007/978-981-96-0935-2_2.

[12] N. Alnahawi, D. Haas, E. Mauß, and A. Wiesmaier, *SoK: PQC PAKEs - cryptographic primitives, design and security*, Cryptology ePrint Archive, Paper 2025/119, 2025.

[13] D. Taylor, T. Perrin, T. Wu, and N. Mavrogiannopoulos, *Using the Secure Remote Password (SRP) Protocol for TLS Authentication*, RFC 5054, Nov. 2007. DOI: 10.17487/RFC5054.

[14] J.-M. Schmidt, *Requirements for Password-Authenticated Key Agreement (PAKE) Schemes*, RFC 8125, Apr. 2017. DOI: 10.17487/RFC8125.

[15] S. Bellovin and M. Merritt, "Encrypted key exchange: Password-based protocols secure against dictionary attacks", in *Proceedings 1992 IEEE Computer Society Symposium on Research in Security and Privacy*, 1992, pp. 72–84. DOI: 10.1109/RISP.1992.213269.

[16] M. Bellare, D. Pointcheval, and P. Rogaway, "Authenticated key exchange secure against dictionary attacks", in *Advances in Cryptology — EUROCRYPT 2000*, B. Preneel, Ed., Berlin, Heidelberg: Springer Berlin Heidelberg, 2000, pp. 139–155, ISBN: 978-3-540-45539-4.

[17] E. Bresson, O. Chevassut, and D. Pointcheval, "Security proofs for an efficient password-based key exchange", in *Proceedings of the 10th ACM Conference on Computer and Communications Security*, ser. CCS '03, Washington D.C., USA: Association for Computing Machinery, 2003, pp. 241–250, ISBN: 1581137389. DOI: 10.1145/948109.948142.

[18] D. Harkins, *Dragonfly Key Exchange*, RFC 7664, Nov. 2015. DOI: 10.17487/RFC7664.

[19] ICAO - International Civil Aviation Organization, *Doc 9303 - machine readable travel documents- part 11: Security mechanisms for mrtds, eighth edition*, https://www.icao.int/publications/Documents/9303_p11_cons_en.pdf, 2021.

[20] M. Abdalla, B. Haase, and J. Hesse, "CPace, a balanced composable PAKE", Internet Engineering Task Force, Internet-Draft draft-irtf-cfrg-cpace-14, Apr. 2025, Work in Progress, 96 pp.

[21] A. Faz-Hernandez, S. Scott, N. Sullivan, R. S. Wahby, and C. A. Wood, *Hashing to Elliptic Curves*, RFC 9380, Aug. 2023. DOI: 10.17487/RFC9380.

[22] W. Ladd, *SPAKE2, a Password-Authenticated Key Exchange*, RFC 9382, Sep. 2023. DOI: 10.17487/RFC9382.

[23] T. Wu, *The SRP Authentication and Key Exchange System*, RFC 2945, Sep. 2000. DOI: 10.17487/RFC2945.

[24] T. Taubert and C. A. Wood, *SPAKE2+, an Augmented Password-Authenticated Key Exchange (PAKE) Protocol*, RFC 9383, Sep. 2023. DOI: 10.17487/RFC9383.

[25] Android Developers, *Microbenchmark*, https://developer.android.com/topic/performance/benchmarking/microbenchmark-overview, retrieved: September, 2025.

[26] Perfetto, *System profiling, app tracing and trace analysis*, https://perfetto.dev/, retrieved: September, 2025.

[27] M. Kojo and T. Kivinen, *More Modular Exponential (MODP) Diffie-Hellman groups for Internet Key Exchange (IKE)*, RFC 3526, May 2003. DOI: 10.17487/RFC3526.

[28] T. Polk, R. Housley, S. Turner, D. R. L. Brown, and K. Yiu, *Elliptic Curve Cryptography Subject Public Key Information*, RFC 5480, Mar. 2009. DOI: 10.17487/RFC5480.

[29] NIST, "Module-lattice-based key-encapsulation mechanism standard", U.S. Department of Commerce, Washington, D.C., Tech. Rep. Federal Information Processing Standards Publication (FIPS) 203, 2024. DOI: 10.6028/NIST.FIPS.203.

Towards Automated Penetration Testing Using Inverse Soft-Q Learning

Dongfang Song Yuhong Li Ala Berzinji Elias Seid
Department of Computer and Systems Sciences, Stockholm University
Stockholm, Sweden
Email: {yh2025, alabe, elias.seid}@dsv.su.se

***Abstract*—Penetration testing (pentesting), a proactive defensive practice for identifying vulnerabilities and supporting cybersecurity management, has traditionally been conducted manually due to its heavy reliance on specialized knowledge of human experts. In this paper, we propose PT-ISQL, an automated PenTesting approach based on Inverse Soft-Q Learning (ISQL), an imitation learning algorithm that enables efficient policy learning from expert demonstrations. PT-ISQL trains an agent to take optimal actions when interacting with the pentesting environment by effectively mimicking expert behavior. Our evaluation shows that PT-ISQL achieves high performance using significantly fewer expert demonstrations compared with generative adversarial imitation learning approaches. Furthermore, it demonstrates faster convergence, improved stability, and reduced training overhead. These results suggest that PT-ISQL is a promising and practical solution for scalable, automated penetration testing.**

Keywords*—*penetration testing; deep reinforcement learning; imitation learning; inverse soft-Q learning; PT-ISQL.

I. INTRODUCTION

Penetration testing, commonly referred to as pentesting, is a proactive cybersecurity measure that involves simulating real-world attacks on computer systems, networks, or applications to identify vulnerabilities before they can be exploited by malicious actors. By mimicking the tactics, techniques, and procedures of actual attackers, pentesters can uncover weaknesses in systems and applications, providing insights to mitigate them and helping organizations prioritize their security strategies before real attacks occur.

Pentesting is one of the most essential cybersecurity controls. It is not a one-time activity but a continuous process that organizations must conduct regularly. The frequency of testing is typically determined by risk assessments and the organizations' operational structure. Traditionally, pentesting is a highly manual process, requiring skilled and experienced professionals to plan, execute, and adapt attacks based on system reconnaissance and responses. The manual nature of this process, combined with the increasing complexity and scale of modern IT infrastructures, makes frequent and comprehensive testing both costly and time-consuming.

As a result, researchers have begun investigating methods to automate pentesting, with the goal of increasing testing speed, reducing dependence on skilled professionals, and making the process easy to conduct. Recent work can be broadly categorized into two main approaches.

One involves the use of Large Language Models (LLMs), such as GPT-based systems [1] and deep learning agent-based systems [2][3], to use the extensive domain knowledge inherent in LLMs to automate pentesting. Although LLM-based pentesting approaches have proven highly effective in reducing manual intervention and enhancing automation, they still face notable challenges and inefficiencies inherent to LLMs, such as limited pentesting knowledge, context loss [1], unstructured data generation and efficiency [4].

The other category uses Reinforcement Learning (RL) to discover novel attack paths and adapt to dynamic environments. Among these approaches, one class, such as [5]-[7], relies on attack graphs. However, applying attack graphs to real-world, dynamic pentesting scenarios is challenging, as they require comprehensive and often unavailable system knowledge. In contrast, the other class, such as [8], uses exploitable machines to train a deep reinforcement learning model to automate the pentesting process. Nevertheless, deep RL methods often face challenges related to large state spaces and high-dimensional discrete action spaces, which complicate the training process in pentesting scenarios [9]. Moreover, the use of random exploration during the early stages of training can further introduce instability, potentially causing the model to fail to converge.

Recently, Imitation Learning (IL) has been used in automating pentesting [4] [10] [11]. IL[12], a special form of reinforcement learning, infers the reward function by modeling expert behaviour rather than relying on direct feedback from the environment. The agent learns a policy through expert demonstrations. The approaches presented in [4] [10] [11] have shown that IL can improve the performance of automated pentesting by incorporating expert knowledge. However, these approaches often face challenges in agent training, either too complex or requiring a vast amount of expert data, which is hard to gain in practice.

In this paper, we proposed PT-ISQL, an automated pentesting approach based on Inverse Soft-Q Learning (ISQL), which simplifies the process of IL by learning a soft Q-function that implicitly captures both the reward and the policy without using the complex adversarial training process. Our contributions are as follows:

- We propose an architecture for realizing automated pentesting based on ISQL;
- We implement a method for encoding pentesting tasks and actions, demonstrating that ISQL can be effectively used in automating pentesting;
- We conduct thorough experiments in a simulated network to evaluate the proposed PT-ISQL approach, and provide an in-depth analysis to the results.

The remainder of the paper is organized as follows. In Section II, we review the related work, focusing on comparing our approach with state-of-the-art approaches for pentesting based on reinforcement and imitation learning. In Section III, we present the proposed PT-ISQL approach, including the system architecture and detailed methodological steps. In Section IV, we elaborate the experiments and provide an analysis of the results. We conclude the paper and describe the future work in Section V.

II. Related Work

As mentioned above, LLMs have recently been used to automate pentesting. For example, PentestGPT [1] uses three modules, Reasoning, Generation, and Parsing to represent the specific roles typically found within penetration testing. It introduces a Pentesting Task Tree (PTT) derived from the cybersecurity attack tree to encode the ongoing status of tests and guide the subsequent actions. To overcome limitations such as limited pentesting knowledge and insufficient automation, PentestAgent [2] was proposed, which uses multi-agent collaboration to cover all phases of the pentesting lifecycle, thereby greatly reducing the need for human intervention. Although these studies have shown strong potential for automating penetration testing tasks, they also suffer from critical limitations inherent to LLMs. These include the need for vast amounts of high-quality training data, shallow task understanding, limited context windows, and lack of persistent memory. Such constraints pose huge risks in security-critical domains like pentesting. Particularly, the inability to perform long-term planning and retain stateful knowledge may hinder performance in complex tasks such as multi-step exploit chaining and privilege escalation.

We chose to use IL with limited amount of expert knowledge to automate pentesting, aiming to build compact, robust and reliable pentesting systems. In the following sections, we focus on state-of-the-art approaches using RL and IL to automate the pentesting process.

A. Pentesting based on Reinforcement Learning (RL)

In RL, an agent learns to make decisions by interacting with an environment, making it well-suited for pentesting which requires evaluating the current situation and then taking appropriate actions. As a result, many studies have applied RL to automate pentesting, such as [5]-[8]. In these approaches, the system under test is modeled as the Environment, and the pentester is the Agent. The interaction of the tester and the system is considered as the Action and results in the state change. Various techniques, including deep RL, have been used to address the complexity of RL problems for pentesting.

For example, [5] presented a method for identifying optimal attack path using a Deep Q-Network (DQN), based on a network topology generated from Shodan data and an attack tree constructed using MulVAL [13]. The traditional attack tree representation was improved by transforming it into a transition matrix, which was then used for DQN training. However, in real-world scenarios, the topology of the target network is often unknown or only partially accessible, limiting the applicability of such approaches.

Deep Exploit [14] is a pentesting tool that uses an advanced deep RL algorithm, Asynchronous Advantage Actor Critic (A3C), to exploit vulnerable servers automatically. In [8], a pentesting framework was developed based on Deep Exploit, and the influence of the number of neural networks on exploitation success rates was evaluated. However, real-world pentesting environments and complex network systems often involve a large, discrete action space, posing challenges for the training and convergence of deep RL models. For instance, algorithms like DQN select the action with the highest predicted value as the optimal choice. Unlike environments such as games, where actions are relatively deterministic and limited in scope, pentesting involves greater uncertainty and a more complex, discrete set of actions and outcomes. Furthermore, in large action spaces, multiple actions may have similar or identical values, leading to ambiguity and suboptimal decisions [15]. These limitations hinder the effective use of RL for pentesting, especially in realistic and dynamic environments.

B. Pentesting based on Imitation Learning (IL)

IL [12] is a specialized form of RL. Traditional RL relies on trial and error, with the agent receiving feedback from its environment in the form of rewards or penalties. In contrast, IL enables an agent to learn a policy directly from expert demonstrations by modeling expert behavior and inferring the underlying reward function being implicitly optimized. IL is particularly useful when it is easier for an expert to demonstrate the desired behavior than to define a reward function that would lead to the same behaviour, or when learning the policy from scratch is difficult. This makes IL especially well-suited for complex tasks such as pentesting.

A Generative Adversarial IL (GAIL) method was proposed in [16], where the reward function is learnt by measuring the similarity between an agent's and an expert's behavior. GAIL-PT [9], which combines GAIL and Deep Exploit, was developed to build an automatic pentesting framework. It addresses the challenge of high-dimensional action space by using the GAIL algorithm. GAIL-PT performs well in small-scale network environments (with or without honeypots), and large-scale networks, showing the potential of using IL for automated pentesting. However, the training process of GAIL requires careful tuning of hyperparameters and techniques, such as gradient penalization. Moreover, GAIL-PT is prone to overfitting with expert trajectory distributions and may not generalize well to different environments.

In the framework (i.e., DQfD-AIPT) [11], a method using expert knowledge is proposed. It combines transformed abstract expert knowledge with collected pentesting traces over various network scenarios. It provides a different method for solving the overfitting problem. However, despite using a less complex algorithm, this method requires a large amount of expert data to build the expert database.

Compared with these studies, our approach uses a more efficient way to train a pentesting agent, which requires far fewer expert demonstrations while converges more quickly.

III. Pentesting based on Inverse Soft-Q Learning

A. System Architecture

IL has developed into three main methods, Behaviour Cloning (BC), Direct Policy Learning (DPL) and Inverse Reinforcement Learning (IRL). BC is the simplest form of

IL, using supervised learning on expert data. It is widely used but can lead to cascade errors. DPL requires the presence and interaction with an expert. IRL, on the other hand, aims to infer the environment's reward function from expert demonstrations and then uses RL to discover the optimal policy—one that maximizes the inferred reward function.

ISQL is a recent method for implementing IRL, incorporating soft Q-Learning into the inverse learning process. ISQL has been shown to require less expert demonstration data to achieve comparable performance. Moreover, it considers stochastic or noisy expert actions. Thus, we chose ISQL to automate pentesting. Figure 1 illustrates the basic architecture of our automated pentesting framework based on ISQL: PT-ISQL. It consists of three main components. The Pentesting Environment represents the network environment where vulnerabilities are assessed by using the automated pentesting approach. It is the environment with which the RL agent and human experts interact during the pentesting. The environment returns the corresponding state information after each action taken by the agent or expert.

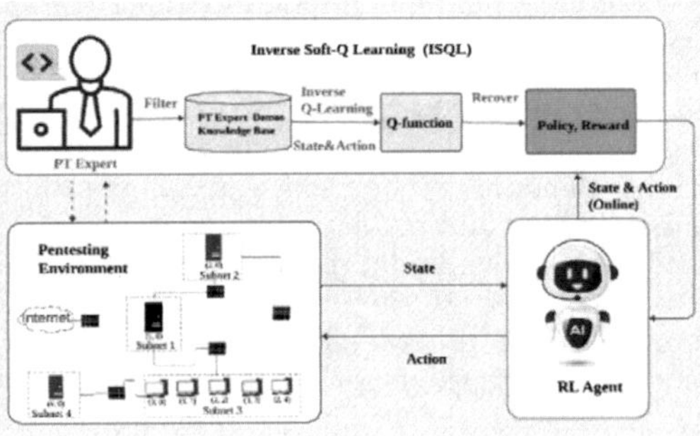

Figure 1. System architecture for PT-ISQL.

The ISQL component is the core of our system, implementing the ISQL algorithm tailored for pentesting. It interacts with the Pentesting Environment and generates the information used by the RL Agent. Expert demonstrations are first collected, consisting of recorded sequences of actions taken by human security experts or earlier runs of an RL agent during attempts to discover and exploit vulnerabilities in the Pentesting Environment. These demonstrations capture high-quality, goal-directed behaviours, such as exploiting services, vulnerability detection, and escalating privileges. Then, the resulting state-action pairs are used in the training process to get a soft Q-function, which enables the model to infer both the reward function and the policy that best explain the experts' behaviours. This process allows the RL agent to imitate expert strategies by learning from their demonstrations, even when the experts' behaviours are stochastic or suboptimal.

Using the learned policy, the RL Agent component interacts with the Pentesting Environment, navigating networks and selecting actions, such as scanning, exploiting, escalating privileges, or exfiltrating data, much like a fully autonomous AI red team agent. Since ISQL allows for stochastic behaviour (a soft policy), the agent can randomize attack sequences, adapt to defensive changes, such as patched systems or Intrusion Detection Systems (IDS), and make context-aware decisions that evolve over time. In addition, because the reward function captures underlying intent (e.g., reaching high-value targets, or staying undetected), the agent can generalize its knowledge to unseen network topologies or adapt to different vulnerabilities.

Through the interaction of these three components, fully automated pentesting can be achieved.

B. *Inverse Soft-Q Learning for Pentesting*

The PT-ISQL process consists of three main steps:

Step 1: process expert demonstrations. For each trajectory τ in the set of expert demonstrations D_{expert}, the state-action pairs (s, a) are extracted. These pairs are then used as inputs for the reward and Q networks.

Step 2: conduct iterative training via ISQL. Instead of learning a policy from a reward function, ISQL simplifies the process of the IRL by learning a Q-function that implicitly captures both the reward and the policy without using the complex adversarial training process. The goal of this step is to learn rewards and Q-values that align with expert behaviour. The target of the Q-function is computed based on the current reward $r(s,a)$, the expected value of the next state's Q-values and a soft entropy term $-\alpha \log \pi(a|s)$, where $\pi(a|s)$ is the policy derived from the Q-values using a softmax function, scaled by the entropy temperature α. This reflects the fact that experts not only try to perform well (i.e., high rewards) but also act stochastically and robustly, avoiding always picking the single "best" action. It balances the reward maximization and exploration through entropy. Namely

$$Q_{target}(s,a) = r(s,a) + \gamma \, \mathrm{E}_{a'} [Q(s',a')] - \alpha \log \pi(a'|s') \quad (1)$$

$$\pi(a|s) = \mathrm{softmax}\,(Q(s,a)/\,\alpha) \quad (2)$$

Figure 2 shows the pseudocode of this step.

Algorithm 1 Inverse soft Q-Learning (ISQL) for Pentesting

Require:

Input: Expert trajectories $\mathcal{D}_{\mathbf{expert}} = \{(s, a, s')\}$, states **s**, Actions **a**, discount factor γ, entropy temperature α, learning rate η, total iterations T

//Expert trajectories $\mathcal{D}_{\mathbf{expert}}$ are from pentesting environment;

//states **s**, such as configuration, vulnerability information of all hosts (open ports, access level...) ;

//Actions **a**, such as scans, exploits, or privilege escalations etc. similar to expert behavior.

Ensure:

Output: Learned Q-function $Q_\theta(s, a)$ from which policy $\pi(a|s) \propto \exp(Q_\theta(s, a)/\alpha)$ can be derived

Initialize Q-function $Q_\theta(s, a)$ with parameters θ

for $t = 1$ to T **do**

  Sample batch $\{(s, a, s')\} \sim \mathcal{D}_{\mathbf{expert}}$

  Compute soft values: $V(s') \leftarrow \alpha \cdot \log \sum_{a'} \exp(Q_\theta(s', a')/\alpha)$

  Compute reward: $\hat{r} \leftarrow (Q_\theta(s, a) - \gamma V(s'))$

  Compute loss:

$$\mathcal{L} \leftarrow -E[\hat{r}] + E[Q_\theta(s, a) - \gamma V(s')] + \frac{1}{4\alpha} E[\hat{r}^2]$$

  Update Q-function parameters: $\theta \leftarrow \theta - \eta \nabla_\theta \mathcal{L}$

end for

Figure 2. Pseudocode of the ISQL training for pentesting.

Step 3: agent execution. The trained agent can now use the learned policy to act in the environment autonomously, performing pentesting tasks, such as discovering attack paths, exploiting systems, and chaining exploits toward high-value targets, which enables realistic and adaptive red teaming.

IV. Evaluation and Analasys

A. *Experiement Setup*

We implemented the proposed approach in a virtual machine running Kali Linux. MiniConda (Version 24.1.2) was used to set up the Python virtual environment for building the three components of PT-ISQL. We used the NetworkAttack Simulator (NASim, Version 0.12.0) [17] to simulate the Pentesting Environment. In order to compare our work with [9], we have chosen the "small-honeypot" network.

The topology of our experimental network is shown in Figure 3. The network consists of four subnetworks with a total of eight hosts, one of which is a honeypot. The hosts run two types of operating systems (Linux and Windows) and three types of services (HyperText Transfer Protocol-HTTP, Secure SHell-SSH, and File Transfer Protocol-FTP). Hosts (2, 0) and (4, 0) are valuable assets (i.e., sensitive hosts) in the network, each assigned a reward value of 100. Node (3, 2) is a honeypot machine with a value of -100. The RL agent is expected to avoid exploiting honeypots. Firewalls filter specific types of services between subnets, and each action makes a cost for the agent.

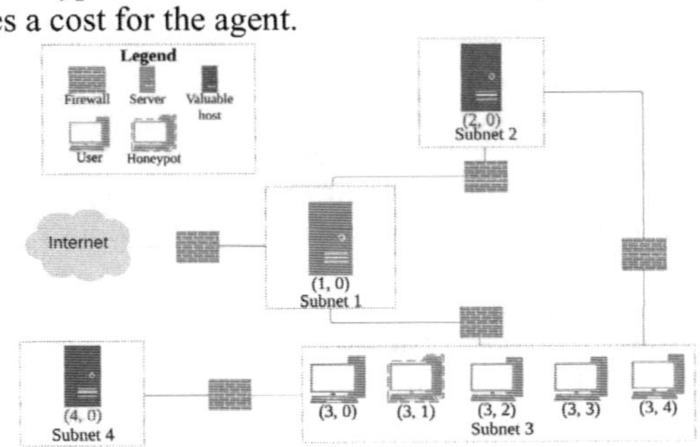

Figure 3. Topology of the experimental network.

The agent aims to maximize its score by reaching the sensitive hosts while minimizing cost. There are four types of scanning actions for getting information from each host: OSScan, Service Scan, ProcessScan, and SubnetScan. In addition, the agent can perform exploitation and privilege escalation actions for specific services and processes. The total number of actions is 72 and states is 24576. The available actions are listed in Table I, with each action associated with a different cost. Moreover, each action has a probability of success, indicating the difficulty of exploiting certain vulnerabilities. However, whether an action succeeds depends not only on this probability but also on factors such as firewall rules, the network topology, and the host's configuration.

TABLE I. Actions that can be taken by agents

Action name	OS	Cost	Probability	Access
SSH-EXP	Linux	3	0.9	User
FTP-EXP	Windows	1	0.6	User
http-EXT	/	2	0.9	User
Tomcat-PE	Linux	1	1	Root
Daclsvc-PE	Windows	1	1	Root
Subnet-Scan	/	1	1	/
OS-Scan	/	1	1	/
Service-Scan	/	1	1	/
Process-Scan	/	1	1	/

Table II lists the hyperparameters used for expert demonstration data generation using RL and agent training. A three-layer SimpleQ Network model was chosen for ISQL. A total of 1000 expert trajectories were extracted. To control the quality of the expert demonstrations, a reward threshold was used to filter the expert demonstrations data.

TABLE II. Hyperparameters for expert data generation and agemt training

Hyperparameter	Value
Learning rate	0.0001
Batch size	64
Discount factor,	0.9
Hidden layer size	128
Replay memory size	1000000
Initial memory size	10000
Target network update frequency	4
Initial temperature parameter	1
Max steps per episode	1000

B. *Evaluation Metrics*

We evaluated the performance of PT-ISQL from the perspectives of both imitation learning and automated pentesting. We first discuss the key factors that influence the performance of the ISQL algorithm in the context of pentesting in Sections C and D, then evaluate the proposed PT-ISQL approach according to the following three metrics.

Honeypot invasion probability. It is the likelihood that a pentesting agent is deceived into interacting with a honeypot. It serves as an indicator of the pentesting approach's stealth and precision. A high probability suggests that the pentesting approach cannot well distinguish real targets from decoys, while a low probability indicates more accurate reconnaissance and smarter exploitation strategies. Frequent hitting of honeypots implies a low ability to uncover real vulnerabilities. In our tests, a honeypot is considered invaded if the returned reward is less than -100. In such cases, the invasion probability is set to 1.0 (100%); otherwise, it is 0. The average honeypot invasion probability is computed over 10 episodes (i.e., pentesting rounds) for each evaluation.

Average reward. In ISQL, an agent that receives a high cumulative reward is likely following expert-level strategies, taking efficient and goal-directed actions while avoiding risky or low-value behaviors. Reward accumulation directly reflects several aspects of performance: success rate (i.e., whether the goal is reached), efficiency (i.e., fewer steps to reach the goal) and stealthiness (i.e., fewer alerts triggered or honeypots invaded). Therefore, we use the average cumulative reward of 10 episodes to measure the performance of the proposed PT-ISQL approach.

Goal-reached probability. The goal of our tests in the simulated network is to reach the valuable hosts (2, 0) and (4, 0). Whether the goal is reached or not is recorded after each episode. If the goal is reached, the probability is set to 1.0 (100%); otherwise, it is 0. The goal-reached probability is calculated as the average value over 10 episodes.

In our tests, the learning steps are set to 20000 as default, and the evaluation interval is set to 200 steps. But for the tests in Section E, the numbers are increased to 100000 and 1000, respectively, to accommodate the extended training requirements of deep reinforcement learning. We describe our experiments and analyze the results in Sections C to E below.

C. Influence of the Threshold of Expert Demonstrations

To study the influence of expert demonstration quality on the performance of PT-ISQL, we use a threshold to filter the expert demonstration data. We observed that when the threshold is reduced to 21, the agent's mean reward is considerably lower than that of the expert demonstrations. To illustrate the influence of this threshold, we compared the results using two values: 21 (low threshold) and 100 (high threshold). For each threshold, varying numbers of expert demonstrations were used to train the agent. The average reward and standard deviation are calculated after 2000 steps, when all rewards had converged.

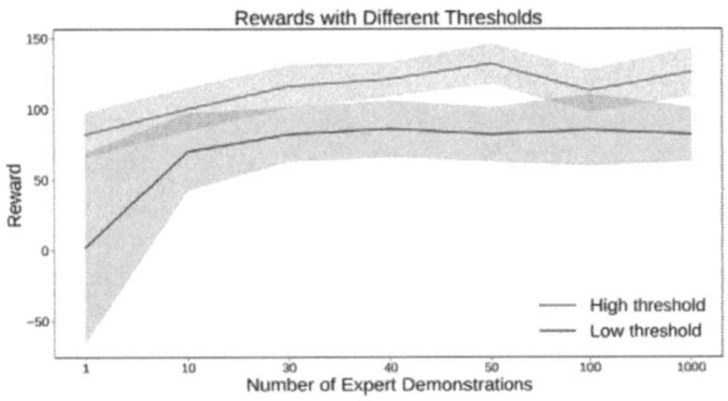

Figure 4. Rewards under different thresholds (solid lines-average values).

Figure 4 shows the rewards with different numbers of expert demonstrations under two threshold settings. When the reward threshold is low (21), the average reward and standard deviation of all the experiments are 98.80 and 41.14, respectively. When the threshold is high (100), the average reward and the standard deviation improved to 134.86 and 21.23, respectively. These results indicate that higher-quality expert data (i.e., higher threshold) leads to both higher average rewards and more stable performance, regardless of the number of demonstrations used. However, even in the high-threshold case, the agent's mean reward remains lower than that of the expert data.

D. Number of Reruired Expert Demonstrations

Due to the difficulty of obtaining expert data in practice, the minimum required number of expert demonstrations is an important factor affecting the usability of IL algorithms. To investigate this in the context of our PT-ISQL, we measured the reward when using different numbers of expert demonstrations: 1, 10, 30, 40, 50, 100, and 1000, under both low and high threshold settings. We observe the minimum number of expert demonstrations when the reward reaches a stable required value.

As shown in Figure 5, the rewards converge around 2000 steps in all settings. When the number of expert demonstrations is 1, the rewards are low and fluctuate heavily. Table III presents the average reward with standard deviation for different numbers of expert demonstrations after convergence (2000 steps). The results show that when the number of expert demonstrations exceeds 30, the performance becomes stable and consistent.

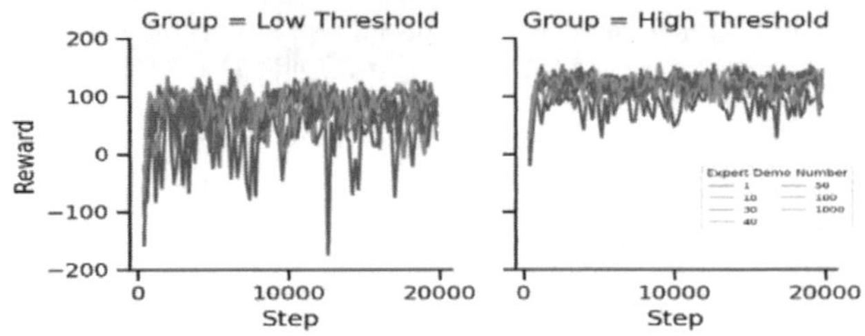

Figure 5. Rewards of different number of expert demonstrations.

TABLE III. AVERAGE REWARD WITH STANDARD DEVIATION UNDER DIFFERENT NUMBER OF EXPERT DEMONSTRATGIONS

No. Expert demo	Rewards - low threshold	Rewards - high threshold
1	2 ± 67	82 ± 16
10	70 ± 27	100 ± 15
30	82 ± 19	116 ± 15
40	86 ± 20	121 ± 12
50	82 ± 19	132 ± 14
100	85 ± 25	113 ± 15
1000	82 ± 19	126 ± 17

To further analyze convergence speed, we examined the relationship between the number of episodes completed and the number of training steps. After convergence (around 2000 steps), a higher number of episodes within a fixed number of training steps indicates faster convergence and thus a shorter duration for completing the automated pentesting task.

As shown in Figure 6, under the low-threshold setting, using 50 expert demonstrations results in a convergence speed nearly identical to that achieved with 100 or even 1000 expert demonstrations. Under the high-threshold setting, the number of expert demonstrations can be reduced to 40 while still achieving the convergence speed of the 100 and 1000 demonstration cases. Additionally, when completing 100 episodes, the time required with 30 expert demonstrations under the high-threshold condition is shorter than that under the low-threshold condition.

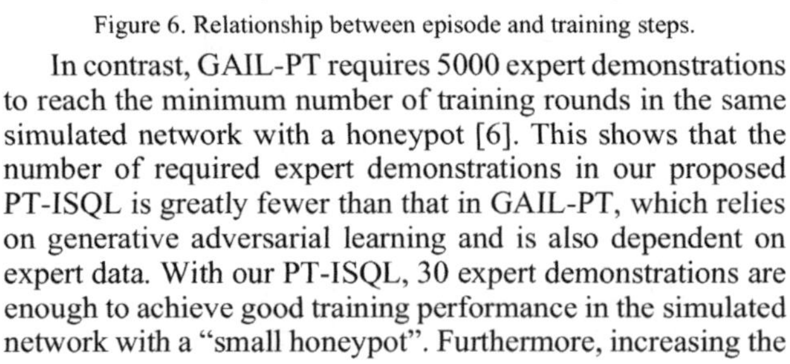

Figure 6. Relationship between episode and training steps.

In contrast, GAIL-PT requires 5000 expert demonstrations to reach the minimum number of training rounds in the same simulated network with a honeypot [6]. This shows that the number of required expert demonstrations in our proposed PT-ISQL is greatly fewer than that in GAIL-PT, which relies on generative adversarial learning and is also dependent on expert data. With our PT-ISQL, 30 expert demonstrations are enough to achieve good training performance in the simulated network with a "small honeypot". Furthermore, increasing the number or the quality threshold of expert demonstrations can further increase the converging speed of training.

E. Comparison of ISQL with Simple Q-Learning

To demonstrate the advantages of the ISQL algorithm in our PT-ISQL approach, we compared the pentesting performance using ISQL with that using Simple Q-Learning (a reinforcement learning method). The three pentesting metrics were examined across varying training steps. In this experiment, the high-threshold expert data was used, with 50 expert demonstrations provided. For each algorithm (with ISQL denoted as iq, and Simple Q-Learning as rl), five runs were conducted, and the results were averaged for the comparison of each metric.

Honeypot Invasion Probability

Figure 7 illustrates the honeypot invasion probability of five runs. The solid line represents the mean value, with the shaded area denoting the standard deviation. The results show that using ISQL greatly reduces the probability of honeypot invasion compared with deep reinforcement learning. This finding aligns with the results reported in DQfD-AIPT [11], where using expert demonstrations also led to significantly fewer interactions with honeypots. Nevertheless, in their study, the agent interacted with the honeypot during the early stages, i.e., before convergence.

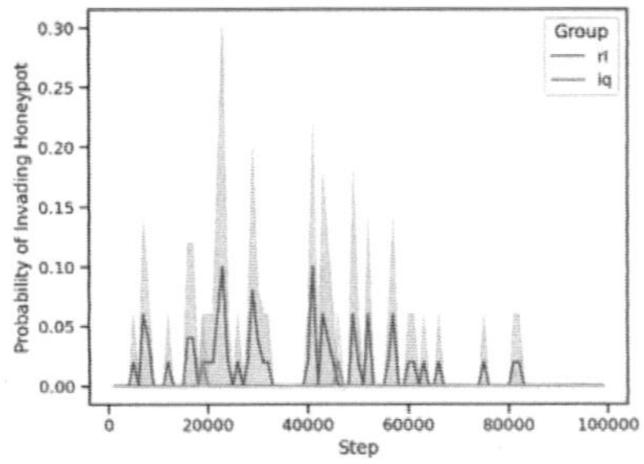

Figure 7. Probability of honeypot invasion of ISQL and Simple Q-Learning.

Average Reward

As shown in Figure 8, the rewards obtained using ISQL are both high and stable from the early stage of training. In addition, the reward is consistent across runs as indicated by the small shaded area. In contrast, when using the reinforcement learning algorithm, the reward is highly unstable across different runs. In fact, some runs fail to converge even after 100000 steps. This trend is consistent with the results reported in [9] and [11].

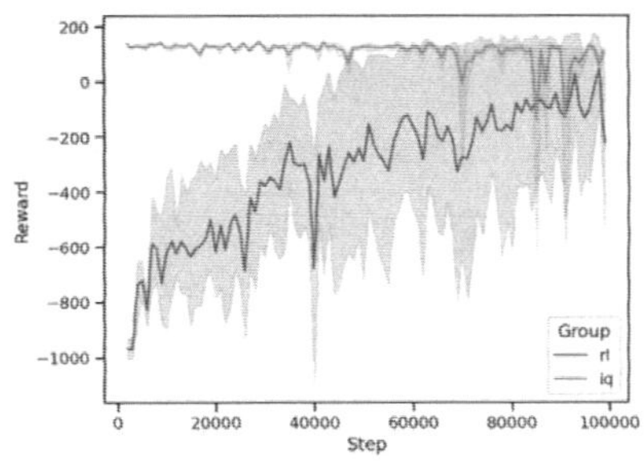

Figure 8. Rewards of ISQL and Simple Q-Learning.

Goal-Reached Probability

Figure 9 shows the average goal-reached probability with standard deviation (shaded area) over five runs using both algorithms. The results demonstrate that ISQL achieves much higher goal-reaching performance and requires far fewer training steps compared with Simple Q-Learning. ISQL achieves high goal-reaching performance even from the early stage of training, as it can quickly learn effective strategies from expert demonstrations.

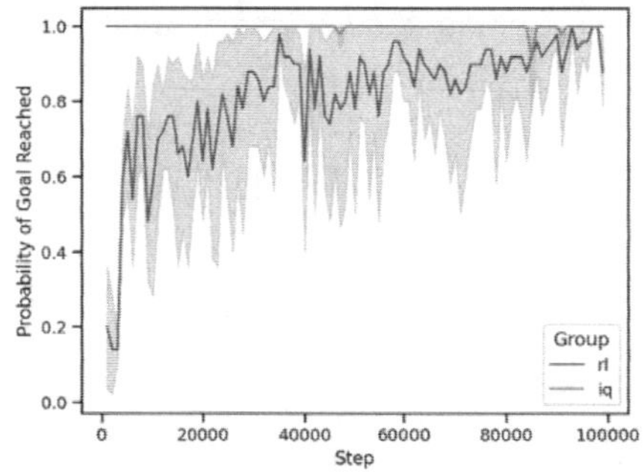

Figure 9. Goal reached probability of ISQL and Simple Q-Learning.

However, the performance of ISQL may degrade with excessive training. As seen in Figure 8 and Figure 9, after around 20000 steps, the reward begins to fluctuate more, and the goal-reaching rate declines. In contrast, Simple Q-Learning shows slower and less stable learning. Even after 100000 steps, the algorithm has not fully converged: the continued upward trend in the goal-reaching probability indicates that learning is still in progress.

V. Conclusions and Future Work

In this paper, we proposed an automatic pentesting approach based on ISQL. Our approach uses soft Q-Learning to infer the reward function implicitly optimized by human experts, while requiring significantly less expert data compared with other reinforcement learning methods based on expert demonstrations. Evaluation results show that our PT-ISQL approach is much faster than that of the general deep reinforcement learning method, such as Simple Q-Learning. The performance of the trained PT-ISQL agent is comparable to that of human experts. The required number of expert demonstrations is largely reduced compared with GAIL-PT (50 vs 5000), making PT-ISQL a more data-efficient and practical solution for automated pentesting.

However, the experiments conducted in the paper are limited in a simulation environment with a small network, and the trained agent's transferability to different situations has not been assessed. Future work is to evaluate PT-ISQL in a more realistic simulation environment and to test it in real-world networks. This includes training agents on real expert demonstrations data, and integrating PT-ISQL with frameworks such as Deep Exploit, with the goal of making PT-ISQL a fully functional and deployable automated pentesting tool. Qualitative comparisons with LLM-based agents, such as PentestGPT, is also a future work.

REFERENCES

[1] G. Deng et al., "PentestGPT: Evaluating and Harnessing Large Language Models for Automated Penetration Testing," In proc. of 33rd USENIX Security Symposium (USENIX Security 24), pp.847–864.

[2] X. Shen et al., "Pentest Agent: Incorporating LLM Agents to Automated Penetration Testing", arXiv:2411.05185v1 [cs.CR], Nov. 7, 2024.

[3] A. Happe and J. Cito, "Getting pwn'd by AI:penetration testing with large language models," In Proc. of the 31st ACM Joint European Software Engineering Conference and Symposium on the Foundations of Software Engineering, pp.2082–2086.

[4] H. Kong et al., "VulnBot: Autonomous penetration testing for a multi-agent collaborative framework", arXiv:2501.13411v1 [cs.SE] 23 Jan. 2025

[5] Z. Hu, R. Beuran, and Y. Tan, "Automated penetration testing using deep reinforcement learning," in 2020 IEEE European Symposium on Security and Privacy Workshops (EuroSPW), pp. 2-10, IEEE, 9 2020.

[6] I. Jabr, Y. Salman, M. Shqair, and A. Hawash, "Penetration testing and attack automation simulation: deep reinforcement learning approach," An-Najah University Journal for Research, Apr. 2024, pp. 7-14. DOI:10.35552/anujr.a.39.1.2231

[7] J. Yi and X. Liu, "Deep reinforcement learning for intelligent penetration testing path design," Applied Sciences, vol. 13, p. 9467, Aug. 2023.

[8] L. V. Hoang et al., "Leveraging deep reinforcement learning for automating penetration testing in reconnaissance and exploitation phase," in Int. Conf. on Computing and Communication Technologies, pp. 41-46, IEEE, 12 2022.

[9] J. Chen, S. Hu, H. Zheng, C. Xing, and G. Zhang, "Gail-PT: An intelligent penetration testing framework with generative adversarial imitation learning," Computers Security, vol. 126, p. 103055, 3 2023.

[10] F. M. Zennaro and L. Erdődi, "Modelling penetration testing with reinforcement learning using capture-the-flag challenges: tradeoffs between model-free learning and a priori knowledge" IET Information Security, vol.17, pp.441-457, 5 2023.

[11] Y. Wang et al., "Dqfd-aipt: An intelligent penetration testing framework incorporating expert demonstration data," Security and Communication Networks, vol. 2023, pp. 1-15, 5. 2023.

[12] M. Zare, P. M. Kebria, A. Khosravi, and S. Nahavandi, "A survey of imitation learning: Algorithms, recent developments, and challenges," IEEE Transactions on Cybernetics, vol.54, pp. 7137-7168, Dec. 2024.

[13] X. Ou, S. Govindavajhala and A. W. Appel, "Mulval: A logic-based network security analyzer," in Proc. of USENIX security symposium, vol. 8, pp. 113-128, 2005.

[14] T. Isao, "Deep exploit," 2018. https://github.com/13o-bbr-bbq/machine_learning_security/blob/master/DeepExploit/README.md / [retrieved: Sept. 2025]

[15] G. Farquhar et al., "Growing action spaces," in Proc. of the 37th International Conference on Machine Learning, vol. 119, pp. 3040-3051, PMLR, 5 2020.

[16] J. Ho and S. Ermon, "Generative adversarial imitation learning," Advances in neural information processing systems, vol. 29, pp. 4572-4580, Dec. 2016.

[17] J. Schwartz and H. Kurniawati, "Autonomous penetration testing using reinforcement learning," CoRR, vol. abs/1905.05965, 2019.

Hidden-Non-Malicious-Dummies for Evaluation of Defense Mechanisms of Industrial Control System against Steganographic Attacks

Robert Altschaffel, Stefan Kiltz, Jana Dittmann
Otto-von-Guericke University of Magdeburg
Magdeburg, Germany
e-mail: firstname.lastname@iti.cs.uni-magdeburg.de
Tom Neubert, Laura Buxhoidt, Claus Vielhauer
Brandenburg University of Applied Sciences
Brandenburg (Havel), Germany
e-mail: firstname.lastname@th-brandenburg.de
Mathias Lange, Rüdiger Mecke
Magdeburg-Stendal University of Applied Sciences
Magdeburg, Germany
e-mail: firstname.lastname@h2.de

***Abstract*—Cyber-Security in Industrial Control Systems (ICS) is a topic of growing relevance. Attack scenarios include the exfiltration of critical process data, the infiltration of commands and the manipulation of the controlled physical processes. Machine learning based detection mechanism are employed against these attacks. However, such machine learning based approaches rely on training data. This paper addresses two core challenges with regards to such machine learning approaches: 1. the required training data containing such attacks is usually difficult to obtain and 2. information about the detection rates is necessary in order to deploy the mechanisms for detection in a fashion benefiting security incident management. As such, this paper discusses an approach to generate such training data containing hidden non-malicious-dummy data representing attacks for five different attack scenarios, means to ensure that these dummies do not negatively affect the system under test, different strategies for injection and detection. This synthetically generated facility-specific data is then used for evaluating the usefulness of such machine learning detection approaches in ICS security management.**

Keywords-SCADA; hidden-non-malicious-dummy; cyber-security

I. INTRODUCTION

Industrial Control Systems (ICS) are under a rising threat from cyber-attacks, as shown by the trends identified in [1]. ICS processes directly affect the physical world (hence, they are often referred to as cyber-physical systems). An attack on the security of an ICS might compromise the safety of the surrounding facility, staff, bystanders or even those dependent on the services of the facility. As discussed in [1], Advanced and Persistent Threat actors (APTs) play a significant role in this threat scenario.

APTs are able to use advanced techniques including steganographic means to facilitate illicit communication flows (e.g., to infiltrate malicious payload, to exfiltrate data about the facility or for outright command&control of deployed malware). Such steganographic means are included in the MITRE ATT&CK Matrix [2] under the technique *Data Obfuscation: Steganography*. Another example from Desktop IT is the use of (primitive) steganographic means in the the widely-spread malware campaign SteganoAmor (see [3]).

Commonly, machine learning based detection mechanics are employed to counter attacks on ICS. Such approaches rely on the presence of training data including those of cyber-attacks in order to create models able to discern between legitimate network behavior and attacks.

Obtaining such training data faces different challenges (e.g., the data in itself contains critical information about the facility and is hence not made available to outsiders, the data is always facility-specific, some facilities might not have monitored any cyber attacks).

Hence, means to create 'known-bad' training data without compromising a given facility are necessary to support detection mechanisms. As such, this paper discusses an approach to generate such training data containing hidden non-malicious-dummy data representing attacks. Furthermore, the marking of these hidden-non-malicious dummies in a way to prevent any harm during testing procedures is discussed.

This paper furthermore explores the use of an Open Source Machine Learning suite to protect against attacks using steganographic means. The generation of a facility-specific training data set as well as the training of models. These models and their application is then evaluated.

This paper is structured as follows: After this introduction, Section II provides an overview on ICS terminology, communication protocols addressed within this paper and steganograpy employed in ICS. Section III describes the various scenarios of non-malicious-dummies and as well as their injection and their detection. Section IV discusses the creation of a test set and how it can be used to evaluate a detected approach. V discusses the results of the evaluation. Section VI provides the conclusion and a discussion on how to mark hidden non-malicious-dummies in the future to ensure that no facilities are damaged during security tests.

II. State-of-the-Art

This section provides a brief background on Industrial Control Systems (ICS) in general, the network protocol OPC UA commonly used in ICS, the terminology of steganography and the conjunction of ICS and steganograpy.

A. Industrial Control Systems (ICS)

ICS govern industrial processes. They encompass sensors (to measure the physical world), actuators (to affect the physical world), computing units (to calculate the intended control signals for the actuators based on sensor readings and operator input) and networking enabling all the communication required between these components. The computing units are generally known as Programmable Logic Controllers (PLCs). Other components also employed within the context of ICS comprise Human-Machine-Interfaces (HMI) that are used by operators to access sensor readings or to affect the actuators.

Various terms are used to describe the domain of ICS: Operational Technology (OT) or SCADA (Supervisory Control and Data Acquisition) describe functions and parts common in ICS. Field device is another term often used for ICS components located in a production field.

To enhance descriptive accuracy, we use the Purdue Enterprise Reference Architecture (PERA) [4]. The PERA describes the system hierarchy common to ICS in six levels. The exact definition and naming of these levels shifted over the years, but [5] identifies the following levels: *Level 0 - Process* (sensors and actuators involved in the basic manufacturing process), *Level 1 - Basic Control* (controllers that direct and manipulate the manufacturing process), *Level 2 - Area Supervisory Control* (Cell/Area zone runtime supervision and operation) (incl. operator interfaces or alarms), *Level 3 - Site Manufacturing Operations and Control*, *Level 4 - Site Business Planning and Logistics* (basic business administration tasks), and *Level 5 - Enterprise* (centralized IT systems and functions). These levels are grouped into specific zones. Levels 0, 1 and 2 are grouped into the *Cell/Area Zone*. Levels 0, 1, 2 and 3 represent the *Manufactoring Zone*. Levels 4 and 5 comprise the *Enterprise Zone*. The use of these levels of the control hierarchy enables a more accurate description than the terms ICS, OT or SCADA. In this paper, we are concerned with the levels 0-2 (The *Cell/Area Zone*).

B. OPC Unified Architecture Industrial Control Systems (OPC UA)

Within the *Manufacturing Zone*, the use of ICS-specific communication protocols is common. One of these protocols is the OPC Unified Architecture (OPC UA) protocol. OPC UA is an open standard (including an open source reference implementation) to facilitate the communication between various ICS components. TCP/IP is often used as a foundation for the network connection [6].

OPC UA follows a client/server-model. A range of clients connects to a specific OPC UA server. On *Control Hierarchy Level 1*, the OPC UA server is usually provided by a computing unit (the PLC) with the sensors and actuators connected as clients to this server.

C. Steganography in ICS

According to the recent work of [7]: "*Steganography is the art and science of concealing the existence of information transfer and storage*". Steganography has several subdomains such as: *text steganography*, *digital media steganography*, *file system steganography* and *cyber-physical systems steganography*. Each of these exemplary subdomains has different characteristics and requirements. The relevant subdomain for steganography in ICS is cyber-physical systems steganography and is characterized by a limited channel capacity and ICS-specific network protocols. There is usually a lower amount of available data for a potential embedding in ICS networks compared to traditional IT networks. Additionally, transmitted network packets are usually significantly smaller in ICS since only few (sensor) values or meta-data are transferred. ICS-specific network protocols, like Modbus TCP or OPC UA, are often encapsulated in TCP/IP (or other transport protocols). This creates the opportunity to utilize the data fields of the ICS-specific protocols in addition to TCP/IP protocol headers [8]. A further domain-specific characteristic is that the ICS-specific payload is transmitted unencrypted in many or at least some cases, because ICS are often considered closed networks.

From the attackers point of view, the embedding of hidden information can be realized by steganographic techniques (e.g, manipulating network packets payload by altering time intervals, time stamps or sensor values on least significant digits in specific selected packets). The attackers goal is that the packets seem inconspicuous for a potential warden (e.g., intrusion detection system) observing the network traffic.

A unified definition of terms and their applicability in steganographic context is provided in [7].

D. Steganograhic Attack Vectors in ICS

Since the last decade, stealthy malware or information hiding based malware is increasingly used by attackers, confirmed for example by the attack vectors presented in [2]. The well-known Stuxnet-Attack [9] proves that attackers use information hiding techniques to compromise ICS or cyber-physical systems since the last decade. During the attack, lnk-files have been utilized as cover data and in-memory code injections have been used to conceal the attack. Further attacks with stealthy malware on ICS, like the Ukrainian [10] and the Indian power grid attack [11], show that attacks on ICS and other cyber-physical systems are more and more common.

Basically, stealthy malware uses steganographic techniques to embed and inject or extract data in ICS. Therefore, attacker use stealthy malware to stay undetected for as long as possible to establish command and control channels (e.g., to trigger malfunctions or to exfiltrate confidential data).

Additional relevant attack vectors for information hiding based malware in ICS are discussed in [12].

III. HIDDEN-NON-MALICIOUS-DUMMIES

The central aim of this paper is to provide 'known-bad' training data of cyber-attacks containing steganographic means without compromising a given facility. These training data encompasses the network communication of an ICS. Hence, we face some general conceptional requirements for this data:

- **The data must be facility-specific**: Facilities come in diverse configurations, each leading to a different base line communication behavior. The inclusion of different sensors and actors leads to a differences in communication behavior, which could lead to the detection of anomalous behavior by using non-facility-specific data even if no attack and no steganographic communication is present at all.
- **The data must be attack-specific**: A dummy can have specific properties or requirements due to the category of an attack (see Section III-A).
- **The resulting data must not trigger any damage to the facility in question**: A dummy must never damage or destroy a target system.
- **The data must contain steganographic communication**: As we aim to evaluate a security measure's capability of detecting attacks containing steganographic communication, the inclusion of steganographic communication is necessary.

We term such training data as containing *hidden-non-malicious-dummies*. Our terminology comprises two parts: The non-malicious-dummies itself, and the hiding mechanism (provided by steganographic means).

A. The Non-Malicious-Dummy

The non-malicious-dummy is the message itself transmitted by stenographic means. As stated before, this message must not trigger harm to the specific facility. On the other hand, the message should mimic properties of messages used in cyber-attacks. Different types of attacks might affect the requirements for these non-malicious-dummies.

These attacks generally fall under the following broad categories:

- **Infiltration**: Data is infiltrated into the ICS. This data would include malicious commands, malicious binary code or manipulated documentation.
- **Exfiltration**: Confidential data is exfiltrated from the ICS into another network. This typically includes data like network scan information or process data used as reconnaissance for follow-up attacks or lateral movement in the scope of a complex cyber-attack scenario (e.g., as described by the Cyber Kill Chain [13]). Other potential targets include source code, binary objects or construction documents.
- **Command and Control** (C&C, C2): general command&control communication involving a two-way communication (e.g., queries and results).

These categories motivate five scenarios for the use of specific types of non-malicious-dummy messages. These scenarios aim at covering a broad range of these potential categories:

- **Scenario$_1$: Plain text documents**; this could be relevant during an exfiltration. This would include automatically generated text or placeholder text (e.g., Lorem Ipsum)
- **Scenario$_2$: Multimedia Files**, those could also be relevant mostly for exfiltration scenarios. This comprises placeholder files in standard document formats (e.g., JPEG for images, PDF for documents).
- **Scenario$_3$: Binary Codes**; this could be relevant for exfiltration or infiltration scenarios. This includes binary files, which include the common headers for the respective architecture but do not cause any malicious execution.
- **Scenario$_4$: C&C Control Commands**; this could be relevant for a Command and Control scenario. It includes a list of common unspecific command words used in the context of controlling deployed malicious software in plain text, e.g., *START*, *SET*, *TRANSFER*. These will have no function without deployed malware on the communication partners.
- **Scenario$_5$: Control Commands & Sensor readings**; this could be relevant in all categories. This scenario requires the greatest knowledge of the ICS in question since it encompasses sensor readings and control commands that do not affect the ICS in question (e.g., sensor readings from sensors not present within the ICS).

Furthermore, it must be ensured that the non-malicious-dummies do not cause any harm to the systems tested. This can be supported by marking the non-malicious-dummy, which is discussed in VI.

B. Injection of hidden non-malicious-dummies

In this section, we specify how hidden non-malicious-dummies without malicious effect can be injected into realistic, legitimate network traffic cover data without causing damage to the ICS. We identify the following approaches:

- **Direct injection:** For the direct injection of hidden non-malicious-dummies into the running network traffic of an ICS a corrupted setup with a "man-in-the-middle" (MitM) is required and should be modeled as a non-malicious simulation in a research lab. In this injection method, the non-malicious simulation can use scripts that select, intercept, modify and then forward selected network packets.
- **Injection through network recording:** Based on the Synthetic Steganographic Embedding (SSE) concept presented in [14], recorded network traffic from ICS can be subsequently modified synthetically. The SSE-concept offers the possibility to embed hidden information everywhere in recorded network cover data with a fast embedding pace near real time. The SSE-concept has two synthetic embedding options. Synthetic Embedding Option A (SEO_A) focuses on a high embedding pace and SEO_B on a more comfortable and easier to handle embedding, due to access to structural elements of a network packet.

In the evaluation of this work, the steganographic hidden non-malicious-dummies are injected into the cover data through network recording using SEO_A as part of the SSE-concept.

C. Detection of hidden non-malicious-dummies

Several detection approaches [8], [15], [16] of steganographic techniques used by attackers have been elaborated. A general overview of potential defense mechanisms for steganographic network data is introduced in [17]. Additionally, an extended analysis testbed for steganographic network data to evaluate detection and defense mechanisms is presented in [8]. Machine learning driven approaches based on handcrafted feature spaces with as much discriminatory power as possible are well-suited for the detection of steganographic network data because they offer the opportunity for a comprehensive and explainable classification of samples (i.e., steganographic network data). In our evaluation (see Section IV), we train a classifier based on an existing handcrafted feature space to distinguish between steganographic network data samples with embedded hidden non-malicious-dummies and cover network data samples.

IV. Conceptual Approach for an Evaluation Setup for Hidden-Non-Malicious-Dummies

In this section, we present our evaluation setup including our evaluation goals and metrics (Section IV-A), our evaluation data with our laboratory setup and a potential attack vector (Section IV-B), our exemplary steganographic embedding method which is used encode the hidden non-malicious-dummies into cover data and the resulting captured evaluation data (Section IV-C). Additionally, the detection approach for our evaluation is briefly outlined (Section IV-D).

A. Evaluation Goals and Metrics

In our evaluation, the goal is to determine if a selected state-of-the-art detection approach (Section IV-D) is able to detect samples with exemplary embedded hidden non-malicious-dummies and if the approach can distinguish between a sample with embedded hidden non-malicious-dummies and an unaltered cover data sample. To achieve our goals, we split our evaluation data with a 5-fold cross validation (Figure 1). For the determination of the performance of the detection approach we use the following well-known forensic success- and error rates:

- **True Positive Rate** (**TPR**, number of correctly classfied altered samples (with embedded dummy) in relation to number of all altered samples),
- **True Negative Rate** (**TNR**, number of correctly classfied unaltered samples in relation to number of all unaltered samples),
- **False Miss Rate** (**FMR**, number of incorrectly classfied altered samples in relation to number of all altered samples) and
- **False Alarm Rate** (**FAR**, number of incorrectly classfied unaltered samples in relation to number of all unaltered samples).

The determined classification performance of the used detection approach is presented in Section V.

B. Evaluation Data including Laboratory Setup and Attack Vector

For the evaluation of the detectability of exemplary hidden non-malicious-dummies, an uncompromised laboratory ICS setup is required to record uncompromised network traffic, i.e., cover data. As discussed in Section III-B), we use this cover

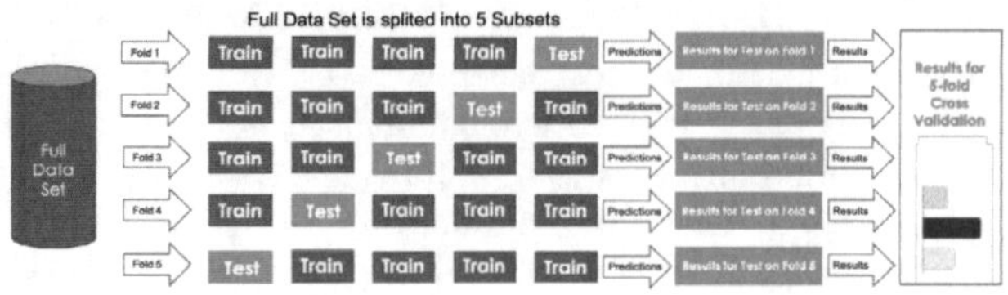

Figure 1. Generic description of the 5-fold cross validation process

data for the embedding of the introduced hidden non-malicious-dummies. We inject the dummies afterwards into the cover data recording with the previously mentioned SSE-concept from [14] without the need to compromise our laboratory ICS setup. To record uncompromised cover data, we build an ICS setup with multiple components, visualized in Figure 2.

This CP-Lab is a customizable educational system that integrates current Industry 4.0 standards. The system is made up of two islands, each consisting of four different modules (module describes a combination of base module, application module and Siemens TOUCH HMI) (see Figure 2). The two islands are physically connected by the transport robot called "ROBOTINO". This robot transports the pallet carriers between the two islands. The base module consists of a control cabinet with the control technology for the conveyor belt and the application module, which has task-specific components, e.g., a press, a drill, a magazine and even a Festo UR-5 robot. Only "The Branch" module is controlled by a FESTO PLC (one for each island). The others have a SIMATIC ET 200 Open Controller with a CPU 1515 SP. Each module is connected to a Siemens SCALANCE XB008 switch via PROFINET [**pn**]. The switches are in turn connected with each other via a central switch, which bundles all data traffic between the host computer and the system. This allows each module to communicate with each other. The OPC-UA server, a web store and a Manufacturing Execution System (MES) are located on the host computer. The host computer focuses on controlling a single production line or section, while the MES controls the entire production process. Both systems require data acquisition, process control and visualization to improve production. After start-up, the system is in automatic mode. In this operating mode, the conveyor belts move the pallet carriers permanently. During this time, all modules communicate permanently with the host computer, transmitting the position of the pallet carriers to the host computer and waiting for new commands, such as an order triggered by the MES. No SIEM systems exist in this test setup during the test period in order to document the effects of attacks on an unprotected system and to generate test data. For documentation purposes a switch with a mirror port connecting the host computer and the modules is integrated. The switch mirrors all traffic to a mirror port where it is recorded using a notebook running Wireshark [**wireshark**].

Our recorded cover data REC_{Cover} capture from this setup is roughly 25 minutes long and includes 4.961 relevant OPC UA packets (9.922 packets in total). In a potential attack scenario, the server is corrupted via a supply-chain attack and responds to

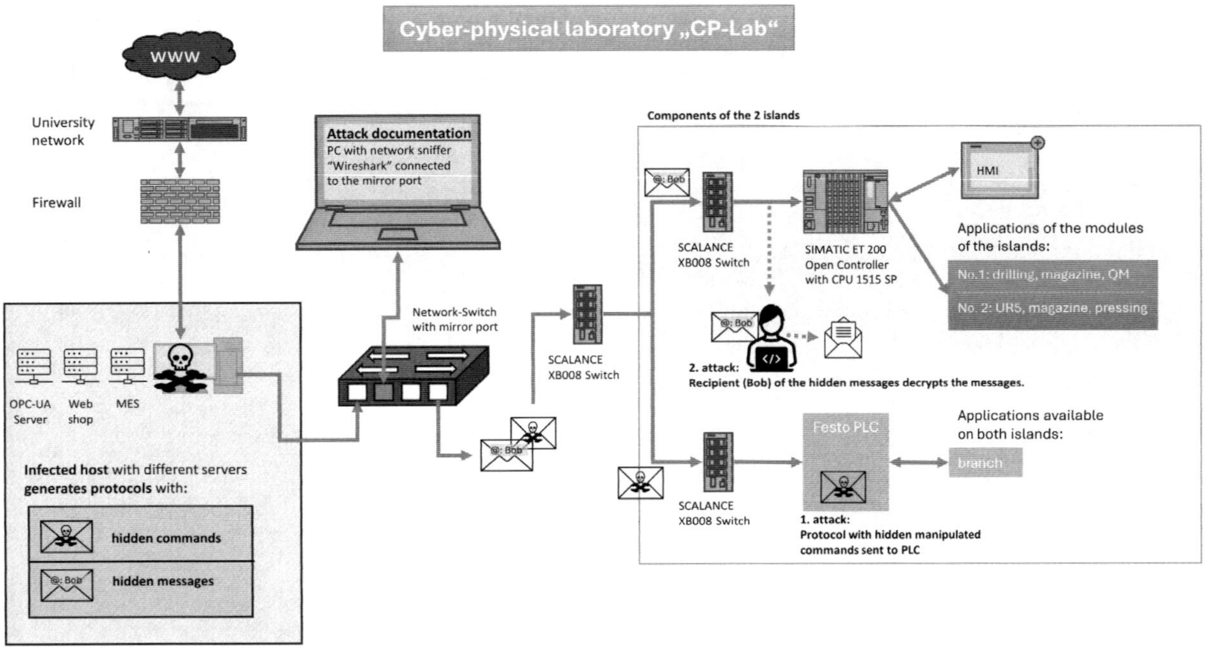

Figure 2. CP-Lab Setup for the recording of the uncompromised cover data. The communication path in the attack scenario used for evaluation is highlighted.

specific requests with timing delays, which embeds the hidden-malicious-dummy. An accomplice can decode the embedded message by accessing the mirror port of the switch, see Figure 2. For our evaluation, we duplicate REC_{Cover} to obtain the exact same data into which we embed our hidden non-malicous dummies. We embed synthetically created non-malicious data into the recorded data with the SSE-concept, introduced in [14], for a fast and easy embedding near real time afterwards, without risking a corruption of the deployed hardware. We embed the following exemplary dummy message: "*Set Valv1 390 Sleep 5 Set Valv1 400 Sleep 5 Set Valv1 405 Set Valv2 200 Sleep 15 Set Valv1 390 Sleep*" representing **Scenario$_5$: Control Commands & Sensor readings**. The resulting recording with included steganographic hidden-non-malicious-dummies is called REC_{Stego} and has the same number of packets as REC_{Cover}. The next subsection describes the steganographic embedding method used to inject the non-malicious data into the network data.

C. Steganographic Embedding Method for use in our scenario

To embed the hidden non-malicious-dummy into the network data, a state-of-the-art steganographic embedding method from [18] is used. This method utilizes network packet timestamps to embed hidden information. In this work, we use the protocol-specific OPC UA timestamp for an embedding. In the initial method from [18], the microsecond digits of a timestamp were altered (Example: $T_i = 08 : 00 : 00.123\mathbf{456}789$) to embed the hidden information. In this work, we have to adjust the approach due to unavailability in our setup's recording. We use the the digits in the millisecond range for embedding (Example: $T_i = 09 : 00 : 00.\mathbf{123}000000$), because they represent the three least significant values in the timestamp. The embedding methods embeds a bitstream into the data, which can be converted afterwards into an ASCII-message. For the embedding three consecutive OPC UA server timestamps (read requests) are modified (T_i , T_{i+1} , T_{i+2}). For timestamp T_i the first millisecond digit position ms_1 is modified, for T_{i+1} the second millisecond digit ms_2 and for T_{i+2} the third one ms_3. The following three timestamps of this component stay untouched (T_{i+3} , T_{i+4}, T_{i+5}) to ensure more unobtrusiveness. The approach uses the digit '4' to embed bit = 0 and digit '9' to embed bit=1. This means in three consecutive timestamps the following digit positions are altered into '4' or '9' to embed bit = 0 or bit = 1: $T_i = ms_1$, $T_{i+1} = ms_2$ and $T_{i+2} = ms_3$. For more details, see [18].

D. Detection Approach and resulting Data Set for Evaluation

For the detection of the hidden non-malicious-dummies, we build a logistic model tree classifier with WEKA 3.8 [19], which uses a handcrafted feature space from [15]. The feature space performs a frequency analysis of occurrence for the digits *0* to *9* on selected digit positions and a selected number of packets. In this work, we perform the frequency analysis on the OPC UA timestamps of the server packets on the millisecond digit positions ms_1, ms_2 and ms_3. Thus, we determine 10 features for each of the three digit positions with values ranging from 0.0 to 1.0. This results in a 30-dimensional feature space with the addition of a label for each vector, i.e., sample ('cover' or 'stego'). With this feature extractor, we iterate through relevant OPC UA server packets in both data sets REC_{Cover}

and REC_{Stego}. We extract a feature vector after analyzing 20 relevant packets. As introduced in Section IV-B, we have 4.961 relevant packets per recording, which results in 248 samples for both recordings REC_{Cover} and REC_{Stego}. In Section V, the evaluation results are presented.

V. Evaluation Results

As introduced in Section IV-A, we perform a 5-fold cross validation with our selected detection approach (Section IV-D) to determine if the approach is able to distinguish between cover data samples (unaltered) and steganographic data samples with embedded hidden non-malicious-dummies. The performance of the approach is measured with TPR, TNR, FMR and FAR. The resulting rates are visualized in Figure 3. The classification results of the approach are presented in Table I.

TABLE I. Confusion Matrix of 5-fold cross validation

Classification Results of Detection Approach		
classified as $->$ actual (248)	REC_{Cover}	REC_{Stego}
REC_{Cover}	**214**	34
REC_{Stego}	26	**222**

The approach is able to detect 222 out of 248 samples with embedded hidden non-malicious-dummies. This results in TPR = 0.895 and FMR = 0.105. Additionally, the detection approach classifies 214 of 248 unaltered cover data samples correctly, this leads to TNR = 0.862 and FAR = 0.138. Overall the approach has an accuracy of 0.879, derived from 436 of 496 correctly classified samples. For an initial detection approach the performance is decent but should be improved in future work, e.g., with a novel feature space. Especially, a better FAR would be critical for a real world application.

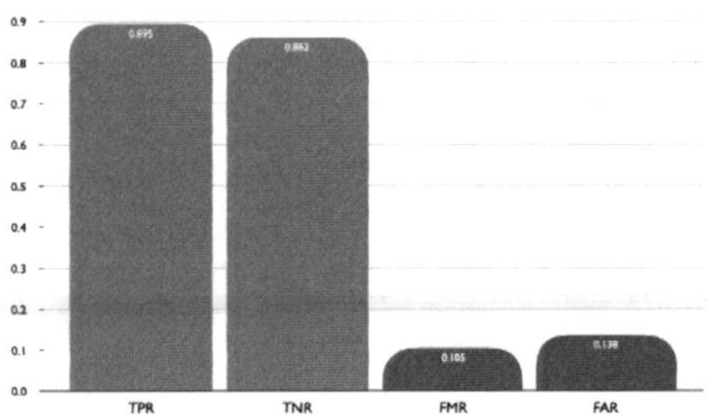

Figure 3. TPR, TNR, FMR and FAR of detection approach determined with 5-fold cross validation

VI. Conclusion and Future Work

This paper serves as starting point for the creation of a comprehensive definition of dummies that can be used to test and simulate attacks in ICS networks with the goal to improve detection and reaction of this threat.

However, it must be ensured that these dummies must not have any harmful effect on networks to prevent possible misuse. For this, it is necessary to establish a corresponding standard in future work. Such a standard should specify which requirements hidden-non-malicious-dummies must meet, as well as a systematic classification of such dummies, the definition and agreement of suitable protection mechanisms, the definition of areas of application and the identification of relevant user groups. In addition, potential extensions to the dummy definition that have not yet been addressed in this article must be considered.

The requirements formulated in this work have shown that the design of the dummies depends largely on their specific properties and purposes. These properties can differ significantly from one another, which means that the respective dummies also pose different potential hazards. Therefore it seems plausible to define different hazard classes for dummies.

The classification of the messages in hidden communication used by attackers can also support the attribution of real attacks against ICS. The motivation of some of proposed communication scenarios comes from the analysis of attack scenarios occurring in theoretical considerations as well as practical cases investigated during the work in the project ATTRIBUT [20]. For this project, measures to identify the Communication Scenario pursued by an attacker are an aspect of future work.

Marking of the hidden-non-malicious-dummies

One of the most important focal points of future work will be the inclusion of suitable protection mechanisms. Protection mechanisms have to be defined in close coordination with existing standards for security information and event management (SIEM) systems - both in the context of ICS and for enterprise/business IT. This is necessary to the risk of misuse or misappropriation of the dummies.

Any individual using so-called hidden-non-malicious-dummies, or test dummies in general, must commit - provided they act without malicious intent - to explicitly marking the protocols they use as dummies. While this approach may initially seem contradictory, particularly in the context of hidden channel attacks, it should be understood as a preventive security measure intended to mitigate the risk of such dummies being misused for offensive purposes.

For testing purposes, monitoring systems can be configured to ignore specific markers or tags. This enables the evaluation of relevant attack characteristics and their potential impact - as well as the detectability of hidden-non-malicious-dummies - without compromising the integrity of the testing environment.

Various protocol-marking methods are already established in enterprise IT. One such method is tagging, as implemented in tagged VLANs according to IEEE 802.1Q, where additional fields are inserted into the Ethernet protocol's data section to carry VLAN-specific tags. Another approach is labeling, such as through Quality of Service (QoS) labels, which allow certain protocols to be prioritized in network traffic. These mechanisms could also be applied to hidden-non-malicious-dummies by defining standardized procedures to identify and distinguish misused dummies within network environments.

Furthermore, protocol-level marking—such as IP header marking—offers an additional option. For instance, the Type of Service (ToS) field in the IP header could be extended to introduce, define, and standardize a new service type labeled "DUMMY," thereby enabling a consistent and identifiable classification of such dummy traffic.

The range of possible measures to prevent misuse is significantly broader than those outlined in this context. There remains a considerable need for continued research and discourse on how, and to what extent, protective mechanisms can, should, and must be implemented in practice.

At the same time, it is important to acknowledge that absolute protection against misuse can never be fully guaranteed. Nevertheless, the residual risk can be substantially reduced through the conscious selection and implementation of appropriate safeguards—provided that researchers remain aware of their ethical responsibilities and adhere to the principles of responsible cyber-security research.

Acknowledgment

This work has been performed in the scope of the project "SYNTHESIS - Synthetically generated data segments with hidden malicious code functions for safety analysis in nuclear control technology" with the grant number FKZ: 1501666A which is funded by the Federal Ministry for the Environment, Nature Conservation, Nuclear Safety and Consumer Protection (BMUV). The motivation for the Communication Scenarios originates from considerations for the project ATTRIBUT which has been supported by the Agentur für Innovation in der Cybersicherheit GmbH. The Agentur für Innovation in der Cybersicherheit GmbH did not interfere in the research process and its results.

Author shares: All authors: fundamental discussion. RA: formalization of non-malicious dummies and injection methods. TN & LB: conception of the detection approach, implementation of the embedding code, injecting of the non-malicious dummies & experimental evaluation. TN & CV: General conception of SSE, embedding scheme & the evaluation methodology. ML: Creation on recordings; considerations on marking of resulting test sets.

References

[1] Dragos, Inc., "2025 OT/ICS Cybersecurity Report", 2025, Accessed: Sep. 15, 2025. [Online]. Available: https://hub.dragos.com/hubfs/312-Year-in-Review/2025/Dragos-2025-OT-Cybersecurity-Report-A-Year-in-Review.pdf?hsLang=en.

[2] MITRE, "MITRE ATT&CK: Techniques - Data Obfuscation: Steganography", Apr. 2025, Accessed: Sep. 15, 2025. [Online]. Available: https://attack.mitre.org/techniques/T1001/002/.

[3] A. Badaev and K.Naumova, "Steganoamor campaign: Ta558 mass-attacking companies and public institutions all around the world", *https://www.ptsecurity.com/ww-en/analytics/pt-esc-threat-intelligence/steganoamor-campaign-ta558-mass-attacking-companies-and-public-institutions-all-around-the-world/*, 2024.

[4] T. Williams, "An overview of pera and the purdue methodology", *https://link.springer.com/content/pdf/10.1007/978-0-387-34941-1_8.pdf*, 1996.

[5] Rockwell Automation, "Converged plantwide ethernet (cpwe) design and implementation guide", *https://literature.rockwellautomation.com/idc/groups/literature/documents/td/enet-td001_-en-p.pdf*, 2011.

[6] OPC-Foundation, "Unified architecture", 2008, Accessed: Sep. 15, 2025. [Online]. Available: https://opcfoundation.org/about/opc-technologies/OPC%20UA/.

[7] S. Wendzel et al., "A generic taxonomy for steganography methods", *Association for Computing Machinery; ACM 1557-7341/2025/4-ART*, Jul. 2025. DOI: https://doi.org/10.1145/3729165.

[8] T. Neubert, E. Schueler, H.Ullrich, L. Buxhoidt, and C. Vielhauer, "Extended analysis, detection and attribution of steganographic embedding methods in network data of industrial controls systems", *International Journal on Advances in Security, ISSN:1942-2636 online: https://www.thinkmind.org/library/Sec/Sec_v18_n12_2025/sec_v18_n12_2025_10.html*, 2025.

[9] D. Kushner, "The real story of stuxnet", *https://spectrum.ieee.org/the-real-story-of-stuxnet, last access: 19/09/2024*, 2013.

[10] R. M. Lee, M. J. Assante, and T. Conway, "Analysis of the cyber attack on the ukrainian power grid", SANS Institute, Tech. Rep., 2016.

[11] Dragos, Inc., "Assessment of reported malware infection at nuclear facility", 2019, Accessed: Sep. 15, 2025. [Online]. Available: https://www.dragos.com/blog/industry-news/assessment-of-reported-malware-infection-at-nuclear-facility/.

[12] T. Neubert and C. Vielhauer, "Kill chain attack modeling for hidden channel attack scenarios in industrial control systems", *21st IFAC World Congress, Berlin, Germany, July 11-17, Submission 1475*, 2020.

[13] Lockheed Martin, "Https://www.lockheedmartin.com/en-us/capabilities/cyber/cyber-kill-chain.html", Apr. 2025, Accessed: Sep. 15, 2025. [Online]. Available: https://www.lockheedmartin.com/en-us/capabilities/cyber/cyber-kill-chain.html.

[14] T. Neubert, B. Peuker, L. Buxhoidt, E. Schueler, and C. Vielhauer, "Synthetic embedding of hidden information in industrial control system network protocols for evaluation of steganographic malware", *Tech. Report, arXiv, https://doi.org/10.48550/arXiv.2406.19338*, 2024.

[15] T. Neubert, A. J. C. Morcillo, and C. Vielhauer, "Improving performance of machine learning based detection of network steganography in industrial control systems.", *In the Proceedings of 17th International Conference on Availability, Reliability and Security (ARES 2022), Article No.: 51, pp. 1 - 8, August 23– 26, 2022, Vienna, Austria. ACM, New York, NY, USA, 8 pages. https://doi.org/10.1145/3538969.3544427*, 2022.

[16] M. Massimo Guarascio, M. Marco Zuppelli, N. Nunzio Cassavia, G. Manco, and L. Caviglione, "Detection of network covert channels in iot ecosystems using machine learning", *In Proceedings of Italian Conference on Cybersecurity, Rome, Italy, https://api.semanticscholar.org/CorpusID:253270269*, 2021.

[17] L. Caviglione, "Trends and challenges in network covert channels countermeasures", *DOI: 10.3390/app11041641*, 2021.

[18] T. Neubert, C. Kraetzer, and C. Vielhauer, "Artificial steganographic network data generation concept and evaluation of detection approaches to secure industrial control systems against steganographic attacks", *In The 16th International Conference on Availability, Reliability and Security (ARES 2021), August 17–20, 2021, Vienna, Austria. ACM, New York, NY, USA, 9 pages. https://doi.org/10.1145/3465481.3470073*, 2021.

[19] M. Hall, "The weka data mining software: An update.", *In SIGKDD Explorations*, 2009.

[20] ATTRIBUT, "Project ATTRIBUT", Accessed: Sep. 15, 2025. [Online]. Available: https://omen.cs.uni-magdeburg.de/itiamsl/english/attribut/attribut.html.

The Balanced Chance & Cyber-Risk Card: Extending Reichmann's Multidimensional Controlling Framework for C-Level Steering in SMEs

Alexander Lawall
IU International University of Applied Sciences
Erfurt, Thüringen, Germany
e-mail: alexander.lawall@iu.org

Maik Drozdzynski
IU International University of Applied Sciences
Erfurt, Thüringen, Germany
e-mail: maik.drozdzynski@iu.org

***Abstract*—Cyber threats pose a growing strategic challenge for German Small and Medium-Sized Enterprises (SMEs), yet existing management control systems offer limited tools to integrate cybersecurity into executive steering. This paper introduces the Balanced Chance & Cyber-Risk Card (BCCR-Card) – an extension of Reichmann's multidimensional controlling framework – designed to embed cyber-specific Key Performance Indicators (KPIs) and Key Risk Indicators (KRIs) into a five-dimensional control structure. By aligning operational metrics (e.g., Mean Time To Detect (MTTD), patch latency) with strategic indicators (e.g., Cyber Value at Risk (CyVaR), Expected Annual Loss (EAL)), the BCCR-Card bridges technical cybersecurity telemetry and C-level decision-making. The framework supports role-specific dashboards and maps directly to standards, such as ISO 31000, National Institute of Standards and Technology (NIST) Cybersecurity Framework (CSF) 2.0, and Corporate Stabilisation and Restructuring Act (StaRUG) compliance requirements. A tiered KPI logic and scenario-based stress testing ensure traceability and audit readiness. The model transforms cybersecurity from a siloed IT concern into a board-level control dimension, enabling risk-informed leadership and resilience planning. While further empirical validation is needed, the BCCR-Card offers a scalable foundation for integrating cyber risk into enterprise performance management.**

Keywords-Cyber Risk Management; Enterprise Risk Management (ERM); Risk Controlling in SMEs; Management Control Systems; Cybersecurity Metrics; Balanced Scorecard.

I. INTRODUCTION

Over the past decade, the risk landscape for German enterprises has been reshaped by cybercrime. In 2024, the Federal Criminal Police Office recorded 131,391 domestic cybercrime offences – 9% more than in 2023 – and 950 officially reported ransomware incidents [1]. The economic impacts are equally notable: according to Bitkom's Wirtschaftsschutz 2024, cyberattacks alone (exclusive of other forms of white-collar crime) caused € 178.6 billion in losses on Germany's economy, while eight out of ten firms experienced at least one successful attack within the preceding twelve months [2].

The cyber threats continue to grow. The Federal Office for Information Security (BSI) identified a daily average of 309,000 new malware variants in its 2024 situation report – an increase of 26% year-on-year [3]. These attacks translate directly into balance-sheet risks: IBM's Cost of a Data Breach 2024 puts the mean loss per breach in Germany at USD 5.31 million, up from USD 4.67 million a year earlier [4]. Perceptions inside companies are converging with these figures; the Hiscox Cyber Readiness Report 2024 notes that 67% of surveyed firms faced more attacks than in the prior year and a majority classify their cyber risk exposure as "high" [5].

As a consequence, cybersecurity has moved onto the management agenda of controlling departments. Controlling founder Horváth lists cyber risk management, alongside Environmental, Social and Corporate Governance (ESG) reporting, among the fastest-growing controlling disciplines for CFOs in 2024 [6]. Yet existing research still lacks an integrated steering framework that treats cyber risks on an equal footing with classical corporate-risk categories. The Balanced Chance & Risk Card proposed in 2000 [7] and updated alongside the Law on Control and Transparency in the Corporate Sector (KonTraG) in 2001 [8, pp. 282] by German controlling pioneer Reichmann offers a conceptual anchor as a breakthrough in risk-management, but has so far not been extended with cyber-specific KRIs. Likewise, the risk-controlling process by German leading risk-management researcher Diederichs provides a systemic approach and does not yet incorporate the distinctive dynamics of cyber-threat scenarios [9, pp. 189].

Adding to the urgency, the StaRUG, in force since January 1st, 2021, obliges German SMEs of any legal form to establish an early-warning system for existential risks, implicitly requiring a proportionate risk-controlling architecture [10]. Cyber threats now constitute the most prominent risk class within this mandate, which significantly emphasizes the need to establish a corporate cyber risk integrated controlling framework to guarantee optimized steering capabilities.

This study closes the identified gap by introducing a BCCR-Card – an extension of the Reichmann framework that embeds quantifiable cyber KRIs and aligns them with traditional financial and operational metrics. Building on the classical risk-controlling cycle (identification, assessment, steering, monitoring), we (i) derive a set of cyber-specific steering indicators, (ii) integrate them into the BCR-Card, and (iii) demonstrate applicability through a mid-sized manufacturing case. The result is a practicable concept that enables top management and controllers alike to treat cyber risks as a first-class steering dimension within the regular corporate reporting.

The remainder of the paper is structured as follows. Section II reviews the theoretical foundations of corporate risk management, Reichmann's multidimensional controlling framework, and the Balanced Chance and Risk Card. Section III presents the proposed BCCR-Card as a cyber risk-oriented extension, detailing its dimensions, KPIs/KRIs, and cause-effect logic. Section IV discusses limitations, implications, and directions for future research. Section VI concludes by summarizing the contributions and positioning the BCCR-Card as a scalable tool for embedding cyber risk into enterprise performance management.

II. Theoretical Foundation

A. Corporate Risk Management

In managerial accounting, risk management refers to the systematic handling of uncertainties that may impair, or enhance, the achievement of corporate objectives [9]. From an expected-value perspective, risk is the dispersion of potential outcomes around a planned value [7]. Hopkin further argues that modern frameworks must recognize the upside of uncertainty and integrate opportunity management into corporate steering [11, p.472].

The legal framework in Germany mandates an enterprise-wide early-warning system:

1) Section 91(2) of the Stock-Corporation Act, enacted through the KonTraG (1998), obliges listed boards to detect developments that could threaten their going concern [12].
2) The StaRUG (effective January 1st, 2021) extends this duty to all limited-liability entities by requiring "continuous crisis detection" [10].

However, the key challenge remains that, although the StaRUG formally requires early-crisis detection, even for small private limited companies (GmbHs), enforcement still operates through civil and insolvency liability rather than administrative penalties. Accordingly, a GmbH that fails to establish such a system exposes itself to potential civil or insolvency claims and may incur less favourable insurance terms or downgraded ratings from banks and rating agencies.

The international guidelines refine the process. ISO 31000:2018 embeds risk management within governance structures, while Committee of Sponsoring Organizations of the Treadway Commission Enterprise Risk Management (COSO ERM) 2017 operationalises a four-step cycle of (i) Identify, (ii) Assess, (iii) Respond, and (iv) Monitor [13].

Following this tradition, Diederichs draws a clear line between risk management (strategic orientation) and risk controlling (information supply and steering). Risk controlling comprises (i) quantitative appraisal through scenario and sensitivity analyses, (ii) portfolio aggregation into metrics, such as Value at Risk, and (iii) stakeholder-specific reporting to boards and operational units [9].

This paper adopts this canonical four-phase model as its methodological basis, but focuses on a critical gap: digital threat scenarios. Recent German threat reports show high malware volumes and escalating breach costs. Traditional taxonomies must be expanded to encompass cyber risks, ensuring compliance with statutory requirements and alignment with evolving technological realities.

B. Multidimensional Controlling Concept by Reichmann

The multidimensional controlling concept developed by Thomas Reichmann is considered a reference model in German-language management control, because it integrates functional responsibilities, information logic, and time horizons within a single, coherent framework [14, pp. 21]. At its core, controlling is defined as an IT-supported, decision-oriented management service: every decision-maker should receive exactly the information that matches their task, planning horizon, and area of responsibility.

The model is built around a data cube with three orthogonal dimensions. (i) Functional view (e.g., cost- and profit-, financial, or procurement controlling) allocates information along the value chain and thus provides an impact-oriented perspective. (ii) Information categories separate monetary profit- and cash-flow figures from operational quantity and quality data, enabling quantitative metrics to be combined with qualitative early-warning indicators. (iii) Time horizons distinguish strategic, tactical, and operational scopes; consequently, short-term variance analyses and long-term trend observations can coexist within the same data model.

Reichmann links the cube to a three-level information pyramid to keep the data volume manageable [14, pp. 13]. On the accounting layer, raw booking and voucher data are captured. The reporting layer aggregates these into management reports featuring plan/actual comparisons. At the top, the key-figure layer compresses the data further into leading and structural ratios, among them the RL ratio system designed by Reichmann and Lachnit [14, p. 87], which provides rapid steering impulses. Data flow is strictly bottom-up for aggregation and top-down for target values, ensuring consistency between operational detail and strategic metrics.

The concept is practically relevant due to its integration blueprint, where each dimension assumes a distinct role in the IT architecture. Fact and dimension tables in a data warehouse map functions, information categories, and time horizons. Extract, Transformation and Load (ETL)-processes transport booking data up to the key-figure layer and dashboards. Planning, actual, and forecast values can therefore be compared across all levels without media or aggregation breaks. In practice, boards decide based on top-level KPIs (Return on Investment, working-capital ratio, etc.), while divisional managers drill down to variance reports. Meanwhile, operational controllers still work with itemized lists.

Finally, the concept supports early-warning and scenario analyses: qualitative indicators (e.g., Threats or market-trend signals) are stored as a distinct information category and can be combined with monetary KPIs. Organisations thus detect opportunities and risks earlier and can simulate response options before effects appear in the income statement.

In summary, Reichmann's multidimensional concept provides a robust bridge between a company's goal system and its technical implementation, allowing for traceable aggregation from primary data to key figures and providing role-specific access to the exact level of information granularity required for sound management decisions.

Reichmann's merit lies not only in having proposed a controlling framework in the mid-1980s, but also in designing it to stay compatible with future technologies and thus continuously extensible. Although conceived decades ago, the model is regularly adapted to new industries and technologies, allowing emerging controlling sub-disciplines, such as risk management, to be integrated without altering its core. For example, Drozdzynski embeds medical performance data and BI dashboards into the system- and application-layers of Reichmann's cube for a hospital context [15], while Liebe and Drozdzynski extend the framework to health-and-social-care organisations [16]. These adaptations demonstrate that the cube's general part remains comparable across sectors, whereas its special part can be customised with domain-specific metrics.

C. Balanced Chance & Risk Card

The Balanced Chance and Risk Card (BCRC) was introduced by Reichmann as an extension of the Balanced Scorecard (BSC) to meet the tighter German regulatory requirements for integrated risk management, such as KonTraG, at the beginning of the 2000s [17] [8]. Diederichs subsequently operationalised the concept for controlling practice and anchored it in the German "Controlling" journal [18]. The instrument combines value-based management, the BSC logic, and systematic opportunity-and-risk control within a single reporting artefact.

Several authors recommend a six-step implementation procedure: (i) define strategic goals per perspective, (ii) derive appropriate performance KPIs, (iii) identify and evaluate the main opportunities and risks (probability $\times$ impact), (iv) link KPIs with the respective opportunities/risks to obtain risk-adjusted targets and actuals, (v) specify measures, owners and milestones, and (vi) install a rolling review cycle (monthly or quarterly). This procedure merges strategy progress, risk exposure, and action effectiveness into a single management view.

While the BCRC is conceived as an entirely risk-oriented steering framework, recent applications mention cyber threats only in passing as a subset of generic operational risks and provide neither dedicated KRIs nor tailored control routines for them [18]. Considering the accelerating frequency, networked propagation and potentially existential financial impact of contemporary cyber incidents, it is timely and methodologically warranted to give cybersecurity risks disproportionate analytical weight within the BCRC [19]. Section II-D therefore examines the nature and managerial relevance of cybersecurity risks as a prerequisite for their systematic integration into the card.

D. Cybercrime & Cybersecurity

Recent research highlights the importance of integrating real-time Cyber Threat Intelligence (CTI) into dynamic risk management systems to enable situational awareness [20]. A semantic web technology-based architecture is introduced to create a dynamic risk assessment system at operational, tactical, and strategic levels [21]. A further development is the concept with an ontology-driven real-time risk management approach that encompasses anomaly detection and cataloging vulnerabilities [22]. The requirement for automated technologies to offer situational awareness solutions for National Cyber Operation Centers is pointed out by [23]. An example in practice suggests a Metrics Visualization System that can dynamically visualize network security incidents and correlate them with risk levels [24]. Collectively, these studies emphasize the potential for real-time, standardized operational cyber threat metrics to enhance decision-making across hierarchy levels, from administrators to the C-suite, through a more timely and accurate assessment of an organization's cybersecurity position.

CTI has proved to be an essential way of supplementing cybersecurity and risk management in organizations. CTI significantly increases threat detection, response, and risk management capability [25]. CTI provides evidence-based insight into the threats to facilitate proactive risk mitigation in critical infrastructure [26]. CTI can be integrated into campaigns for raising awareness against cyberattacks, especially in the banking sector, through the use of tactical, operational, and strategic intelligence [27] [20]. In response to the need for real-time risk analysis, a semantic-based architecture using Web Ontology Language (OWL) and Semantic Web Rule Language (SWRL) has been proposed, such as Structured Threat Information eXpression (STIX) v2.0 for the structured exchange of threat information [21]. Despite its advantages, there are barriers to CTI adoption, including technological constraints and the absence of executive sponsorship. These issues need to be overcome through extensive awareness programs, executive participation, and systematic training efforts [25].

III. A Cyber Risk-Oriented Extension of the Reichmann Framework

A. Limitations of Classical Risk Assessment Models in Cyber Contexts

Classical risk-assessment frameworks have challenges in cyber domains for four core reasons. First, scarce loss data leave actuarial or scenario models without reliable frequency and severity inputs citeElingSchnell2022. Second, traffic-light heat maps compress complex threats into ordinal colours, masking value at stake and skewing priorities [28]. Third, adversarial tactics evolve weekly, so annual risk registers are inappropriate, as European Union Agency for Cybersecurity (ENISA) 2024 survey warns [29]. Fourth, cloud and supply-chain interdependence creates cascade-prone losses; single-asset Value at Risk (VaR) thus understates extremes [30]. Embedding cyber KRIs in Reichmann's multi-dimensional controlling framework, especially into the BCR-Card, ties exposure to profitability-liquidity goals and helps close these gaps.

B. A Structured Controlling Concept for Cyber Metrics

Modern organisations face data overload and goal conflicts. An integrated controlling concept mitigates both by

(i) aligning metrics with strategic objectives, (ii) enforcing a common language for financial and non-financial data, and (iii) enabling transparent, audit-ready decision trails [31, pp. 7] [32, pp. 5]. Research shows that companies with coherent management-control systems achieve higher decision quality and risk resilience than those using ad-hoc indicator sets [33, pp. 30].

Applying this logic to cybersecurity avoids metric issues: isolated dashboards might track patch rates or incident counts, yet without linkage to profitability and liquidity, they lack managerial traction. Embedding cyber-risk KPIs into Reichmann's cube – e.g., as an additional information category on the system layer – ensures goal congruence (security spend vs. value at risk), comparability (cross-unit benchmarking), and governance compliance (StaRUG early-warning duties). Hence, a structured concept is not academic ornamentation but a prerequisite for turning raw cyber data into actionable, strategy-consistent steering information.

The proposed framework introduces cyber resilience as a fifth dimension besides the well-known four dimensions: finance, growth, internal processes, and customer/market. Clear roles and responsibilities ensure accountability, like the Chief Executive Officer (CEO)/ Chief Financial Officer(CFO) owns capital allocation and is in charge of gaining profitability and driving financial return. The top management, e.g., Vice President Sales (VPS), owns the Market/Customer perspective. The Chief Information Security Officer (CISO) operates the technical control loop and supplies metrics alongside the perspective *cyber resilience*. The following concept will not discuss the steering capabilities of the balanced scorecard in general, but will focus on the steering levers in the field of cyber risk management.

C. Extension Modules for the Cyber Risk-Oriented BCRC

Building on the original BCRC, five enhancements build a foundation in the context of handling cyber risks:

1) Add a dedicated **Cyber Resilience** perspective. This fifth view elevates cyber threats to the same strategic level as Finance, Customer, Process and Learning, following the Balanced Scorecard logic already adopted by security leaders.
2) Embed **cyber-specific KRIs** into every perspective. Examples include CyVaR under Finance, Customer-trust indices under Customer/Market, Mean Time to Patch for Processes, and secure-coding coverage in Learning.
3) **Cross-walk** each KRI to NIST Cybersecurity Framework (CSF 2.0). Mapping metrics to the Identify-Protect-Detect-Respond-Recover-Govern functions provides audit-ready consistency and international comparability.
4) Introduce a **scenario- and stress-test layer**. A cyber scenario sheet quantifies best-likely-worst losses and mirrors the board-level logic of a cyber-risk balance sheet.
5) Apply **dynamic weighting and alerting**. Weekly (or faster) refreshes of KRI scores from Security Operations Center (SOC) telemetry, threat intelligence feeds, and vulnerability scanners keep the BCRC heat-map aligned with the shifting threat landscape.

D. KPIs in Cybersecurity

A tiered KPI system is essential, aligning *strategic KPIs* for top management with *operational metrics* for CISOs, middle management, and IT administrators to effectively integrate cybersecurity into corporate steering, particularly in SMEs.

Strategic KPIs, such as the CyVaR, Expected Annual Loss, or a Cyber Resilience Index, translate technical risks into financial terms [34] [8]. These figures support board-level steering decisions and ensure compliance with regulatory duties, such as those mandated by the StaRUG, which requires continuous monitoring of existential threats [10].

Operational KPIs, including (MTTD), Mean Time to Respond (MTTR), and Patch Compliance Rate, measure the effectiveness of technical controls. A decreasing MTTD, for example, indicates faster breach detection, while increasing patch compliance reflects reduced vulnerability exposure [28] [35]. These indicators, typically monitored via SOC dashboards, inform tactical actions and feed into higher-level summaries.

A *role-specific allocation* of KPIs ensures managerial relevance: while C-levels need aggregated dashboards on residual risk, CISOs interpret trends in departmental exposure, and SOC staff focus on technical telemetry. Reichmann's multidimensional controlling model supports this by aggregating data bottom-up while cascading targets top-down [14].

KPIs should map onto international standards to ensure auditability and governance alignment. The NIST CSF 2.0 recommends outcome-based metrics across its core functions (Identify, Protect, Detect, Respond, Recover, Govern) [36] [37], while ISO/IEC 27001 and ISO/IEC 27004 call for structured monitoring and evaluation of Information Security Management System (ISMS) performance [38]. Mapping MTTD to "Detect" or patch compliance to "Protect" enhances traceability and facilitates compliance checks.

We propose a practical KPI pyramid logic:

1) **Strategic layer (CEO/CFO):** e.g., CyVaR, residual cyber risk index, compliance readiness.
2) **Tactical layer (CISO/Chief Information Officer (CIO):** e.g., maturity scores, awareness coverage, open vulnerabilities.
3) **Operational layer (SOC/Admin):** e.g., phishing susceptibility, patch latency, intrusion attempts.

At the base, CTI provides real-time data (e.g., vulnerability alerts, attack vector trends) [25] [21]. These are aggregated into composite indicators, such as a Threat Intelligence Index, which informs middle and upper management of current threat exposure and supports adaptive countermeasures.

Furthermore, distinguishing between *gross (inherent)* and *residual (net)* cyber risk is essential. This enables management to assess the effectiveness of existing controls. For example, if the inherent ransomware risk is high, but the residual risk is low due to segmentation and offline backups, no immediate investment is needed. German legal standards under

KonTraG and StaRUG explicitly require this level of risk quantification [12] [10].

In summary, embedding cyber KPIs into a multidimensional controlling system bridges technical telemetry and strategic steering. For SMEs, this approach is not only methodologically sound but regulatory-aligned, promoting a risk-aware leadership culture with measurable security accountability.

E. The Balanced Chance & Cyber Risk Card

Table I translates Reichmann's multidimensional framework into a five-perspective dashboard that makes cyber risks "board-ready". Each perspective shows *value drivers* (KPI) and *residual-risk indicator* (KRI). The Finance row anchors the card with the Return on Capital Employed (ROCE) [14, p. 131] and the ratio EAL/Earnings Before Interest and Taxes (EBIT), while *CyVaR95%-intensity* expresses cyber exposure to the revenue [39]. Market & Customer links digital availability to loyalty by pairing the Net-Promoter-Score with service downtime. Internal Processes connects OEE to vulnerability management. Learning & Growth captures the human attack surface; and the dedicated Cyber-Resilience view merges technical readiness (MTTR, MTTD) with an aggregate Cyber-Resilience-Index [29]. Horizons (strategic, tactical, operational) follow Reichmann's time axis, ensuring that indicators are reported at the level where they can be acted upon.

All KPIs/KRIs should use a three-step traffic-light logic. The limits depend on the branch and the individual business, but as a rule of thumbs, one can firstly go with the following suggestion:

- **Green:** on or better than target;
- **Yellow:** target–10% (warning);
- **Red:** $\geq$ 10% deviation, triggering an escalation to the next management tier and a liquidity stress-test in line with StaRUG early-warning duties.

F. Illustrative Cause–Effect Chains

Chain 1: Patch backlog → Production efficiency → Financial impact: A rising patch latency (Red at >14 days) increases exploit probability; the resulting micro-outages degrade OEE. Each OEE point lost raises unit cost by 0.4%, reducing ROCE and lifting CyVaR95%. If CyVaR passes the 5%-of-revenue threshold, the Finance cell flips to Yellow, prompting additional patch sprints and a review of the cyber-insurance cap.

Chain 2: Phishing awareness → Incident detection → Resilience: Quarterly awareness training pushes the phishing click-rate below 5% (Green). MTTD for phishing drops from 48h to 12h, which, with unchanged MTTR, cuts the Cyber Resilience Index gap by 7 points. When the index exceeds the 80-point target, the Resilience perspective turns Green, signalling sufficient buffer to keep CyVaR and EAL/EBIT within Finance targets.

These chains demonstrate how the BCCR-Card connects technical metrics to profitability and liquidity, enabling top management to prioritise cyber investments on a value-at-risk basis while satisfying the integrative control logic advocated by Reichmann.

IV. Discussion and Outlook

The BCCR-Card integrates cyber exposure to Reichmann's profitability–liquidity logic, yet several reservations remain. First, the proposal models frequencies and loss-severities; data scarcity and under-reporting continue to limit the statistical confidence of CyVaR and EAL estimates [39]. Second, the traffic-light logic simplifies dynamic attack surfaces into discrete states; abrupt threshold effects may hide early trend deterioration. Third, transferring the card across industries requires recalibrating KPIs/KRIs, e.g., patch latency is less relevant for cloud-natives than for Operational Technology (OT) environments, which challenges cross-company benchmarking.

Future research should focus on four components: (i) *Empirical validation*: multi-case studies that track KPI/KRI trajectories over 12-18 months could test whether red-or-yellow signals indeed precede financial variance. (ii) *Automated data feeds*: integrating Security Information and Event Management (SIEM) and Enterprise Resource Planning (ERP) streams via Application Programming Interfaces (APIs) will reveal how latency and data-quality issues distort CRI and CyVaR. (iii) *Artificial Intelligence (AI)-driven scenario generation*: Large Language Models could widen the threat catalogue beyond historical events and improve tail-risk estimation. (iv) *ESG-Cyber overlaps*: regulators increasingly frame cybersecurity as a governance pillar; embedding ESG metrics into the BCCR-Card would extend its relevance for integrated reporting. Addressing these gaps will raise the explanatory power of the card and help verify whether the hypothesised cause–and–effect chains hold across organisational contexts [33] [29].

V. SME Adoption, Generalizability, and Lessons Learned

This section offers a concise methodology for SMEs, discusses generalizability beyond the German context, and summarizes lessons learned alongside future technical work from applying the BCCR-Card.

A. Methodology for SME Adoption

Effective use of the BCCR-Card starts with clear ownership and cadence at C-level, typically shared between finance and security leadership (e.g., CFO and CISO), with a monthly review focused on decisions rather than dashboards. Organizations select a small set of indicators. Ideally, no more than two per perspective to preserve attention on what moves value and resilience. Each indicator is defined in one sentence (scope, unit, and aggregation), assigned a single quarterly target, and governed by stable green/yellow/red thresholds to allow trend interpretation. A minimal measurement layer reuses existing sources such as ticketing, endpoint management, SIEM, and backup reports, complemented by plausibility checks and

TABLE I
THE BALANCED CHANCE & CYBER RISK CARD

Perspective	Responsability	Horizon	KPI/KRI	Target
Finance	CEO / CFO	strategic *> 3 Years*	ROCE CyVaR95%-intensity EAL / EBIT	ROCE $\geq$ 10% CyVaR95 $\leq$ 5% EAL / EBIT $\leq$ 10%
Market & Customer	Top Management	strategic-tactical *1-3 Years*	Net Promoter Score (NPS) Service downtime per customer (in min/yr)	NPS $\geq$ 60 Downtime $\leq$ 30 min
Internal Processes	Middle Management	tactical-operational *Quarter-1 Year*	Overall Equipment Effectiveness (OEE) Patch latency of critical systems (in days) Patch-Compliance-Rate (PCR)	OEE $\geq$ 85% Latency $\leq$ 14d PCR $\geq$ 95%
Learning & Growth	Team Level	operational *month-year*	Training hours per employee and year Phishing click-through rate (in %)	$\geq$ 24h $\leq$ 5%
Cyber Resilience	CISO & IT ops	operational-strategic *Day-Year*	Cyber Resilience Index (CRI) MTTR MTTD Backup-restore success rate (in %)	$\geq$ 80% MTTR $\leq$ 2h MTTD $\leq$ 24h $\geq$ 98%

temporary proxies where data coverage is incomplete. Two tabletop scenarios (e.g., ransomware and supplier outage) are used to translate operational signals into financial exposure via EAL and CyVaR. Approved actions are tracked against loss reduction and expenses, with quarterly reporting of EAL/EBIT and the ROCE of controls. In practice, SMEs can achieve a viable first loop within 90 days by fixing ownership and thresholds, assembling a single-page card with the most accessible data, running two scenarios, and replacing estimates with measured values as coverage improves.

B. Generalizability

While our examples reference German regulation, the design itself widely adopted frameworks (NIST CSF and ISO/IEC 27001) and governance principles compatible with COSO ERM. Sector characteristics primarily affect indicator choice (e.g., they choose the KPI liquidity ratio instead of ROCE) and data availability. The cause–and–effect logic and the financial coupling through EAL and CyVaR remain invariant. Very small companies can reduce scope to a single value stream without undermining the control logic.

C. Lessons Learned and Challenges

Across pilots, too many indicators weaken focus, frequent threshold changes flasify trends, and incomplete telemetry invites false precision if point estimates are reported without ranges. Persistently red signals require explicit decision mapping, a quick fix, structural control, or risk acceptance, to avoid loss. Finally, finance and security communities use different vocabularies. The BCCR-Card works as a shared language when explanations stay close to economics and risk awareness.

VI. CONCLUSION AND FUTURE WORK

This study presents the Balanced Chance & Cyber-Risk Card as a novel extension of Reichmann's multidimensional controlling framework, addressing a critical gap in cyber risk integration for German SMEs. By embedding cyber-specific Key Risk Indicators and Key Performance Indicators into a five-dimensional control structure, the model enables a seamless translation of technical security telemetry into strategic, tactical, and operational steering metrics. The framework aligns with regulatory imperatives, such as StaRUG, ISO 31000, and NIST CSF 2.0, ensuring compliance-readiness while enhancing auditability and executive decision-making.

Through role-specific dashboards, cause–effect chains, and scenario-based stress testing, the BCCR-Card enables the C-suite to quantify cyber resilience and align investments with value-at-risk priorities. It makes cybersecurity a core component of enterprise performance management. The framework offers a basis for empirical validation, AI-driven scenarios, and ESG integration. Ultimately, the BCCR-Card embeds cyber risk into measurable, board-level control-bridging financial steering with digital threat management.

REFERENCES

[1] Bundeskriminalamt, "Bundeslagebild Cybercrime 2024 [Federal Situation Report Cybercrime 2024]," Bundeskriminalamt, Wiesbaden, Germany, Tech. Rep., Jun. 2025, [retrieved: July, 2025]. [Online]. Available: https://www.bka.de/DE/AktuelleInformationen/StatistikenLagebilder/Lagebilder/Cybercrime/2024/CC_2024.html

[2] Bitkom e. V., "Wirtschaftsschutz 2024 - Cybercrime in der deutschen Wirtschaft [Economic Protection 2024 - Cybercrime in the German Economy]," Bitkom e. V., Berlin, Germany, Tech. Rep., Aug. 2024, [retrieved: July, 2025]. [Online]. Available: https://www.bitkom.org/Presse/Presseinformation/Angriffe-auf-die-deutsche-Wirtschaft-nehmen-zu

[3] Bundesamt für Sicherheit in der Informationstechnik, "Die Lage der IT-Sicherheit in Deutschland 2024 [The State of IT Security in Germany 2024]," Bundesamt für Sicherheit in der Informationstechnik, Bonn, Germany, Tech. Rep., Nov. 2024, [retrieved: July, 2025]. [Online]. Available: https://www.bsi.bund.de/SharedDocs/Downloads/DE/BSI/Publikationen/Lageberichte/Lagebericht2024.html?nn=129410

[4] IBM Security, "Cost of a Data Breach Report 2024," IBM Security, Armonk, NY, USA, Tech. Rep., 2024, [retrieved: July, 2025]. [Online]. Available: https://www.ibm.com/reports/data-breach

[5] Hiscox, "Cyber Readiness Report 2024," Hiscox Ltd., London, U.K., Tech. Rep., 2024, [retrieved: July, 2025]. [Online]. Available: https://hiscoxdedrupal.prod.acquia-sites.com/sites/default/files/documents/hiscox-cyber-readiness-report-2024.pdf

[6] Horváth & Partners Management Consultants, "CFO Study 2024: The CFO's Path to a data Driven Company," Horváth & Partners, Stuttgart, Tech. Rep., Jul. 2024, [retrieved: July, 2025]].

[Online]. Available: https://www.horvath-partners.com/en/media-center/studies/cfo-study-2024-the-cfos-path-to-a-data-driven-company

[7] T. Reichmann and S. Form, "Balanced Chance- and Risk-Management," *Controlling – Zeitschrift für erfolgsorientierte Unternehmenssteuerung*, vol. 12, no. 4/5, pp. 189–198, 2000.

[8] T. Reichmann, "Die Balanced Chance- and Risk-Card: Eine Erweiterung der Balanced Scorecard [The Balanced Chance and Risk Card: An Extension of the Balanced Scorecard]," in *Risikomanagement nach dem KonTraG – Aufgaben und Chancen aus betriebswirtschaftlicher und juristischer Sicht*, K. W. Lange and F. Wall, Eds. München: Franz Vahlen, 2001, pp. 282–303.

[9] M. Diederichs, *Risikomanagement und Risikocontrolling [Risk Management and Risk Controlling]*, 5th ed. München: Franz Vahlen, 2023.

[10] Bundesrepublik Deutschland, "Gesetz über den Stabilisierungs- und Restrukturierungsrahmen für Unternehmen (Unternehmensstabilisierungs- und -restrukturierungsgesetz – StaRUG) [Law on the Stabilization and Restructuring Framework for Companies (Corporate Stabilization and Restructuring Act – StaRUG)]," Bundesgesetzblatt I, Nr. 66, 29. Dez. 2020, S. 3256–3340, Dec. 2020, [retrieved: July, 2025]. [Online]. Available: https://www.gesetze-im-internet.de/starug/BJNR325610020.html

[11] P. Hopkin and C. Thompson, *Fundamentals of Risk Management: Understanding, Evaluating and Implementing Effective Enterprise Risk Management*, 6th ed. London: Kogan Page, 2022.

[12] Bundesrepublik Deutschland, "Aktiengesetz (AktG) [Stock Corporation Act]," Bundesgesetzblatt I 1965, S. 1089; zuletzt geändert durch Art. 1 Gesetz vom 21. Dez. 2023, BGBl. I 2023 Nr. 394, Sep. 1965, [retrieved: July, 2025]. [Online]. Available: https://www.gesetze-im-internet.de/aktg/BJNR010890965.html

[13] *Risk Management-Guidelines (ISO 31000:2018)*, International Organization for Standardization Std., Feb. 2018.

[14] T. Reichmann, M. Kißler, and U. Baumöl, *Controlling mit Kennzahlen: Die systemgestützte Controlling-Konzeption [Controlling with Key Figures: The System-Supported Controlling Concept]*, 9th ed. München: Franz Vahlen, 2017.

[15] M. Drozdzynski, *Das neue Business Intelligence-gestuetze Krankenhaus-Controlling [The New Business Intelligence-Supported Hospital Controlling]*. Baden-Baden: Nomos, 2020.

[16] M. Liebe and M. Drozdzynski, "IT-gestützte Ausgestaltung einer GeSo-spezifischen mehrdimensionalen Controlling-Konzeption [IT-Supported Design of a Health and Social Care-Specific Multidimensional Controlling Concept]," *Controlling – Zeitschrift für erfolgsorientierte Unternehmenssteuerung*, vol. 30, no. 4, pp. 31–40, 2018.

[17] R. S. Kaplan and D. P. Norton, "The Balanced Scorecard – Measures That Drive Performance," *Harvard Business Review*, vol. 70, no. 1, pp. 71–79, 1992.

[18] M. Diederichs, "Balanced Chance- & Risk-Card," *Controlling*, vol. 16, no. 12, pp. 703–705, 2004.

[19] ISACA. (2024, Apr.) How CISOs Can Take Advantage of the Balanced Scorecard Method. [retrieved: July, 2025]. [Online]. Available: https://www.isaca.org/resources/news-and-trends/industry-news/2024/how-cisos-can-take-advantage-of-the-balanced-scorecard-method

[20] A. Lawall and P. Beenken, "A Threat-Led Approach to Mitigating Ransomware Attacks: Insights from a Comprehensive Analysis of the Ransomware Ecosystem," in *Proceedings of the 2024 European Interdisciplinary Cybersecurity Conference*, ser. EICC '24, S. Li, K. Coopamootoo, and M. Sirivianos, Eds. New York, NY, USA: Association for Computing Machinery, 2024, pp. 210–216. [Online]. Available: https://doi.org/10.1145/3655693.3661321

[21] R. Riesco and V. A. Villagrá, "Leveraging cyber threat intelligence for a dynamic risk framework: Automation by using a semantic reasoner and a new combination of standards (stix™, swrl and owl)," *International Journal of Information Security*, vol. 18, no. 6, pp. 715–739, 2019.

[22] C. Sánchez-Zas, V. A. Villagrá, M. Vega-Barbas, X. Larriva-Novo, J. I. Moreno, and J. Berrocal, "Ontology-based approach to real-time risk management and cyber-situational awareness," *Future Generation Computer Systems*, vol. 141, pp. 462–472, 2023.

[23] R. Graf, F. Skopik, and K. Whitebloom, "A decision support model for situational awareness in national cyber operations centers," in *2016 international conference on cyber situational awareness, data analytics and assessment (CyberSA)*. IEEE, 2016, pp. 1–6.

[24] T. Väisänen, S. Noponen, O.-M. Latvala, and J. Kuusijärvi, "Combining real-time risk visualization and anomaly detection," in *Proceedings of the 12th European Conference on Software Architecture: Companion Proceedings*, 2018, pp. 1–7.

[25] J. Smallman, "The effectiveness of cyber threat intelligence in improving security operations," *Journal of Artificial Intelligence General science (JAIGS) ISSN:3006-4023*, vol. 5, no. 1, p. 189–209, Jul. 2024. [Online]. Available: https://ojs.boulibrary.com/index.php/JAIGS/article/view/193

[26] H. Kure and S. Islam, "Cyber threat intelligence for improving cybersecurity and risk management in critical infrastructure," *Journal of Universal Computer Science*, vol. 25, no. 11, pp. 1478–1502, 2019.

[27] R. A. Firdaus, N. A. Rakhmawati, and F. Samopa, "A state-of-the-art review of cyber threat intelligence awareness programs in mitigating bank cyber attacks," in *2024 IEEE International Symposium on Consumer Technology (ISCT)*. IEEE, 2024, pp. 648–654.

[28] S. Myerson, "Why Heat Maps Fail for Cybersecurity Risk Management," Gartner, Inc., Research Note G00734212, September 2023.

[29] European Union Agency for Cybersecurity (ENISA), "ENISA Threat Landscape 2024," Athens, Tech. Rep., 2024, [retrieved: July, 2025]. [Online]. Available: https://www.enisa.europa.eu/publications/enisa-threat-landscape-2024

[30] M. Eling, U. Kühn, and H. Gruber, "Modelling Systemic Cyber Risk: Accumulation and Cascade Effects in Interconnected IT Ecosystems," *Journal of Risk Finance*, vol. 24, no. 1, pp. 1–26, 2023.

[31] R. N. Anthony and V. Govindarajan, *Management Control Systems*, 13th ed. New York: McGraw-Hill Education, 2017.

[32] R. Simons, *Levers of Control: How Managers Use Innovative Control Systems to Drive Strategic Renewal*. Boston: Harvard Business School Press, 1995.

[33] K. A. Merchant and W. A. V. der Stede, *Management Control Systems: Performance Measurement, Evaluation and Incentives*, 5th ed. Harlow: Pearson, 2021.

[34] A. Orlando, "Cyber risk quantification: Investigating the role of cyber value at risk," *Risks*, vol. 9, no. 10, p. 184, 2021.

[35] D. S. D. White, "Limiting vulnerability exposure through effective patch management: threat mitigation through vulnerability remediation," Ph.D. dissertation, Rhodes University, 2006.

[36] J. Edwards, *A comprehensive guide to the NIST cybersecurity framework 2.0: Strategies, implementation, and best practice*. John Wiley & Sons, 2024.

[37] "NIST Cybersecurity Framework 2.0 (Draft)," 2024, [retrieved: July, 2025]. [Online]. Available: https://www.nist.gov/cyberframework

[38] "ISO/IEC 27004: Information security management – Monitoring, measurement, analysis and evaluation," [retrieved: July, 2025]. [Online]. Available: https://www.iso.org/standard/73906.html

[39] M. Eling and W. Schnell, "Ten Key Questions for Cyber Risk Modelling: A Systematic Review and Research Agenda," *The Geneva Papers on Risk and Insurance-Issues and Practice*, vol. 47, no. 3, pp. 366–401, 2022.

Supporting the Security Modelling in Operational Technology by identifying capacities of Hidden Channels in ICS protocols

Robert Altschaffel, Sönke Otten, Stefan Kiltz, Jana Dittmann
Otto-von-Guericke University of Magdeburg
Magdeburg, Germany
e-mail: firstname.lastname@ovgu.de

***Abstract*—A domain affected by a rising threat landscape is Operational Technology (OT) and adjacent cyber-physical domains like Internet of Things (IoT). With the increased threat to OT, the need for security modelling in this domain grows. Security modelling requires reliable data about attack vectors and threats for optimal results. In this paper, we want to contribute to this data by presenting our approach to model the capacity of hidden channels in the OT-domain. This modelling is based on the systematic exploration of hidden channels in the MQTT network protocol, the creation of dedicated tools and the resulting data sets in order to investigate the capacity of these hidden channels within a control network. The approach is used to identify the capacity for 5 hidden channels usable in the MQTT protocol.**

***Keywords*-security modeling; iot; hidden channels.**

I. INTRODUCTION

Industrial Control Systems (ICS) are facing rising threats, as shown by the trends identified in [1]. ICS are also, commonly referred to as Operational Technology (OT), are characterized by directly affecting physical processes. Hence, when an ICS is attacked, the result might endanger the safety of all the entities in the sphere of influence of the respective ICS. Actors posing as Advanced and Persistent Threats (APTs) play a significant role in this threat scenario (as demonstrated in [1]).

Advanced threat actors also use advanced techniques like hidden channels for aspects like malware infiltration, exfiltration of confidential data or command and control. This is exemplified by the inclusion of the technique *Data Obfuscation: Steganography* in the MITRE ATT&CK Matrix [2] and continuing overhauls. Another example is the widely-spread malware campaign SteganoAmor [3].

To protect against this threat, awareness and correct identification of the extent of danger originating from a threat are required. This includes the modelling of security and threats. Such security modelling requires reliable data about attack vectors and threats for optimal results. In this paper, we want to contribute to this data by presenting our approach to model the capacity of hidden channels in the OT-domain. This modelling is based on the systematic exploration of hidden channels in the Message Queuing Telemetry Transport (MQTT) network protocol [4] widely used in OT, the creation of dedicated tools and the resulting data sets in order to investigate the capacity of these hidden channels within a control network. The approach identifies the capacity for 5 hidden channels usable in the MQTT protocol and discusses countermeasures against these channels.

This paper is structured as follows: Section II will present some fundamentals. Section III describes the approach to identify the capacity of hidden channels as a foundation for security modelling after providing an overview on hidden channels in MQTT. Section IV discusses the technical implementation of the capacity measurement. Section V presents the results of the theoretical and practical considerations. Section VI discusses countermeasures against the hidden channels presented in this work. Section VII provides a summary and an outlook on future work.

II. STATE OF THE ART

This section provides a brief overview on the terminology of hidden channels, hidden channels in ICS protocols and a brief overview on MQTT.

A. Hidden channels

Hidden Channels describe the use of techniques for hiding the communication altogether. This is often referred to as steganography. In general terms, a hidden message is concealed within legitimate cover communication.

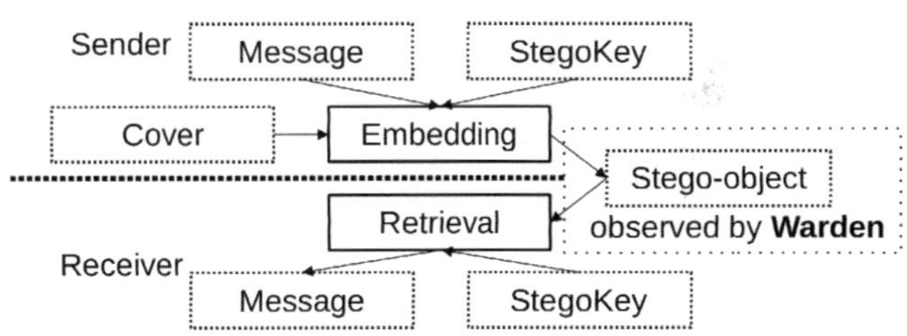

Figure 1. Entities and pipeline for concealed communication using a hidden channel

Figure 1 provides an overview on the general communication. On the sender side, a message is embedded into a Cover object. This process is parametrized by a StegoKey, which might include information about, e.g., embedding position or encoding. The resulting Stego-object is then transferred to the receiver of the message. The warden embodies the position of any security mechanism investigating the cover channel. The receiver then uses the knowledge of the StegoKey to obtain the message.

B. ICS and MQTT fundamentals

ICS control processes in the physical world by measuring them with sensors, affecting them with actuators and using computing units to process sensor readings into control commands for the actuators. The same fundamentals hold true for the domain of IoT; the primary difference being the scale and objectives. In each case, such control networks rely on regular communication between these components using specialized protocols. For this paper, we use MQTT [4], which is a simple and compact protocol used in broad range of applications usually evolving around measuring (and potentially controlling) physical processes.

MQTT employs a client-server structure. Clients (**MQTT Clients**) connect to a server (**MQTT Broker**) and send or receive messages assigned to specific **Topics**. Clients regularly sending such messages to a given topic are sometimes referred to as **Publishers**. Messages are received by clients by subscribing to a specific topic. The Broker forwards any message by legitimate publisher to any client, which is referred to as a **Subscriber**.

C. Hidden Channels in ICS Protocols

Generalized hidden channels in network communication are described as patterns in [5]. These patterns are applied to the domain of ICS protocols in [6]. Closely following the concepts described in [5], [6] describes two primary groups - covert timing channels and covert storage channels.

The covert timing channels include 8 of the overall 18 patterns. All of these 8 patterns create a covert channel in common traffic by using different techniques for altering the timing of messages. Therefore, they transmit the hidden data trough e.g., manipulating the timing of massages or packets.

The covert storage channels manipulate the data transmitted in order to enable a hidden communication. This data could include header fields or certain aspects of the legitimate payload.

III. Identifying the Capacity of Hidden Channels in MQTT as a Foundation for Security Modelling

This section describes our approach to discern the capacity of hidden channels in MQTT.

A. Hidden channels in MQTT

The systematic approach presented in [6] can be an applied to the MQTT and leads to the identification of a set of potential patterns viable for hidden communication.

This feasibility is based on two essential aspects:

- The ability to implement a proof of concept of this pattern within the MQTT protocol. Specifically, the question is whether this pattern can be implemented at all in the MQTT protocol. An example of this would be the patterns **S4: Random Value**. This pattern uses a random value in the metadata of a message to fill it with pseudo-randomized values in order to encode the hidden message. However, this is not possible in MQTT, since MQTT does not contain metadata with random values (unlike, for example, TCP/Modbus).
- The feasibility also refers to the use of the implemented pattern under real-world conditions or in real deployment scenarios. A good example of this is **T6: Retransmission**. This pattern encodes the hidden message through artificial retransmissions. It is very easy to implement in MQTT, but it is difficult to use under real-world conditions, since natural retransmissions occur very frequently in those environments.

This investigation and the technical details of the specific patterns are beyond the scope of this paper - an overview on the results is presented in Figure 2.

Pattern from Mazurczyk et al. (2018)		Findings for MQTT	
ID	Pattern	Feasibility under optimal conditions	Realistic applicability
T1	Inter-packet Times	easy	hard
T2	Message Timing	easy	hard
T3	Rate/ Throughput	medium	hard
T4	Artificial Loss	medium	hard
T5	Message Ordering	easy	medium
T6	Retransmis-sion	easy	medium-hard
T7	Frame Collision	not possible	not possible
T8	Temperature	not possible	not possible
S1	Size Modulation	not possible	not possible
S2	Sequence Modulation	not possible	not possible
S3	Add Redundancy	not possible	not possible
S4	Random Value	not possible	not possible
S5	Value Modulation	easy	hard
S6	Reserved/ Unused	not possible	not possible
S7	Payload Field Size Modulation	easy	easy-medium
S8	User-data Corruption	easy	medium
S9	Modify Redundancy	hard	not possible
S 10	User-Data Value Modulation and Reserved/	easy	easy

Figure 2. Results of the systematic approach from [6] based on [5] applied to MQTT. 10 hidden channels are identified as potentially viable.

In this work, we focus on the steps necessary to discern the capacity of the following 5 patterns selected from those deemed viable:

- **T2: Message Timing**
  The "Message Timing" pattern describes a technique that uses variations in the timing of messages to encode hidden information. In MQTT, the Publisher can modify this timing by altering the intervals between messages and the frequency with which they are sent.
- **T5: Message Ordering**
  The "Message Ordering" pattern transmits hidden information by altering the sequence of packets or messages within a communication flow. In MQTT, the Publisher can modify the arrangement of messages quite easily to encode such hidden data.
- **T6: Retransmission**
  The "Retransmission" pattern encodes hidden information through artificial retransmissions. In MQTT, this can be implemented quite easily while it introduces challenges. Retransmissions also occur naturally in real-world scenarios. As a result, distinguishing between intentional and naturally occurring retransmissions can make decoding the hidden message difficult.
- **S7: Payload Field Size Modulation**
  This pattern encodes hidden information by altering the size of the payload field. In MQTT, the payload field size is not explicitly defined in the protocol metadata. It depends on the chosen data type for transmission. However, this technique can still be implemented in a modified form by changing the actual size of the payload. For example, in an MQTT-based temperature measurement, additional decimal places could be added to subtly increase the payload size and encode hidden data.
- **S10: User-data Value Modulation and Reserved/Unused**
  This pattern encodes hidden information by modifying the payload in a way that is not significant or visible in the actual data. This is typically achieved by altering the least significant bits (LSBs) of the payload data. In real-world MQTT applications, the transmitted data usually consists of sensor measurements. Therefore, modifying the LSB of, for example, a temperature reading can be done quite easily and remains very unobtrusive.

B. *Identifying the capacity of Hidden Channels*

The capacity of hidden channels can be evaluated by using theoretical analysis and confirmed by practical evaluation results.

1) Theoretical Analysis of the capacity of Hidden Channels: The theoretical analysis involves the investigation of the specific pattern. The following questions serve as a baseline:

- **Identifying the type of message providing capacity** As a first step, the type of messages used for the encoding of the steganographic messages are identified. This could be messages only transmitted once per connection (e.g., messages during the establishment of a connection), multiple times (e.g., messages used to perform a more common occurrence, like subscribing to a specific topic in the case of MQTT) or messages that occur with every sensor reading transmitted.
- **Quantifying the occurrence of the type of messages providing capacity** The occurrence of the specific message for a given scenario is quantified, e.g., how often is a sensor reading being transmitted.
- **Identifying the capacity within a single message** After the amount of available messages is identified, the capacity within a single message is determined.

With these questions answered, the theoretical capacity of a hidden channel can be calculated by multiplying the occurrence of the type of messages providing capacity with the individual capacity of these messages.

2) Practical analysis of the capacity of hidden channels: The theoretical capacity requires confirmation and refinement using practical tests. These are also useful to identify special cases within a given communication scenario. For this, we chose a common application for the MQTT protocol in the context of IoT: climate control.

The transmission of steganographic messages within this use case is monitored. The basic structure of the test consists of 3 components:

- A temperature sensor acting as Publisher that is also acting as Sender and as such embeds the hidden message into the transmission of temperature readings which are used as Cover,
- A Broker,
- A thermostat acting as Subscriber and Receiver of the hidden message.

This setup is connected using a common network switch to create a closed network to prevent unwanted influences (e.g., packet loss, third-party network traffic). With this setup, a steganographic message of 1000 symbols is transmitted and the duration of the transmission monitored.

IV. Measuring the Capacity

Following this general outline, the test procedure is as follows: For every pattern we run two tests with different cover datasets (**CD**) as cover data. **CD1** and **CD2** each contain 1000 temperature measurements, which are collected from a real temperature sensor for a realistic variance in the measurements. This allows for an increased repeatability of the test.

During the communication between Publisher, Broker and Subscriber, the test data is collected on the device running the Broker software by using network capturing software (this setup is shown in Figure 3). In addition, the retrieved hidden message on the receiver end is obtained and compared against the embedded hidden message on the sender end to evaluate successful embedding and retrieval.

A. *Technical Implementation*

The following section outlines and explains the technical details, such as the selection of hardware and software. The aim of this section is to ensure both the traceability of the decisions made during the hardware and software selection process and the reproducibility of the experiment.

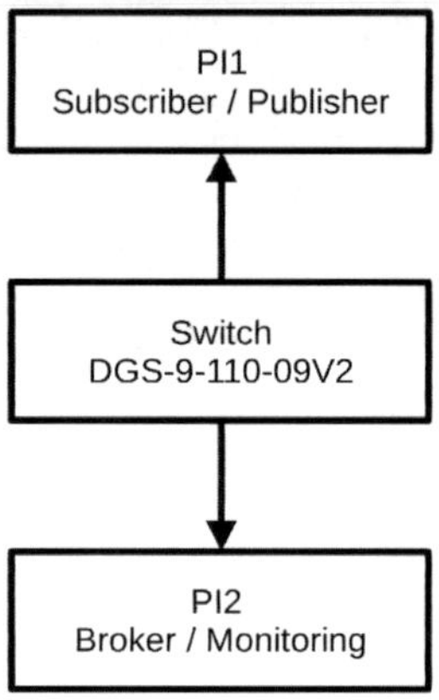

Figure 3. Setup of the test environment for the practical measurements of the capacity of the hidden channels in MQTT.

The following hardware components are chosen: A Raspberry Pi 3 is selected for both the Publisher and the Subscriber, as this device meets the technical requirements and offers a simple and accessible user interface. A Raspberry Pi 4 is used to monitor network traffic and to run the Broker. Additionally, to provide a closed network, a D-Link DGS-1100-09V2 switch is used, which features a monitoring port for observing network traffic.

The Publisher and Subscriber are located on the same device. This does not pose a problem, as the MQTT architecture allows publishers and subscribers to communicate independently with the Broker. There is no direct logical connection between the Publisher and the Subscriber; only between each client and the Broker. There for the Publisher and Subscriber communicate independently with the Broker. The Broker itself operates independently and serves as a central component for communication between clients. Furthermore, this setup simplifies the test environment without compromising the validity of the test data.

The software consists of the following components:

- The operating system used on the Raspberry Pis [7] is Raspberry Pi OS 5.2 (64 bit version) [8]. Raspberry Pi OS was chosen because it is compatible with all common MQTT clients, brokers, and tools, while also offering an accessible and flexible platform for software development.
- Wireshark version 4.4.2 [9] is used to record network traffic, as it captures and logs network data in realtime. Additionally, Wireshark supports MQTT, making it particularly suitable for analysis. Each implementation on the receiver side includes functions that record all transmitted messages and the decoded bits at runtime and save them in a text file for later evaluation.
- Apache ActiveMQ Artemis [10] is used as the Broker, as it enables complex applications and is Open Source software.
- The programming language Python with version 3.13.1[11] is chosen for the implementation of the MQTT clients and the patterns, as it is well-suited due to its extensive libraries and easy integration of MQTT frameworks.
- The framework used is "paho-mqtt" version 2.1.0 [12], which provides an interface for implementing MQTT clients. Additional libraries used include "datetime" or "date" for capturing and recording metadata, "json" for processing data sets, and "struct" for data conversion.

These libraries and tools are chosen for the development of the implementations because they enable efficient and flexible programming.

V. Evaluation

The theoretical capacity of 5 selected hidden patterns is identified before performing the practical measurements using the setup described before. The results of both the theoretical considerations and the practical measurements are shown in Figure 4.

Pattern from Mazurczyk et al. (2018)		Findings for MQTT			
ID	**Pattern**	**Feasibility under optimal conditions**	**Realistic applicability**	**theoretical capacity**	**measured capacity**
T2	Message Timing	easy	hard	1 bit / packet	0,999 bit / packet
T5	Message Ordering	easy	medium	1 bit / flow	0,999 bit / packet
T6	Retransmission	easy	medium-hard	1 bit / time unit	0,66 bit / packet
S7	Payload Field Size Modulation	easy	easy-medium	3 bit / packet	1 bit / packet
S10	User-Data Value Modulation and Reserved/ Unused	easy	easy	1 bit / packet	1 bit / packet

Figure 4. Findings from the theoretical analysis and practical measurements of the capacity of 5 selected hidden channels in MQTT.

The primary observation is, that the practical capacity is lower than the theoretical capacity. This is caused by the difference between the theoretical applicability of a hidden channel - under optimal conditions - and the applicability in a realistic communication setting. In general, the application in a realistic setting is more difficult. Effects like network latency or retransmissions of failed packets interfere with some types of hidden channels. An example is the notably lower capacity of the hidden channel **T6** during the measurement.

A notable effect is the difference in measure and theoretical capacity in channel **S7: Payload Field Size Modulation**. This channel cannot be realized in MQTT as described, because MQTT does not define a fixed payload-field-size in its metadata. The payload size depends on the chosen data format of the transmitted payload and is adjusted flexibly to the payload's actual length. In typical MQTT scenarios, payloads are sensor readings that usually share the same data type and have similar sizes. By artificially manipulating the payload content, a variation of the "payload field size" in a broader sense could therefore be achieved. The theoretical capacity must consequently be determined for each use case. In the context of our experimental series, the payload consists of a float representing temperature sensor data recorded in the twenties (20–30 °C) with up to three decimal places. Thus, up to three additional decimal places could be used covertly to encode a hidden message unobtrusively, which corresponds to a theoretical capacity of up to 3 bits per packet. The measured capacity, however, is 1 bit per packet. This discrepancy is due to the simple implementation used, in which a 0 encodes a common payload size and a 1 encodes a significantly larger payload; using this scheme, 1,000 messages transmitted 1,000 bits. While this implementation has the disadvantage of lower capacity, it is substantially simpler and less conspicuous.

This shows that theoretical consideration alone is not able to provide a sufficient baseline for security modelling in the domain of hidden channels in ICS networks.

VI. Security Measures

The threat discussed in this work requires means to protect against it. Such measures are highly pattern-specific. Some patterns, e.g., timing patterns like **T6: Retransmission** or **T5: Message Ordering**, can be detected effectively through network monitoring using tools such as Wireshark [9] or specialized heuristics. With careful analysis, certain regularities can be identified by examining the order and frequency of messages. In particular, **T5** is readily detectable in this way, since changes in message ordering are not typical and therefore more conspicuous.

Detection is more challenging for payload-storage patterns (**S7–S10**). These can only be identified through deeper network analysis, which requires decrypting individual packets and inspecting their contents. An example is **S10: User-data Value Modulation and Reserved/Unused** by examining individual packets in Wireshark and performing detailed analysis, one may discover a characteristic pattern and thereby not only identify the covert channel and its associated pattern but potentially also decode the hidden message.

It has to be considered that, depending on the specific implementation, unambiguous identification of the pattern and the hidden channel and, above all, correct decoding of the hidden message may be difficult or impossible without background knowledge of the specific implementation details.

VII. Discussion

This work discusses how the capacity of hidden channels in MQTT networks employed in ICS can be identified by theoretical consideration and practical measurements. The tests show that the theoretical consideration has to be supplemented by practical measurements in order to accommodate the effects of real control networks. The considerations performed in this paper help support security modelling by providing a baseline of the extent of hidden communication an attacker could hide in MQTT communication.

The work is performed in a very limited network setting and would benefit from the use of a more complex network setup. Such a setup should follow are more realistic communication scenario including many more publishers and subscribers as well as the effect and the effect of latency and packet loss. Latency and packet loss could affect the capacity of hidden communication, although some MQTT brokers use various QOS mechanisms in some configurations to address latency and packet loss, which in turn affect specific hidden channels. E.g. Pattern **S10** is directly affected since some QoS features use the fields employed by this pattern. Also, packet loss might affect the transmission quality in the hidden channels itself, depending on the pattern. Pattern **T6** is affected to a great degree by natural retransmissions caused by the network quality. For other patterns, the flag *DUB* used in MQTT could be used to prevent impacts. In our setup, no transmission errors are detected.

Also only a subset of the potentially viable hidden channels in MQTT is evaluated, leaving the remaining channels open for future work.

Additionally, other protocols also have relevance in the field of Industrial Control Systems and might also be subject to hidden channels. We deem the approach presented in this paper to be usable for other protocols, even though the specific implementation of the specific patterns would vary and some patterns are not applicable to all common ICS protocols. Modbus/TCP is discussed in [6].

Acknowledgement

This work has been performed in the scope of the project "SYNTHESIS - Synthetically generated data segments with hidden malicious code functions for safety analysis in nuclear control technology" with the grant number FKZ: 1501666A which is funded by the Federal Ministry for the Environment, Nature Conservation, Nuclear Safety and Consumer Protection (BMUV).

Author shares: All authors: fundamental discussion, exchange of ideas, refinement. RA: outline, background, theoretical concept. SO: theoretical and practical adaptation of the concepts from [6] to MQTT as student work, technical implementation (setup, evaluation and hidden channels), evaluation as student work. SK: initial IT-landscape design and test. JD: Input to the general design of hidden channels derived from [6].

References

[1] Dragos, Inc., "2025 OT/ICS Cybersecurity Report", 2025, Accessed: Sep. 15, 2025. [Online]. Available: https://hub.dragos.com/hubfs/312-Year-in-Review/2025/Dragos-2025-OT-Cybersecurity-Report-A-Year-in-Review.pdf?hsLang=en.

[2] MITRE, "MITRE ATT&CK: Techniques - Data Obfuscation: Steganography", Apr. 2025, Accessed: Sep. 15, 2025. [Online]. Available: https://attack.mitre.org/techniques/T1001/002/.

[3] A. Badaev and K. Naumova, "SteganoAmor campaign: Ta558 mass-attacking companies and public institutions all around the world", 2024, Accessed: Sep. 15, 2025. [Online]. Available: https://www.ptsecurity.com/ww-en/analytics/pt-esc-threat-intelligence/steganoamor-campaign-ta558-mass-attacking-companies-and-public-institutions-all-around-the-world/.

[4] MQTT.org, "MQTT: The Standard for IoT Messaging", 2024, Accessed: Sep. 15, 2025. [Online]. Available: https://mqtt.org/.

[5] W. Mazurczyk, S. Wendzel, and K. Cabaj, "Towards deriving insights into data hiding methods using pattern-based approach", *ARES 2018, 13th International Conference on Availability, Reliability and Security; Hamburg, Germany, August 27 - August 30, ISBN: 978-1-4503-6448-5*, pp. 1–10, 2018.

[6] K. Lamshöft and J. Dittmann, "Assessment of Hidden Channel Attacks: Targetting Modbus/TCP", *IFAC-PapersOnLine*, vol. 53, no. 2, pp. 11 100–11 107, 2020, 21st IFAC World Congress, ISSN: 2405-8963. DOI: https://doi.org/10.1016/j.ifacol.2020.12.258.

[7] Raspberry Pi Foundation, "Raspberry Pi", 2025, Accessed: Sep. 15, 2025. [Online]. Available: https://www.raspberrypi.com/.

[8] Raspberry Pi Foundation, "Raspberry Pi software", 2025, Accessed: Sep. 15, 2025. [Online]. Available: https://www.raspberrypi.com/software/.

[9] Wireshark Foundation, "Wireshark", 2024, Accessed: Sep. 15, 2025. [Online]. Available: https://www.wireshark.org.

[10] Apache Software Foundation, "Activemq artemis", 2025, Accessed: Sep. 15, 2025. [Online]. Available: https://activemq.apache.org/components/artemis/.

[11] Python Software Foundation, "Python", 2025, Accessed: Sep. 15, 2025. [Online]. Available: https://www.python.org/.

[12] Eclipse Foundation, "Paho-mqtt", 2025, Accessed: Sep. 15, 2025. [Online]. Available: https://pypi.org/project/paho-mqtt/.

Artificial Intelligence or Artificial Stupidity? The Inability of Small LLMs to Reason, Even Given the Correct Answer!

Salvatore Vella
Department of Computer Science
Toronto Metropolitan University
Toronto, Canada
e-mail: sal.vella@torontomu.ca

Salah Sharieh
Department of Computer Science
Toronto Metropolitan University
Toronto, Canada
salah.sharieh@torontomu.ca

Alex Ferworn
Department of Computer Science
Toronto Metropolitan University
Toronto, Canada
aferworn@torontomu.ca

***Abstract*—Small Large Language Models (LLMs) are now integrated into devices we use every day, but their reliability under prompt variations remains understudied. We see them on cell phones and many other devices. We present a study of prompt variation in small LLMs, focusing on the effect of prompt formatting changes on multiple-choice reasoning tasks, even when the prompt provides the correct answer. We evaluate LLaMA-3 (1B and 4B), Google Gemma (1B and 4B), Alibaba Qwen (1.5B and 3B), Microsoft Phi-3 (4B), IBM Granite (2B) and the smaller OpenAI models (gpt-4o-mini, gpt-4.1-mini, gpt-4.1-nano) on the CommonsenseQA and OpenBookQA benchmarks. Our findings reveal that reordering of answer choices causes statistically significant performance drops, even when the correct answer is explicitly present in the prompt. For very small models, the results are dramatic. Statistical tests, including paired t-tests and McNemar's test, are used to confirm the significance of the results. These results suggest that smaller LLMs rely on heuristics rather than reasoning, as they fail to grasp the correct answer even when it is explicitly provided. This prompt-order sensitivity, where providing the correct answer, is a unique attack surface in LLM systems, allowing adversaries to manipulate prompt structure to create errors. This work suggests additional testing is needed before deploying LLM-based systems.**

Keywords-large language models; bias; threat.

I. Introduction

This paper presents the results of an experiment testing whether small LLMs reason, pattern-match, or employ other heuristics.

Small Large Language Models (LLMs) with fewer than 4 billion parameters are being introduced across many parts of our everyday lives. Small LLMs reside on cell phones for tasks such as summarizing emails, are integrated into home systems, and are used in healthcare. With their increased usage, a focus on their robustness and reliability is necessary, especially as these are integrated into safety-critical systems. We study the impact of prompt changes on model performance.

Recent work has shown that even large models exhibit prompt sensitivity. This effect has not been systematically measured in small models that are now deployed on personal devices.

One question that also needs to be posed is whether these models reason or pattern-match. By reasoning, we refer to a model's ability to draw inferences or apply logical rules beyond surface-level correlations, memorized patterns, or simple heuristics.

We present a study of prompt variation in small LLMs, focusing on the effect of prompt formatting changes on multiple-choice reasoning tasks, even providing the correct answer in the prompt. We evaluate LLaMA-3 (1B and 4B), Google Gemma (1B and 4B), Alibaba Qwen (1.5B and 3B), Microsoft Phi-3 (4B), IBM Granite (2B) and the smaller OpenAI models (gpt-4o-mini, gpt-4.1-mini, gpt-4.1-nano) on the CommonsenseQA and OpenBookQA benchmarks. If a model is truly reasoning, minor changes in prompt layout or answer order should not substantially affect its output. We ask the same multiple-choice question four ways:

- **Base prompt:** The multiple-choice question is asked as-is, with no additions to the prompt.
- **Example prompt:** An example multiple-choice question is asked and answered in the prompt, followed by the actual question. This is a few-shot example using a generic question.
- **Simple Primed prompt:** The same multiple-choice question is asked and answered as an example in the prompt, followed by the same question again. The correct answer appears in the same position both times.
- **Reverse Primed prompt:** The same multiple-choice question is asked and answered as an example in the prompt, but the correct answer is placed in a different position than in the actual question that follows.

To illustrate, Figures 1 and 2 show an example for the Simple and Reverse prompt styles where the correct answer is included but in the same and different positions as the target question.

Our experiment investigates the robustness of small LLMs by presenting the same question in various prompt formats, including cases where the correct answer is explicitly provided. The goal is to test the reasoning ability of the small LLMs:

- Does providing the answer in the same position improve performance? This gives the correct answer, and one would expect it to.
- Does providing the answer, but in a different position, improve performance? There is a small amount of reasoning required, and one would expect that LLMs would be able to perform this simple reasoning.

Our results show that even trivial prompt reordering leads to major statistically significant performance drops, suggesting

```
You are a Multiple Choice answering assistant.
Provide the answer in JSON format like this: {"answer": "answer"}

Question:
The sun is responsible for
Choices:
A: puppies learning new tricks
B: children growing up and getting old
C: flowers wilting in a vase
D: plants sprouting, blooming and wilting
Answer: D

Answer with one letter.
Question: The sun is responsible for
Choices:
A: puppies learning new tricks
B: children growing up and getting old
C: flowers wilting in a vase
D: plants sprouting, blooming and wilting
Answer:
```

Figure 1: Simple Correct Answer Prompt Example.

```
You are a Multiple Choice answering assistant.
Provide the answer in JSON format like this: {"answer": "answer"}

Question:
The sun is responsible for
Choices:
A: plants sprouting, blooming and wilting
B: flowers wilting in a vase
C: children growing up and getting old
D: puppies learning new tricks
Answer: A

Answer with one letter.
Question: The sun is responsible for
Choices:
A: puppies learning new tricks
B: children growing up and getting old
C: flowers wilting in a vase
D: plants sprouting, blooming and wilting
Answer:
```

Figure 2: Reverse Correct Answer Prompt Example.

that small LLMs do not generalize from demonstrations as expected. The smallest of the LLMs has the largest impact, and in some cases, its performance drops below that of simply guessing the answer.

Our key contributions are:

- **Comprehensive evaluation**: We measure the effect of prompt order variations on several multiple-choice question and answer datasets and a number of smaller LLMs. We compare baseline prompts to permuted versions and quantify the changes in accuracy.
- **Statistical analysis**: We apply paired t-tests and McNemar's tests to rigorously assess performance differences. Results show significant accuracy drops due to prompt perturbations in most cases.
- **Prompt-order bias**: We analyze the frequency of answer shifts, revealing that a substantial fraction of questions yield a different prediction when answer positions are swapped.
- **Threat modelling**: We formalize prompt-order sensitivity as an attack surface. An adversary could exploit this by reformatting prompts (or answer keys) to manipulate model outputs in critical systems.
- **Mitigation strategies**: We discuss possible defences, including prompt normalization, adversarial instruction tuning, and ensemble prompting.
- **Ethical discussion**: We discuss implications such as bias amplification (e.g., if models favour last-mentioned options, this could amplify systemic biases) and the risks of adversarial misuse.

By highlighting these vulnerabilities and proposing countermeasures, we aim to inform safer deployment of LLMs in cybersecurity-relevant settings.

The paper is organized as follows: Section II reviews related work, Section III presents the methodology used, Section IV presents the results, Section V provides some discussion of the results, and Section VI provides the conclusion and future work.

II. LITERATURE REVIEW

This section will explore some of the key topics that are used in this paper.

Large Language models, such as those developed by Brown et al. [1], have emerged as a technology that can assist in addressing various problems with their ability to generate language.

LLMs use prompts as their interface. Jiang et al. [2] have explored improving model performance using variations of prompts to create a new prompt. Zhao et al. [3] have explored the issue of prompt sensitivity and showed that with GPT-3, performance could vary widely and was caused by bias for specific answers - data common in the training data or near the end of the prompt. Webson and Patrick [4] show that prompt phrasing, even irrelevant prompts, can improve the performance of GPT-3. These results raise questions about whether the model accurately interprets the prompt's meaning. Our study focuses on small models versus large models, as these small models will become pervasive.

The sensitivity to prompt format in reasoning tasks has also been studied. In-context learning is a method to provide examples for the model to learn from before asking a question. Min et al. [5] have examined in-context learning using GPT-3 and found that any context, even those with random labels, improves performance. Ye and Durrett studied whether adding explanations to the prompt improved the performance of GPT-3 and several other models. They found these models had minimal performance improvements with explanations added. Lu et al. [6] studied the reordering of prompts using GPT-3 and found that reordering examples and answer choices can dramatically change performance. In contrast to larger model studies, our study focuses on small models.

The behaviour of large language models has also been studied. Suri et al. [7] have studied heuristics that LLMs use. It found that GPT-3 judged the likelihood of two events occurring together higher than either alone. Additionally, it found that an item would be more effective when presented positively and that an owned item was more effective than a newly found one. All of these biases were consistent with human participants. Chung et al. [8] found that fine-tuning models can improve performance. [9] has studied positional bias and found that large language models exhibit positional bias, that is, performance changes when the position of the correct answer in a question is changed. Vella et al. [10] have demonstrated positional bias in a number of small LLMs, some with dramatic results.

In this study, we use multiple-choice question and answer datasets. These are simple to use and provide direct answers from the large-magnitude models that are easy to evaluate. We utilize OpenBookQA [11], a dataset for elementary school knowledge of facts that incorporates reasoning, and CommonsenseQA [12], a dataset for commonsense reasoning. These are direct multiple-choice questions and answers with OpenBookQA having four options and CommonsenseQA having five options for each question.

Attacks through prompt injections have also been studied. Wallace et al. [13] show how large language models are sensitive to pre-pending and appending text to a prompt.

The reasoning of large language models has been studied. Ma et al. [14] have created a mathematical benchmark and evaluated larger models (with over 70 billion parameters), showing that performance varies widely. Shojaee et al. [15] have recently generated interest with their study from Apple, which examines both the final answers and the reasoning in a game-playing scenario. The study finds that both standard and reasoning models perform poorly on complex scenarios. In this study, we simplify the requirements for reasoning to just being able to distinguish the correct answer when it is moved.

The literature review summarizes prior research on prompt sensitivity, positional bias, and reasoning, and this highlights evidence of format-dependent behaviour. Whereas prior studies have focused on larger models [3], this study extends that work by focusing on small LLMs and demonstrating that their reasoning failures under prompt variation are much more severe than those observed in larger models.

III. METHODOLOGY

The objective of the study is to evaluate how small LLMs demonstrate reasoning ability or whether they rely on simple heuristics. We also test their robustness to changes in prompt format, including cases where the correct answer is provided. This study also has implications for prompt injection attacks, as the same techniques can be used to alter model performance.

We use the following models:

- Meta LLaMA-3.2 (1B and 4B) [16]
- Google Gemma 3 (1B and 4B) [17]
- Alibaba Qwen 2.5 (1.5B and 3B) [18]
- Microsoft Phi 3 (4B) [19]
- IBM Granite 3.3 (2B) [20]
- OpenAI GPT models (gpt-4o-mini, gpt-4.1-mini, gpt-4.1-nano) [21]

We use the following benchmark datasets and 2000 questions from each:

- **CommonsenseQA**: A benchmark that tests commonsense reasoning with five answer choices per question.
- **OpenBookQA**: A benchmark that focuses on elementary school-level science facts that are combined with reasoning and have four answer choices per question.

Four prompt conditions are used:

- **Base** – Standard multiple-choice question without context or examples.
- **Example** – An example not related to the target question is added to the prompt, followed by the target question.
- **Simple Primed** – The target question is answered as an example, followed by the target question.
- **Reverse Primed** – The target question is asked as an example with the answer provided in a different position than the target question's correct answer.

The evaluation procedure is as follows:

- All models were tested on the same set of questions under each condition.
- Accuracy was measured as the proportion of correct predictions.

Statistical testing was conducted to determine which results are statistically significant:

- Paired t-tests used to compare accuracy differences between conditions.
- McNemar's test is used to examine the significance of prediction shifts when answers are reordered.

We use the following interpretation criteria:

- Substantial drop in performance from Base to Reverse Primed → evidence of prompt-order bias.
- High sensitivity across conditions → suggests lack of deep reasoning.

There are security implications for being able to generate wrong answers from a large language model:

- Consider providing the correct answer in the wrong order as an adversarial attack vector
- Consider prompt-order sensitivity as an adversarial attack vector.
- Proposed mitigations such as prompt normalization and ensemble prompting.

IV. RESULTS

This section provides the results of the experiment. Tables I and II provide the raw percent complete under each condition. These are the percentages correct for each condition.

A. Overall Performance Trends

All models exhibited high sensitivity to the prompt format, with accuracy varying across the four prompt methods: Base, Simple Primed, Reverse Primed, and Example Primed. Tables I and II provide the results of the raw accuracy for each method, and Figures 3 and 4 provide the heat maps for the results.

We note the following:

- There is a wide variety of accuracy performance. The larger models, as expected, outperform the smaller models.
- Providing the correct answer in the same order as the target question improved performance for all models. For

TABLE I. COMMONSENSEQA ACCURACY BY PROMPT CONDITION

Model	Base	Simple	Reverse	Example
gemma-3-1b	42.10	91.65	7.30	38.05
gemma-3-4b	64.70	96.40	43.35	62.15
gpt-4.1-mini	79.45	92.75	87.05	78.45
gpt-4.1-nano	73.30	96.80	84.15	71.70
gpt-4o-mini	78.75	90.60	85.80	77.10
granite-3.3-2b-instruct	64.90	92.85	73.35	64.70
llama-3.2-1b-instruct	52.10	96.70	9.20	26.10
llama-3.2-3b-instruct	65.95	97.05	55.55	61.85
phi-3-mini-4k-instruct	72.85	96.35	84.30	67.70
qwen2.5-1.5b-instruct-mlx	62.60	89.30	52.10	61.10
qwen2.5-3b-instruct	72.25	96.05	69.25	72.85

TABLE II. OPENBOOKQA ACCURACY BY PROMPT CONDITION

Model	Base	Simple	Reverse	Example
gemma-3-1b	41.90	95.70	10.35	29.80
gemma-3-4b	66.15	97.35	61.95	65.65
gpt-4.1-mini	89.40	96.00	94.80	89.30
gpt-4.1-nano	80.50	98.00	96.40	79.15
gpt-4o-mini	87.30	93.95	93.35	85.60
granite-3.3-2b-instruct	68.30	94.50	82.10	65.65
llama-3.2-1b-instruct	44.80	99.15	8.30	22.65
llama-3.2-3b-instruct	67.00	98.90	69.15	61.45
phi-3-mini-4k-instruct	80.40	98.25	90.05	78.35
qwen2.5-1.5b-instruct-mlx	60.05	88.60	65.15	55.50
qwen2.5-3b-instruct	65.85	96.80	75.45	66.45

all models, regardless of size, the performance improved to almost 90%+ accuracy for all models.

- Providing the correct answer in a different order than the target produced mixed results
  - For the very smallest models, the 1 billion parameter models, providing the correct answer in the prompt but in a different order, causes catastrophic results with accuracy rates dropping to well below those of choosing randomly.
  - For the small models with 2 billion and 3 billion parameters, the drops are significant, though better than guessing randomly.
  - For the larger OpenAI models, the drops are smaller, though still statistically significant. Even these larger models struggle to reason between when the answer is given in the same position as the target or in a different position. GPT-4o-mini for the OpenBookQA dataset is the only case where the difference is not statistically significant.
- Adding an example drops the score for all except one model.

Figures 5 and 6 provide the graphics of the perturbation across prompt types for CommonsenseQA and OpenBookQA. That is, what is the difference from the baseline with each of the prompt types? We see that the results improve for all models and both datasets. We can graphically see the dramatic drop when the small models are presented with the correct answer in a different order.

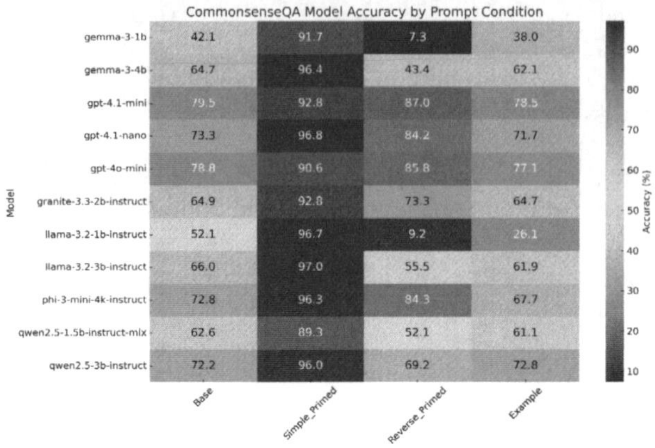

Figure 3: CommonsenseQA Model Accuracy by Prompt Condition.

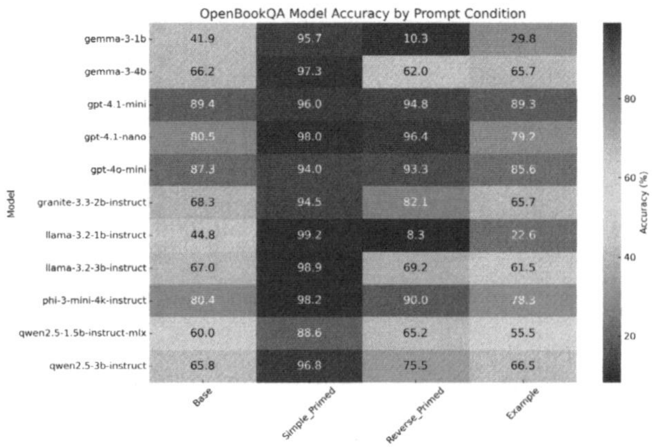

Figure 4: OpenBookQA Model Accuracy by Prompt Condition.

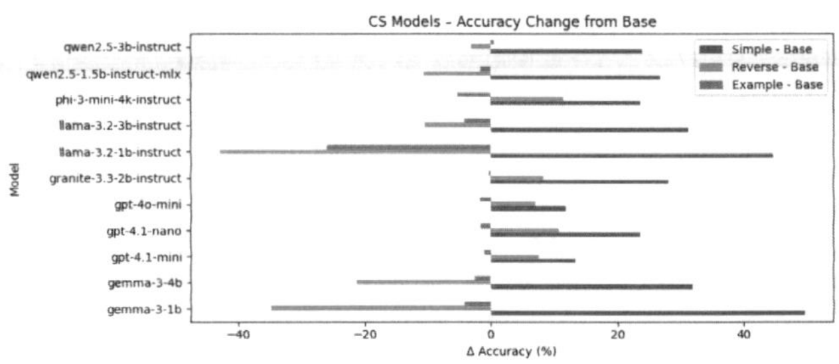

Figure 5: CommonsenseQA Model Perturbation by Prompt Condition.

The Reverse Primed prompts (where a correct QA example was given but the example's correct answer was deliberately placed in a different option position than the actual question's correct option) caused a drastic decrease in accuracy for all models compared with providing the answer in the proper

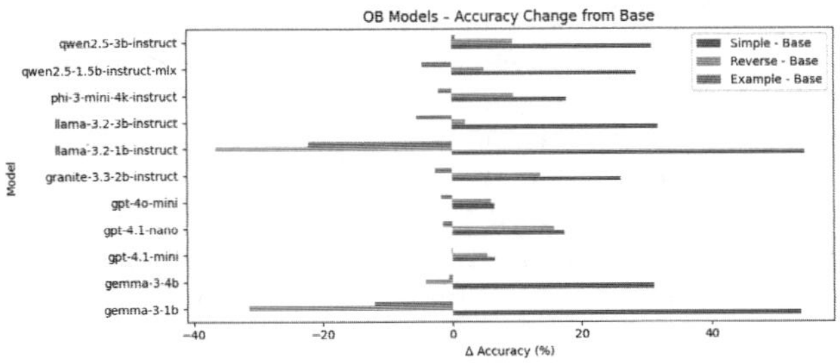

Figure 6: OpenBookQA Model Perturbation by Prompt Condition.

position.

In some cases, performance under Reverse Priming fell well below the Base accuracy, revealing a prompt-order bias. For instance, Meta LLaMA-3 1B, which answered 52% of CommonsenseQA questions correctly with no prompt, managed only about 9% correct under Reverse Priming – a drop of 41 percentage points, leaving it worse than a random guess (20%). Google Gemma 1B was even more misled: its accuracy plunged from 42% (Base) to roughly 7% on CommonsenseQA when given a misaligned example, falling below the 20% chance level. In other words, Gemma-1B answered more questions incorrectly than it would have by guessing uniformly at random, indicating that the incorrect prompt systematically biased its predictions. Similarly, on OpenBookQA, as well, both of these small models dropped to 8.3% and 10.4% respectively - and well below the random guess of 25% for OpenBookQA.

Examining the confusion matrices for LlaMa-3-1B and Gemma-1B in both OpenBookQA and CommonsenseQA, we can observe that the model employs a heuristic that selects the answer previously provided in the prompt. If the answer in the example was 'A', the model chooses 'A' as the answer for the target regardless of where the correct target answer is. This seems to be a simple matching of the word answer versus reasoning, where the correct answer is in the target question.

B. Statistical Significance

In this section, we will discuss some of the statistical tests conducted. In Tables III and IV, we present the t-tests of the Base prompt with no changes to each of the other prompt types.

We find that for Simple and Reverse, where answers are provided, the results are statistically significant for most models. qwen2.5-3b-instruct for CommonsenseQA and llama-3.2-3b-instruct for OpenBookQA are the two that are not. We also note that many of the results from the Example prompt, where we add an example, are not statistically significant.

We also use McNemar's Test, which is a test on paired values to test whether the distributions of two answer sets are statistically significantly different from each other. We present these in Tables V and VI. This shows the difference between the Base answers and each of the prompt types. We

TABLE III. PAIRED T-TEST P-VALUES FOR COMMONSENSEQA

Model	Simple	Reverse	Example
gemma-3-1b	0.000	0.000	0.000
gemma-3-4b	0.000	0.000	0.004
gpt-4.1-mini	0.000	0.000	0.121
gpt-4.1-nano	0.000	0.000	0.031
gpt-4o-mini	0.000	0.000	0.006
granite-3.3-2b-instruct	0.000	0.000	0.809
llama-3.2-1b-instruct	0.000	0.000	0.000
llama-3.2-3b-instruct	0.000	0.000	0.000
phi-3-mini-4k-instruct	0.000	0.000	0.000
qwen2.5-1.5b-instruct-mlx	0.000	0.000	0.186
qwen2.5-3b-instruct	0.000	0.022	0.487

TABLE IV. PAIRED T-TEST P-VALUES FOR OPENBOOKQA

Model	Simple	Reverse	Example
gemma-3-1b	0.000	0.000	0.000
gemma-3-4b	0.000	0.005	0.566
gpt-4.1-mini	0.000	0.000	0.850
gpt-4.1-nano	0.000	0.000	0.057
gpt-4o-mini	0.000	0.000	0.004
granite-3.3-2b-instruct	0.000	0.000	0.002
llama-3.2-1b-instruct	0.000	0.000	0.000
llama-3.2-3b-instruct	0.000	0.120	0.000
phi-3-mini-4k-instruct	0.000	0.000	0.003
qwen2.5-1.5b-instruct-mlx	0.000	0.000	0.000
qwen2.5-3b-instruct	0.000	0.000	0.540

see that the p-values for all the simple and all but one of the reverse comparisons are less than 0.05, indicating a statistically significant difference. Even in many cases where we provide a simple example, it results in a statistically significantly different distribution.

V. DISCUSSION

Several observations can be made from the results.

The first is that the smaller LLMs exhibit prompt-order bias and are dependent on heuristics. The difference in performance between answering in the correct order and obtaining worse

TABLE V. COMMONSENSEQA: MCNEMAR'S TEST P-VALUES

Model	Simple	Reverse	Example
CS-gemma-3-1b	0.000	0.000	0.000
CS-gemma-3-4b	0.000	0.000	0.005
CS-gpt-4.1-mini	0.000	0.000	0.140
CS-gpt-4.1-nano	0.000	0.000	0.037
CS-gpt-4o-mini	0.000	0.000	0.008
CS-granite-3.3-2b-instruct	0.000	0.000	0.856
CS-llama-3.2-1b-instruct	0.000	0.000	0.000
CS-llama-3.2-3b-instruct	0.000	0.000	0.000
CS-phi-3-mini-4k-instruct	0.000	0.000	0.000
CS-qwen2.5-1.5b-instruct-mlx	0.000	0.000	0.201
CS-qwen2.5-3b-instruct	0.000	0.025	0.524

TABLE VI. OPENBOOKQA: MCNEMAR'S TEST P-VALUES

Model	Simple	Reverse	Example
OB-gemma-3-1b	0.000	0.000	0.000
OB-gemma-3-4b	0.000	0.006	0.606
OB-gpt-4.1-mini	0.000	0.000	0.925
OB-gpt-4.1-nano	0.000	0.000	0.067
OB-gpt-4o-mini	0.000	0.000	0.005
OB-granite-3.3-2b-instruct	0.000	0.000	0.002
OB-llama-3.2-1b-instruct	0.000	0.000	0.000
OB-llama-3.2-3b-instruct	0.000	0.128	0.000
OB-phi-3-mini-4k-instruct	0.000	0.000	0.004
OB-qwen2.5-1.5b-instruct-mlx	0.000	0.000	0.000
OB-qwen2.5-3b-instruct	0.000	0.000	0.575

results when answering in a different order, even though both cases yield the proper result, is an indication of position bias and the use of simple heuristics, such as matching the answer in the prompt before the question. This reasoning mimics Clever Hans [22] in which performance is good when superficial patterns match expectations.

The second is that the smallest of the models, the one-billion-parameter models, prioritize pattern matching over reasoning. Performance for the 1-billion-parameter models drops well below random guessing. Examining the confusion matrix, we see that these small models match the answer provided in the prompt and disregard any reasoning. This finding raises doubts about the reasoning ability of large language models, as they can be easily fooled.

The third point is that the sensitivity to prompt changes raises serious concerns about malicious usage, fairness and ethics. Different answers to equivalent prompts indicate that testing and validation must be comprehensive before an application is deployed into production.

VI. CONCLUSION AND FUTURE WORK

Several conclusions can be drawn from this work.

This study demonstrates that small LLMs employ heuristics that lead to prompt sensitivity. Small models, all of the models here, have differences between answers provided in the same or different orders. The smallest of models have catastrophic results, dropping below random guessing. The results indicate that these models exhibit some form of pattern matching rather than actual reasoning.

The second is that, while larger models perform better, they all rely on heuristics rather than reasoning. We can see this from the results, where the correct answer is presented in the same or different order. This is simple reasoning that most humans would understand.

The third is that the results of this study undermine the trustworthiness of smaller models and limit their practical deployment. Models should answer consistently across prompts that are essentially the same. The fact that they rely on heuristics poses risks in higher-risk applications where these models make safety-critical decisions.

We had expected some reasoning issues with the Reverse Primed condition, but the fact that several models performed worse than random was a surprising finding.

Future work will expand this analysis to include mitigating prompt sensitivity and ensemble prompting using multiple models. Benchmarks will also need to be established so that application builders can test LLMs and applications before deployment.

REFERENCES

[1] T. B. Brown *et al.*, "Language models are few-shot learners", *arXiv preprint arXiv:2005.14165*, 2020.

[2] Z. Jiang, F. F. Xu, J. Araki, and G. Neubig, "How can we know what language models know?", *Transactions of the Association for Computational Linguistics*, vol. 8, pp. 423–438, 2020. DOI: 10.1162/tacl_a_00324.

[3] T. Z. Zhao, E. Wallace, S. Feng, D. Klein, and S. Singh, "Calibrate before use: Improving few-shot performance of language models", *arXiv preprint arXiv:2102.09690*, 2021. DOI: 10.48550/arXiv.2102.09690.

[4] A. Webson and E. Pavlick, "Do prompt-based models really understand the meaning of their prompts?", in *Proceedings of the 2022 Conference of the North American Chapter of the Association for Computational Linguistics: Human Language Technologies*, Seattle, USA: Association for Computational Linguistics, 2022. DOI: 10.18653/v1/2022.naacl-main.167.

[5] S. Min, M. Lewis, L. Zettlemoyer, and H. Hajishirzi, "Rethinking the role of demonstrations: What makes in-context learning work?", in *Proceedings of the 2022 Conference on Empirical Methods in Natural Language Processing*, Abu Dhabi, United Arab Emirates: Association for Computational Linguistics, 2022. DOI: 10.18653/v1/2022.emnlp-main.759.

[6] Y. Lu, M. Bartolo, A. Moore, S. Riedel, and P. Stenetorp, "Fantastically ordered prompts and where to find them: Overcoming few-shot prompt order sensitivity", in *Proceedings of the 60th Annual Meeting of the Association for Computational Linguistics (Volume 1: Long Papers)*, Dublin, Ireland: Association for Computational Linguistics, 2022. DOI: 10.18653/v1/2022.acl-long.556.

[7] G. Suri, L. R. Slater, A. Ziaee, and M. Nguyen, "Do large language models show decision heuristics similar to humans? a case study using gpt-3.5", *Journal of Experimental Psychology: General*, 2023.

[8] H. W. Chung *et al.*, "Scaling instruction-finetuned language models", *arXiv preprint arXiv:2210.11416*, 2022. DOI: 10.48550/arXiv.2210.11416.

[9] P. Pezeshkpour and E. Hruschka, "Large language models sensitivity to the order of options in multiple-choice questions", *arXiv preprint arXiv:2308.11483*, 2023. DOI: 10.48550/arXiv.2308.11483.

[10] S. Vella, F. Hussain, S. Sharieh, and A. Ferworn, "Where you say matters: A study of positional bias of small llms", in *Proceedings of the 2025 IEEE World AI IoT Congress (AIIoT)*, To appear, New York City, USA: IEEE, May 2025.

[11] T. Mihaylov, P. Clark, T. Khot, and A. Sabharwal, "Can a suit of armor conduct electricity? a new dataset for open book question answering", in *Proceedings of the 2018 Conference on Empirical Methods in Natural Language Processing (EMNLP)*, Association for Computational Linguistics, 2018, pp. 2381–2391. DOI: 10.18653/v1/D18-1260.

[12] A. Talmor, J. Herzig, N. Lourie, and J. Berant, "Commonsenseqa: A question answering challenge targeting commonsense knowledge", in *Proceedings of the 2019 Conference of the North American Chapter of the Association for Computational Linguistics: Human Language Technologies (NAACL-*

HLT), Minneapolis, USA: Association for Computational Linguistics, 2019. DOI: 10.48550/arXiv.1811.00937.

[13] E. Wallace, S. Feng, N. Kandpal, M. Gardner, and S. Singh, "Universal adversarial triggers for attacking and analyzing nlp", *arXiv preprint arXiv:1908.07125*, 2021. DOI: 10.48550/arXiv.1908.07125.

[14] Q. Ma, Y. Wu, X. Zheng, and R. Ji, "Benchmarking abstract and reasoning abilities through a theoretical perspective", *arXiv preprint arXiv:2505.23833*, 2025. DOI: 10.48550/arXiv.2505.23833.

[15] P. Shojaee *et al.*, "The illusion of thinking: Understanding the strengths and limitations of reasoning models via the lens of problem complexity", *arXiv preprint arXiv:2506.06941*, 2025.

[16] Meta AI, *Introducing LLaMA 3.2: Multimodal intelligence at the edge*, https://ai.meta.com/blog/llama-3-2-connect-2024-vision-edge-mobile-devices/, Accessed: Oct. 10, 2025, 2024.

[17] Google DeepMind, *Gemma 3: Multimodal models for developers*, https://developers.googleblog.com/en/introducing-gemma3/, Accessed: Oct. 10, 2025, 2025.

[18] Alibaba DAMO Academy, *Qwen 2.5: Stronger open models with agent capabilities*, https://www.forbes.com/sites/torconstantino/2025/01/29/alibaba-unveils-qwen-25-a-deepseek-rival/, Accessed: Oct. 10, 2025, 2025.

[19] Microsoft Research, "Phi-3: A family of open language models", *arXiv preprint arXiv:2404.14219*, 2024, Accessed: Oct. 10, 2025.

[20] IBM Research, *Granite 3.3 language models: Open, powerful, and enterprise-ready*, https://www.ibm.com/granite/docs/models/granite/, Accessed: Oct. 10, 2025, 2025.

[21] OpenAI, *Gpt-4.1 and gpt-4o-mini: Fast, efficient, and powerful*, https://openai.com/index/gpt-4-1/, Accessed: Oct. 10, 2025, 2025.

[22] L. Samhita and H. J. Gross, "The "Clever Hans phenomenon" revisited", *Communicative & Integrative Biology*, vol. 6, no. 6, e27122, 2013. DOI: 10.4161/cib.27122.

Improving Crypto-Agility in Operational Technology through Exchangeable Smart Cards

Tobias Frauenschläger and Jürgen Mottok
Laboratory for Safe and Secure Systems (LaS³)
OTH Regensburg
93053 Regensburg, Germany
e-mail: {tobias.frauenschlaeger, juergen.mottok}@oth-regensburg.de

***Abstract*—As industrial and Operational Technology (OT) systems face increasing cryptographic demands, including migration to post-quantum cryptography, the need for crypto-agility has become critical. However, retrofitting constrained embedded devices with new cryptographic capabilities is often impeded by hardware limitations, high certification costs, and operational complexity. In this work, we propose a modular architecture that externalizes cryptographic functionality through exchangeable smart cards. This decouples algorithm support and key storage from the host platform, enabling secure and flexible upgrades. We implement and evaluate this concept using resource-constrained embedded devices and a prototype smart card that supports both traditional and post-quantum algorithms. Our results demonstrate that even full cryptographic offloading is feasible with the constraints of OT environments and that the resulting overhead remains acceptable in typical deployment scenarios. We further analyze the security of the interface between the host and the smart card and outline protection mechanisms based on secure channels suitable for OT deployment.**

Keywords-Crypto-Agility; Smart Cards; Operational Technology; Post-Quantum Cryptography; Key Management; Security.

I. INTRODUCTION

The importance of robust security in *Operational Technology* (OT) environments has increased significantly. As industrial systems become increasingly interconnected, they face a growing threat landscape that demands proactive and future-proof security measures [1][2]. At the same time, the impending introduction of *Post-Quantum Cryptography* (PQC) is becoming not only a technical necessity but also a regulatory requirement [3]–[5]. This transition poses considerable challenges for many existing OT systems, particularly those characterized by legacy hardware and limited upgradability.

While software-based cryptographic updates are often technically feasible, they are frequently avoided in practice due to the high cost and complexity of device recertification processes. Furthermore, many OT devices are constrained in terms of processing power and memory capacity. As a result, deploying newer and more computationally demanding cryptographic algorithms is often impractical without significant hardware modifications. Yet, *Crypto-Agility*, the ability to rapidly adopt and switch between cryptographic primitives and protocols, is increasingly considered a significant requirement in security architectures of OT systems [6].

Public-key cryptography and Public-Key Infrastructures (PKIs) are fundamental to many essential security features, such as authentication, encryption, and digital signatures. However, managing cryptographic keys in a secure and scalable way remains a complex task. Bootstrapping trust, securely storing private keys, and maintaining PKIs are non-trivial challenges, particularly when device manufacturers and system operators are distinct entities, with operators often lacking deep cryptographic expertise. Dedicated hardware-based security tokens, such as *Hardware Security Modules* (HSMs), *Secure Elements* or *Trusted Platform Modules* (TPMs), are a proven solution for secure key storage, offering tamper-resistant environments for sensitive operations [7]. However, in Embedded and OT environments, such tokens are typically deployed as soldered chips within a device, inheriting the upgrade issues.

Smart Cards as an exchangeable form of dedicated security tokens have been widely adopted in various domains, such as corporate IT, healthcare, and eGovernment, for user authentication and secure key storage. These devices offer an attractive balance between strong security guarantees and deployment flexibility. By externalizing key storage and key management functions from a host device, smart cards simplify the overall system architecture and reduce the complexity of security-critical software updates. This separation would be particularly valuable in OT contexts, where partial hardware upgrades (e. g., inserting a new smart card) could provide support for modern cryptographic algorithms without requiring intrusive modifications to the host device. Pre-installing cryptographic material, such as keys and certificates, on smart cards further simplifies the bootstrapping process.

To address the challenges of upgrading cryptographic capabilities in OT environments, we propose an architecture based on *exchangeable smart cards*. By decoupling key management and algorithm support from the host device in a modular way, smart cards provide a path toward crypto-agility, enabling gradual migration to modern cryptographic standards without requiring deep changes to existing hardware or firmware, while potentially easing device recertification. The main contributions of this work are:

1) *Algorithm Agnosticism*: Our approach allows the adoption of new cryptographic algorithms without requiring their implementation on the host device, reducing complexity and easing certification.
2) *Flexible Key Deployment*: Our approach enables secure provisioning of trust anchors, certificate chains, private keys, and symmetric pre-shared keys.

3) *Evaluation on Constrained Devices*: We demonstrate and evaluate deployment on resource-constrained hardware.
4) *OT-Specific Security Analysis*: We assess the architecture's security against the unique threats and constraints of OT environments.

The remaining paper is structured as follows. In Section II, related work is discussed. Section III then presents our approach on using exchangeable smart cards for crypto-agility. This is followed by a description of our technical implementation in Section IV and the evaluation on resource-constrained devices in Section V. Furthermore, Section VI presents a security analysis of our approach and proposes possible solutions. Finally, the paper is concluded in Section VII.

II. Related Work

A. Key-Management and Bootstrapping

The secure deployment and renewal of cryptographic credentials in distributed systems, such as OT and IoT, has been a long-standing challenge. Various protocols, such as EST [8], ACME [9], or SCEP [10], have been developed to automate certificate enrollment within PKI infrastructures. Furthermore, the protocol BRSKI [11] and its extension for alternative enrollment protocols BRSKI-AE [12] enable secure bootstrapping of new devices into an existing PKI. Recent research has proposed improvements to make PKI automation more applicable to constrained environments such as OT. These include improved architectural concepts, namely zoned segmentation, decentralized trust anchors, and communication improvements such as more lightweight protocols or compact certificate encodings to reduce overhead in industrial or embedded contexts [13]–[17]. However, the implications of these automation functionalities on crypto-agility are not yet covered explicitly in the literature. In addition, factory-based provisioning techniques using device-unique secrets have been explored to facilitate secure bootstrapping of identity and key material in IoT deployments [18][19].

B. Hardware Offloading of Secrets in OT and IoT

The use of dedicated hardware components to secure long-term secrets is well established. TPMs, smart cards, and HSMs are commonly used to protect private keys against both physical and logical attacks. These technologies are widely deployed in TLS-based systems, including those targeting industrial and IoT applications [20]–[24]. All works consider the improved protection of long-term secrets as the main advantage of such offloading, without elaborating on the influence on crypto-agility.

In particular, the work of Urien has explored the integration of smart cards across various use cases [25]–[30]. These efforts demonstrate the scalability and modularity of smart card-based security tokens when used for identity management and key protection. However, these approaches often rely on highly specialized or proprietary interfaces, leading to significant integration overhead into security libraries. Furthermore, the topic of crypto-agility is not directly addressed in his works.

C. Other Approaches for Crypto-Agility

In [6], crypto-agility challenges and solution approaches specific to OT systems are investigated, with a particular focus on hardware-based approaches. Among the promising solutions for enhancing cryptographic flexibility in OT environments are *Field-Programmable Gate Arrays* (FPGAs) and *SmartNICs*. FPGAs allow in-field reconfiguration of cryptographic functions, enabling updates to algorithms without replacing hardware components. This is especially important for inert systems with long upgrade cycles. Similarly, for some device types, SmartNICs offer a way to offload cryptographic operations from host devices to programmable network interfaces, reducing the load on host systems while enabling support for new algorithms. However, while these technologies offer significant potential for crypto-agility, their applicability in OT is limited by integration complexity and cost.

III. Crypto-Agility Using Smart Cards

In this section, we elaborate on the improvements for crypto-agility by decoupling security functionality from host hardware onto smart cards. First, Subsection III-A outlines how such tokens are integrated into devices. Then, the crypto-agility enhancements are presented in Subsection III-B.

A. Smart Card Integration

The integration setup of a smart card into a host device is depicted in Figure 1. Smart cards can be connected to host systems via various physical interfaces, such as ISO 7816-3 [31] (typically in SIM card ID-000 form factor), I²C or SPI (for circuit-level integration), USB (via external readers and the CCID protocol), or embedded within secure SD cards. Regardless of the interface, communication typically follows the ISO 7816-4 standard [32] using Application Protocol Data Units (APDUs) to send commands and receive their responses.

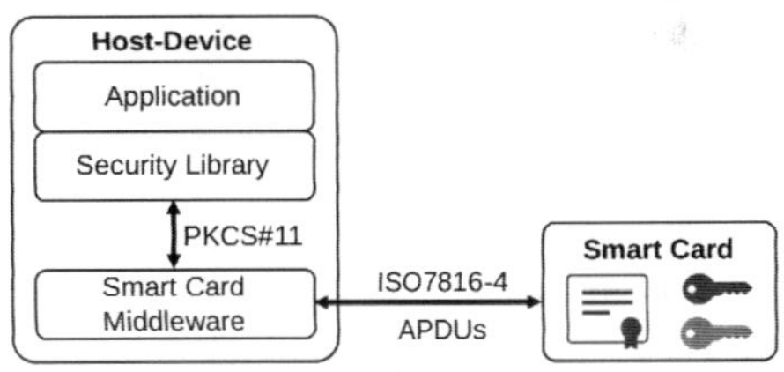

Figure 1. Integration of a smart card into a host device via middleware and standardized interfaces.

To abstract the low-level details of APDU communication, the host device typically uses a middleware layer that interfaces with the smart card and exposes a standardized API to applications. One widely adopted standard is PKCS#11 [33], which defines a common and generic interface for accessing cryptographic tokens. Through this interface, cryptographic artifacts, such as public and private keys, certificates, or symmetric pre-shared keys (PSK), are managed as opaque objects. Operations, e. g., signature generation or data encryption, are invoked through this abstraction and executed on the token without exposing sensitive material to the host.

In typical deployments, a security library, such as one that implements TLS or other protocols for secure communications, interacts with the middleware to utilize smart card functionality. The middleware then translates PKCS#11 operations into card-specific APDUs. While manufacturers often provide proprietary middleware specifically for their products, there are also vendor-neutral implementations that support a wide range of smart cards [34].

Smart cards are usually pre-provisioned before their deployment. They may already contain keys, certificates, or other cryptographic material necessary for the device's operation. Importantly, from the perspective of the application, the integration is mostly transparent. After initialization, operations reference specific objects on the card using identifiers or labels, enabling a modular and loosely coupled design.

To ensure secure access to stored cryptographic material, smart cards typically enforce access control mechanisms. The most common protection method is the use of a personal identification number (PIN), which must be presented by the host device to authenticate and authorize access to the card. Only after successful verification of the PIN is the host authorized to perform operations on protected objects, including the use of private keys or the modification of stored certificates. Furthermore, many cards delete their secret data after a specific number of invalid PIN entries. These mechanisms ensure that unauthorized usage is prevented even if the card is stolen. A thorough security discussion is conducted in Section VI.

Finally, the use of pre-personalized smart cards for specific devices also provides a practical solution to the challenge of provisioning device-unique cryptographic secrets during manufacturing. This approach eliminates the need for key generation and injection on the factory floor, streamlining production while maintaining strong security guarantees.

B. Enhancing Crypto-Agility through Smart Cards

The use of smart cards for storing and operating on cryptographic material significantly enhances the cryptographic resilience of OT systems. Long-term artifacts, such as private keys, certificates, or PSKs, can be stored securely on the smart card. These secrets remain non-extractable, and all sensitive operations are executed directly on the card. This architecture protects against unauthorized access or tampering and simplifies the management of cryptographic assets.

Smart cards are well-suited for the operational realities of OT environments. They enable secure provisioning during manufacturing, support lifecycle operations such as credential renewal or revocation, and reduce the operational burden on field devices. Furthermore, their use aligns well with established maintenance workflows and regulatory requirements in the OT domain (e. g., IEC 62351 for the energy grid [35] or IEC 62443 for industrial systems [36], in which hardware-based security is prescribed for specific security levels).

Beyond their role in secure storage, smart cards offer significant advantages in enhancing the crypto-agility of OT systems due to their physical exchangeability. When cryptographic credentials need to be updated (e. g., due to expiry, compromise, or organizational changes), the smart card can be replaced without modifying the host device or its software, assuming the new card provides compatible artifacts with the same identifiers. Even when new identifiers are introduced, only minimal reconfiguration is required.

Support for new cryptographic algorithms can also be added via updated smart cards. In such cases, the host system does not need to implement the new algorithm itself. Instead, it must support the smart card interface to invoke the desired functionality. Typically, this involves updating the host middleware to a version that supports the new APDUs and extends the PKCS#11 interface accordingly. Security libraries interfacing via PKCS#11 usually require only minor adjustments to leverage these extensions due to the generic nature of the API.

This model allows OT devices to adopt new cryptographic standards, such as PQC algorithms, with minimal software changes, streamlining integration and reducing the scope of costly recertification. Since smart cards and their operating systems are often certified as platforms under established security standards (e. g., Common Criteria [37] or FIPS 140 [38]), their integration into existing systems allows manufacturers and operators to reuse these platform certifications within a composite product evaluation of the complete device (host + smart card). As a result, recertifications after modifications to the smart card or the middleware on the host can be much simpler and faster compared to the deployment of the cryptographic functionality solely in software on the host. This significantly reduces both development and compliance overhead, particularly in regulated environments often found in OT. Furthermore, by isolating cryptographic operations from the application logic, smart cards offer a clean separation of concerns, which simplifies security audits and enables clearer security boundaries in system designs. In the context of long-lived OT deployments, this modular approach supports phased upgrades of cryptographic functionality, allowing systems to remain secure and standards-compliant throughout their lifetime. However, each modification of the middleware or the card application interface requires re-evaluation of the composed product, which can limit the extent of certification reuse. In practice, this means that compatible middleware and timely vendor support for new cryptographic features are essential for realizing these benefits.

An alternative to PKCS#11 is the more recently introduced Generic Trust Anchor API (GTA-API) [39]. This API provides a higher-level abstraction between cryptographic applications and the underlying trust anchors. Unlike PKCS#11, which requires applications to be updated with new identifiers or mechanisms when supporting new cryptographic algorithms, the GTA-API offers algorithm-agnostic integration. This enables applications, such as TLS libraries, to transparently benefit from updated smart card capabilities without requiring code changes. This also further decreases the need for recertification due to reduced host-side software changes. While GTA-API holds promise for improving crypto-agility even further, its software ecosystem is still emerging, and integration into production environments remains future work.

IV. Implementation

To demonstrate the practical viability of our proposed crypto-agility enhancement, we implemented a migration scenario from traditional public-key cryptography to PQC on embedded OT devices. This scenario leverages the smart card-based integration architecture described in Section III, allowing cryptographic capabilities to be updated and extended without modifying the host application or firmware. The selected use case involves secure communication over the TLS protocol, which is representative of widely deployed security solutions in industrial and critical infrastructure environments.

Our implementation includes two classes of target devices that reflect the heterogeneity of real-world OT deployments. The first group comprises microprocessor-based platforms running a full Linux operating system. The second group consists of resource-constrained microcontroller-based systems running a real-time operating system (RTOS). In both cases, the devices act as host platforms connected to a smart card, according to the architecture of Subsection III-A.

On each host, a middleware exposes a PKCS#11 interface to the TLS application and handles the low-level APDU communication with the smart card. To support PQC algorithms, our implementation is based on the new version 3.2 of the PKCS#11 standard [33], which introduces identifiers and mechanisms for newly standardized PQC algorithms ML-KEM, ML-DSA, and SLH-DSA. The support in application code for this version was implemented as part of this work.

On the application side, we selected WolfSSL as the TLS library due to its ability to scale across a wide range of hardware, from low-end microcontrollers to high-performance embedded systems, and its established support for PKCS#11 integration. We extended WolfSSL with support for the new version 3.2 interface and incorporated PQC support for the algorithms ML-KEM and ML-DSA. These extensions enable the library to offload sensitive cryptographic operations to the smart card without exposing private key material to the host.

For the middleware layer, we used a prototype implementation provided by Eviden that supports PKCS#11 v3.2 features, including integration with PQC-enabled smart cards. The PQC-capable smart card itself is a prototype developed by Eviden. The interface between this card and the host is based on ISO 7816-3. It supports both traditional cryptographic algorithms (RSA, ECC) and selected PQC algorithms (ML-KEM and ML-DSA). This coexistence of legacy traditional and quantum-safe algorithms on the same platform demonstrates the ability to support a phased migration strategy, a core aspect of crypto-agility in OT deployments.

In addition to support for public-key cryptography, the system also enables the use of symmetric PSKs stored on the smart card. This feature is particularly relevant for use cases requiring an additional layer of security besides public-key cryptography. For TLS integration, the smart card performs key derivation using the PSK object, as required by the TLS 1.3 key schedule. A detailed analysis of PSK integration using external security tokens is presented in [40].

To evaluate the system in practice, we developed lightweight TLS client and server applications that utilize the smart card for various cryptographic operations during the handshake:

- All trusted root certificates are retrieved from the smart card and used as trust anchors for peer authentication.
- A complete certificate chain, consisting of an entity certificate and required intermediate certificates, is read from the card for identity presentation.
- The private key corresponding to the entity certificate is used for handshake signature generation. To ensure that the key remains protected, the TLS handshake transcript (the data to be signed for the handshake signature during authentication) is sent to the smart card, which performs the signing operation internally and returns only the resulting signature.
- If required, the smart card also provides a symmetric PSK for use in the TLS key schedule, computing a session secret without revealing the underlying key material.

In the current implementation, all certificates, both roots and the device chain, are retrieved from the smart card during system initialization and cached in host memory for use during the TLS handshake. As these certificates contain only public data, their potential exposure through a host vulnerability does not present a confidentiality risk. However, storing them in host memory increases the potential attack surface, as compromised or vulnerable host software could tamper with these artifacts. A more secure approach would involve retrieving the certificate chain on demand during the TLS handshake, thereby reducing the window of exposure. Additionally, the signature verification for peer authentication using a root public key should ideally be performed directly on the smart card, preventing the trust anchors from ever being exposed to or manipulated by the host. However, realizing such functionality requires significant modifications to the WolfSSL library and is therefore left for future work.

The host-side software stack has been implemented for two environments: Linux and the embedded RTOS Zephyr. On Linux, the system interfaces with the smart card via USB using the standard CCID protocol. On embedded platforms running Zephyr RTOS, the smart card is accessed directly through the ISO 7816-3 interface. Both implementations are functionally equivalent and demonstrate that the proposed architecture is suitable for a range of hardware classes typically found in OT systems. This hardware-agnostic approach illustrates the effectiveness of smart card-based decoupling, allowing cryptographic upgrades and algorithm changes to be realized without significantly modifying the host software stack. As a result, long-term maintainability is significantly improved.

Finally, custom PKI tooling was developed to support provisioning and bootstrapping tasks. This includes the generation of PQC key pairs and X.509 certificates directly on the smart card prototype, enabling secure device initialization without exposing sensitive material outside the token. In the future, this functionality must be integrated into established PKI systems to use PQC-enabled smart cards in production environments.

V. Evaluation and Feasibility Assessment

To assess the practical feasibility of our smart card-based crypto-agility architecture, we evaluate the performance impact of using an external smart card for cryptographic operations in a typical OT deployment scenario. In line with common OT communication patterns, where long-lived secure connections are typical, we emphasize that connection establishment and initialization occur infrequently. Therefore, our evaluation aims to demonstrate that the overhead introduced by smart card offloading remains acceptable for various typical OT applications. The following subsections detail our measurement setup and present results for handshake time, memory usage, and initialization time, which are critical for constrained embedded systems.

A. Measurement Setup

All measurements are conducted on the microcontroller (MCU) STM32H743ZI from STMicroelectronics (ARM Cortex M7, 480 MHz clock), running Zephyr RTOS version 4.2. Two smart cards from Eviden are used (ID-000 SIM card form factor), connected via an ISO 7816-3 interface directly to the MCU: the commercial CardOS DI V5.3, which is only capable of traditional public-key cryptography, and the prototype of the new CardOS V8 smart card with PQC support mentioned in Section IV. By using both smart cards for the traditional measurements, the possible improvements through upgrading a card in the field while using the same algorithm are shown.

For traditional public-key cryptography, the SECP256R1 elliptic curve is used ("ECC"), while ML-DSA 44 serves as the representative PQC algorithm ("PQC"). The certificate infrastructure consists of a hierarchical PKI with a root certificate authority (CA) and a single intermediate CA that issues device (entity) certificates, resulting in a three-element certificate chain. In all configurations, the TLS key exchange uses traditional ECDHE with the SECP256R1 curve.

B. TLS Handshake Time

TLS handshake time is measured in a mutually authenticated setup, with the MCU acting as the TLS server and the client being a Raspberry Pi 4 running Linux (Raspberry Pi OS Lite, kernel 6.12). The client uses software-only artifacts, while the server is evaluated in three configurations:

1) *Software-only* ("SW-only"): All cryptographic operations are executed in software on the MCU.
2) *Card-signing*: The TLS handshake signature is computed on the smart card; verification of peer certificates is performed on the MCU.
3) *Full offload*: All signature generations and verifications (three per handshake) are delegated to the smart card.

Table I summarizes the measured time-to-first-byte (TTFB) values across all test configurations. Each value represents the average of 100 handshake runs within an isolated network with a round-trip time of about 0.3 ms, measuring the time from the start of the handshake to the receipt of the first application-layer byte on the client side.

TABLE I. TTFB results for ECC and PQC (in milliseconds).

Setup	SW-only	Card-signing	Full offload
ECC (V5.3)	22.92	221.43	3619.67
ECC (V8)		137.78	2961.33
PQC	49.19	453.52	4148.81

The software-only configuration provides a performance baseline for each cryptographic algorithm. As expected, the TTFB increases when cryptographic operations are offloaded to the smart card. The card-signing configuration introduces moderate latency as the handshake transcript must be transmitted to the smart card, and the generated signature is read by the host. The full offload configuration adds a large additional delay, since in addition to signing, all peer signature verifications are delegated to the card. These operations require importing the peer's public keys, verifying the signatures, and removing the imported keys again, adding several round-trips over the card interface in addition to the computations.

The ECC setup consistently shows lower latency than PQC across all configurations. This difference reflects the higher processing requirements and larger data sizes associated with PQC, especially in its current state of maturity. While ECC benefits from decades of optimization and mature hardware-supported implementations, PQC support is still emerging. The current PQC smart card prototype relies on pure software implementations for PQC algorithms. Additionally, PQC artifacts, such as signatures and public keys, are significantly larger, further contributing to transmission and processing delays. Nevertheless, the results demonstrate that even full offload of PQC operations is technically feasible and remains within acceptable bounds for many OT applications, where handshakes occur infrequently and connections are long-lived.

In addition, the reduced ECC measurement results for the newer prototype smart card indicate the potential future improvements possible through an agile system architecture using exchangeable smart cards. Only by upgrading to a newer smart card generation without any software changes (as long as the artifacts on the card use the same identifiers as on the old one), performance can be improved substantially. This also indicates that the currently larger latency of the PQC algorithms will be reduced in the future.

C. Memory Overhead

The peak heap memory usage during the TLS handshake execution is shown in Table II, measured on the MCU platform. For both the commercial smart card and the prototype, the same middleware is used. One of the expected advantages of smart card-based cryptography is the ability to offload computation and reduce memory pressure on the host. However, the current implementation of the middleware has not yet been optimized for resource-constrained embedded deployment. As a result, the measured peak memory usage in the smart card-based configurations is noticeably higher than in the software-only baselines, which are well optimized by WolfSSL for embedded targets.

TABLE II. PEAK HEAP MEMORY USAGE (IN KB).

Configuration	Peak RAM
ECC - Software-only	20.664
ECC - Full offload	36.320
PQC - Software-only	50.832
PQC - Full offload	67.496

The increased memory footprint is primarily attributed to internal buffering, data marshalling, and generic logic within the middleware. These aspects are expected to be significantly reduced through tailored memory management, removal of unnecessary buffers, and streamlined protocol logic. Importantly, the long-term benefits of the smart card-based approach remain valid even with current results and are expected to improve as the implementation matures.

D. Initialization Latency

Finally, Table III shows the initialization latency for both ECC and PQC setups on the MCU platform. This includes middleware startup, smart card initialization, and sequential certificate readout (root, intermediate, and entity certificates).

TABLE III. INITIALIZATION LATENCY (IN MILLISECONDS).

Algorithm	Duration
ECC (V5.3)	999.47
ECC (V8)	859.68
PQC	2920.36

In the SW-only setup, initialization takes less than 1 ms for both algorithms. The difference between the ECC variants again indicates improvements through a newer smart card. The large increase in the PQC setup is mainly due to the significantly larger size of PQC artifacts transmitted through the slow ISO 7816-3 interface. For instance, the PQC entity certificate is around 4182 bytes, compared to just 590 bytes for ECC. Nonetheless, initialization occurs only once per system boot or after a smart card replacement, making it a rare event in OT environments. Given this infrequency, the added latency is acceptable and does not affect ongoing runtime performance.

E. Summary

The evaluation confirms that the use of exchangeable smart cards for cryptographic operations in TLS is feasible on resource-constrained embedded OT devices. While the use of smart cards introduces additional latency during handshake and initialization, these overheads are bounded and acceptable in many OT environments in which secure sessions are long-lived, devices rarely reboot, and safety considerations permit it. The results further demonstrate that even PQC algorithms can be integrated via smart cards without requiring host-side cryptographic implementations. Although the current performance results for PQC are worse than those of ECC due to the unoptimized state of the implementations, future adjustments are expected to improve performance. Overall, the findings validate the practical viability of achieving crypto-agility through smart cards in constrained OT deployments.

VI. SECURITY CONSIDERATIONS

The proposed smart card-based crypto-agility architecture significantly improves modularity and hence longevity in OT systems. However, the use of exchangeable smart cards connected to host devices also introduces new security challenges, particularly when the interface between the host and the smart card is left unprotected. This section analyzes the resulting threat landscape (Subsection VI-A), outlines mitigation strategies (Subsection VI-B), and discusses the achieved security level with extended protections in place (Subsection VI-C).

A. Threat Model

We consider a representative OT deployment in which multiple devices communicate over secure channels, such as TLS. Each device participates in a PKI and contains root certificates, a device-specific certificate chain, and a private key. Optionally, one or more symmetric PSKs may be used. All cryptographic artifacts are stored on a smart card attached to the host device. We assume that the smart card's internal storage is secure, with its tamper resistance being evaluated and certified, and that direct extraction or manipulation of its contents is infeasible.

The smart card serves as the secure execution environment for cryptographic operations, including digital signatures using private keys and symmetric key derivation based on PSKs, and enables peer authentication, either via certificate-based trust anchors or through possession of symmetric PSKs. An attacker's primary goals are to compromise this setup by

- Extracting private keys or PSKs stored on the smart card,
- Modifying trusted root certificates or identity-related data on the card,
- Breaking message integrity or impersonating one peer to enable eavesdropping or man-in-the-middle attacks.

The currently considered setup relies on PIN-based access control: the host device must present a shared PIN to the smart card to enable the retrieval or use of stored cryptographic artifacts for operations such as key exchange, authentication, or signing. However, this mechanism exhibits a critical security flaw. While the PIN may be stored in a secure storage within the host, it is transmitted in plaintext via APDUs during runtime. A local attacker with access to the communication interface between host and card can eavesdrop on the PIN, allowing unauthorized access to the smart card and its stored artifacts. As a result, we identify the following attack scenarios:

1) *Communication Tampering*: An attacker intercepts and modifies the APDU messages between the host and the smart card. This allows the attacker to forge operations, such as generating signatures for malicious data or substituting data read from the card (e. g., certificates).
2) *Smart Card Theft*: If the smart card is physically removed from the host and connected to a malicious device, the attacker can use its credentials to impersonate the original device (host + smart card) in the network.

3) *Malicious Smart Card Insertion*: A manipulated smart card is inserted into the host device. This card may be programmed to leak secrets or respond incorrectly to authentication or signing requests.

These threats highlight the need for a secure association between the host and the smart card, as well as protected communication between them. For our elaborations in the following section, we assume that such a pairing process can be performed within a trusted provisioning environment, enabling the deployment of suitable cryptographic mechanisms.

B. Secure Pairing between Host and Smart Card

To mitigate the threats described above, we propose to establish a cryptographic coupling between the host and the smart card during a secure pairing process. This approach prevents unauthorized hosts or smart cards from being accepted and protects the integrity and confidentiality of all communications between them. Our design is based on two main requirements:

- *Mutual Authentication*: During each session, the host and the smart card must authenticate each other to prevent impersonation or rogue device usage.
- *Secure Channel Establishment*: All APDU exchanges must be cryptographically protected to guarantee message authenticity, integrity, and confidentiality.

To achieve this, the host and the smart card are provisioned with a shared symmetric secret during the secure pairing phase. This secret is then used to derive ephemeral session keys for authenticated encryption of APDU traffic. Furthermore, knowledge of the session keys derived from this secret implicitly authenticates both peers. Public-key cryptography could alternatively be used to establish mutual trust, but managing host-side key material reintroduces the complexity that our smart card-centric design seeks to avoid. Therefore, we prefer symmetric approaches for simplicity and performance.

Two standardized protocols are suitable for this purpose, which are already available in various commercial products:

- *Secure Channel Protocol 03* (SCP03) [41]: Widely adopted in commercial smart cards, SCP03 uses static PSKs to derive session keys for message encryption and authentication. It does not require public-key cryptography and has been formally verified for security [42].
- *Password Authenticated Connection Establishment* (PACE) [43][44]: Originally developed for eIDs and ePassports, PACE maps a user-provided password (or PIN) to a session key using a combination of symmetric and ephemeral public-key cryptography. While more complex and reliant on public-key operations, PACE has also been formally proven secure [45][46]. However, it requires adaptation for use with PQC algorithms [47][48].

Among these, SCP03 provides a lightweight and efficient solution that aligns well with the constraints and goals of OT environments. It supports symmetric authentication, message encryption, and integrity protection without introducing asymmetric key management overhead. In contrast, PACE offers comparable security guarantees, especially if adapted for PQC in the future, but comes with significantly higher complexity due to its use of ephemeral public-key cryptography and more comprehensive protocol steps. While technically feasible, this added complexity makes PACE less attractive for resource-constrained OT systems where simplicity, footprint, and integration effort are critical design considerations.

C. Resulting Protection Level

By integrating a secure communication protocol between the host and the smart card, sensitive APDUs can be cryptographically protected. Protocols like SCP03 and PACE are supported by many commercial smart card platforms, allowing integration into the described architecture with only moderate implementation effort. As a result, communication tampering is impossible, and an attacker is prevented from using a stolen smart card in a malicious device or inserting a malicious smart card, as long as the shared symmetric secret is protected.

Although the secure channel protocols introduce additional processing overhead due to the protection of each exchanged APDU, the impact on overall system performance is expected to be minimal. Since they rely solely on symmetric cryptography, the computational cost is low. Furthermore, the limited speed of the host $\leftrightarrow$ smart card interface further renders the cryptographic overhead less influential compared to the latency of the communication.

Regarding the protection of the shared symmetric secret, the secure internal storage of the smart card is considered secure, ensuring that its stored artifacts remain confidential and tamper-resistant. However, it is assumed that the pairing process itself is performed in a trusted environment. In practice, this assumption may not always hold: while some OT setups allow for secure provisioning before or even after initial deployment, others might require pairing in less controlled field environments. The design of pairing mechanisms that remain secure under such operational constraints represents an important challenge for future research. For the scope of this work, we neglect the detailed pairing process and focus on the security properties once a trusted pairing has been established. In total, overall system security now depends on the protection of the shared symmetric secret on the host.

Modern embedded platforms often include secure storage capabilities within their SoCs. While typically less robust and less rigorously certified than smart card storage, these mechanisms still raise the attacker's cost significantly. Physical access and dedicated setups for side-channel measurements are usually required to extract keys from host memory [49]–[51], and such intrusions are infeasible during normal device operation. In addition, in OT systems, unexpected downtime or physical tampering is likely to trigger rapid alerts or inspections. This further raises the bar for a successful attack.

In summary, the proposed protection scheme eliminates the transmission of PINs in plaintext, ensures mutual trust between the host and the smart card, and protects all exchanged messages. The resulting system achieves crypto-agility, enabling modular upgrades and long-term maintainability in OT environments without expanding the attack surface.

VII. Conclusion and Future Work

This paper introduced a smart card-based architecture to enable crypto-agility in OT systems. By decoupling cryptographic algorithm support and key management from the host device, our approach addresses the challenges of deploying modern cryptography, such as PQC, on constrained and long-lived embedded platforms.

We demonstrated that new cryptographic algorithms can be integrated without requiring host-side implementation, supporting *algorithm agnosticism* and reducing the scope for recertification. Our architecture supports *flexible deployment of cryptographic artifacts*, including both asymmetric key pairs and symmetric keys, using standardized APIs and pre-personalized smart cards. We validated the approach through *practical implementation* on resource-constrained microcontrollers and showed that handshake latency and memory usage remain acceptable in common OT scenarios. Finally, we conducted an *OT-specific security analysis*, addressing the risks of smart card exchangeability and proposing secure pairing mechanisms between hosts and smart cards.

Future work will explore the integration of commercially available smart cards to replace the current prototype and extend support to additional cryptographic algorithms and formats. The implementation of secure communication protocols, such as SCP03 and PACE, together with the creation of the secure pairing process, will further strengthen the protection of sensitive operations between the host and the smart card. Additionally, the emerging GTA-API offers a promising abstraction to simplify application-side integration and will be investigated as a next step toward maximizing crypto-agility.

Acknowledgments

The presented work is part of the research project *KRITIS Scalable Safe and Secure Modules* (KRITIS³M), which is funded by the Project Management Jülich (PtJ) and the German Federal Ministry for Economic Affairs and Climate Action (BMWK) under funding code 03EI6089A.

References

[1] P. Viorel, *Preparing ICS for Future Threats with Quantum-Resistant Cybersecurity*, Nov. 2024. [Online]. Available: https://www.iiot-world.com/ics-security/cybersecurity/preparing-ics-future-threats-quantum-cybersecurity/ (Retrieved: 09/04/2025).

[2] Waterfall team, *How Industrial Cybersecurity Works in 2025*, Jun. 2025. [Online]. Available: https://waterfall-security.com/ot-insights-center/ot-cybersecurity-insights-center/industrial-cyber-security/ (Retrieved: 09/04/2025).

[3] A. Ribeiro, *EU begins coordinated effort for Member States to switch critical infrastructure to quantum-resistant encryption by 2030*, Jun. 2025. [Online]. Available: https://industrialcyber.co/regulation-standards-and-compliance/eu-begins-coordinated-effort-for-member-states-to-switch-critical-infrastructure-to-quantum-resistant-encryption-by-2030/ (Retrieved: 09/04/2025).

[4] National Cyber Security Centre, *Timelines for migration to post-quantum cryptography*. [Online]. Available: https://www.ncsc.gov.uk/guidance/pqc-migration-timelines (Retrieved: 09/04/2025).

[5] Cybersecurity & Infrastructure Security Agency (CISA), *Post-Quantum Considerations for Operational Technology*, Jun. 2025. [Online]. Available: https://www.cisa.gov/resources-tools/resources/post-quantum-considerations-operational-technology (Retrieved: 09/04/2025).

[6] T. Frauenschläger and J. Mottok, "Problems and New Approaches for Crypto-Agility in Operational Technology", in *12th European Congress Embedded Real Time Systems - ERTS 2024*, Jun. 2024. [Online]. Available: https://hal.science/hal-04614197.

[7] M. Khan, M. Ilyas, and O. Bayat, "Enhancing IoT Security Through Hardware Security Modules (HSMs)", in *2024 International Conference on Intelligent Computing, Communication, Networking and Services (ICCNS)*, IEEE, Sep. 2024, pp. 278–282. DOI: 10.1109/iccns62192.2024.10776375.

[8] M. Pritikin, P. E. Yee, and D. Harkins, *Enrollment over Secure Transport*, RFC 7030, Oct. 2013. DOI: 10.17487/RFC7030.

[9] R. Barnes, J. Hoffman-Andrews, D. McCarney, and J. Kasten, *Automatic Certificate Management Environment (ACME)*, RFC 8555, Mar. 2019. DOI: 10.17487/RFC8555.

[10] P. Gutmann, *Simple Certificate Enrolment Protocol*, RFC 8894, Sep. 2020. DOI: 10.17487/RFC8894.

[11] M. Pritikin, M. Richardson, T. Eckert, M. H. Behringer, and K. Watsen, *Bootstrapping Remote Secure Key Infrastructure (BRSKI)*, RFC 8995, May 2021. DOI: 10.17487/RFC8995.

[12] D. von Oheimb, S. Fries, and H. Brockhaus, *BRSKI with Alternative Enrollment (BRSKI-AE)*, RFC 9733, Mar. 2025. DOI: 10.17487/RFC9733.

[13] J. Astorga, M. Barcelo, A. Urbieta, and E. Jacob, "How to Survive Identity Management in the Industry 4.0 Era", *IEEE Access*, vol. 9, 2021. DOI: 10.1109/access.2021.3092203.

[14] J. Höglund, S. Lindemer, M. Furuhed, and S. Raza, "PKI4IoT: Towards public key infrastructure for the Internet of Things", *Computers & Security*, vol. 89, Feb. 2020, Publisher: Elsevier BV. DOI: 10.1016/j.cose.2019.101658.

[15] J. Höglund and S. Raza, "LICE: Lightweight certificate enrollment for IoT using application layer security", in *2021 IEEE Conference on Communications and Network Security (CNS)*, Oct. 2021, pp. 19–28. DOI: 10.1109/CNS53000.2021.9705036.

[16] J. Höglund *et al.*, "AutoPKI: Public key infrastructure for IoT with automated trust transfer", *International Journal of Information Security*, vol. 23, no. 3, pp. 1859–1875, Jun. 2024, Publisher: Springer Science and Business Media LLC. DOI: 10.1007/s10207-024-00825-z.

[17] M. El-Hajj and P. Beune, "Decentralized Zone-Based PKI: A Lightweight Security Framework for IoT Ecosystems", *Information*, vol. 15, no. 6, May 2024, Publisher: MDPI AG, ISSN: 2078-2489. DOI: 10.3390/info15060304.

[18] Q. Zhang, Y. He, Y. Xiao, X. Zhang, and C. Song, "OTA-Key: Over the Air Key Management for Flexible and Reliable IoT Device Provision", *IEEE Transactions on Network and Service Management*, vol. 22, no. 2, Apr. 2025, arXiv:2412.11564 [cs]. DOI: 10.1109/TNSM.2024.3515212.

[19] Fortanix, *Secure Manufacturing of IoT Devices*. [Online]. Available: https://www.fortanix.com/resources/solution-briefs/secure-manufacturing-of-iot-devices (Retrieved: 09/04/2025).

[20] C. Lesjak *et al.*, "Securing smart maintenance services: Hardware-security and TLS for MQTT", in *2015 IEEE 13th International Conference on Industrial Informatics (INDIN)*, 2015, pp. 1243–1250. DOI: 10.1109/INDIN.2015.7281913.

[21] A. J. Paverd and A. P. Martin, "Hardware Security for Device Authentication in the Smart Grid", in *Smart Grid Security*, Springer Berlin Heidelberg, 2013, pp. 72–84, ISBN: 978-3-642-38030-3.

[22] O. Kehret, A. Walz, and A. Sikora, "Integration of Hardware Security Modules into a Deeply Embedded TLS Stack", *In-*

ternational Journal of Computing, vol. 15, pp. 22–30, Mar. 2016. DOI: 10.47839/ijc.15.1.827.

[23] R. Matischek and B. Bara, "Application Study of Hardware-Based Security for Future Industrial IoT", in *2019 22nd Euromicro Conference on Digital System Design (DSD)*, 2019, pp. 246–252. DOI: 10.1109/DSD.2019.00044.

[24] O. Gilles, D. G. Pérez, P. A. Brameret, and V. Lacroix, "Securing IIoT communications using OPC UA PubSub and Trusted Platform Modules", *Journal of Systems Architecture*, vol. 134, p. 102 797, Jan. 2023. DOI: 10.1016/J.SYSARC.2022.102797.

[25] P. Urien, "Innovative TLS 1.3 Identity Module for Trusted IoT Device", in *2021 IEEE 18th Annual Consumer Communications & Networking Conference (CCNC)*, 2021, pp. 1–4. DOI: 10.1109/CCNC49032.2021.9369656.

[26] P. Urien, "On Line Secure Elements: Deploying High Security Keystores and Personal HSMs", in *2023 International Conference on Computing, Networking and Communications (ICNC)*, 2023, pp. 450–455. DOI: 10.1109/ICNC57223.2023.10074066.

[27] P. Urien, "Revisiting Multi-Factor Authentication Token Cybersecurity: A TLS Identity Module Use Case", in *2024 International Conference on Computing, Networking and Communications (ICNC)*, 2024, pp. 33–38. DOI: 10.1109/ICNC59896.2024.10556005.

[28] P. Urien, "Innovative Open On-Line Secure Elements Providing Secure Storage and Trusted Computing Resources: Invited Paper", in *2024 Ninth International Conference On Mobile And Secure Services (MobiSecServ)*, vol. CFP24RAC-ART, 2024, pp. 1–6. DOI: 10.1109/MobiSecServ63327.2024.10759976.

[29] P. Urien, "A New Approach for Crypto Off-loading Based on Personal HSM", in *2023 7th Cyber Security in Networking Conference (CSNet)*, Montreal, QC, Canada: IEEE, Oct. 2023, pp. 23–26. DOI: 10.1109/csnet59123.2023.10339762.

[30] P. Urien, "Personal HSM, Privacy for Subscribers in 5G/6G Networks", in *2022 1st International Conference on 6G Networking (6GNet)*, Paris, France: IEEE, Jul. 2022, pp. 1–6. DOI: 10.1109/6gnet54646.2022.9830453.

[31] ISO/IEC JTC 1/SC 17, "Identification cards — Integrated circuit cards — Part 3: Cards with contacts — Electrical interface and transmission protocols", International Organization for Standardization, Standard ISO/IEC 7816-3:2006, Nov. 2006.

[32] ISO/IEC JTC 1/SC 17, "Identification cards — Integrated circuit cards — Part 4: Organization, security and commands for interchange", International Organization for Standardization, Standard ISO/IEC 7816-4:2020, May 2020.

[33] D. Bong and G. Scott, *PKCS #11 Specification Version 3.2*, OASIS Standard, Apr. 2025. [Online]. Available: https://docs.oasis-open.org/pkcs11/pkcs11-spec/v3.2/pkcs11-spec-v3.2.html.

[34] OpenSC team, *OpenSC*, Jul. 2025. [Online]. Available: https://github.com/OpenSC/OpenSC (Retrieved: 09/04/2025).

[35] International Electrotechnical Commission, "Power systems management and associated information exchange – Data and communications security", Standard IEC/TS 62351:2025, 2025.

[36] International Electrotechnical Commission, "Industrial communication networks – Network and system security", Standard IEC/TS 62443:2009, 2009.

[37] ISO/IEC JTC 1/SC 27, "Information technology — Security techniques — Evaluation criteria for IT security", International Organization for Standardization, Standard ISO/IEC 15408-1/2/3:2020, Dec. 2020.

[38] National Institute of Standards and Technology (US), "Security requirements for cryptographic modules", National Institute of Standards and Technology, Washington, D.C., Tech. Rep., 2019. DOI: 10.6028/nist.fips.140-3.

[39] ISO/IEC JTC 1/SC 41, "Internet of Things (IoT) — Generic trust anchor application programming interface for industrial IoT devices", International Organization for Standardization, Standard ISO/IEC TS 30168:2024, May 2024.

[40] T. Frauenschläger, L. Füreder, and J. Mottok, "Enhancing Quantum-Safe Cryptography in TLS: The Role of Pre-Shared Keys", in *2025 International Conference on Applied Electronics (AE)*, IEEE, Sep. 2025.

[41] GlobalPlatform Technology, *Secure Channel Protocol 03*, Apr. 2020. [Online]. Available: https://globalplatform.org/specs-library/secure-channel-protocol-03-amendment-d-v1-2.

[42] M. Sabt and J. Traoré, "Cryptanalysis of GlobalPlatform Secure Channel Protocols", in *Security Standardisation Research. Lecture Notes in Computer Science*, Springer International Publishing, 2016, pp. 62–91. DOI: 10.1007/978-3-319-49100-4_3.

[43] Federal Office for Information Security, *BSI TR-03110: Advanced Security Mechanisms for Machine Readable Travel Documents and eIDAS Token*, 2016. [Online]. Available: https://www.bsi.bund.de/EN/Themen/Unternehmen-und-Organisationen/Standards-und-Zertifizierung/Technische-Richtlinien/TR-nach-Thema-sortiert/tr03110/tr-03110.html?nn=909310 (Retrieved: 09/04/2025).

[44] ICAO, *Doc 9303: Machine Readable Travel Documents*, 2021. [Online]. Available: https://www2023.icao.int/publications/Documents/9303_p11_cons_en.pdf (Retrieved: 09/04/2025).

[45] J. Bender, M. Fischlin, and D. Kügler, "Security Analysis of the PACE Key-Agreement Protocol", in *Information Security. ISC 2009. Lecture Notes in Computer Science*, Springer Berlin Heidelberg, 2009, pp. 33–48. DOI: 10.1007/978-3-642-04474-8_3.

[46] J.-S. Coron, A. Gouget, T. Icart, and P. Paillier, "Supplemental Access Control (PACE v2): Security Analysis of PACE Integrated Mapping", in *Cryptography and Security: From Theory to Applications. Lecture Notes in Computer Science*, Springer Berlin Heidelberg, 2012, pp. 207–232. DOI: 10.1007/978-3-642-28368-0_15.

[47] N. Alnahawi, J. Alperin-Sheriff, D. Apon, G. T. Davies, and A. Wiesmaier, *NICE-PAKE: On the Security of KEM-Based PAKE Constructions without Ideal Ciphers*, Cryptology ePrint Archive, Paper 2024/1957, Publication info: Preprint., 2024. [Online]. Available: https://eprint.iacr.org/2024/1957 (Retrieved: 07/15/2025).

[48] N. Alnahawi *et al.*, *Post-Quantum Cryptography in eMRTDs: Evaluating PAKE and PKI for Travel Documents*, Cryptology ePrint Archive, Paper 2025/812, Publication info: Preprint., 2025. [Online]. Available: https://eprint.iacr.org/2025/812 (Retrieved: 07/15/2025).

[49] T. Krachenfels, T. Kiyan, S. Tajik, and J.-P. Seifert, "Automatic extraction of secrets from the transistor jungle using Laser-Assisted Side-Channel attacks", in *30th USENIX Security Symposium (USENIX Security 21)*, USENIX Association, Aug. 2021, pp. 627–644, ISBN: 978-1-939133-24-3. [Online]. Available: https://www.usenix.org/conference/usenixsecurity21/presentation/krachenfels.

[50] K. Murdock *et al.*, "Plundervolt: Software-based Fault Injection Attacks against Intel SGX", in *2020 IEEE Symposium on Security and Privacy (SP)*, 2020, pp. 1466–1482. DOI: 10.1109/SP40000.2020.00057.

[51] H. Lohrke, S. Tajik, T. Krachenfels, C. Boit, and J.-P. Seifert, "Key Extraction Using Thermal Laser Stimulation: A Case Study on Xilinx Ultrascale FPGAs", *IACR Transactions on Cryptographic Hardware and Embedded Systems*, pp. 573–595, Aug. 2018. DOI: 10.46586/tches.v2018.i3.573-595.

A Modular and Flexible OPC UA Testbed Prototype for Cybersecurity Research

Sebastian Kraust, Peter Heller and Jürgen Mottok
Laboratory for Safe and Secure Systems (LaS³)
OTH Regensburg
93053 Regensburg, Germany
e-mail: {sebastian.kraust | peter2.heller | juergen.mottok}@oth-regensburg.de

Abstract—**The security assessment of Industrial Control Systems (ICS) is becoming increasingly challenging due to their growing complexity and interconnectivity. Traditional penetration testing is often impractical in live environments due to the risk of operational disruption, making testbeds essential for evaluating security mechanisms, analyzing threats, and developing defense strategies. However, existing testbeds tend to be static and difficult to quickly adapt to a wide variety of scenarios. To address these limitations, we propose a modular and flexible ICS testbed that enables rapid reconfiguration of the testbed composition in order to test a wide variety of scenarios. Our open-source approach leverages containerized applications as building blocks, allowing users to create and modify the testbed with minimal effort. We show how to use the provided components to construct testbeds and how our approach can be used as a tool for accommodating penetration tests.**

Keywords-testbed; OPC UA; cybersecurity; penetration testing.

I. Introduction

The increasing complexity and interconnectivity of Industrial Control Systems (ICS) require extensive security assessments. This is no trivial task considering the rapidly evolving attack surface and the widespread use of devices and protocols without security features. Penetration tests offer a way to actively assess a system's security status but are not practical in live environments due to the risk of damaging equipment and endangering human life. Testbeds address this issue by providing a safe environment for evaluating security mechanisms, analyzing cyber-physical threats, and developing defense strategies. However, existing testbeds are often static in nature, tightly coupled to specific architectures, or require extensive effort to modify, making them unsuitable for adapting them to the specific needs for a given scenario. Most notably, this rigidity limits their usefulness for assessing threats to one's own system, which might be vastly different from a prefabricated testbed.

To address this issue, we introduce a novel ICS testbed prototype designed for maximum modularity and flexibility, enabling rapid restructuring and reconfiguration to accommodate various attack vectors and system configurations. The basic idea is to provide a set of building blocks in the form of containerized applications, from which a wide variety of testbed compositions can be created with minimal manual effort. By making the testbed components freely available, we hope to facilitate the sharing of problematic scenarios, insights, and custom testbed extensions within the research community.

In this paper, we first describe our design process along with the relevant literature in Section II. Then, we present the basic concept and components in Section III, and create and modify a basic testbed. We also show how containers can be swapped to enable security tests with certain vulnerabilities. We summarize the paper and provide an outlook for future work in Section IV.

II. Design Process and Related Work

Prior to introducing the testbed, we provide the relevant context regarding the project environment in which it was developed, and highlight topics and issues we encountered that influenced our design.

The idea for a new type of testbed was developed within the context of a research project focusing on improving the cyber resilience of critical infrastructure systems. Key elements include the exploration of new active and passive cyber security techniques for industrial environments powered by artificial intelligence. We conducted extensive literature research to find a suitable testbed that we could recreate. However, this turned out to be difficult due to lack of information or accessibility. As a result, we decided to develop our own environment to have total control over a system while launching realistic attacks. During this process, we first noticed an evident lack of literature that addresses testbed design in industrial environments. Most publications touch upon it only very briefly and instead cite a real system or a reference model as the inspiration, as shown in [1]. As a result, we decided to document our thought process during the development process.

The first task was to choose a common industrial protocol with known vulnerabilities, working exploits, and readily accessible toolkits and SDKs. Ultimately, OPC Unified Architecture (OPC UA) was selected as the primary protocol for a number of reasons: first, it is well defined in the open standard IEC 62541 [2] and comes with a plethora of security-relevant features, such as encryption, authentication, and certificate management. Second, it supports the creation of complex hierarchical system architectures, which are high-value targets for adversaries due to their highly interconnected monitoring and control devices. Lastly, OPC UA fits well into the context of our research project and has a significant share of usage in industry and research. We also realized that flexibility would play an important role during design, due to the great number of existing implementations of the protocol and the extensive configuration capabilities. Secondary protocols for simulating other legitimate applications in an ICS environment and additional noise are planned to be included in the future, but are not a focal point.

TABLE I. COMPARISON OF TESTBED FEATURES

Feature	MiniCPS [13]	DHALSIM [14]	MOTRA [12]
Focus	ICS network simulation, SDN	Impact analysis of ICS traffic events on physical process simulation	Penetration testing
Network fidelity	high	high	low (focus on OPC UA)
Physical process fidelity	low	high (EPANET, water-only)	low
Deployment	single host (Mininet)	single host co-sim	single/multi host (Docker)
Swap implementation/version	codebase modification	codebase modification	Docker images/tags

OPC UA provides a framework in which complex information can be modeled and accessed with standardized services [3][4]. The most basic building blocks are called *nodes*, which are used to construct more complex structures, such as hierarchical data types and objects. The entirety of all node instances is called the *address space*, which defines a standard way of structuring the nodes within in a tree-like fashion. This achieves a consistent way for servers to present data to clients. Initially, we focused on building prototypes of virtual devices for a custom water treatment testbed with different OPC UA software stacks and versions to enable certain vulnerabilities. For all these variants, we manually created all required nodes within the address space. Although we achieved near-identical behavior, the resulting tree structure was not exactly the same, making quick one-to-one replacements of devices during our penetration tests unfeasible. Furthermore, maintaining the different stack versions written in their respective programming languages required significant amounts of time and effort. Fortunately, OPC UA also allows the address space and custom extensions to be modeled using XML. Through the use of tools like the *OPC UA Model Compiler*, the source code for specific implementations can be generated automatically using a common modeling language. Most available stacks support these extensions; thus we can use a standardized way of building and maintaining devices by using XML-based models and configurations. This simplified the workflow and allowed us to verify a variety of vulnerabilities.

Developing interchangeable implementations was merely the initial phase in establishing a versatile framework. Subsequently, we needed to tackle their deployment. Container technology was the first solution to be considered as it allows packaging software to be developed and deployed independently of the underlying hardware. It can even be deployed on embedded platforms with built-in support for different platforms, such as x86 and ARM64. It also guarantees reproducible results, as it leaves no room for errors regarding software versions, installed tool chains, etc., and simplifies exchanging implementations by replacing containers. Other advantages include implicit versioning through tags, easy software sharing with the research community, and, to a certain extent, the ability to recreate testbeds and verify results independently. In addition, many network simulation tools, such as GNS3, natively support container integration, which facilitates the creation of complex architectures. Finally, the flexibility to replace any container through a real component makes it easy to expand from a virtual to a hybrid setup.

The ability to grow into a hybrid setup turns out to be very relevant, as commercial, proprietary products often use reference implementations as a basis. In 2021, OTORIO [5] released their latest research on OPC UA attack surface, mapping out supply chain dependencies for a number of major manufacturers. Based on the specification available from the standard body (IEC 62541 [2]), there have been different releases of the OPC UA Core Stack for public use. Before this, there have been different stacks (namely: .NET legacy, ANSI C legacy, JAVA legacy) that are not officially supported anymore. As OTORIO has shown, there is a significant relationship between the reference stack implementations and the selected OPC UA SDKs. The foundation reference implementations and core stacks have been partly used to design or build commercial and open source SDKs for products by different OEMs [5]. Due to the ability to include such products in a hybrid setup, we can also evaluate vulnerabilities in these proprietary stacks.

Finally, further aspects that we came across during development are configuration and bootstrapping issues. While the underlying protocol has been verified to be securely designed and audited by several bodies (BSI [6], Kaspersky [7], Claroty [8]), proper configuration, bootstrapping, and personnel training are still major issues [9]–[11]. Furthermore, certain implementations are characterized by incomplete feature sets and potentially confusing documentation. As a result, we started to vary the configurations in addition to the software stack itself.

Considering these issues in conjunction with the aforementioned lack of testbed design literature, we implement the penetration testing-focused methodology for deriving testbeds proposed by Kraust et al. [1] as a proof of concept. It introduces an iterative, protocol-agnostic approach that gradually builds up a complex testbed from individual devices. During each iteration, penetration tests including their respective goals are defined and executed. The following iterations build on the knowledge gained, which allows the user to create more complex attacks over time. To be able to do this, the testbed must be modular in nature. As a consequence, we analyzed the OPC UA protocol in terms of its features and capabilities, which allowed us to extract the basic building blocks of a testbed centered around this protocol. We then used the so-called *Model Compiler* to translate XML files with the specified nodes of OPC UA devices into actual source code across different implementations. In this way, we were able to create applications with the same interface that use various software stacks underneath. These building blocks are currently available on Github [12]. We will explain the full extent of the available software in the following section. In this paper, we will use these building blocks to actually construct an exemplary water treatment testbed.

To conclude this section, we want to briefly address how this testbed concept distinguishes itself from other approaches in the ICS domain that also emphasize flexibility and reproducibility instead of using a static setup. For this comparison, we have chosen to use MiniCPS [13] and DHALSIM [14]. The former is a toolkit that extends Mininet (a network emulator) to emulate realistic ICS networks, providing a physical-layer API for coupling simulations. It was developed in response to the lack of generic simulation environments for cyber-physical systems (CPS), providing a framework that supports physical interactions and industrial protocols while placing a strong focus on software-defined networking (SDN). DHALSIM combines MiniCPS with the EPANET process simulator to achieve high-fidelity co-simulation of water distribution systems in order to study the impact of network anomalies and faults on the process. Table I summarizes the key features and highlights the differences compared to our approach. Although MiniCPS and DHALSIM can be used for cybersecurity analyses, this was not their primary design objective. Consequently, essential penetration testing features, such as quick and easy reconfiguration, multi-host setups, and swapping protocol implementations and software versions, require more time and effort. MOTRA was developed with these needs in mind, focusing on protocol-level interactions and semantics rather than high network-level fidelity.

III. The Testbed

The goal of this section is to introduce the reader to the overall testbed concept and to highlight how researchers can build a testbed tailored to specific scenarios. We divide our presentation into two parts: first, we introduce the overall concept and the building blocks. Second, we build up an exemplary testbed from scratch and show how the modular approach can be used to modify the system with minimal effort to perform a specific penetration test.

A. Concept and Components

The concept of a flexible testbed through the use of containers allows users to test specific setups and configurations, and enables reproducible experiments across cybersecurity practitioners. This requires careful consideration of how to split testbeds into reusable chunks. During our initial tests, we often found ourselves in the situation of needing another already existing component, such as another sensor or actuator. As a result, packaging software units that perform a certain function was the obvious choice. The exemplary testbed used in this paper is shown in Figure 1a, where these units (hereinafter referred to as *Components*) are shown as white boxes. For the chosen OPC UA protocol, they can be derived in part from the protocol specification, such as discovery or global services.

In addition to the pure functionality, the next most relevant properties for penetration testing considerations are the underlying software stacks and the respective versions. Generally, components (e. g., the valve-server) can be realized using different implementations. Depending on the stack used, specific vulnerabilities exist and can be exploited. Closely related to this is the selection of the exact software version. As developers constantly patch their software to improve security, many real-world systems do not receive timely updates and continue to run with outdated versions. We account for this issue by allowing for the specification of a certain version. As a result, we package components according to these three parameters as separate containers, which is reflected in the suggested naming scheme in the following section. We decided to use Docker as the containerization solution, as it is freely available, well-known, and feature-rich.

Before explaining the usage of the suggested testbed, we provide a rough description of the workflow and the components shown in Figure 1a. Please note that unless stated otherwise, all components communicate using the OPC UA protocol. In principle, the functionality could be replicated using any other suitable protocol.

In essence, the testbed simulates a closed, single water tank system as shown in Figure 1b. It has a static outflow and an adjustable inflow through a pump. The water level is kept between an upper limit (V_{max}) and a lower limit (V_{min}) by activating the pump when the water level falls below V_{min} and deactivating it upon reaching V_{max}. The water level in the tank is monitored by a single fill level sensor. Depending on the current level, water purification chemicals are added by activating a valve. The control of the valve, logging, and monitoring functionalities are realized by the architecture shown in Figure 1a. In the following, we take a closer look at the individual components.

watertank-simulation - This component implements the simulation of the physical process of the tank in Python. This simplified version is derived from a real process of a water treatment facility. The current implementation features pump control to keep the water level between the allowed minimum and maximum. The pump is modeled to show PT2 behavior. The current tank fill level is reported to the levelsensor-server via an OPC UA client. For simplicity reasons, there is currently no feedback loop regarding the concentration of water treatment chemicals. The communication between the simulation and the connected servers can be made invisible

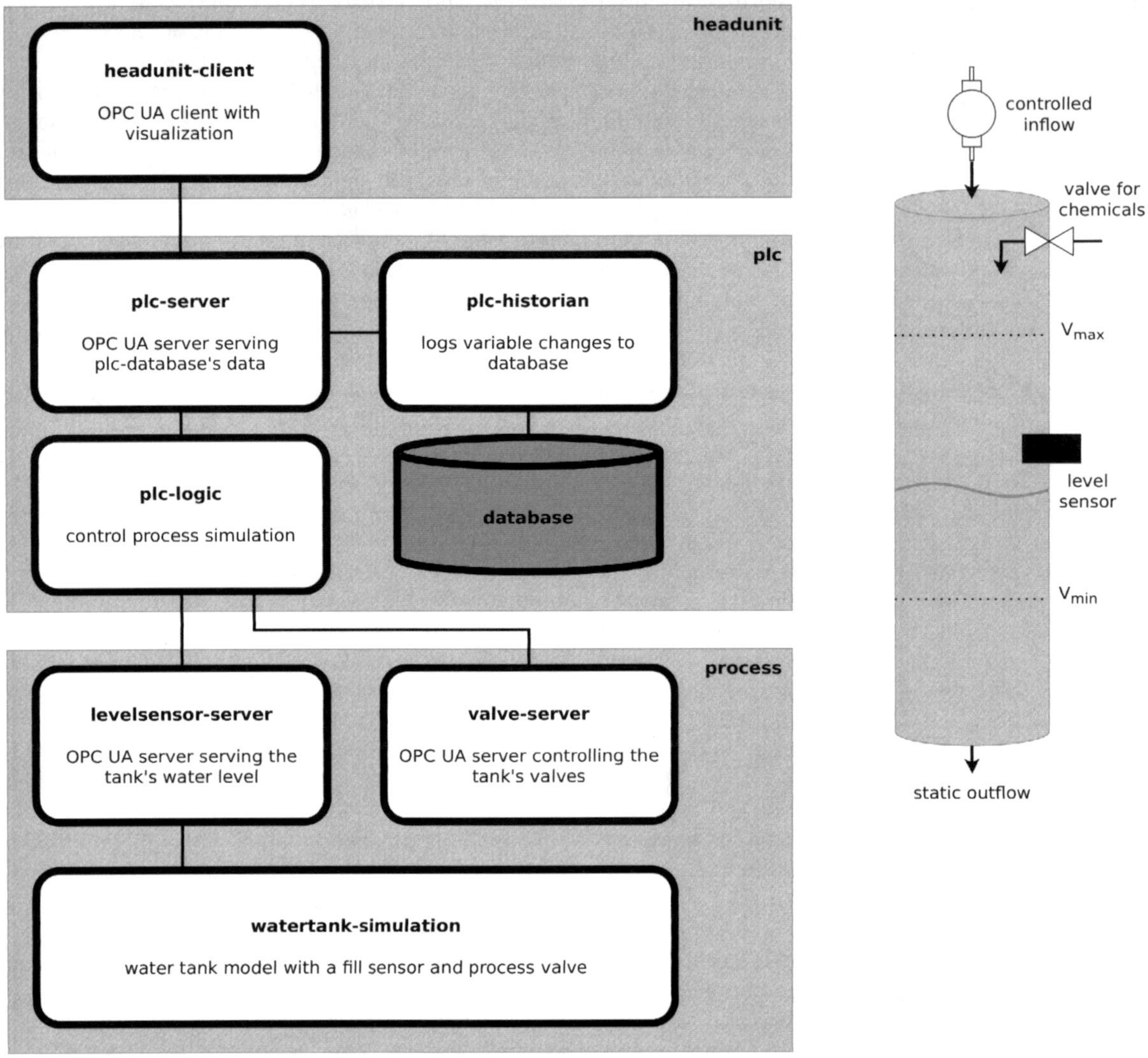

(a) Schematic representation of the testbed architecture

(b) Schematic representation of the simulated water tank system

Figure 1. Schematic representations of the testbed architecture and the simulated water tank system

to the host networks by using internal Docker networks while simultaneously decoupling the simulation and the server application code. The realism of the simulations was of lesser concern due to the testbed's focus on penetration testing.

levelsensor-server - This OPC UA server hosts the current sensor readings of the water level sensor. Depending on the requirements of the production network, the security configuration can be adjusted as needed. Another design consideration was the implementation of internal sensor value updates. We went with network-based communication for interacting with the simulation instead of using hard-coded callbacks in each custom server. This allows us to decouple the simulation from the server entirely, which simplifies replacing containers.

valve-server - The second OPC UA server allows the control of actuators in the system, which is currently just the valve for adding treatment chemicals. The valve status does not propagate back to the simulation, but we plan to extend the simulation to include this feature in the future. As for levelsensor-server, security features can be enabled as needed.

plc-logic - This component encapsulates the logic of activating and deactivating the valve depending on the current reading of the level sensor. It opens a connection to both the valve-server and the levelsensor-server and subscribes to changes in the water level variable. This triggers the latter to send a message to the logic client, where the reading is first written into a queue and evaluated asynchronously in another

```yaml
services:
  headunit-dashboard:
    container_name: "headunit-dashboard"
    hostname: "headunit-dashboard"
    image: dashboard:latest
    environment:
      - SERVER_URI=opc.tcp://172.17.1.1:4840
    build:
      context: ${IMAGE_REPO_URL}#main:opcua/
          dashboard/python-opcua-asyncio/latest
    ports:
      - "8050:8050"
```

Figure 2. compose.yaml file for headunit

thread. Depending on the value, the valve position is changed by writing a new value to the valve-server. Any changes to either the water level or the valve position are also written to the plc-server. This allows other devices (the headunit in our case) to assess process data without having to directly interact and possibly interrupt the process level servers. Lastly, the water level thresholds for opening and closing the valves used by the logic component can be configured. For this purpose, it is informed if new values are written to the plc-server and adopts the values as soon as possible.

plc-historian - The historian acts as a recording mechanism for all relevant process parameters by writing them into a persistent database. The current implementation uses the file-based, lightweight SQLite database for simplicity reasons, which is made accessible to the container via volumes. The current implementation is not packaged as a container to allow easier replacement with the user's database of choice, and is therefore depicted in gray in Figure 1a. The historian subscribes to all relevant variables on the plc-server and is triggered upon receiving new values.

plc-server - This third OPC UA server allows systems of the upper layers to access process data for monitoring and planning purposes. In contrast to the production network servers, this instance simulates interactions with enterprise clients, e. g., encrypted and authenticated connections for administrative tasks or read-only connections for dashboards. Authorized users may also set certain properties that influence the simulation.

headunit-client - This client simulates a control station for visualizing and monitoring the underlying process through a web GUI. It also allows for setting certain process-relevant parameters, such as the threshold values. It connects to the plc-server via a secure connection.

Please note that these currently available components are implemented with different software stacks and versions. We only implemented what is currently needed for this proof-of-concept, but it is planned to add more containers. Another notable point is that we will add containers for network noise in the future, in order to simulate more realistic networks.

B. Building a Testbed

In this section, we present how the previously defined building blocks can be orchestrated and deployed. As we use Docker, the orchestration tool of choice is Docker Compose [15]. It allows the management of multi-container applications on a single host by using a declarative YAML file. It allows users to define services (containers), networks, and volumes that are then automatically configured and created upon starting the Compose application. Every physical device that is part of the testbed uses its own compose file. This gives the user maximum freedom in terms of distributing services across devices. We intentionally decided against using multi-host orchestration tools, such as Docker Swarm or Kubernetes, as this would introduce additional unwanted traffic that is normally not found in industrial environments.

```yaml
services:
  plc-server:
    container_name: "plc-server"
    hostname: "plc-server"
    image: node-server:latest
    build:
      context: ${IMAGE_REPO_URL}#main:opcua/server/
          nodejs-node-opcua/latest
      args:
        NODESET_MODEL: "PLC.NodeSet2.xml"
        ...
    ports:
      - "4840:4840"
    networks:
      - plc-net

  plc-historian:
    container_name: "plc-historian"
    hostname: "plc-historian"
    image: historian:latest
    environment:
      - SERVER_URI=opc.tcp://plc-server:4840
    volumes:
      - /tmp/docker/database:/database
    build:
      context: ${IMAGE_REPO_URL}#main:opcua/
          historian/python-opcua-asyncio/latest
    networks:
      - plc-net
    depends_on:
      - plc-server

  plc-logic:
    container_name: "plc-logic"
    hostname: "plc-logic"
    image: plc-logic:latest
    environment:
      - PS_URI=opc.tcp://plc-server:4840
      - LSS_URI=opc.tcp://172.17.0.1:4840
      - VS_URI=opc.tcp://172.17.0.2:4840
    build:
      context: ${IMAGE_REPO_URL}#main:opcua/plc-
          logic/python-opcua-asyncio/latest
    networks:
      - plc-net
    depends_on:
      - plc-server

networks:
  plc-net:
    name: plc-net
    external: false
```

Figure 3. compose.yaml file for plc

```
services:
  levelsensor-server:
    container_name: "levelsensor-server"
    hostname: "levelsensor-server"
    image: node-server:latest
    build:
      context: ${IMAGE_REPO_URL}#main:opcua/server/
          open62541/latest
      args:
        NODESET_MODEL: "Tank.NodeSet2.xml"
      ...
    ports:
      - "4840:4840"
    networks:
      - levelsensor-net

  water-tank-simulation:
    container_name: "water-tank-simulation"
    hostname: "water-tank-simulation"
    image: water-tank-simulation:latest
    environment:
      - SERVER_URI=opc.tcp://levelsensor-server
          :4840/KRITIS3M/
    build:
      context: ${IMAGE_REPO_URL}#main:opcua/water-
          tank-simulation/python-opcua-asyncio/
          latest
    networks:
      - levelsensor-net
    depends_on:
      - levelsensor-server

networks:
  levelsensor-net:
    name: levelsensor-net
    external: false
```

Figure 4. compose.yaml file for process

To demonstrate the usage, we again consider the system shown in Figure 1a. Therein, we divided the system into three groups: headunit, plc, and process. This indicates a reasonable division of the testbed across different devices, which are Raspberry Pi 4's. The headunit could be assumed to be a monitoring workstation, the plc replicates the behavior of a real programmable logic controller, and the process encapsulates the interfaces with the low-level process devices. As a result, we would need a total of three compose files, which are presented below. Please note that the exact usage could deviate as the software matures, so please consult the online documentation for the latest version.

This first compose file in Figure 2 configures the services of the headunit device. The string for the *build* key points to path within the Github repository, which is comprised of the 4-tuple *protocol*, *component*, *library/stack*, and *version*. In this instance, the client is implemented using the latest version of the *asyncua* Python library. Our applications are configured by certain exposed environment variables (*environment*), in this case, the address of the plc-server on another physical device to which the client connects. As this application provides a graphical monitoring interface, it allows access via the host on port 8050 in this example.

The PLC application shown in Figure 3 is more complex, as

```
  tempsensor-server:
    container_name: "tempsensor-server"
    hostname: "tempsensor-server"
    image: node-server:latest
    build:
      context: ${IMAGE_REPO_URL}#main:opcua/server/
          open62541/latest
      args:
        NODESET_MODEL: "Temp.NodeSet2.xml"
      ...
    ports:
      - "4841:4840"
    networks:
      - levelsensor-net
```

Figure 5. compose.yaml file extension for additional sensor

it currently consists of three separate services that communicate over a private network *plc-net*. By using these networks, we expose ports only if it is necessary, and addressing within the network can be done by referencing the container names. The OPC UA servers in our implementation are able to load a number of different nodesets, depending on their task. This is specified by the *NODESET_MODEL* argument, and therefore avoids building the server anew every time the nodes change. Due to the fact that we are currently using SQLite, we have to mount the database file into the container using *volumes*.

Lastly, the production process application with the simulation is shown in Figure 4. It is demonstrated how internal container networks (in this example *process-net*) can be used to separate simulation-specific network traffic from the testbed-facing interfaces of the host system. Therefore, it isolates simulation and additional tools from the testbed system. It can also be seen that the same server implementation is used, but another nodeset is loaded upon startup. Please note that we omitted the valve server for the sake of clarity.

The described exemplary setup can be easily modified. For example, suppose that the system is upgraded by including a second sensor to measure the water temperature. To replicate this in the testbed, it is sufficient to modify the process compose file by adding a service as shown in Figure 5.

Modularity was a key requirement to support our concept for designing testbeds as proposed in [1]. By starting with a minimal setup initially and gradually adding functionality through additional containers, we can support a bottom-up approach when creating testbeds. This means that penetration tests are initially conducted in a relatively simple environment (e. g., only a server-client pair), and the following tests can build upon these layers of understanding. This is more feasible than coming up with complex scenarios straight away.

Another feature of the design is the redistribution of services between physical devices. This can easily be done by moving a service to another compose file and adjusting the environment variables if necessary. This is especially interesting for recording network data at specific nodes. By restructuring the setup, the desired connection can be exposed and recorded by inserting a network tap.

Lastly, adjusting the setup for a certain penetration test

```
plc-server:
  # change old version to new
  # build: "plc-server/node-opcua/latest"
  build: "plc-server/node-opcua/v2.73.0"
  ...
plc-server:
  container_name: "plc-server"
  ...
  build:
    # change old version to new
    # context: ${IMAGE_REPO_URL}#main:opcua/server
        /nodejs-node-opcua/latest
    context: ${IMAGE_REPO_URL}#main:opcua/server/
        nodejs-node-opcua/v2.73.0
  ...
```

Figure 6. modify image to enable vulnerabilities

is straightforward: first, the necessary implementation and version must be selected. This is as easy as searching for the relevant CVEs, and selecting the vulnerable software. Then, the image for the affected container is modified. For example, CVE-2022-21208 describes a Denial-of-Service attack against implementations using the node-opcua package. Before version 2.74.0, this causes the server to crash if an attacker continuously sends big chunks of data to the server. Simply modifying the version within the compose file enables the vulnerability, as shown in Figure 6.

We currently support the most common open-source implementations of OPC UA, namely open62541 (written in C), node-opcua (NodeJS), opcua-asyncio (Python), locka99/opcua (rust), and UA-.NETStandard (C#). Over time, we are planning to expand on the available stacks.

IV. Conclusion and Future Work

This paper proposes a modular and flexible testbed approach to facilitate easier and faster reconfigurations for penetration testing purposes. First, we put our approach into context by providing design considerations, relevant literature, and issues that we encountered. Next, we introduced our testbed approach by defining the building blocks of the modular design. Then, these were combined into an exemplary testbed. Lastly, we showed how the ability to quickly change the architecture, implementation, and configuration can be used to leverage penetration testing activities.

The next steps include open-sourcing of our testbed complete with an example configuration. We will also expand the number of available components in order to enable the modeling of more complex scenarios. We will use the knowledge gained to construct a testbed with a sufficient number of features to create an ICS dataset for intrusion detection research.

Acknowledgment

The presented work is part of the research project *KRITIS Scalable Safe and Secure Modules* (KRITIS³M), which is funded by the Project Management Jülich (PtJ) and the German Federal Ministry for Economic Affairs and Climate Action (BMWK) under funding code 03EI6089A.

References

[13] D. Antonioli and N. O. Tippenhauer, "MiniCPS: A Toolkit for Security Research on CPS Networks," in *Proceedings of the First ACM Workshop on Cyber-Physical Systems-Security and/or PrivaCy*, ser. CPS-SPC '15, New York, NY, USA: Association for Computing Machinery, 2015, pp. 91–100, ISBN: 978-1-4503-3827-1. DOI: 10.1145/2808705.2808715.

[14] A. Murillo *et al.*, "High-Fidelity Cyber and Physical Simulation of Water Distribution Systems. I: Models and Data," May 2023, Publisher: CISPA. DOI: 10.60882/cispa.25460440.v1.

[12] Laboratory for Safe and Secure Systems, "MOdular Testbed for Researching Attacks (MOTRA) - setups," [Online]. Available: https://github.com/Laboratory-for-Safe-and-Secure-Systems/motra-setups (Retrieved: 09/08/2025).

[1] S. Kraust, P. Heller, and J. Mottok, "Concept for designing an ICS testbed from a penetration testing perspective," in *2025 IEEE European Symposium on Security and Privacy Workshops (EuroS&PW)*, ISSN: 2768-0657, Jun. 2025, pp. 561–568. DOI: 10.1109/EuroSPW67616.2025.00071.

[2] OPC Foundation, "OPC UA Online Reference - Released Specifications," 2025, [Online]. Available: https://reference.opcfoundation.org/ (Retrieved: 09/08/2025).

[3] F. Pauker, T. Frühwirth, B. Kittl, and W. Kastner, "A Systematic Approach to OPC UA Information Model Design," *Procedia CIRP*, vol. 57, pp. 321–326, 2016, ISSN: 22128271. DOI: 10.1016/j.procir.2016.11.056.

[4] S. Friedl, C. von Arnim, A. Lechler, and A. Verl, "Generation of OPC UA Companion Specification with Eclipse Modeling Framework," in *2020 16th IEEE International Conference on Factory Communication Systems (WFCS)*, Apr. 2020, pp. 1–7. DOI: 10.1109/WFCS47810.2020.9114448.

[5] E. Jacob, "A Broken Chain: Discovering OPC UA Attack Surface and Exploiting the Supply Chain," Dec. 2021, [Online]. Available: https://i.blackhat.com/USA21/Wednesday-Handouts/us-21-A-Broken-Chain-Discovering-OPC-UA-Attack-Surface-And-Exploiting-The-Supply-Chain.pdf (Retrieved: 09/08/2025).

[6] BSI, "OPC-UA Security Analysis," Bundesamt für Sicherheit in der Informationstechnik, Tech. Rep., 2022.

[7] P. Cheremushkin and S. Temnikov, "OPC UA Security Analysis," Kaspersky Lab, Security Analysis, 2018.

[8] Team82, "Exploring the OPC Attack Surface," 2020, [Online]. Available: https://claroty.com/team82/research/white-papers/exploring-the-opc-attack-surface (Retrieved: 09/08/2025).

[9] A. Erba, A. Müller, and N. O. Tippenhauer, "Security analysis of vendor implementations of the OPC UA protocol for industrial control systems," in *Proceedings of the 4th Workshop on CPS & IoT Security and Privacy*, ser. CPSIoTSec '22, New York, NY, USA: Association for Computing Machinery, Nov. 7, 2022, pp. 1–13, ISBN: 978-1-4503-9876-3. DOI: 10.1145/3560826.3563380.

[10] L. Roepert, M. Dahlmanns, I. Fink, J. Pennekamp, and M. Henze, "Assessing the security of OPC UA deployments," *Proceedings of the 1st ITG Workshop on IT Security*, May 11, 2020, Accepted: 2020-05-11T12:51:19Z ISBN: 9781698020358 Publisher: Universität Tübingen. DOI: 10.15496/publikation-41813.

[11] J. Polge, J. Robert, and Y. L. Traon, "Assessing the impact of attacks on OPC-UA applications in the Industry 4.0 era," in *2019 16th IEEE Annual Consumer Communications & Networking Conference (CCNC)*, Jan. 2019, pp. 1–6. DOI: 10.1109/CCNC.2019.8651671.

[15] Docker, "Docker compose manual," 2025, [Online]. Available: https://docs.docker.com/compose (Retrieved: 09/08/2025).

Towards Post-Quantum-Ready Automated Certificate Lifecycle Management in Operational Technology

Ayham Alhulaibi*, Tobias Frauenschläger† and Jürgen Mottok†
* Maschinenfabrik Reinhausen, 93059 Regensburg, Germany
e-mail: a.alhulaibi@reinhausen.com
† Laboratory for Safe and Secure Systems (LaS³), OTH Regensburg, 93053 Regensburg, Germany
e-mail: {tobias.frauenschlaeger, juergen.mottok}@oth-regensburg.de

Abstract—**Operational Technology (OT) systems increasingly depend on robust and automated certificate lifecycle management to maintain secure operations across long device lifespans and constrained environments. As quantum-capable adversaries emerge, these systems must also support cryptographic agility and prepare for a seamless transition to Post-Quantum Cryptography (PQC). This work presents a crypto-agile, post-quantum-ready testbed architecture that extends existing standards, such as Enrollment over Secure Transport (EST) and Bootstrapping Remote Secure Key Infrastructure (BRSKI), to support hybrid certificates, hardware-based key storage, and protocol flexibility for device bootstrapping and certificate management. A work-in-progress prototype implementation demonstrates support for both traditional and PQC algorithms across device types. Planned evaluations target performance on constrained devices, PQC readiness, and compatibility with alternative protocols. The system lays a foundation for secure and standards-compliant certificate management in future-proof OT deployments.**

Keywords-Post-Quantum Cryptography; Public Key Infrastructure; Automated Device Onboarding; BRSKI; Security Token; Operational Technology Security.

I. INTRODUCTION

The convergence of Information Technology (IT) and Operational Technology (OT) has brought increased efficiency and connectivity to critical infrastructure sectors, such as water supply, energy distribution, and industrial automation. However, this interconnection expands the attack surface and raises the urgency for adopting scalable and robust cybersecurity mechanisms [1]. Among the most critical challenges is the secure provisioning and lifecycle management of device certificates in environments with remaining manual processes [2].

In OT contexts, device onboarding and certificate management must account for long operational lifespans, constrained computational resources, and limited maintenance windows [3]. Compounding these challenges is the increasing need to prepare for quantum-capable adversaries, which threaten to break widely deployed, traditional cryptographic schemes, such as Rivest–Shamir–Adleman (RSA) and Elliptic Curve Digital Signature Algorithm (ECDSA) [4][5]. Ensuring long-term security in OT deployments thus requires not only Public Key Infrastructure (PKI) automation but also cryptographic agility and support for transitioning to PQC [6].

In order to address these challenges, we currently work on a testbed to evaluate the migration to PQC for the entire certificate lifecycle management (enrollment, renewal, revocation, and algorithm migration) within OT environments, including automated device onboarding. Our proposed architecture extends existing standards by addressing two key requirements missing or underexplored in prior work: (i) support for hardware-based secure key storage through a generic and agile interface, and (ii) end-to-end readiness for PQC, including hybrid certificates that combine traditional and PQ algorithms for transitional security [7]. In this context, *crypto-agility* refers to a system's ability to support multiple cryptographic algorithms throughout its lifetime without requiring major redesign or loss of interoperability [8]. By supporting crypto-agility and standard-compliant interfaces, the system enables future-proof, maintainable deployments without requiring protocol redesigns or vendor-specific extensions.

This paper presents a work-in-progress report on the design and early implementation of this testbed. Our main contributions are as follows:

- A system architecture for automated certificate lifecycle management in OT environments, combining secure onboarding, renewal, and revocation processes with cryptographic agility and hardware-backed key protection.
- A modular prototype implementation with support for PKCS#11-based security tokens and hybrid post-quantum/traditional certificates.
- An evaluation strategy covering both constrained device performance and the system's cryptographic and protocol agility.

The remainder of this paper is structured as follows: Section II presents fundamentals and discusses related work. Section III presents the final system architecture with its key components. Section IV outlines the current implementation status. Section V describes the remaining future work. Finally, Section VI concludes the paper.

II. BACKGROUND AND RELATED WORK

PKIs are critical for securing industrial and OT systems, enabling authenticated communication and device identity management. In such environments, automated certificate provisioning is essential to replace manual processes that are error-prone and difficult to scale. A foundational protocol for certificate management in such systems is EST [9]. EST defines a secure, certificate-based protocol for retrieving Certification Authority (CA) certificates, requesting new client certificates, and renewing or rekeying existing ones. EST is widely used in automated certificate provisioning workflows, as it supports mutual TLS authentication and standard X.509 certificate [10] handling.

In order to enable secure and automated device onboarding, the Internet Engineering Task Force (IETF) specified the BRSKI protocol [11], which builds on EST. In BRSKI, a new device (the *pledge*) presents its manufacturer-issued *Initial Device Identity certificate* (IDevID) to a *domain registrar* (the operator's administrative and security boundary, whose identity is represented by the *pinned-domain-cert*). The registrar then contacts the *Manufacturer Authorized Signing Authority* (MASA), which returns a signed voucher (a data object containing metadata [12]) that binds the pledge to the local domain (i. e., the local OT network). This voucher allows the pledge to verify the registrar's identity (via the *pinned-domain-cert* and a pre-installed MASA root certificate). Once trust is established, the pledge uses EST to request its *local operational certificate* (LDevID), completing the onboarding. Several extensions and variations of BRSKI have been proposed to support broader use cases. *BRSKI-AE* [13] enables the use of alternative enrollment protocols, such as CMPv2 [14]. Furthermore, extensions introduce support for registrar-initiated onboarding (BRSKI-PRM) or enable the usage of more efficient encoding formats (cBRSKI). Together, these variants support a range of network conditions, device capabilities, and operational constraints.

In order to protect private keys, OT systems increasingly rely on hardware security tokens, partly even required by regulations like IEC 62443 [15]. The PKCS#11 interface [16] provides a standard interface to such tokens, including Hardware Security Modules (HSMs), Trusted Platform Modules (TPMs), smart cards, and secure elements. It abstracts key storage, signing, and other cryptographic operations, ensuring tamper-resistant credential protection and interoperability across vendors.

Existing work has explored the applicability of BRSKI in industrial and resource-constrained environments. Heinl *et al.* [2] analyze BRSKI adoption in OT networks in accordance with IEC 62443, creating a testbed similar to ours. They also add support for hardware-based security tokens in the form of TPMs. However, their setup misses a generic interface for security tokens and does not consider the PQC migration. Krieger *et al.* [17] demonstrate an embedded BRSKI client running on a microcontroller. While suitable for Bluetooth Low Energy-based constrained networks, it does not address the challenges of PQ readiness or hardware-based key storage. Rüst *et al.* [18] present an implementation of cBRSKI for wireless building automation devices using mbedTLS and support for various secure elements. They note the integration overhead of vendor-specific interfaces and call for harmonization, a gap we address through standardized PKCS#11 support. Again, the PQC migration is not addressed.

In contrast to prior work, our approach focuses explicitly on *post-quantum readiness* and *cryptographic agility*, enabling the use of hybrid classical/PQ certificates and hardware-based key storage. This positions our system as a forward-looking solution for scalable and future-proof device onboarding and PKI certificate lifecycle management in critical OT environments. Building on these foundations, we introduce an architecture designed to integrate crypto-agility and secure key storage into standard onboarding and lifecycle management protocols.

III. System Architecture and Design

Figure 1 depicts our complete, post-quantum-ready onboarding and certificate management architecture for OT networks. The design follows the BRSKI protocol layered over EST, with targeted extensions to support PQC and hardware-based key protection. For deterministic and low-complexity deployments, we omit automatic registrar discovery via mDNS/DHCP and instead preconfigure pledges with the registrar address. The architecture comprises four core components:

Pledge: A constrained embedded device to be onboarded. It holds a pre-installed IDevID certificate and initiates the BRSKI workflow. The pledge supports traditional and post-quantum key types and is capable of generating hybrid or PQC-only Certificate Signing Requests (CSRs) for EST enrollment. Secure key storage is provided via PKCS#11-based tokens, including TPMs or secure elements. All BRSKI and EST interactions are protected with a PQC-enabled Transport Layer Security (TLS) client stack, enabling both backward compatibility and security against future adversaries.

Registrar: The designated onboarding coordinator within the operator domain. It terminates BRSKI and EST requests from pledges, communicates with the MASA to validate voucher requests, and relays certificate enrollment messages to the CA. The registrar supports hybrid TLS handshakes to accommodate PQC-ready pledges. It enforces local policy decisions (e. g., which pledges to accept) and handles certificate issuance with the CA.

Certificate Authority (CA): Responsible for issuing LDevID certificates based on authenticated enrollment requests received via EST. The CA supports hybrid and PQC-only certificates. It is integrated with a PKCS#11 interface to manage key material in security tokens. This ensures keys are protected and compliance with security regulations is achieved.

MASA: Validates pledges and issues vouchers, binding them to a domain registrar. While MASA is typically vendor-operated and external, our prototype includes a minimal MASA implementation with PQC support for voucher signing and TLS. Its goal is to enable local testing of end-to-end onboarding flows without focusing on full MASA lifecycle functionality.

Our architecture emphasizes *crypto-agility* and *hardware security* as key design goals. PKCS#11 integration ensures compatibility with a wide range of security tokens and simplifies token management across the stack. By supporting hybrid certificates and PQC-native flows at every layer (TLS, voucher validation, and enrollment), our system enables future-proof certificate lifecycle management for OT environments facing both legacy compatibility and quantum-capable threats.

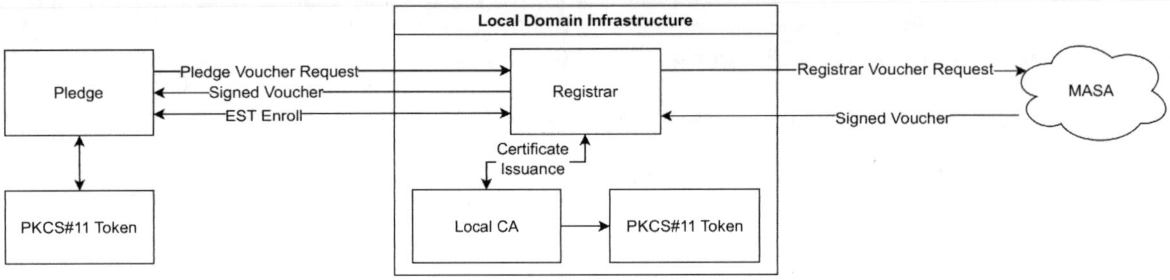

Figure 1. Testbed architecture with the various logical components required to cover the full certificate lifecycle.

While the depicted components in Figure 1 follow the standard BRSKI/EST layering, our work introduces the following targeted extensions:

- Support for PQC-enabled TLS handshakes and hybrid certificates across pledge, registrar, and CA.
- Integration of PKCS#11-based secure key storage in both resource-constrained pledges and backend components.
- PQC support for voucher handling and issuance within the MASA

These additions ensure crypto-agility and post-quantum readiness and are highlighted in the prototype implementation described in Section IV.

IV. Implementation Status

A. Platform Support

Our current prototype implementation is developed in Go [19] and targets Linux and Windows platforms. Both the EST server and the pledge client are based on a fork of an open-source EST implementation [20]. This fork has been extended to support BRSKI functionality, hybrid and post-quantum cryptography, and integration with PKCS#11-based security tokens. The prototype includes an EST server extended with registrar functionality for BRSKI, a pledge client implementing EST and BRSKI voucher exchange, and a minimal MASA implementation for testing.

All components use the WolfSSL library for cryptographic operations via wrapper bindings, including TLS, X.509 [10] handling, and PQC algorithm support. The system is designed to enable automated onboarding in OT environments, with particular focus on cryptographic agility and secure key storage. A lightweight C-based pledge implementation targeting microcontrollers (e. g., with the Real-Time Operating System Zephyr) is under active development and forms an essential part of future work.

B. BRSKI Workflow and Voucher Handling

The implementation supports the complete BRSKI voucher exchange flow. The registrar handles authenticated voucher requests from pledges and validates the incoming messages using the pledge's IDevID certificate. After verifying pledge identity and request integrity, the registrar constructs the registrar voucher request, encapsulating domain metadata and pledge identity. This request is forwarded to the MASA, which verifies the registrar's credentials and issues a signed voucher containing a *pinned-domain-cert*. The registrar forwards the voucher to the pledge to complete the trust establishment.

Voucher artifacts are encoded and signed using Cryptographic Message Syntax (CMS) [21]. PQC support for CMS is still under development [22][23], and is not yet implemented in our prototype. Supporting PQC-capable CMS structures is an essential item on our roadmap.

C. Enrollment and Certificate Lifecycle Support

After successful voucher validation, the pledge initiates certificate enrollment via EST. In our implementation, the registrar and CA are combined into a single application with modular separation between protocol handling and certificate logic. The registrar manages EST endpoints, including CA certificate distribution, CSR attribute provisioning, and enrollment via mutually authenticated TLS (mTLS). The CA is designed for cryptographic agility and lifecycle flexibility. It supports:

- Issuance of traditional, PQC-only, and hybrid X.509 certificates [10], based on configurable templates.
- Template-driven control of signature algorithms, validity periods, and metadata constraints.
- Hardware-based signing via PKCS#11 tokens.

Lifecycle operations include:

- Certificate renewal and rekeying, including transitions between algorithm profiles (e. g., classical→hybrid→PQC).
- Revocation via Certificate Revocation List (CRL) and Online Certificate Status Protocol (OCSP), with future extensions for transparency logging and PQC awareness.
- Backward-compatible fallback modes to support legacy devices during migration.

The full EST flow already supports PQC, both for the TLS handshake and for issued certificates, while ensuring backward compatibility for legacy clients. This ensures compatibility during the transition period and provides a robust foundation for long-term cryptographic resilience in OT deployments.

V. Planned Future Work

A. Evaluation of Constrained Clients

Our primary evaluation target is the microcontroller-based pledge implementation, as it represents the most resource-constrained component in the proposed architecture. The evaluation will focus on metrics relevant to embedded OT devices:

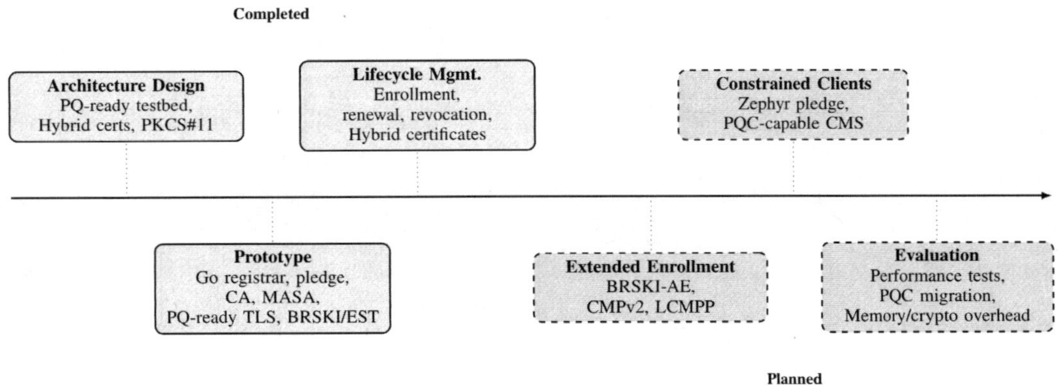

Figure 2. Roadmap of contributions (green) and planned extensions (blue).

- Enrollment performance: Time required to complete voucher acquisition and certificate enrollment over EST.
- Memory usage: Stack and heap consumption during onboarding and certificate renewal.
- Hardware-backed key operations: Comparison of cryptographic performance with and without secure key storage.

Initial tests using Zephyr on representative microcontroller platforms will guide optimizations of the pledge client and its integration with constrained TLS and PKI libraries.

B. Enrollment Flexibility and PQ Transition

Our planned future work will also extend the system to support alternative enrollment workflows using BRSKI-Alternative Enrollment (BRSKI-AE), enabling the integration of certificate management protocols, such as Certificate Management Protocol (CMPv2) and lightweight profiles like Lightweight CMP (LCMPP) [24]. This allows comparative analysis of EST-based and alternative enrollment approaches, particularly in scenarios with asynchronous provisioning or intermittent network connectivity.

In parallel, we plan to evaluate the system's cryptographic agility by transitioning from traditional to hybrid and post-quantum certificates. Planned experiments include the migration of IDevID and LDevID certificates to post-quantum formats, as well as lifecycle testing of hybrid certificates, covering renewal and revocation processes.

Together, these extensions will assess the testbed's readiness for long-term cryptographic transitions and its ability to support diverse PKI profiles across industrial use cases.

VI. Conclusion

This work presents a crypto-agile, post-quantum-ready certificate management architecture tailored for OT environments. Building on standardized protocols, such as BRSKI and EST, our system enables secure and automated device onboarding, coupled with full certificate lifecycle support. A key feature of the architecture is its support for hybrid and PQC-only certificates, allowing gradual migration without disrupting legacy compatibility. The integration of PKCS#11-based secure key storage further strengthens credential protection and aligns with regulatory requirements in critical infrastructure.

By decoupling enrollment and transport mechanisms from specific cryptographic primitives, the system remains adaptable to future algorithmic changes. Planned extensions, such as constrained pledge evaluations, PQC support in CMS, and the integration of alternative enrollment protocols via BRSKI-AE (e. g., CMPv2) to enable secure air-gapped provisioning. Ultimately, this work lays the foundation for long-term, crypto-agile PKI deployments in OT systems, enabling secure, automated, and standards-aligned certificate management in the post-quantum era.

To clearly separate outcomes from open directions, Figure 2 summarizes our contributions to date and places them in the context of the planned extensions. This roadmap highlights the concrete results of the present work while outlining the future steps towards full post-quantum readiness.

Acknowledgments

The presented work is part of the research project *KRITIS Scalable Safe and Secure Modules* (KRITIS³M), which is funded by the Project Management Jülich (PtJ) and the German Federal Ministry for Economic Affairs and Climate Action (BMWK) under funding code 03EI6089A.

References

[1] Waterfall team, *How Industrial Cybersecurity Works in 2025*, Jun. 2025. [Online]. Available: https://waterfall-security.com/ot-insights-center/ot-cybersecurity-insights-center/industrial-cyber-security/ (Retrieved: 09/04/2025).

[2] M. P. Heinl, A. Reuter, S. N. Peters, and M. Bever, "Leveraging BRSKI to Protect the Hardware Supply Chain of Operational Technology: Opportunities and Challenges", in *Proceedings of the 40th ACM/SIGAPP Symposium on Applied Computing*, ser. SAC '25, Association for Computing Machinery, May 2025, pp. 245–254. DOI: 10.1145/3672608.3707707.

[3] M. P. Heinl, M. Pursche, N. Puch, S. N. Peters, and A. Giehl, "From Standard to Practice: Towards ISA/IEC 62443-Conform Public Key Infrastructures", in *Computer Safety, Reliability, and Security*, Springer Nature Switzerland, 2023, pp. 196–210. DOI: 10.1007/978-3-031-40923-3_15.

[4] C. Gidney, *How to factor 2048 bit RSA integers with less than a million noisy qubits*, arXiv:2505.15917 [quant-ph], May 2025. DOI: 10.48550/arXiv.2505.15917.

[5] C. Chevignard, P.-A. Fouque, and A. Schrottenloher, "Reducing the Number of Qubits in Quantum Factoring", in *Advances in Cryptology – CRYPTO 2025*, Y. Tauman Kalai and S. F. Kamara, Eds., vol. 16001, Series Title: Lecture Notes in Computer Science, Springer Nature Switzerland, 2025, pp. 384–415. DOI: 10.1007/978-3-032-01878-6_13. [Online]. Available: https://link.springer.com/10.1007/978-3-032-01878-6_13 (Retrieved: 09/05/2025).

[6] P. Viorel, *Preparing ICS for Future Threats with Quantum-Resistant Cybersecurity*, Nov. 2024. [Online]. Available: https://www.iiot-world.com/ics-security/cybersecurity/preparing-ics-future-threats-quantum-cybersecurity/ (Retrieved: 09/04/2025).

[7] J. Fan *et al.*, "Impact of post-quantum hybrid certificates on PKI, common libraries, and protocols", *International Journal of Security and Networks*, vol. 16, no. 3, pp. 200–211, 2021. DOI: 10.1504/IJSN.2021.117887.

[8] T. Frauenschläger and J. Mottok, "Problems and New Approaches for Crypto-Agility in Operational Technology", in *12th European Congress Embedded Real Time Systems - ERTS 2024*, Jun. 2024. [Online]. Available: https://hal.science/hal-04614197.

[9] M. Pritikin, P. E. Yee, and D. Harkins, *Enrollment over Secure Transport*, RFC 7030, Oct. 2013. DOI: 10.17487/RFC7030.

[10] ITU-T, *Recommendation ITU-T X.509*, Oct. 2019. [Online]. Available: https://www.itu.int/rec/T-REC-X.509-201910-I/en.

[11] M. Pritikin, M. Richardson, T. Eckert, M. H. Behringer, and K. Watsen, *Bootstrapping Remote Secure Key Infrastructure (BRSKI)*, RFC 8995, May 2021. DOI: 10.17487/RFC8995.

[12] K. Watsen, M. Richardson, M. Pritikin, and T. Eckert, *A Voucher Artifact for Bootstrapping Protocols*, RFC 8366, May 2018. DOI: 10.17487/RFC8366.

[13] D. von Oheimb, S. Fries, and H. Brockhaus, *BRSKI with Alternative Enrollment (BRSKI-AE)*, RFC 9733, Mar. 2025. DOI: 10.17487/RFC9733.

[14] T. Mononen, T. Kause, S. Farrell, and D. C. Adams, *Internet X.509 Public Key Infrastructure Certificate Management Protocol (CMP)*, RFC 4210, Sep. 2005. DOI: 10.17487/RFC4210.

[15] International Electrotechnical Commission, "Industrial communication networks – Network and system security", Standard IEC/TS 62443:2009, 2009.

[16] D. Bong and G. Scott, *PKCS #11 Specification Version 3.2*, OASIS Standard, Apr. 2025. [Online]. Available: https://docs.oasis-open.org/pkcs11/pkcs11-spec/v3.2/pkcs11-spec-v3.2.html.

[17] J. Krieger, T. Hilbig, and T. Schreck, "Device Identity Bootstrapping in Constrained Environments: A BLE-Based BRSKI Extension", in *2025 20th European Dependable Computing Conference (EDCC)*, IEEE Computer Society, Apr. 2025, pp. 93–99. DOI: 10.1109/EDCC66201.2025.00024.

[18] A. Rüst, A. R. D. Schellenbaum, T. Schläpfer, C. Stauffer, and O. Camenzind, "Authenticating wireless nodes in building automation : Challenges and approaches", in *Wireless Congress: Systems & Applications*, Nov. 2018. DOI: 10.21256/ZHAW-2750.

[19] The Go Project, *The Go Programming Language*. [Online]. Available: https://go.dev/ (Retrieved: 09/05/2025).

[20] GlobalSign, *Globalsign/est*, May 2025. [Online]. Available: https://github.com/globalsign/est (Retrieved: 09/05/2025).

[21] R. Housley, *Cryptographic Message Syntax (CMS)*, RFC 5652, Sep. 2009. DOI: 10.17487/RFC5652.

[22] S. Ben, R. Adam, and D. V. Geest, "Use of the ML-DSA Signature Algorithm in the Cryptographic Message Syntax (CMS)", Internet Engineering Task Force, Internet-Draft draft-ietf-lamps-cms-ml-dsa-06, Jul. 2025, Work in Progress, 30 pp. [Online]. Available: https://datatracker.ietf.org/doc/draft-ietf-lamps-cms-ml-dsa/06/.

[23] M. Ounsworth, J. Gray, M. Pala, J. Klaußner, and S. Fluhrer, "Composite ML-DSA for use in X.509 Public Key Infrastructure and CMS", Internet Engineering Task Force, Internet-Draft draft-ietf-lamps-pq-composite-sigs-07, Jul. 2025, Work in Progress, 198 pp. [Online]. Available: https://datatracker.ietf.org/doc/draft-ietf-lamps-pq-composite-sigs/07/.

[24] H. Brockhaus, D. von Oheimb, and S. Fries, *Lightweight Certificate Management Protocol (CMP) Profile*, RFC 9483, Nov. 2023. DOI: 10.17487/RFC9483.

Quantifying Persuasion – A Comparative Analysis of Cialdini's Principles in Phishing Attacks

Alexander Lawall
IU International University of Applied Sciences
Erfurt, Thüringen, Germany
e-mail: alexander.lawall@iu.org

***Abstract*—This paper presents a mixed-method investigation into how psychological persuasion is operationalized in phishing attacks, with a specific focus on Cialdini's six principles of influence. A qualitative analysis of authentic spear-phishing emails was integrated with a quantitative study of 300 phishing samples across ten attack types to address three research questions. The findings show that while *scarcity* is the most frequently used tactic, it does not significantly predict user compromise. Instead, *liking* and *authority* emerge as the most effective predictors of phishing success, based on a robust regression model. These results reveal a mismatch between the most commonly used and the most behaviorally potent influence strategies. The study contributes empirical evidence for the strategic deployment of persuasion in phishing and proposes implications for awareness training, Natural Language Processing (NLP)-enhanced detection, and psychologically informed defense design.**

Keywords-Phishing; Social Engineering; Cialdini's Principles of Influence; Behavioral Security; Cyber Security.

I. Introduction

A. Motivation and Background

Phishing has remained one of the most prevalent and financially damaging forms of cybercrime since its emergence in the 1990s [1]. Despite continuous advancements in technical countermeasures, attackers consistently exploit the human element, which remains the weakest link in cybersecurity. Recent statistics show that up to 80% of security breaches are attributed to human error, underscoring the need for behavioural and psychological countermeasures alongside technical controls [2].

Current phishing campaigns frequently use psychological manipulation rather than exploiting technical vulnerabilities [3] [4]. Specifically, attackers embed persuasive elements within their messages to increase credibility [5]. Among the most robust frameworks for analyzing these manipulations are the six principles of social influence developed by Robert Cialdini: *Reciprocity*, *Liking*, *Social Proof*, *Authority*, *Scarcity*, and *Commitment/Consistency* [6] [7] [8]. These principles have been widely adopted by attackers in phishing, spear-phishing, and vishing campaigns, making them critical to understanding adversarial social engineering.

B. Research Objectives and Questions

This study aims to investigate how psychological persuasion, particularly Cialdini's principles, is operationalized in phishing attacks, and to determine which principles are most strongly associated with successful compromise. Prior work in this area either focuses on case-based interpretations of real and hypothetical phishing emails [9] [10], or applies statistical modeling to large corpora of phishing incidents [11] [12]. However, there is a lack of research that integrates both qualitative and quantitative perspectives to comparatively evaluate the psychological mechanics behind phishing efficacy.

The following research questions address this gap:

RQ1 *"How are Cialdini's principles of influence exploited in real-world phishing and spear-phishing attacks?"*

RQ2 *"What is the statistical prevalence of each principle across phishing types?"*

RQ3 *"Which principles are most strongly associated with victim compromise, and why?"*

C. Contribution and Structure

This paper contributes a mixed-methods analysis of persuasion in phishing attacks by (1) synthesizing how Cialdini's six principles manifest in phishing attacks, (2) quantifying their intensity and frequency across multiple phishing modalities, and (3) modeling their predictive power for user compromise using the statistical relationship between the application principle and the success of the phishing. The findings highlight a critical gap between commonly used tactics (e.g., scarcity) and the most behaviorally effective ones (liking and authority), offering implications for awareness training, Natural Language Processing (NLP)-based detection, and psychologically informed defenses.

The remainder of the paper is structured as follows. Section II reviews related work on persuasion in phishing and positions this contribution within existing literature. Section III introduces the theoretical background on Cialdini's framework and phishing typologies. Section IV describes the qualitative and quantitative methods used. Section V presents the empirical results, while Section VI discusses implications for cybersecurity practice. Section VII concludes with a summary and outlook for future research.

II. Related Work

Research on phishing attacks highlights the role of social engineering and psychological manipulation as key drivers of victim compromise. Among the most widely used frameworks for examining these tactics are Cialdini's six principles of influence. Prior work demonstrates that these principles are systematically exploited across diverse phishing modalities, yet their behavioral potency varies considerably.

Content analyses and simulations consistently find *authority* and *social proof* to be the most prevalent principles. Taib et al. [13] conducted a meta-analysis of over 56,000 participants and 81 studies, showing that authority-based manipulations not only dominate phishing messages but also lead to significantly higher compromise rates. Similarly, Ahmad et al. [14] found that man-in-the-middle phishing attacks employ social proof in 76.1% of cases and liking in 74.6%, illustrating the systematic use of group conformity and familiarity cues. In spear-phishing, Uehara et al. [15] documented authority usage rates as high as 96.1% and scarcity in 41.1% of attacks, highlighting the tailoring of principles to hierarchical and urgent contexts. By contrast, reciprocity (16.4%) and commitment/consistency (1–2%) remain less common, though their use is increasing over time in certain contexts [5].

While principle prevalence is well documented, fewer studies directly assess their effectiveness in predicting compromise. Experimental research shows authority consistently yields high success rates. Bona and Paci [16] report a 21.5% compromise rate in organizational phishing exercises driven by authority cues, while Butavicius et al. [17] confirm its dominance across spear-phishing contexts. Social proof also emerges as a strong predictor, particularly in finance and public sector settings where conformity to peer behavior or industry norms is salient [18]. Liking is less frequently used in generic phishing but has proven highly effective in personalized contexts such as vishing or social media-based attacks, where rapport and similarity cues are stronger. Scarcity shows mixed results: although frequent, it may suffer from diminishing returns due to user desensitization in environments saturated with urgency cues [5] [19]. Reciprocity appears context-dependent, being more effective among older adults [20], but in some cases correlates negatively with compromise likelihood, possibly reflecting heightened awareness of unsolicited "favors".

The literature also shows contextual and demographic moderators shaping susceptibility. Lawson et al. [21] and subsequent studies suggest that personality traits interact with persuasion tactics, while age is a strong predictor of susceptibility to reciprocity-based influence [20]. Organizational culture and industry also affect outcomes: Tian et al. [18] demonstrate that authority cues are especially effective in finance and public administration, whereas liking is more influential in non-financial contexts. Furthermore, attack modality influences principle application, i.e., scarcity dominates in low-bandwidth channels like SMS, while liking and commitment gain prominence in richer contexts such as spear-phishing and vishing.

More recent research indicates the evolving nature of phishing. AI-generated phishing campaigns increasingly combine multiple principles, blending emotional tone with contextual realism [22] [23]. Longitudinal analyses reveal that while reciprocity and social proof are declining in prevalence, scarcity and commitment/consistency are on the rise, suggesting attacker adaptation to user awareness over time [5]. Hybrid strategies that combine principles, such as authority with scarcity or liking with social proof, have been shown to produce synergistic effects [24].

Despite extensive empirical work, existing studies often focus either on prevalence (content analysis) or effectiveness (experiments and field tests), but rarely integrate both perspectives. Moreover, few studies systematically compare principles across diverse phishing modalities while simultaneously modeling their predictive power for compromise. This creates a critical gap between descriptive and causal insights. Addressing this gap, this paper contributes a mixed-method approach, combining qualitative analysis of authentic phishing emails with quantitative modeling of 300 samples across ten attack types. This integration enables a more nuanced assessment of both the strategic deployment and behavioral impact of Cialdini's principles in phishing attacks.

III. Theoretical Foundation

A. Cialdini's Principles of Influence

Robert Cialdini's theory of persuasion outlines six core psychological principles that shape human decision-making and compliance [6]. These principles are frequently exploited in phishing campaigns and form the analytical backbone of this study.

1) **Reciprocity:** People feel obligated to return a favor, even if unsolicited [25]. In phishing, this manifests through fake services or alerts that prompt the victim to "reciprocate" by providing credentials or completing tasks. For example, attackers may offer help (e.g., account recovery) and then request sensitive information as a return favor.
2) **Liking:** Users are more likely to comply with requests from individuals or brands they find likable or familiar. Attackers mimic social proximity by impersonating colleagues, friends, or well-known brands to reduce suspicion [26]. This principle strongly correlates with compromise likelihood [13].
3) **Social Proof:** Individuals tend to follow behaviors exhibited by others, especially in uncertain situations. Phishing emails exploit this by referencing peer behavior, testimonials, or organizational norms to create urgency and legitimacy [27].
4) **Authority:** Compliance increases when messages appear to originate from legitimate authority figures. This is a dominant principle in spear-phishing, CEO fraud, and Business Email Compromise (BEC) attacks where attackers impersonate superiors or institutions [17].
5) **Scarcity:** Limited-time offers or threats of loss trigger urgency. Phishing emails frequently use deadline pressure ("act now") or warnings of account suspension to rush decision-making [5]. Scarcity combined with authority significantly amplifies manipulation.
6) **Commitment and Consistency:** Once a target agrees to a small action, they are more likely to continue with larger requests to remain consistent with prior behavior [28]. Phishing often begins with innocuous clicks or confirmations, gradually escalating to credential theft [29].

These principles are not mutually exclusive and are often combined strategically in phishing scenarios [30]. They represent well-documented psychological heuristics that adversaries exploit to bypass cognitive defenses.

B. Social Engineering and Phishing Taxonomy

Social Engineering refers to the manipulation of human behavior to gain unauthorized access or extract confidential data. Unlike technical exploits, social engineering targets cognitive biases and emotional responses [30] [5].

Phishing, a subclass of social engineering, takes multiple forms depending on delivery method, personalization, and attacker intent [31]. The following taxonomy outlines ten studied phishing/attack types:

1) **Generic Phishing:** Broad, untargeted campaigns often impersonating major services (e.g., banks, delivery services). These rely on volume and simple cues like logos or time-sensitive warnings [32].
2) **Spear-Phishing:** Tailored attacks on individuals, typically leveraging Open-Source Intelligence (OSINT) to personalize content [33]. Spear-phishing has high success rates due to contextual plausibility [34].
3) **Business Email Compromise (BEC):** A subtype of spear-phishing where attackers impersonate executives to fraudulently initiate financial transactions [35]. Authority and urgency dominate these attacks.
4) **CEO-Fraud:** A further specialization of BEC in which attackers spoof high-level executives to manipulate subordinates into performing unauthorized tasks, often financial [36]. Strongly driven by authority and obedience heuristics.
5) **Whaling:** A form of spear-phishing targeting high-profile individuals such as C-level executives or board members [37]. These attacks combine authority with high contextual relevance, often mimicking internal workflows.
6) **Clone-/Dynamite-Phishing:** Involves copying legitimate past communications and resending them with malicious payloads or links. This method exploits trust in established communication patterns and prior context.
7) **Vishing:** Voice-based phishing via phone calls. Attackers impersonate authorities or support personnel [38]. Vishing exploits real-time pressure, often employing the commitment and authority principles.
8) **Quishing:** QR-code phishing attacks that exploit users' trust in QR-based scenarios. Quishing bypasses URL verification and often embeds commitment through routine-seeming steps [39].
9) **Smishing:** SMS-based phishing that mimics alerts from banks, couriers, or apps. Its scarcity and urgency lead to quick, unreflective responses [40].
10) **AI-Based Phishing:** Uses Large Language Models (LLM) or Generative AI to create highly convincing and personalized phishing content at scale [22]. These attacks increasingly integrate emotional tone, contextual cues, and stylistic mimicry, enhancing the persuasiveness of principles like liking and authority [23].

Human factors in cybersecurity remain critical. Attackers increasingly adapt their strategies to exploit known psychological vulnerabilities, not just technological gaps. These include cognitive overload, authority bias, time pressure, and familiarity illusions [41]. Understanding how influence principles manifest across phishing variants is essential for designing more effective awareness training and detection mechanisms.

IV. Methodology

A. Case-Based Qualitative Analysis

A qualitative case study approach was employed based on real spear-phishing examples to explore how Cialdini's influence principles are operationalized. Therefore, authentic spear-phishing emails were drawn from documented APT campaigns and original email scenarios, each designed to exemplify Cialdini's six principles. Each case was examined through critical textual analysis, focusing on linguistic markers, attacker strategy, and contextual cues that demonstrated the activation of psychological triggers. The qualitative analysis aimed to answer how each principle is exploited in practice. This analysis provides both validity and conceptual diversity.

B. Quantitative Content Analysis

A content analysis was conducted to statistically assess the prevalence and intensity of the six principles across different phishing methods. The dataset comprised 300 phishing emails, evenly distributed across the ten attack types (cf. Section III-B). Each email was manually coded using a predefined scale (0-5) for the six principles. Coding followed a deductive scheme grounded in Cialdini's theory, and a structured coding guide ensured inter-case consistency. This method allowed for fine-grained measurement of psychological influence intensity and variation across modalities. Friedman tests were performed, followed by pairwise Wilcoxon signed-rank tests with Bonferroni correction to assess within-group variance and test for statistically significant differences between principles within each attack type. The Friedman test was selected because the study design involved repeated measures across the same set of phishing samples evaluated on six related persuasion principles. Unlike ANOVA, which assumes normality, the Friedman test is a non-parametric equivalent suitable for ordinal or non-normally distributed data. Following this, Wilcoxon signed-rank tests with Bonferroni correction were applied for pairwise comparisons. This choice reflects their suitability for dependent samples where measurements are related (i.e., the same phishing email coded for multiple principles) and where assumptions of parametric tests (normal distribution, homoscedasticity) are not met.

C. Regression and Statistical Evaluation

A multiple linear regression model was developed using Ordinary Least Squares (OLS), with the dependent variable being the compromise rate per attack type to quantify the relationship between principles and phishing success. The independent variables were the principle intensity scores per email, resulting in a total of 300 observations with six predictors.

The model was validated using standard assumptions checks. Multicollinearity was tested via Variance Inflation Factors (VIF), heteroskedasticity was assessed via the Breusch-Pagan test, and normality of residuals via Q-Q plots and histograms. Due to violations of homoskedasticity and residual normality, robust HC3 standard errors were applied. Significant predictors were identified based on $p < 0.05$. Positive predictors of phishing success are confirmed via confidence intervals. In summary, non-parametric tests were employed for within-group comparisons due to the ordinal nature and non-normal distribution of principle intensity scores, while regression modeling with robust errors allowed us to examine predictive relationships at the continuous level, compensating for assumption violations. Together, these methods ensured both robustness and interpretability for behavioral security data.

D. Limitations and Ethical Considerations

The mixed-methods approach has inherent limitations. The qualitative case study relies on subjective interpretation of attacker intent and message construction, which may limit reproducibility. The quantitative analysis is limited by its reliance on public datasets (i.e., PhishTank, OpenPhish, APWG eCrime Exchange), which may underrepresent more sophisticated or covert phishing techniques.

From an ethical standpoint, the dual-use nature of this research: the insights gained into manipulation strategies could potentially be misused. However, the aim is to empower defenders to recognize and mitigate socially engineered threats. No Personally Identifiable Information (PII) was included, and all real phishing emails used were publicly disclosed by security researchers.

V. Results and Discussion

A. Patterns of Influence in Phishing

The qualitative analysis of real-world phishing emails revealed strategic and differentiated use of Cialdini's influence principles. For example, attackers exploiting *authority* frequently impersonated C-level executives or institutional leaders, incorporating formal signatures and authoritative tone to enforce compliance. A spear-phishing email targeting the Afghan National Security Council used institutional logos and urgency to simulate government hierarchy.

Liking was exploited via impersonation of familiar senders, such as colleagues or friends, while *social proof* was invoked through phrases suggesting peer compliance (e.g., "your team has already updated credentials"). The framework was further expanded through scenarios that demonstrated nuanced manipulations, such as using perceived similarity or shared values to activate *commitment and consistency*.

B. Statistical Prevalence Across Attack Types

The quantitative analysis of 300 phishing samples (10 attack types × 30 emails each) across ten attack types revealed distinct patterns in the intensity and distribution of influence principles. Table I summarizes the median influence scores of the ten attack types. It is important to note that descriptive frequency counts alone could not establish whether observed differences across principles were statistically reliable. The Friedman and Wilcoxon tests thus provided a rigorous basis for determining whether the differences in principle intensity were significant rather than artifacts of sample variation. It highlights that influence principles are functionally adapted to each attack type. For example, scarcity dominates in smishing and generic phishing due to limited message length, while authority and commitment prevail in BEC, CEO-fraud, and Whaling scenarios. Thus, influence principles are selected based on attack modality, channel limitations (e.g., SMS vs. email), and attacker objectives.

TABLE I
RELEVANCE OF CIALDINI'S PRINCIPLES BY ATTACK TYPE (MEDIAN)

Attack Type	*Reciprocity*	*Commit./Consist.*	*Social Proof*	*Liking*	*Authority*	*Scarcity*
Generic Phishing	0.00	3.00	0.00	0.00	2.00	5.00
Spear-Phishing	0.00	3.00	0.00	0.00	3.50	5.00
BEC	0.00	4.50	0.00	1.00	4.00	5.00
CEO-Fraud	0.00	5.00	0.00	1.00	5.00	5.00
Whaling	0.00	5.00	0.00	1.00	5.00	5.00
Vishing	0.00	4.50	0.00	1.00	4.00	5.00
Clone-/Dyn.-Phish.	0.00	3.00	0.00	0.00	2.00	5.00
Quishing	0.00	2.50	0.00	0.00	2.00	4.00
Smishing	0.00	2.00	0.00	0.00	2.00	5.00
AI-based Phishing	0.00	3.00	0.00	1.00	4.00	5.00

The principle of *scarcity* was the most consistently applied, with a median intensity of 5 across the attack types. *Authority* and *commitment and consistency* were also prevalent, especially in BEC, CEO-fraud, and Whaling attacks, where hierarchical compliance and task escalation were common. Conversely, *reciprocity*, *social proof*, and *liking* were less frequently used overall, though they appeared more often in high-personalization scenarios such as vishing and AI-enhanced phishing.

C. Regression Results: Compromise Correlation

The OLS regression model, fitted to the dataset with HC3 robust standard errors, demonstrated statistically significant relationships between principle intensity and compromise rates. The adjusted R^2 of the model was 0.126. This means that about 12.6% of the variance in the dependent variable (i.e., compromise rate) is explained by the independent variables (i.e., the six Cialdini principle intensity scores), which is acceptable for behavioral modeling in cybersecurity contexts. All VIF values were below 1.4, indicating low multicollinearity between the six independent variables (Cialdini's princi-

TABLE II
SUMMARY OF INFLUENCE PRINCIPLE PREVALENCE AND STATISTICAL EFFECT
*STATISTICALLY SIGNIFICANT AT $p < 0.05$; **HIGHLY SIGNIFICANT AT $p < 0.001$.
REGRESSION MODEL: OLS WITH HC3 ROBUST STANDARD ERRORS, $N = 300$, $R^2 = 0.126$.

Cialdini's Principle	Median Intensity	Prevalence (%)	Regression Coefficient β	p-value
Reciprocity	0	11.3%	−0.0263	0.0234*
Liking	1	34.0%	0.6030	<0.001**
Social Proof	0	9.7%	0.0091	0.210
Authority	4	63.7%	0.2011	0.018*
Scarcity	5	72.1%	0.0118	0.081
Commitment/Consistency	3	58.0%	0.0142	0.092

ples). This suggests that each Cialdini principle is relatively independent as a predictor. These six persuasion principles are statistically distinct in the dataset, so you can trust the individual effects estimated by the regression model.

Table II summarizes the statistical influence of each of Cialdini's principles on user compromise rates across the 300 phishing emails. The analysis confirms that not all principles contribute equally to phishing success. *Liking* demonstrates the strongest and most statistically significant effect ($\beta = 0.6030$, $p < 0.001$), supporting the hypothesis that affective closeness, familiarity, or interpersonal mimicry substantially increase user compliance. Similarly, *authority* is a significant predictor ($\beta = 0.2011$, $p = 0.018$), consistent with prior findings that impersonation of executives, IT staff, or institutional figures drives user obedience, especially under hierarchical pressure.

Interestingly, *reciprocity* showed a statistically significant negative association with compromise likelihood ($\beta = -0.0263$, $p < 0.0234$), suggesting that overt attempts to provide "favors" may arouse user suspicion in phishing contexts, potentially due to increasing awareness of this manipulation tactic. *Scarcity* ($\beta = 0.0118$, $p < 0.081$) and *commitment/consistency* ($\beta = 0.0142$, $p < 0.092$), despite being highly prevalent in the samples, did not yield statistically significant predictive power within the model. This discrepancy between frequency and predictive strength highlights an important insight: frequent use of an influence tactic does not necessarily imply behavioral efficacy.

Overall, these findings offer empirical grounding for prioritizing *liking* and *authority* in both phishing detection mechanisms and user awareness training, while also suggesting diminishing returns for overused tactics like *scarcity* unless contextually embedded with realism.

D. Dominant Principles and Interactions

Figure 1 presents six linear regression plots, each modeling the relationship between the intensity of a specific Cialdini principle and the corresponding phishing compromise rate. The results reveal substantial variation in behavioral effectiveness. *Liking* demonstrates the strongest positive correlation: higher affective or personalized cues are associated with increased compromise rates, supporting the regression model's identification of liking as the most effective principle. *Authority* also shows a positive linear trend, consistent with its significant regression coefficient, confirming that hierarchical impersonation and institutional tone enhance persuasive success. In contrast, *scarcity*, despite being the most frequently used principle in the dataset, exhibits no meaningful trend, suggesting user desensitization to urgency-based manipulations. *Reciprocity* even displays a negative correlation, possibly reflecting increased user skepticism toward unsolicited favors. *Commitment/Consistency* and *Social Proof* show flat to weakly positive trends, indicating limited predictive utility in isolated message contexts. These results emphasize that influence principle effectiveness is not uniform and may depend on contextual deployment, multimodal layering, or user expectations. Most notably, the data confirm that frequent use does not guarantee behavioral impact.

The statistical findings reveal a decoupling between principle frequency and behavioral effectiveness. Table II shows that *scarcity*, while the most frequently applied principle across all phishing types (median intensity = 5 in 9 out of 10 attack types), did not significantly predict compromise success ($p = 0.081$). In contrast, *liking*, applied in only 34% of the messages, exhibited the strongest statistical association with compromise likelihood ($\beta = 0.6030$, $p < 0.001$).

Similarly, *authority* emerged as both prevalent (63.7%) and significantly effective ($\beta = 0.2011$, $p = 0.018$), particularly in BEC, CEO-Fraud, Whaling, and spear-phishing scenarios where hierarchical power is invoked. Conversely, *reciprocity* (11.3%) showed a negative association with compromise, possibly due to heightened user suspicion of unsolicited "favors" or assistance.

Overall, these findings highlight the importance of focusing not only on principle prevalence but also on behavioral potency and contextual deployment. These findings suggest that the effectiveness of influence principles is highly context-dependent. For instance, while *scarcity* was applied in over 70% of the messages, it showed no statistically significant effect on user compromise. This may be explained by user desensitization in environments where deadline-driven messages are frequent (e.g., corporate inboxes or customer service workflows), reducing perceived urgency. Conversely, *liking*, though less frequent, was particularly effective in personalized or peer-based attacks such as vishing, where social cues are more prominent.

Further, principle efficacy may vary by communication channel: *scarcity* cues are more impactful in constrained formats (e.g., SMS), while *liking* requires richer context or sender familiarity, often found in email or voice interactions.

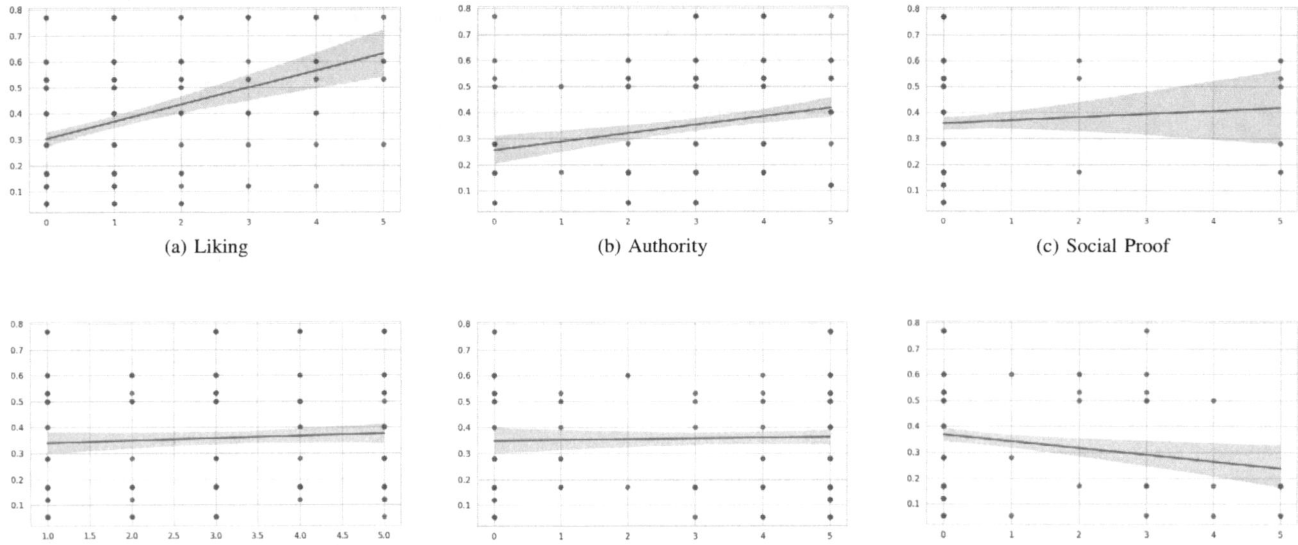

(a) Liking (b) Authority (c) Social Proof

(d) Commitment and Consistency (e) Scarcity (f) Reciprocity

Figure 1. Linear Regression Plots of Cialdini Principle Intensity (x-axis) versus Compromise Rate (y-axis). While *liking* and *authority* show positive correlations, *scarcity* and *reciprocity* display no or negative effects. The red shaded areas indicate 95% confidence intervals around the regression line. They visualize the uncertainty of the estimated relationship: narrow intervals reflect stable effects, while wide intervals suggest weaker or non-significant associations.

Cultural and organizational factors (e.g., power distance, communication formalism) may also moderate response patterns.

E. Cross-Attack Type Comparison

Comparative analysis across attack types revealed the strategic flexibility of attackers in selecting and combining influence principles. Each phishing vector favors a different psychological profile based on channels, user expectations, and social context.

In *Generic Phishing*, *Scarcity* and *authority* dominate through fake account alerts, service disruptions, and impersonated institutions. Messages are brief and rely on fear and urgency. *Spear-Phishing* exhibits high variance in principle application, often combining *liking*, *authority*, and *commitment*. Personalization is derived from OSINT and contextual familiarity. *BEC* relies on formal tone and impersonation of executives to trigger *authority* and *consistency*. Often embedded in regular workflows (e.g., invoice approvals). In *CEO-Fraud*, top-level executives demand confidential action (e.g., fund transfers). Strongly driven by *authority*, hierarchical obedience, and urgency. *Whaling* targets high-ranking individuals (e.g., C-level execs). Incorporates high contextual detail and cues of exclusivity, invoking *authority*, *scarcity*, and *social proof* (e.g., "Board-only access"). *Clone-/Dynamite-Phishing* uses previously legitimate email threads, duplicated with altered links or attachments. Exploits *commitment* and *consistency* by leveraging past trusted interactions. *Vishing* uses real-time voice to exert psychological pressure. Commonly invokes *authority* (e.g., fake IT or bank staff) and *commitment* by escalating task sequences in live interaction. *Quishing* relies on *commitment* and *scarcity* via QR codes embedded in emails or posters. Users are lured into taking quick action with limited time or context to reflect. *Smishing* emphasizes *scarcity* and *urgency* with short, time-pressured messages. Lacks personalization but achieves reach and immediacy. *AI-Based Phishing* enhances *liking*, *social proof*, and mimics human tone more convincingly, posing new detection challenges.

These patterns illustrate that influence principle deployment is not uniform but highly context-sensitive. For example, *scarcity* dominates in low-bandwidth channels like SMS, whereas *liking* and *commitment* are more effective in richer, interaction-heavy environments such as spear-phishing and vishing. The adaptability of persuasion strategies across attack types reinforces the need for context-aware, psychologically informed defense mechanisms in training, detection, and interface design.

VI. IMPLICATIONS FOR CYBERSECURITY PRACTICE

A. Psychological-Aware Security Training

Traditional security awareness programs often focus on technical indicators (e.g., suspicious URLs or attachments), overlooking the psychological mechanisms that drive compliance. The findings demonstrate that *liking* and *authority* are not only prevalent but significantly associated with user compromise. These principles often bypass verification by appealing to trust, familiarity, or hierarchical obedience. Security training must therefore integrate behavioral countermeasures that explain how persuasion operates. For example, users should be taught to question affective signals such as informal greetings from "known" senders or praise followed by requests. Role-playing simulations that mimic real phishing attempts using these principles can foster resistance through experiential learning. Training should also differentiate between the attack types. In high-risk environments (e.g., finance, defense), training must include social engineering reconnaissance awareness and contextual manipulation recognition.

B. Technical Countermeasures and AI Detection

While human awareness is essential, scalable defense requires automated recognition of manipulation patterns. AI-based email filters and NLP can be enhanced to detect rhetorical structures associated with influence principles. For instance, classifiers can be trained to recognize language signaling urgency (scarcity), hierarchical tone (authority), or affective cues (liking) using supervised learning on labeled phishing corpora. As mentioned, current phishing detection systems focus on URL blacklists and attachment scanning. The results suggest that integrating linguistic and psychological features could significantly improve detection precision, especially in text-only or highly targeted attacks. Attention-based models (e.g., transformers) may be particularly effective at identifying subtle combinations of influence tactics across message context.

C. Design Recommendations

Security systems should not only detect threats but also guide users in making safer decisions. Based on the findings, several design strategies are proposed. Contextual warnings can alert users to specific persuasive cues, e.g., "This message may simulate authority", to increase awareness. Cognitive interrupts should be used when requests deviate from normal workflows, such as financial approvals from executives, prompting users to verify intent. Email clients could also highlight rhetorical patterns associated with Cialdini's principles, helping users reassess suspicious messages. For low-bandwidth channels like SMS and QR-based phishing, lightweight NLP can screen for urgency and forcing before users engage.

These interventions represent a move from reactive filtering to proactive behavioral defense, embedding psychological insights into security interfaces to mitigate human-targeted phishing risks created by human cognitive biases.

VII. Conclusion and Future Work

A. Summary of Findings

This study investigated how Cialdini's six principles of persuasion are deployed in phishing attacks and to what extent they contribute to user compromise. To answer RQ1, a qualitative analysis of real phishing emails demonstrated that attackers apply influence principles with strategic intent. *Authority* was often used to simulate hierarchical urgency, *liking* to build interpersonal trust, and *commitment* to create behavioral momentum. Many messages embedded multiple principles, suggesting that psychological synergy enhances manipulation.

In response to RQ2, the quantitative content analysis of 300 phishing messages across ten attack types showed that *scarcity* was the most frequently used principle, with a median intensity of 5 and present in over 70% of cases. *Authority* and *commitment* followed in prevalence, particularly in structured fraud scenarios such as BEC, CEO-fraud, and whaling. In contrast, *liking*, *social proof*, and *reciprocity* were less common but appeared more often in personalized attacks like vishing and AI-based phishing.

For RQ3, a multiple linear regression with HC3 robust standard errors revealed that *liking* ($\beta = 0.6030$, $p < 0.001$) and *authority* ($\beta = 0.2011$, $p = 0.018$) are the most significant predictors of compromise rate. Surprisingly, *scarcity*, despite its high frequency, did not significantly predict compromise ($p = 0.081$), suggesting a behavioral desensitization effect. Moreover, *reciprocity* showed a small but statistically significant negative association ($\beta = -0.0263$, $p = 0.0234$), possibly indicating growing user skepticism toward unsolicited help.

In summary, these results confirm a critical insight: the most frequently used influence principles are not always the most behaviorally effective. Successful phishing campaigns influence targeted psychological manipulation, particularly affective and hierarchical cues, rather than relying solely on urgency or volume. These findings support the need for cognitively grounded defenses and context-aware phishing detection.

B. Methodological Reflection

This study is based on mixed-methods; qualitative scenario analysis has enabled contextual depth, while quantitative regression provided empirical rigor. However, limitations exist. The qualitative portion relied on interpretative judgment, which, while conceptually grounded, lack ecological verification. The quantitative analysis was constrained by the availability of public phishing datasets, limiting granularity and possibly introducing reporting bias. Despite these constraints, this approach enhanced validity, and the consistent convergence of results from both methods strengthens confidence in the core findings.

C. Research Extensions

Several directions offer potential for advancing this work. First, controlled phishing simulations should be used to test user susceptibility to individual influence principles in real time, allowing for causal validation beyond correlational inference. Second, future studies should investigate how influence principles operate across multimodal channels, such as text, voice, and QR code interactions, as attackers increasingly integrate multiple attack vectors. Third, the rise of LLM-generated phishing content requires new approaches to detect psychologically persuasive language at scale. Research should focus on identifying adversarial prompts and developing counter-generation strategies. Lastly, cross-cultural studies are needed to examine how cultural norms shape susceptibility to specific principles, and to assess the global generalizability of the findings in cybersecurity contexts. These extensions can strengthen the understanding of adversarial persuasion and support the development of cognitively informed, culturally robust defense systems.

REFERENCES

[1] N. Daswani and M. Elbayadi, *Big breaches: Cybersecurity lessons for everyone*. Springer, 2021.

[2] Keepnet, "Top 70 Phishing Statistics and Trends You Must Know in 2025," 10 2024, [retrieved: July, 2025]. [Online]. Available: https://keepnetlabs.com/blog/top-phishing-statistics-and-trends-you-must-know

[3] R. T. Wright, M. L. Jensen, J. B. Thatcher, M. Dinger, and K. Marett, "Research note—influence Techniques in Phishing Attacks: An Examination of Vulnerability and Resistance," *Information systems research*, vol. 25, no. 2, pp. 385–400, 2014.

[4] P. Wang and P. Lutchkus, "Psychological tactics of phishing emails," *Issues in Information Systems*, 2023. [Online]. Available: http://dx.doi.org/10.48009/2_iis_2023_107

[5] O. Zielinska, A. Welk, C. B. Mayhorn, and E. Murphy-Hill, "The Persuasive Phish: Examining the Social Psychological Principles hidden in Phishing Emails," in *Proceedings of the Symposium and Bootcamp on the Science of Security*, 2016, pp. 126–126.

[6] R. B. Cialdini, "Principles and Techniques of Social Influence," *Advanced social psychology*, vol. 256, p. 281, 1995.

[7] R. Cialdini, "Principles of Persuasion," *Arizona State University, eBrand Media Publication*, 2001.

[8] R. Cialdini and B. Sagarin, "Principles of interpersonal influence," *Persuasion: Psychological Insights and Perspectives*, pp. 143–169, 01 2005.

[9] J. Wang, T. Herath, R. Chen, A. Vishwanath, and H. R. Rao, "Research Article Phishing Susceptibility: An Investigation into the Processing of a Targeted Spear Phishing Email," *IEEE transactions on professional communication*, vol. 55, no. 4, pp. 345–362, 2012.

[10] P.-E. Arduin, "To Click or not to Click? Deciding to Trust or Distrust Phishing Emails," in *International Conference on Decision Support System Technology*. Springer, 2020, pp. 73–85.

[11] A. Bergholz, J. De Beer, S. Glahn, M.-F. Moens, G. Paaß, and S. Strobel, "New Filtering Approaches for Phishing Email," *Journal of Computer Security*, vol. 18, no. 1, pp. 7–35, 2010.

[12] C. Whittaker, B. Ryner, and M. Nazif, "Large-Scale Automatic Classification of Phishing Pages," in *Ndss*, vol. 10, 2010, p. 2010.

[13] R. Taib, K. Yu, S. Berkovsky, M. Wiggins, and P. Bayl-Smith, "Social Engineering and Organisational Dependencies in Phishing Attacks," in *IFIP conference on human-computer interaction*. Springer, 2019, pp. 564–584.

[14] R. Ahmad, S. Terzis, and K. Renaud, "Getting users to click: a content analysis of phishers' tactics and techniques in mobile instant messaging phishing," *Information & Computer Security*, vol. 32, no. 4, pp. 420–435, 2024.

[15] K. Uehara, H. Nishikawa, T. Yamamoto, K. Kawauchi, and M. Nishigaki, "Analysis of the relationship between psychological manipulation techniques and both personality factors and behavioral characteristics in targeted email," in *International Conference on Advanced Information Networking and Applications*. Springer, 2020, pp. 1278–1290.

[16] M. De Bona and F. Paci, "A real world study on employees' susceptibility to phishing attacks," in *Proceedings of the 15th International Conference on Availability, Reliability and Security*, 2020, pp. 1–10.

[17] M. Butavicius, K. Parsons, M. Pattinson, and A. McCormac, "Breaching the Human Firewall: Social engineering in Phishing and Spear-Phishing Emails," *arXiv preprint arXiv:1606.00887*, 2016.

[18] C. A. Tian, M. L. Jensen, and A. Durcikova, "Phishing susceptibility across industries: The differential impact of influence techniques," *Computers & Security*, vol. 135, p. 103487, 2023.

[19] G. Raywood-Burke, D. M. Jones, and P. L. Morgan, "Maladaptive behaviour in phishing susceptibility: How email context influences the impact of persuasion techniques," 2023.

[20] D. Oliveira, H. Rocha, H. Yang, D. Ellis, S. Dommaraju, M. Muradoglu, D. Weir, A. Soliman, T. Lin, and N. Ebner, "Dissecting spear phishing emails for older vs young adults: On the interplay of weapons of influence and life domains in predicting susceptibility to phishing," in *Proceedings of the 2017 chi conference on human factors in computing systems*, 2017, pp. 6412–6424.

[21] P. A. Lawson, A. D. Crowson, and C. B. Mayhorn, "Baiting the hook: Exploring the interaction of personality and persuasion tactics in email phishing attacks," in *Congress of the International Ergonomics Association*. Springer, 2018, pp. 401–406.

[22] J. Hazell, "Spear Phishing With Large Language Models," *arXiv preprint arXiv:2305.06972*, 2023.

[23] S. C. Matz, J. D. Teeny, S. S. Vaid, H. Peters, G. M. Harari, and M. Cerf, "The Potential of Generative AI for Personalized Persuasion at Scale," *Scientific Reports*, vol. 14, no. 1, p. 4692, 2024.

[24] F. Sharevski and P. Jachim, ""alexa, what'sa phishing email?": Training users to spot phishing emails using a voice assistant," *EURASIP Journal on Information Security*, vol. 2022, no. 1, p. 7, 2022.

[25] C. Happ, A. Melzer, and G. Steffgen, "Trick with Treat–Reciprocity increases the Willingness to communicate Personal Data," *Computers in Human Behavior*, vol. 61, pp. 372–377, 2016.

[26] O. Goga, G. Venkatadri, and K. P. Gummadi, "The Doppelgänger Bot Attack: Exploring Identity Impersonation in Online Social Networks," in *Proceedings of the 2015 Internet Measurement Conference*, 2015, pp. 141–153.

[27] A. Vishwanath, T. Herath, R. Chen, J. Wang, and H. R. Rao, "Why do people get phished? Testing individual differences in phishing vulnerability within an integrated, information processing model," *Decision Support Systems*, vol. 51, no. 3, pp. 576–586, 2011.

[28] J. L. Freedman and S. C. Fraser, "Compliance without Pressure: The Foot-in-the-Door Technique," *Journal of Personality and Social Psychology*, vol. 4, no. 2, p. 195, 1966.

[29] H. Abroshan, J. Devos, G. Poels, and E. Laermans, "Phishing Happens Beyond Technology: The Effects of Human Behaviors and Demographics on Each Step of a Phishing Process," *IEEE Access*, vol. 9, pp. 44 928–44 949, 2021.

[30] A. Ferreira, L. Coventry, and G. Lenzini, "Principles of Persuasion in Social Engineering and Their Use in Phishing," in *International Conference on Human Aspects of Information Security, Privacy, and Trust*. Springer, 2015, pp. 36–47.

[31] A. Lawall and P. Beenken, "A Threat-Led Approach to Mitigating Ransomware Attacks: Insights from a Comprehensive Analysis of the Ransomware Ecosystem," in *Proceedings of the 2024 European Interdisciplinary Cybersecurity Conference*, ser. EICC '24, S. Li, K. Coopamootoo, and M. Sirivianos, Eds. New York, NY, USA: Association for Computing Machinery, 2024, pp. 210–216. [Online]. Available: https://doi.org/10.1145/3655693.3661321

[32] S. Chanti and T. Chithralekha, "A Literature Review on Classification of Phishing Attacks," *International Journal of Advanced Technology and Engineering Exploration*, vol. 9, no. 89, pp. 446–476, 2022.

[33] A. Lawall, "Fingerprinting and Tracing Shadows: The Development and Impact of Browser Fingerprinting on Digital Privacy," in *The Eighteenth International Conference on Emerging Security Information, Systems and Technologies (SECURWARE) 2024*, 2024, pp. 132–140.

[34] A. Sumner and X. Yuan, "Mitigating Phishing Attacks: An Overview," in *Proceedings of the 2019 ACM Southeast Conference*, 2019, pp. 72–77.

[35] T. Nisha, D. Bakari, and C. Shukla, "Business E-mail Compromise — Techniques and Countermeasures," in *2021 International Conference on Advance Computing and Innovative Technologies in Engineering (ICACITE)*. IEEE, 2021, pp. 217–222.

[36] M. J. Conyon and L. He, "Executive Compensation and Corporate Fraud in China," *Journal of Business Ethics*, vol. 134, no. 4, pp. 669–691, 2016.

[37] D. Pienta, J. B. Thatcher, and A. Johnston, "Protecting a Whale in a Sea of Phish," *Journal of Information Technology*, vol. 35, no. 3, pp. 214–231, 2020.

[38] S. I. Hashmi, N. George, E. Saqib, F. Ali, N. Siddique, S. Kashif, S. Ali, N. U. H. Bajwa, and M. Javed, "Training Users to Recognize Persuasion Techniques in Vishing Calls," in *Extended Abstracts of the 2023 CHI Conference on Human Factors in Computing Systems*, 2023, pp. 1–8.

[39] T. Vidas, E. Owusu, S. Wang, C. Zeng, L. F. Cranor, and N. Christin, "QRishing: The Susceptibility of Smartphone Users to QR Code Phishing Attacks," in *International conference on financial cryptography and data security*. Springer, 2013, pp. 52–69.

[40] M. L. Rahman, D. Timko, H. Wali, and A. Neupane, "Users Really Do Respond To Smishing," in *Proceedings of the thirteenth ACM conference on data and application security and privacy*, 2023, pp. 49–60.

[41] J. Jeong, J. Mihelcic, G. Oliver, and C. Rudolph, "Towards an Improved Understanding of Human Factors in Cybersecurity," in *2019 IEEE 5th International Conference on Collaboration and Internet Computing (CIC)*. IEEE, 2019, pp. 338–345.

A Modified Schnorr Sigma Protocol and Its Application to Isogeny-Based Identification

Mahdi Mahdavi[1], Zaira Pindado[2], Amineh Sakhaie[3], and Helena Rifà-Pous[1]
[1] Universitat Oberta de Catalunya (UOC), [2] Barcelona Supercomputing Center (BSC), [3] University of Lisbon
e-mail: {m_mahdavi | hrifa}@uoc.edu zaira.pindado@bsc.es
fc65105@alunos.ciencias.ulisboa.pt

***Abstract*—Quantum computing threatens classical cryptographic protocols like the Schnorr identification scheme, which relies on the Discrete Logarithm Problem (DLP), vulnerable to quantum attacks. In this paper, we propose a modification to the classical Schnorr protocol by redefining the prover response as $r = cu \pm x \bmod q$ instead of $r = u + cx \bmod q$. While this adjustment preserves the arithmetic simplicity of the original protocol, it introduces subtle but significant changes to the protocol's security and verifiability. We analyze its soundness, zero-knowledge properties, extractor functionality, and practical viability, and explore its adaptation into a secure digital signature system under standard cryptographic assumptions. To underscore the practical significance of our approach, we implement the modified protocol within an isogeny-based framework, demonstrating its capacity to enhance an existing identification scheme with respect to both security and efficiency. Our findings illustrate that revisiting classical protocols through judicious modifications can yield more robust, quantum-resistant solutions for applications like blockchain.**

Keywords-Schnorr Protocol; Zero-knowledge proofs; Discrete Logarithm Problem; Isogeny-based cryptography; Post-Quantum Cryptography.

I. INTRODUCTION

Identification protocols are fundamental cryptographic primitives that enable a prover to convince a verifier of their identity by demonstrating knowledge of a secret without disclosing it. These protocols are the foundation for many cryptographic systems, such as authentication frameworks, zero-knowledge proofs, and digital signature algorithms. One of the most celebrated and widely studied identification schemes is the Schnorr identification protocol [1], which offers a simple and elegant construction grounded in the hardness of the Discrete Logarithm Problem (DLP) [2].

The Schnorr protocol is a canonical Σ-protocol that defines the prover's response to the verifier's challenge c as $r = u + cx \bmod q$, where u is a random nonce used in the commitment, x is the prover's secret and c is the challenge. This formulation balances efficiency and security, and forms the basis for many digital signature schemes through the Fiat–Shamir transformation [3].

As a Σ-protocol, Schnorr satisfies three essential properties: completeness, which ensures that an honest prover always convinces the verifier; special soundness, which guarantees that if an adversary can produce two accepting transcripts with the same commitment but different challenges, then it is possible to efficiently extract the secret x, and Honest Verifier Zero-Knowledge (HVZK), meaning that a simulator, given access to the challenge, can generate transcripts that are computationally indistinguishable from real interactions, without knowing the prover's secret.

A. Related work

The Schnorr protocol has been extensively studied and extended in various directions. Fuchsbauer et al. [4] analyzed blind Schnorr signatures and signed ElGamal encryption techniques using the Algebraic Group Model (AGM), demonstrating robust security guarantees under normal assumptions without the use of heuristic arguments.

In the threshold setting, Bacho et al. [5] introduced HARTS, the first threshold Schnorr signature scheme that is simultaneously adaptively secure, robust under full asynchrony, and communication-efficient. HARTS supports high-threshold configurations—where the number of required signers can significantly exceed the corruption threshold—and outputs standard Schnorr signatures using only one asynchronous online round and subcubic communication.

Fukumitsu and Hasegawa [6] demonstrated that Schnorr signatures are secure in the multi-user setting under the AGM, assuming the hardness of the DLP. This multi-user resilience is essential for large-scale deployments, such as public key infrastructures.

In parallel, Fuchsbauer and Wolf [7] proposed a practical, concurrently secure blind signature protocol compatible with standard Schnorr signatures. Their technique ensures system compatibility while introducing predicate blind signatures, enabling signers to impose constraints on signed messages—a feature particularly valuable for privacy-preserving blockchain applications.

In post-quantum cryptography, Galbraith, Petit, and Silva [8] developed two digital signature systems based on the hardness of isogeny problems over supersingular elliptic curves, leveraging a novel identification technique to achieve quantum-resistant security. A key innovation in their work is a novel identification technique that builds upon a well-established computational problem but addresses limitations seen in prior methods. These systems can be converted into secure digital signatures using both classical and quantum-safe approaches, providing a realistic path to efficient post-quantum cryptography solutions. In a related advancement, Baghery et al. [9] adapted the Schnorr sigma protocol to the isogeny-based setting.

These developments illustrate the robustness of the Schnorr paradigm across diverse cryptographic settings. Building on this foundation, we introduce a novel algebraic modification to the protocol's response function to improve efficiency and resilience in isogeny-based, post-quantum identification schemes.

B. Our contribution

In this paper, we propose a novel variation of the Schnorr identification protocol in which the prover's response is computed as $r = cu \pm x \mod q$, fundamentally altering the interaction between the nonce, challenge, and secret. This structural change results in a new verification equation and requires a complete re-evaluation of the protocol's security properties. Unlike minor tweaks, our modification challenges the conventional structure and allows for new analytical insights.

Our main contributions can be summarised as follows.

1) Formal definition and analysis of the modified protocol, reversing the typical dependency between the challenge and the secret. We also prove the security proofs that guarantee the protocol maintains completeness, special soundness, and honest-verifier zero-knowledge.
2) We analyze how the modified response can be adapted for use in non-interactive settings via the Fiat–Shamir heuristic, preserving signature viability.
3) We propose a new post-quantum id protocol based on isogenies using the modified Schnorr protocol.
4) An examination of the proposed Sigma protocol's application within isogeny-based cryptographic systems. Building upon and extending prior work [9], we identify significant advantages, most notably the elimination of the requirement for witnesses at critical proof stages. This refinement enhances protocol resilience by preventing leakage of errors related to the protocol, or witness during execution.

In addition, our modified Schnorr protocol enables the use of the MPC-in-the-Head technique and its advantages, which we leave as an avenue for future work.

This paper is structured as follows. In Section II, we provide the necessary background on Σ-protocols, digital signature schemes, and isogeny-based identification systems. Section III introduces our modified Schnorr protocol in detail, including the new response format and its implications on completeness, special soundness, and honest-verifier zero-knowledge. We also show how our construction leads to a secure digital signature scheme under the Discrete Logarithm Problem and supports non-interactive instantiations via the Fiat–Shamir transform. In Section IV, we extend the modified protocol to an isogeny-based setting, presenting a novel identification scheme that improve upon previous work by eliminating the need for witnesses during critical stages and enhancing resilience against execution errors. Finally, Section V concludes with a summary of our findings and outlines potential directions for future research in post-quantum cryptography.

II. Preliminaries

A. Notation

Let $\mathbb{Z}_q = \mathbb{Z}/q\mathbb{Z}$ denote the set of integers modulo q, being q a positive prime integer and $\mathbb{Z}_q^*$ its multiplicative set. Let $\mathbb{G}$ be a group of order q with generator $g \in \mathbb{G}$.

Let $\mathbb{Z}_N = \mathbb{Z}/N\mathbb{Z}$ denote the ring of integers modulo N, where N is a composite integer with a known prime factorization $N = \prod_{i=1}^{m} q_i^{r_i}$, such that $q_1 < q_2 < \cdots < q_m$ are distinct prime numbers and each $r_i \in \mathbb{N}$.

For any set S, the notation $a \xleftarrow{\$} S$ indicates that the element a is sampled uniformly at random from S. A function $\mu(X)$ from the natural numbers to the non-negative real numbers is *negligible* if for every positive polynomial p there is a constant C such that for all integers $x > C$, we have $\mu(x) < \frac{1}{p(x)}$ [9]. We denote by λ the security parameter.

Discrete Logarithm Problem (DLP). *Given a group $\mathbb{G}$, a generator $g \in \mathbb{G}$ and some element $h = g^x \in \mathbb{G}$, recovering x is called the Discrete Logarithm Problem.*

B. Sigma protocols

Let $V = V(\lambda)$ and $W = W(\lambda)$ be two sets defined with respect to a security parameter λ. Let $\mathrm{R} \subseteq V \times W$ be a **relation** on $V \times W$ that defines a **language** $\mathrm{L} = \{v \in V : \exists w \in W, \mathrm{R}(v; w) = 1\}$. An element $w \in W$ such that $\mathrm{R}(v; w) = 1$ for some $v \in \mathrm{L}$ is called a **witness** for v.

A sigma-protocol (Σ-protocol) for the relation R is a three-round interactive protocol between two Probabilistic Polynomial-Time (PPT) algorithms: a prover $\mathcal{P}$ and a verifier $\mathcal{V}$. The prover holds a witness w for $v \in \mathbf{L}$, and the verifier knows v. The protocol proceeds as follows: $\mathcal{P}$ sends a *commitment* a, $\mathcal{V}$ answers with a *challenge* c, and $\mathcal{P}$ sends a *response* r. The verifier accepts or rejects the proof based on the triple (a, c, r), which is called a transcript of the Σ-protocol.

A Σ-protocol satisfies three properties: completeness, special soundness, and honest verifier zero-knowledge (HVZK).

Completeness. *A Σ-protocol Π with parties $(\mathcal{P}, \mathcal{V})$ is complete for* R*, if for all $(v; w) \in \mathrm{R}$, the honest $\mathcal{V}$ always accepts the honest proof of $\mathcal{P}$.*

Special Soundness. *A Σ-protocol Π has a* special soundness *for* R *if there exists a PPT extractor $\mathcal{E}$ such that, for any $v \in \mathrm{L}$, given two valid transcripts (a, c, r) and (a, c', r') with the same commitment a but different challenges $c \neq c'$, the extractor $\mathcal{E}(a, c, r, c', r')$ outputs a valid witness w such that $(v; w) \in \mathrm{R}$.*

Honest-Verifier Zero-Knowledge (HVZK). *A Σ-protocol Π satisfies* HVZK *for* R *if there exists a PPT simulator* Sim *such that, for all $(v; w) \in \mathrm{R}$, the transcript (a, c, r) generated by $\mathsf{Sim}(v)$ is computationally indistinguishable from a real transcript produced by an honest execution between the prover $\mathcal{P}$ and the verifier $\mathcal{V}$ on input $(v; w)$.*

$\mathcal{P}(g, h; x)$		$\mathcal{V}(g, h)$
samples $u \xleftarrow{\$} \mathbb{Z}_q$		
computes $a = g^u$	$\xrightarrow{a}$	
	$\xleftarrow{c}$	samples $c \xleftarrow{\$} \mathbb{Z}_q^*$
computes $r = u + cx \bmod q$	$\xrightarrow{r}$	computes g^r, h^c
		$\mathcal{V}$'s output: accept or reject
		checks $g^r \stackrel{?}{=} a \cdot h^c$
		if yes, $\mathcal{V}$ accepts; otherwise rejects.

Figure 1. Protocol 1- Schnorr Protocol for relation R_{ID}.

1) Schnorr Identification Protocol: The Schnorr protocol instantiates a Σ-protocol for the relation $\mathrm{R}_{\mathrm{ID}} = \{(g, h; x) \mid h = g^x\}$ with $\mathbb{G}$ a multiplicative group of order q and generator g. Let $x \in \mathbb{Z}_q$ be the secret key (witness) and $h = g^x \in \mathbb{G}$ be the public key. Protocol 1 (see Figure 1) describes the steps of the Schnorr protocol.

The Schnorr protocol satisfies the key properties of a Σ-protocol:

- **Completeness:** If the prover is honest and knows x, then

$$g^r = g^{u+cx} = g^u \cdot (g^x)^c = a \cdot h^c$$

  and the verifier accepts.
- **Special Soundness:** Given two accepting transcripts (a, c, r) and (a, c', r') with $c \neq c'$, we show how the verifier can extract x.First, we have $g^r = a \cdot h^c$ and $g^{r'} = a \cdot h^{c'}$. Then, by operating these two expressions, $g^r g^{-r'} = h^{c-c'}$ we get that the discrete logarithm of h is equal to $(r - r')(c - c')^{-1} \mod q$.
- **HVZK:** There exists a simulator S that, chooses random values $c \xleftarrow{\$} \mathbb{Z}_q^*$ and $r \xleftarrow{\$} \mathbb{Z}_n$, computes:

$$a = g^r \cdot h^{-c}$$

  and outputs a transcript (a, c, r) that is indistinguishable from a real one.

C. Isogeny-Based ID Protocol Using Structured Public Keys

An identification (ID) protocol allows a prover to demonstrate the knowledge of a secret key corresponding to a public key, often formalized as a Σ-protocol over a hard relation. In isogeny-based cryptography, the underlying hardness assumption is the difficulty of computing isogenies between supersingular elliptic curves, a post-quantum hard problem.

Commutative Supersingular Isogeny Diffie–Hellman (CSIDH) [10] was proposed to enhance the efficiency of isogeny-based cryptography by using supersingular elliptic curves over the prime field $\mathbb{F}_p$. The CSI-FiSh signature scheme [11] was developed within the CSIDH framework to provide efficient isogeny-based signatures. It began with a binary challenge space and was later optimized with larger public keys and an improved identification protocol, achieving subsecond signing times.

In [9], the authors propose an efficient isogeny-based identification protocol that extends CSI-FiSh [11], which was previously enhanced in [12] and [13] to support a larger challenge space through the use of structured public keys. This enhancement significantly reduces the soundness error and communication overhead. The protocol is built on Hard Homogeneous Spaces and introduces exceptional and superexceptional sets to ensure extractability and security. A non-interactive signature version is derived via the Fiat–Shamir transform, achieving strong unforgeability in the quantum random oracle model. Additionally, they present trustless key generation techniques using zero-knowledge proofs of well-formedness, making the scheme both efficient and suitable for postquantum cryptographic applications.

Let E_0 be a fixed supersingular elliptic curve over $\mathbb{F}_p$, and let $\mathrm{Cl}(\mathcal{O})$ be the class group of its endomorphism ring $\mathcal{O}$. This group acts freely and transitively on the isogeny class of E_0, defining a Hard Homogeneous Space (HHS). The secret key is an element $x \in \mathbb{Z}_N$, and the public key is $E_1 = [x]E_0$, where $[x]$ denotes the group action via an ideal class.

Classical isogeny-based ID protocols, such as those underlying CSI-FiSh [11], suffer from efficiency issues due to binary challenge spaces. To reduce the soundness error ϵ, they must be repeated λ times, where $\epsilon = 2^{-\lambda}$. The new protocol extends the challenge space to k elements, reducing the soundness error per round to $1/k$, or $1/(2k-1)$ when symmetry (through twisting) is used.

The security of our protocol is based on a hardness assumption: the $(c_0, \ldots, c_{k-1})$-*Vectorization Problem with Auxiliary Inputs*. Detailed definitions and explanations of this issue are presented in [9], which, it should be noted, draws inspiration from papers [14] and [15]. Given a starting curve E_0 and a sequence of images $\{E_i = [c_i x]E_0\}$, where $c_0 = 0$, $c_1 = 1$ and all pairwise differences $c_i - c_j$ (for $i \neq j$) are invertible modulo N. the problem is to recover the secret scalar x, under the assumption that each $c_i \in \mathbb{Z}_N$ and all pairwise differences $c_i - c_j$ are invertible modulo N. This assumption generalizes the discrete logarithm problem with auxiliary inputs to the setting of isogenies and hard homogeneous spaces.

The protocol presented in [9] can be made non-interactive using the Fiat-Shamir transform in the Quantum Random Oracle Model (QROM). This structure enables a tradeoff: larger public keys allow shorter proofs and 14x faster executions than repeated binary-challenge protocols, without compromising post-quantum security or requiring trusted third parties.

D. Hard Homogeneous Space

A Hard Homogeneous Space (HHS), as formulated by Couveignes [12], comprises a finite abelian group $\mathbb{G}$ and a finite set $\mathcal{E}$, equipped with an efficient computable group action

$$\star : \mathbb{G} \times \mathcal{E} \to \mathcal{E}.$$

This action satisfies the following structural properties:

1) **Freeness and Transitivity:** The group action is *free*, which means that for any $E \in \mathcal{E}$ and $g \in \mathbb{G}$, if $g \star E = E$, then g is the identity in $\mathbb{G}$. It is also *transitive*, to ensure that for every pair $E_1, E_2 \in \mathcal{E}$, there exists a $g \in \mathbb{G}$ such that $g \star E_1 = E_2$.
2) **Efficient Operations:** The group operation in $\mathbb{G}$, membership and equality checks in both $\mathbb{G}$ and $\mathcal{E}$, and the group action $\star$ are all efficiently computable. Furthermore, each element in $\mathbb{G}$ has a unique representation that can be computed efficiently, and elements of $\mathbb{G}$ can be sampled uniformly at random.
3) **Hard Computational Problems:** Security in HHS-based cryptosystems relies on the intractability of two core problems:
   - *Vectorization Problem:* Given $E_1, E_2 \in \mathcal{E}$, compute $g \in \mathbb{G}$ such that $g \star E_1 = E_2$.
   - *Parallelization Problem:* Given $E_1, E_2, F_1 \in \mathcal{E}$ with $E_2 = g \star E_1$ for some unknown $g \in \mathbb{G}$, compute $F_2 = g \star F_1$.

In the common special case where $\mathbb{G}$ is a cyclic group of known order N with generator g, the action can be expressed using additive notation as $[a]E := g^a \star E$, where $a \in \mathbb{Z}_N$ and $E \in \mathcal{E}$. This representation satisfies the compositional property

$$[a][b]E = [a+b]E,$$

which is frequently exploited in isogeny-based protocols.

III. Modified Schnorr Protocol

In this section, regarded as the most significant portion of this work, we first present the new protocol based on Schnorr where the response form is specifically one of $r = cu + x$ or $r = cu - x$, previously agreed on between the prover and the verifier. We then proceed to investigate and prove its core properties.

A. Modified Schnorr Protocol

Let $\mathbb{G} = \langle g \rangle$ be a cyclic group of prime order q and g a generator. The following sigma protocol lets the prover convince a verifier about the prover's knowledge of their secret key is $x \in \mathbb{Z}_q$, such that the corresponding public key is $h = g^x \in \mathbb{G}$. More precisely, the sigma protocol is a proof system for the following relation:

$$\mathrm{R_{ID}} = \{(g, h; x) : h = g^x\}.$$

The protocol for relation $\mathrm{R_{ID}}$ is described in Protocol 2 (see Figure 2) in the following, where previously $r = cu + x$ or $r = cu - x$ has been chosen, but use both in the exposition:

The commitment and the challenge steps of our protocol are exactly as Schnorr's. We changed the response of the prover that now is $r = cu \pm x \mod q$, which is send r to V in the final step. In the verification phase, the verifier accepts if $g^r = a^c \cdot h$ in the case of $r = cu + x$, or if $g^r \cdot h = a^c$ in the case of $r = cu - x$.

In the following, we analyse that our modified protocol holds same properties as the original scheme that are the main properties of a sigma protocol.

$\mathcal{P}(g, h; x)$		$\mathcal{V}(g, h)$
samples $u \xleftarrow{\$} \mathbb{Z}_q$		
computes $a = g^u$	$\xrightarrow{a}$	
	$\xleftarrow{c}$	samples $c \xleftarrow{\$} \mathbb{Z}_q^*$
computes $r = cu \pm x \mod q$	$\xrightarrow{r}$	
		computes g^r, a^c
		$\mathcal{V}$'s output: accept or reject
		if $r = cu + x$,
		checks $g^r \stackrel{?}{=} a^c \cdot h$
		if yes, $\mathcal{V}$ accepts; otherwise rejects.
		if $r = cu - x$,
		checks $g^r \cdot h \stackrel{?}{=} a^c$
		if yes, $\mathcal{V}$ accepts; otherwise rejects.

Figure 2. Protocol 2- Modified Schnorr Protocol for relation $\mathrm{R_{ID}}$.

1) Completeness: Let us ensure that an honest prover always passes the verifier's check.

$$g^r = g^{cu+x} = g^{cu} \cdot (g^x) = (g^u)^c \cdot (g^x) = a^c \cdot h.$$

Hence $g^r = a^c \cdot h$, So, the verifier will accept. Thus, completeness holds. For the case $r = cu - x$, the completeness property is established as follows.

$$g^r \cdot h = g^{cu-x} \cdot (g^x) = g^{cu} = (g^u)^c = a^c.$$

2) Special Soundness: To prove *soundness*, we must demonstrate that if an adversary can produce valid responses to two distinct challenges $c \neq c'$ for the same commitment a, then the secret x can be extracted.

Assume the adversary outputs a valid transcript (a, c, r). By rewinding the adversary with the same commitment a but a different challenge c', we obtain a second valid transcript (a, c', r'). Therefore, we have two valid transcripts: (a, c, r), (a, c', r') with $c \neq c'$, and both satisfying the verification equations:

$$g^r = a^c \cdot h \quad \text{and} \quad g^{r'} = a^{c'} \cdot h.$$

We compute

$$(g^r)^{c'} (g^{r'})^{-c} = (a^c h)^{c'} (a^{c'} h)^{-c} = h^{c'-c}. \tag{1}$$

Thus, the secret, which is the Discrete Logarithm of h in the basis g, can be extracted by computing:

$$x = (rc' - r'c) \cdot (c' - c)^{-1} \mod q.$$

This confirms that knowledge of valid responses to two distinct challenges allows extraction of the secret witness x, thereby proving the soundness of the protocol.

Note that we used the verification of the case that the response is, $r = cu + x$, to prove the above equality. In the case where the response is $r = cu - x$, the same relation can be employed to extract x.

3) Honest-Verifier Zero-Knowledge (HVZK): To prove HVZK, we show that the simulator chooses a random challenge c and a random response r, can simulate a valid transcript without knowing the secret x. Given the public parameters g, h, the simulator begins by selecting a random challenge $c \in \mathbb{Z}_q^*$ and a random response $r \in \mathbb{Z}_q$. Then, it computes the commitment $a \in \mathbb{G}$ so that the final transcript (a, c, r) satisfies the verification equation of the verifier.

Specifically, the simulator sets $a = (g^r h^{-1})^{c^{-1}}$ if $r = cu + x$, or $a = (g^r h)^{c^{-1}}$ if $r = cu - x$. This ensures that the verification equation $g^r = a^c \cdot h$ is valid, even if the simulator does not know x. Since both c and r are chosen independently and uniformly at random, and the commitment a is derived deterministically, the simulator output is computationally indistinguishable from that of an honest execution. Consequently, the protocol maintains the HVZK property, assuming the hardness of the discrete logarithm problem and that c is invertible modulo q.

B. Non-Interactive Schnorr and Its Modified Variant

The Fiat–Shamir transformation [3] allows converting interactive identification protocols, such as Schnorr's [16], into non-interactive zero-knowledge proofs (NIZKs). This transformation replaces the verifier's random challenge with a deterministic output derived from a cryptographic hash function, typically modeled as a random oracle. It enables the prover to independently compute the proof without interaction, making it suitable for applications such as digital signatures and proof of key possession.

In both the classical and modified Schnorr protocols, the prover first computes a commitment $a = g^u$, where $u \in \mathbb{Z}_q$ is randomly chosen. The challenge is then generated as $c = \mathcal{H}(a, m)$, where m represents the public data (e.g., a message or context), and $\mathcal{H}$ is a cryptographic hash function. The prover computes the response r using either the classical form $r = u + cx \mod q$ or the modified form $r = cu \pm x \mod q$, depending on the protocol variant.

The final proof consists of the pair (a, r). The verifier reconstructs c from the hash and checks the validity of the proof by verifying the corresponding group equation. This non-interactive approach preserves zero-knowledge and soundness under the random oracle model.

IV. Isogeny-Based ID Protocol Using Modified Schnorr

The isogeny-based identification protocol presented in [9] extends the CSI-FiSh framework by introducing structured public keys, which significantly improve efficiency and reduce the soundness error rate. Although it operates within the Hard Homogeneous Space (HHS) formed by the class group acting on supersingular elliptic curves, the protocol maintains a classic Σ-protocol format with a commitment, challenge, and response reminiscent of the Schnorr identification scheme.

Our modified Isogeny-Based ID Schnorr variant offers a conceptual change by redefining the prover response as $r = cu \pm x \mod q$, in contrast to the traditional $r = u + cx \mod q$. The resulting protocol has completeness, special soundness, and HVZK, making it suitable for efficient Fiat-Shamir-based signature schemes.

A. An Efficient ID Protocol based on Modified Schnorr

Let p be a large prime such that the supersingular elliptic curves over $\mathbb{F}_p$ form a well-connected isogeny graph. Denote by $\mathcal{E}$ the set of $\mathbb{F}_p$-isomorphism classes of supersingular elliptic curves, and let $\mathrm{Cl}(\mathcal{O}) \cong \mathbb{Z}_N$ denote the class group of maximal order $\mathcal{O}$ in a quaternion algebra acting on $\mathcal{E}$ via isogenies.

The pair $(\mathbb{Z}_N, \mathcal{E})$ thus defines a *hard homogeneous space* [12] $(\mathcal{G}, \mathcal{X})$, equipped with a free and transitive action:

$$[a] \star E := \phi_a(E), \quad \text{for } a \in \mathbb{Z}_N,\ E \in \mathcal{E}.$$

Let $E_0 \in \mathcal{E}$ denote a publicly agreed base curve. We assume the existence of a publicly known *exceptional set* $C = \{c_0 = 0, c_1 = 1, \ldots, c_{k-1}\} \subset \mathbb{Z}_N$ such that every pairwise difference $c_i - c_j \in \mathbb{Z}_N^*$ is invertible. This assumption enables the construction of a sound Σ-protocol with extractability. Based on [9], we know that an Exceptional Set is defined as follows.

Definition. *Let $N \in \mathbb{Z}_{>0}$. A subset $C = \{c_0, c_1, \ldots, c_{k-1}\} \subset \mathbb{Z}_N$ is called an* exceptional set *modulo N if all pairwise differences are invertible, i.e., for all $i \neq j$, the element $c_i - c_j \in \mathbb{Z}_N^*$. This set guarantees that for any two distinct challenges $c, c' \in \mathbb{C}$, the value $c - c'$ is invertible modulo N, enabling efficient extraction in Σ-protocols.*

Remark. Given a target size k for an exceptional set and a modulus N, it is sufficient that the smallest prime factor q_1 of N satisfies $q_1 \geq k$. Under this condition, there exists an efficient algorithm, referred to as `XSGen`, capable of generating an exceptional set $C = \{c_0, c_1, \ldots, c_{k-1}\} \subseteq \mathbb{Z}_N$ of size k, in which all pairwise differences $c_i - c_j$ (for $i \neq j$) are invertible modulo N. If $q_1 < k$, one can still construct such a set by restricting the operation to a subgroup of $\mathbb{Z}_N$ in which smaller prime divisors are eliminated. This involves factoring out those small primes so that the minimal prime factor of the resulting subgroup is at least k. The only structural constraint imposed on N is that it must not be k-smooth, that is, N should not be composed entirely of prime factors less than k, which is typically a reasonable assumption for cryptographic applications involving large composite moduli [9].

B. Identification Protocol steps

In the first step for this protocol, we start with Key Generation. The prover samples $x \xleftarrow{\$} \mathbb{Z}_N$ as a secret key, and the public key is $E_x := [x] \star E_0$. The tuple $(E_0, E_x) \in \mathcal{E}^2$ is published, while x remains private to the prover. The identification protocol is a 3-move public-coin Σ-protocol defined by the protocol 3 (see Figure 3) as following steps. This Protocol ensures that the prover demonstrates knowledge of x consistent with the challenge and commitment.

Before detailing the protocol's primary characteristics, it is essential to first outline its underlying structure and associated benefits. Building on the proof techniques presented in [9], it can be readily shown that the set $\mathbf{A}$ in protocol 3 is well-defined and retains its essential properties. For any A_i, a corresponding proof, referred to as a pre-proof, must be

$\mathcal{P}(E_0, C, E_x; x)$		$\mathcal{V}(E_0, C, E_x)$
samples $u \xleftarrow{\$} \mathbb{Z}_N$		
computes		
$\mathbf{A} = \{A_i := [c_i u] \star E_0\}_{i=1}^{k-1}$		
runs pre-proof† π		
	$\xrightarrow{A}$	
		samples $d \xleftarrow{\$} \{0, 1, \ldots, k-1\}$
	$\xleftarrow{d}$	
computes $r = c_d u - x \mod N$		
	$\xrightarrow{r}$	
		computes $[r] \star E_x$
		$\mathcal{V}$'s output: accept or reject
		checks $[r] \star E_x \stackrel{?}{=} A_d$
		if yes, $\mathcal{V}$ accepts;
		otherwise rejects.

Figure 3. Protocol 3- Isogeny Schnorr Protocol for relation R_{ID}.

provided. This pre-proof follows the same approach as the proof techniques in [9], concretely Theorems 5.1 and 5.2 in [9], as well as remark (IV-A).

It is important to note that the protocol presented in [9] operates under idealized assumptions—namely, that all components, including randomness and network integrity, function flawlessly. Under such conditions, any deviation—such as inaccurate randomness or communication failures— during pre-proof can compromise the witness and, consequently, the security of the main protocol by causing information leakage from x.

On the other hand, generating all $E_i = [c_i x]E_0$ in [9] requires invoking the aforementioned theorems and consistently relying on the witness x during the pre-proof construction. However, in the modified isogeny-based Schnorr protocol, this reliance is mitigated by replacing x with u, thereby reducing direct dependence on the witness. In contrast, our modified Schnorr protocol exhibits greater resilience, enabling corrective measures to be taken without undermining its core functionality. More specifically, in the modified isogeny-based Schnorr protocol, it is sufficient to halt execution, select a new value u, and restart the pre-proof and protocol—without affecting the witness. This property significantly enhances the protocol's reliability under failure scenarios or adversarial conditions.

1) Completeness: We know that if the prover follows the protocol honestly, the verifier accepts with probability 1. For our modified Schnorr protocol, given $A_d = [c_d u] \star E_0$, $E_x = [x] \star E_0$, and $r = c_d u - x$, we compute:

$$[r] \star E_x = [c_d u - x] \star [x]E_0 = [c_d u] \star E_0 = A_d.$$

Therefore, the verifier check passes.

2) Special Soundness: We demonstrate that given two valid transcripts for the same commitment and distinct challenges, the prover's secret x can be recovered efficiently. Given two accepting transcripts (A, d, r) and (A, d', r') with $d \neq d'$ and a known set $C = \{c_0 = 0, c_1 = 1, c_2, \cdots, c_{k-1}\}$, we have:

$$[r]\star E_x = A_d = [c_d u]\star E_0 \quad \text{and} \quad [r']\star E_x = A_{d'} = [c_{d'} u]\star E_0$$

note that we can extract c_d and $c_{d'}$ by having d, d' and set C. From the verification equation, one can conclude that $[r]E_x = A_d$ and $[r']E_x = A_{d'}$, and from the pre-proof (or trusted) commitment we know that $A_i = [c_i u]E_0$ for $i = 1, \cdots, k-1$. These imply that we have $[r][x]E_0 = [c_d u]E_0$ and $[r'][x]E_0 = [c_{d'} u]E_0$, so:

$$[r + x]E_0 = [c_d u]E_0 \quad \text{and} \quad [r' + x]E_0 = [c_{d'} u]E_0$$

These imply that:

$$[c_{d'}(r+x)]E_0 = [c_{d'} c_d u]E_0 \quad \text{and} \quad [c_d(r'+x)]E_0 = [c_d c_{d'} u]E_0$$

Since the right part of relations are the same we have:

$$[c_{d'}(r + x)]E_0 = [c_d(r' + x)]E_0$$

It implies that

$$c_{d'} r + c_{d'} x = c_d r' + c_d x \;\Rightarrow$$

$$c_{d'} r - c_d r' = c_d x - c_{d'} x = (c_d - c_{d'})x.$$

Since $d \neq d'$ so $c_d \neq c_{d'}$. Therefore, we can divide both sides to $c_d - c_{d'} \in \mathbb{Z}_N^*$ and then we compute:

$$x = \frac{c_{d'} r - c_d r'}{c_d - c_{d'}} \mod N.$$

This proves extractability and thus special soundness.

3) Honest-Verifier Zero-Knowledge (HVZK): To prove HVZK, we construct a simulator that produces a valid-looking transcript (A, c, r) without knowing the secret key $x \in \mathbb{Z}_N$. Consider that the simulator has a sequence of images $\{E_i = [c_i x]E_0\}$ according to $(c_0, \ldots, c_{k-1})$-Vectorization Problem with Auxiliary Inputs. The simulator selects $u \in \mathbb{Z}_N$ and samples a challenge $d \in \{0, \ldots, k-1\}$, both uniformly at random and set $E_x = [c_d x]E_0 = E_d$. Given random u and sequence $\{E_i = [c_i x]E_0\}$, the simulator calculates $A = \{A_i := [c_i u] \star E_i = [c_i u + c_i x] \star E_0\}_{i=1}^{k-1}$ and sets the response as $r = c_d u$. The resulting transcript (A, d, r) satisfies the verifier check by construction $[r] \star E_x = A_d$ and is identical to a real transcript, thus establishing the HVZK property.

Remark. In [9], the pre-proof phase involves verifying the public set $E_i = [c_i x]E_0$, directly involving the secret x. In contrast, our protocol verifies $E_i = [c_i u]E_0$, where u is a random value unrelated to the secret.

If, during the pre-proof phase in [9], the randomness used in the commitment has insufficient entropy, the verifier could potentially recover the secret x from the response. In our protocol, even if such a weakness occurs, only the random value u could be exposed, without compromising x. In that case, the prover can simply discard u and any related computations, select a fresh random value, and rerun the pre-proof securely.

V. Conclusion and Future Work

We have introduced a modified version of the Schnorr Sigma protocol, redefining the prover's response to reduce its dependency on the secret witness x. This seemingly minor algebraic change leads to meaningful improvements in both the structural and practical aspects of the protocol. Through a formal analysis, we have demonstrated that the modified scheme retains its fundamental security properties—including soundness and zero-knowledge—while offering enhanced robustness and flexibility.

Applying this construction in the isogeny-based setting, we addressed key limitations of an existing identification protocol, particularly those arising from its idealized assumptions and its heavy reliance on the witness during pre-proof generation. By shifting this dependency from x to a fresh random value u, our approach enables safer recovery from randomness failures or communication errors, without compromising the security of the secret key. This resilience to faults and adversarial interruptions marks a significant improvement in the protocol's practicality and reliability for real-world deployment. Moreover, our modification opens the door to applying the MPC-in-the-Head technique, offering potential advantages in efficiency and security. We leave the exploration and formal development of this direction to future work.

Our work illustrates how carefully rethinking classical cryptographic constructions can lead to more robust solutions in post-quantum settings, such as isogeny-based cryptography, and opens the door to further exploration of protocol modifications that enhance security under realistic conditions.

Acknowledgments

This work was supported by the Spanish Ministry of Science and Innovation through the PID2021-125962OB-C31 "SECURING" project. Additional funding was provided by the ARTEMISA International Chair of Cybersecurity (C057/23) and the DANGER Strategic Project of Cybersecurity (C062/23), both funded by the Spanish National Institute of Cybersecurity through the European Union — NextGenerationEU and the Recovery, Transformation, and Resilience Plan. Funded by the European Union. Views and opinions expressed are however those of the author(s) only and do not necessarily reflect those of the European Union or the European Research Council Executive Agency. Neither the European Union nor the granting authority can be held responsible for them. Zaira Pindado is supported by ERC grant (HomE, 101043467).

References

[1] C.-P. Schnorr, "Efficient signature generation by smart cards," *Journal of Cryptology*, vol. 4, no. 3, pp. 161–174, 1991. DOI: 10.1007/BF00196725.

[2] W. Diffie and M. E. Hellman, "New directions in cryptography," *IEEE Transactions on Information Theory*, vol. 22, no. 6, pp. 644–654, 1976. DOI: 10.1109/TIT.1976.1055638.

[3] A. Fiat and A. Shamir, "How to prove yourself: Practical solutions to identification and signature problems," *Lecture Notes in Computer Science*, vol. 263, pp. 186–194, 1987. DOI: 10.1007/3-540-47721-7_12.

[4] G. Fuchsbauer, A. Plouviez, and Y. Seurin, "Blind schnorr signatures and signed elgamal encryption in the algebraic group model," *Lecture Notes in Computer Science*, vol. 12106, pp. 63–95, 2020. DOI: 10.1007/978-3-030-45724-2_3.

[5] R. Bacho, J. Loss, G. Stern, and B. Wagner, *Harts: High-threshold, adaptively secure, and robust threshold schnorr signatures*, To appear in: Advances in Cryptology – ASIACRYPT 2024, Lecture Notes in Computer Science, vol 15486, Springer, Singapore. Edited by KM. Chung and Y. Sasaki, 2025. [Online]. Available: https://doi.org/10.1007/978-981-96-0891-1_4.

[6] M. Fukumitsu and S. Hasegawa, "On multi-user security of schnorr signature in algebraic group model," *Proceedings of the Tenth International Symposium on Computing and Networking Workshops (CANDARW)*, pp. 295–301, 2022. DOI: 10.1109/CANDARW57323.2022.00014.

[7] G. Fuchsbauer and M. Wolf, "Concurrently secure blind schnorr signatures," in *Annual International Conference on the Theory and Applications of Cryptographic Techniques*, Springer, 2024, pp. 124–160.

[8] S. D. Galbraith, C. Petit, and J. Silva, *Identification protocols and signature schemes based on supersingular isogeny problems*, Journal of Cryptology, Volume 33, Pages 130–175, Springer, https://doi.org/10.1007/s00145-019-09316-0, 2020. [Online]. Available: https://doi.org/10.1007/s00145-019-09316-0.

[9] K. Baghery, D. Cozzo, and R. Pedersen, "An isogeny-based id protocol using structured public keys," in *IMA international conference on cryptography and coding*, Springer, 2021, pp. 179–197. DOI: 10.1007/978-3-030-92641-0_9.

[10] W. Castryck, T. Lange, C. Martindale, L. Panny, and J. Renes, "Csidh: An efficient post-quantum commutative group action," in *Advances in Cryptology – ASIACRYPT 2018*, ser. Lecture Notes in Computer Science, vol. 11274, Springer, 2018, pp. 395–427. DOI: 10.1007/978-3-030-03332-3_15.

[11] W. Beullens, T. Kleinjung, and F. Vercauteren, "CSI-FiSh: Efficient isogeny-based signatures through class group computations," in *Advances in Cryptology – ASIACRYPT 2019, Part I*, S. D. Galbraith and S. Moriai, Eds., ser. Lecture Notes in Computer Science, Presented at ASIACRYPT 2019, vol. 11921, Kobe, Japan: Springer, Heidelberg, Germany, Dec. 2019, pp. 227–247. DOI: 10.1007/978-3-030-34578-5_9.

[12] J.-M. Couveignes, *Hard homogeneous spaces*, Cryptology ePrint Archive, Report 2006/291, Preprint, Jul. 2006. [Online]. Available: https://eprint.iacr.org/2006/291.

[13] A. Rostovtsev and A. Stolbunov, "Public-key cryptosystem based on isogenies," *Cryptology ePrint Archive*, 2006.

[14] J. H. Cheon, "Discrete logarithm problems with auxiliary inputs," *Journal of Cryptology*, vol. 23, no. 3, pp. 457–476, Jul. 2010. DOI: 10.1007/s00145-009-9047-0.

[15] T. Kim, "Multiple discrete logarithm problems with auxiliary inputs," in *Advances in Cryptology – ASIACRYPT 2015, Part I*, T. Iwata and J. H. Cheon, Eds., ser. Lecture Notes in Computer Science, vol. 9452, Auckland, New Zealand: Springer, Nov. 2015, pp. 174–188. DOI: 10.1007/978-3-662-48797-6_8.

[16] F. Hao, *Schnorr non-interactive zero-knowledge proof*, RFC 8235, Internet Engineering Task Force (IETF), Informational, Sep. 2017. DOI: 10.17487/RFC8235. [Online]. Available: https://www.rfc-editor.org/info/rfc8235.

Evaluating User Perceptions of Privacy Protection in Smart Healthcare Services

Huan Gua, Elias Seid, Yuhong Li, Fredrik Blix
Department of Computer and Systems Sciences
Stockholm University, Sweden
E-mail: (Huan, elias.seid, Yuhong, Fredrik) @dsv.su.se

Abstract—**As smart healthcare services rapidly evolve, ensuring user privacy has become a critical concern. While prior research has focused extensively on technical solutions, the user perspective on privacy protection remains underexplored. This study addresses that gap by examining how users perceive both technical and organizational privacy protection measures across four smart healthcare service types: wearable devices, mobile health apps, telehealth platforms, and medicine delivery systems. Through a qualitative survey, the study uncovers a duality in user perceptions. Positive perceptions relate to multi-layer technical safeguards, regulatory oversight such as General Data Protection Regulation (GDPR), Health Insurance Portability and Accountability Act (HIPAA), and proactive provider practices, such as transparent privacy policies and breach responses. On the other hand, negative perceptions center on lack of transparency, limited user control, forced consent to privacy terms, and both cognitive and operational barriers to engaging with privacy features. These findings reveal a critical imbalance in user-provider power dynamics and call for user-centric privacy strategies that balance protection with usability. The study contributes to theoretical advancements in privacy calculus, Technology Acceptance Model (TAM), and Unified Theory of Acceptance and Use of Technology (UTAUT) by refining constructs, such as perceived control, facilitating conditions, and transparency. Practical recommendations are offered to guide more inclusive, adaptable, and empowering privacy solutions in smart healthcare contexts.**

Keywords-privacy protection measures; privacy-preserving techniques; smart healthcare; users' perception.

I. Introduction

Smart cities embody the integration of digital technologies into urban systems, with smart healthcare emerging as a key sector. By leveraging sensors, Internet of Things (IoT) devices, and data analytics, smart healthcare aims to enhance service delivery and quality of life, particularly in response to urbanization challenges such as population growth [1]-[4]. Users are central to this ecosystem, both as data contributors and service beneficiaries. However, the diverse and sensitive nature of the data collected, particulary personal health data—necessitates robust privacy protection. Healthcare has become a primary target for data breaches, leading to heightened privacy concerns and user avoidance behaviors that hinder adoption and effectiveness [5]-[11]. This study focuses on users' perceptions of privacy protection in smart healthcare, particularly in terms of technical (e.g., encryption) and organizational (e.g., privacy policies) measures. Given their role as data owners, patients' engagement is vital to the success of smart healthcare services [12][13]. However, despite the availability of privacy-preserving technologies like blockchain, homomorphic encryption, and secure multi-party computation, users often lack awareness or confidence in these tools. The effectiveness of such measures is influenced not only by their technical strength but also by users' psychological perceptions of security [10][13][14][15].

User perceptions—shaped by factors such as perceived control, information risk, and expected societal benefits—significantly influence their willingness to disclose data and use smart healthcare services [16][17][18]. Technology acceptance models like UTAUT have been used to explore these dynamics, showing that while users recognize the benefits of digital health services, privacy and trust issues remain critical barriers to adoption [19][20]. These concerns are not just technical but deeply human, highlighting the need to bridge the gap between system design and user expectations. Despite growing attention, many studies still overlook the user's perspective on privacy protection. Limited awareness, passive consent, and a lack of empowerment persist due to the unequal power dynamics between users and service providers [13][21][22]. Effective communication of data protection measures is lacking, preventing users from making informed privacy decisions [23][24]. To advance smart healthcare adoption, future systems must prioritize transparency, user education, and privacy frameworks that align with user preferences and perceptions. This study aims to contribute by deepening the understanding of these user-centered concerns and informing more inclusive privacy strategies. To help users better protect and control their privacy, it is essential to improve the communication of privacy protection measures to users and raise their privacy awareness. The first step in this process is ensuring they perceive the privacy measures in place. Thus, it is crucial to address the research problem underlying this paper, namely, to understand users' perceptions of privacy protection measures in smart healthcare services. The paper is organized as follows. Section II outlines related work, theoretical foundations, and the research methodology. Section III presents the results, Section IV discusses their implications, and Section V concludes with key insights and future directions.

R.Q: How do users perceive privacy protection measures in smart healthcare services? The study aims to explore users' concerns and expectations when perceiving privacy protection measures in smart healthcare services. Understanding users' nuanced feelings is essential for designing privacy safeguards that are user-oriented, ensuring better alignment with users' privacy needs.

II. RESEARCH BASELINE

Smart healthcare has emerged as a response to the increasing strain on traditional healthcare systems caused by population growth and rising disease prevalence. Leveraging technologies such as the Internet of Things (IoT), Artificial Intelligence (AI), and mobile cloud computing, smart healthcare enhances communication, facilitates remote monitoring, and supports personalized treatment, diagnosis, and prevention efforts [25][26]. These services are broadly categorized into domains like location tracking, telehealth, mobile health, AI-driven diagnostics, and robotic systems [27]. Among these, five key application types are emphasized: tracking tools (e.g., Apple Watch), telehealth platforms (e.g., BetterHelp), AI-powered diagnostic systems (e.g., IBM Watson Health), integrated health information systems (e.g., Epic Systems), and medicine delivery platforms (e.g., Amazon Pharmacy). This study focuses on four types of smart healthcare services—wearable devices, mobile health management apps, telehealth platforms, and medicine delivery systems—due to their widespread user adoption and diverse data handling. These services directly involve users in managing vital signs, lifestyle data, medical records, and prescriptions. For example, wearable devices like Apple Health gather physiological data, while telehealth platforms support virtual consultations. These applications offer close user interaction, in contrast to more provider-centric systems such as Electronic Health Record (EHRs) or AI-assisted surgery, which are excluded from the study's scope. The selected services provide a relevant and practical basis for examining users' perceptions of privacy protection in smart healthcare.
Privacy Protection Measures: Smart healthcare systems face ongoing challenges in safeguarding user privacy throughout the data lifecycle, despite the many benefits they offer [11] [28]. To address these concerns, researchers have proposed various privacy protection strategies, including both technical and organizational measures. Organizational approaches such as privacy-by-policy, privacy-by-architecture, and privacy-by-design aim to embed privacy into system design, policy compliance, and user interactions from the outset [30]–[32]. These are further supported by regulatory frameworks like the GDPR and HIPAA, which enforce strict legal standards for personal health data handling. Organizational mechanisms such as consent management, transparency, and auditing play a key role in maintaining accountability and building trust [3]. Technically, privacy is protected through cryptographic methods, anonymization, data masking, access control, and advanced techniques like federated learning, homomorphic encryption, and secure multi-party computation [33]. Blockchain is also recognized for its privacy-enhancing attributes, including decentralization and transparency [6]. However, these measures often fall short in practice due to limited user control and inconsistent implementations across centralized and decentralized environments [23]. Many existing solutions remain too provider-centric, failing to fully address user needs or empower them in managing their own data [6, 11]. As such, there is a pressing need for privacy strategies that incorporate users' perspectives more effectively and bridge the gap between technical safeguards and user-centric privacy experiences.

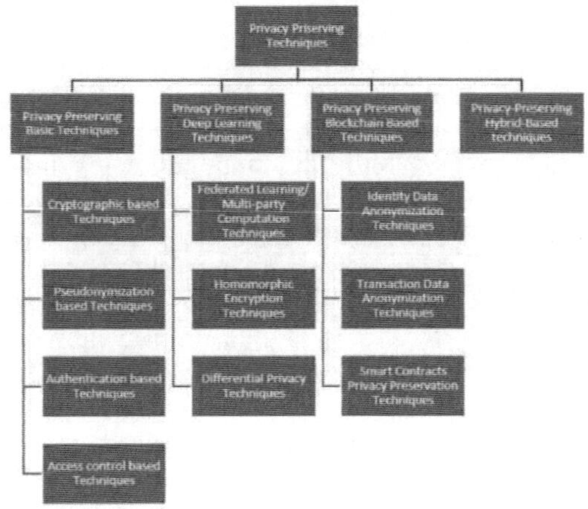

Figure 1. Privacy-preserving Techniques Taxonomy [33]

Theories and Factors Shaping Users' Perception and Adoption: Users' perceptions significantly influence their intention to adopt smart healthcare services, as outlined in established frameworks like the Technology Acceptance Model (TAM) and the Unified Theory of Acceptance and Use of Technology (UTAUT) [35][36]. TAM focuses on perceived usefulness and ease of use, while UTAUT highlights performance expectancy, effort expectancy, social influence, and facilitating conditions. These models are further enriched by the privacy calculus theory, which balances perceived benefits against privacy risks [37][38]. Research shows that risks such as data misuse, legal vulnerabilities, and lack of control affect users' protective behaviors, while perceived benefits like better healthcare and contributions to research often encourage data sharing [9, 39]. Emotions, cognitive biases, and contextual factors also shape decision-making. Although privacy remains a concern, users often prioritize perceived benefits, especially when immediate rewards or limited privacy knowledge come into play [40]–[42]. Older adults, for instance, tend to accept privacy risks over time, leading to a resigned attitude toward potential misuse [43]. For wearables, adoption hinges on a risk-benefit evaluation tied to data sensitivity and regulatory protections [44]. However, challenges like opaque privacy notices and cognitive overload hinder informed decisions [45–47]. Emerging factors—such as trust in AI, personalization, and digital literacy—further affect adoption, prompting scholars to recommend tailoring acceptance models to specific healthcare contexts [48]–[51]. This study adopts relevant theoretical constructs to capture the nuanced dimensions of user perception in smart healthcare.

A. Method Application

This study employs a qualitative, interview-based survey strategy to explore users' perceptions of privacy protection in smart healthcare services. Qualitative surveys effectively reveal nuanced behaviors, perceptions, and attitudes, making them particularly suitable for understanding complex interactions between privacy risks, benefits, and other factors [52][53]. To ensure rigor and reliability, this study integrates standardized theoretical frameworks, including the taxonomy of privacy-preserving techniques [33], Technology Acceptance Model (TAM), Unified Theory of Acceptance and Use of Technology (UTAUT), and privacy calculus theory, to guide interview design and analysis [54]. These frameworks help structure the interview questions effectively by addressing key constructs such as perceived ease of use, social influence, performance expectancy, perceived usefulness, perceived privacy risks, and perceived benefits. Interviews are conducted individually through audio calls on WhatsApp and WeChat, recorded and transcribed using the iOS Voice Memos application for English and Tongyi.ai for Chinese interviews. Recordings are solely for transcription accuracy and verification purposes, ensuring data reliability. **Sampling:**This study employs non-probability purposive sampling, deliberately selecting participants aged 18–65 from urban areas in Europe, North America, and Asia who possess prior experience with smart healthcare services and basic privacy protection knowledge, ensuring their relevance to the research topic [56]. Probability sampling was not chosen due to the need for informed participants rather than random selection. Ethical considerations and resource constraints excluded minors, individuals over 65, and rural populations, as these groups pose consent challenges or may lack familiarity with smart healthcare [13]. The target sample size is approximately 10 participants, consistent with qualitative research standards indicating saturation typically occurs between 10 to 12 interviews [61] [62]. Interviews lasting 60–90 minutes ensure comprehensive coverage of key points, enhancing study validity despite the limited sample size. Convenience sampling was dismissed due to its potential limitations in participant diversity and relevance [56]. **Data Analysis:** The study analyzes interview data using Thematic Analysis (TA), a widely adopted qualitative method suitable for identifying patterns and themes within interview transcripts [63][64]. Following the six-step process outlined by Braun and Clarke [65], the analysis begins by coding relevant keywords, refining codes to eliminate redundancy, and categorizing them into themes. This study adopts a hybrid thematic approach, primarily utilizing inductive thematic analysis to allow patterns to emerge naturally, complemented by deductive analysis based on constructs from the Technology Acceptance Model (TAM), Unified Theory of Acceptance and Use of Technology (UTAUT), and privacy calculus theory to enhance objectivity and validity [66]-[69]. NVivo software is employed to improve analytical efficiency, data management, and accuracy [70, 71]. Content analysis was considered but not selected due to its limited ability to capture contextual and latent meanings critical to the research [56] [72] [73].

III. Result

This study applied thematic analysis supported by NVivo software, following the structured six-step process outlined by [65]. Initial coding involved careful review of interview transcripts, capturing significant insights and relating these to theoretical frameworks. Notably, participant uncertainties, such as limited knowledge about privacy protection, were documented. The code "Cumbersome Authentication Process" drew upon "perceived ease of use" from the TAM and "effort expectancy" from the Unified Theory of Acceptance and Use of Technology (UTAUT). In total, 21 initial codes emerged. From these codes, themes and subthemes were developed, categorizing user perceptions into positive and negative dimensions. A prominent theme identified was the "Disadvantaged Position of Users in Protecting Their Privacy," with the subtheme "Insufficient Right to be Informed," consistently emphasized by participants. Conversely, positive perceptions were encapsulated under the theme related to "facilitating conditions" from UTAUT, distinguishing between external support (Oversight and Constraints) and internal support (Internal Handling). Redundant codes were subsequently refined, reducing them to 12 cohesive codes. For instance, "Unknown Technical Principles" merged into "Unknown Implementation Process," reflecting users' practical concerns rather than theoretical knowledge. Similarly, "Insufficient Engagement" was incorporated into "Lack of User Data Management," categorized under the subtheme "Insufficient Control." Ultimately, the refined analysis identified three main themes and seven subthemes from the dataset.

A. The Disadvantaged Position of Users in Protecting Their Privacy:

Users' Perceived Vulnerability in Privacy Protection Thematic analysis revealed users feel disadvantaged in safeguarding their privacy within smart healthcare services, reflecting concerns from privacy calculus theory. Despite existing measures, users often lack perceived control and awareness, particularly in three key areas: unknown personnel, unclear implementation processes, and uncertain effectiveness of results. Users expressed concerns about not knowing who accesses their data, especially with vague or opaque privacy policies and multi-party access scenarios. Many feared unauthorized third-party data sharing, particularly for commercial purposes, while showing more openness toward research uses, provided transparency and consent are maintained.

Lack of Transparency Undermines Trust: Participants emphasized that unfamiliar technical implementations (e.g., encryption, anonymization) raise doubts, especially when not clearly explained. Even tech-savvy users sought clarity on compatibility and deployment, while others feared such terms masked hidden costs or misuse. Vague legal language in privacy policies also contributed to uncertainty about data handling. Users wanted clear, example-driven explanations of practices and desired features like access logs, deletion confirmation, and visual cues for encryption. Ultimately, the study highlights how insufficient transparency undermines

TABLE I. THEMES, SUBTHEMES, AND CORRESPONDING CODES

Themes	Subthemes	Codes
The Disadvantaged Position of Users in Protecting Their Privacy	Insufficient Right to be Informed	Unknown Personnel Involved
		Unknown Implementation Process
		Unknown Effectiveness of Results
	Insufficient Control	Lack of User Data Management
		Passive Choice in Privacy Policy
Privacy Reassurance	Oversight and Constraints	Legal Regulations and Audits
	Technical Reliability	Multi-Layer Protection
	Internal Handling	Updates of Privacy Policy
		Thoughtful Data Breach Response
User Experience Barriers	Operational Barriers	Cumbersome Authentication Process
		Unclear Position of the Privacy Policy
	Cognitive Barriers	Long and Obscure Privacy Policy

users' sense of security, making trust in privacy protections contingent on clarity, informed consent, and demonstrable effectiveness. **Users' Limited Control and Data Deletion Challenges:** Participants expressed a strong sense of limited control over their data within smart healthcare services, often feeling reliant on providers who possess technical knowledge and control system configurations. This asymmetry reinforces user vulnerability, as providers determine how and when data is used [45]. While participants desired more autonomy—such as opt-in/out capabilities for data use, the ability to delete records post-service, and clearer management of access rights—these features remain inadequately supported. Even in GDPR-covered regions, deletion processes are often slow, indirect, or poorly designed, further disempowering users. Participants from outside the GDPR context reported even fewer deletion options, highlighting global inconsistencies in privacy control.

Inadequate Consent and Forced Privacy Agreements: Granular consent management was viewed as essential, with users preferring settings that allow them to specify the purpose, scope, and recipients of shared data. However, participants described being forced into "take it or leave it" agreements during account registration, where refusing a privacy policy meant losing access to the service entirely [46]. This coercive design fosters mistrust in both the policies and the providers themselves, though it doesn't always deter usage, especially when the service is deemed necessary. Participants emphasized that privacy policies often serve as compliance tools rather than genuine efforts to respect user preferences [5][46]. To restore meaningful control, users should be empowered to use core services even if they partially or fully reject privacy terms.

B. Privacy Reassurance:

Legal Compliance as a Source of Reassurance: Participants expressed generally positive views toward privacy regulations like the GDPR and HIPAA, associating compliance with increased confidence in smart healthcare services. GDPR compliance, in particular, was seen as a strong indicator of trustworthy data practices due to its well-defined principles, independent oversight, and strict penalties for violations . Some participants emphasized that GDPR offers not only legal assurance but also actionable tools for users to verify compliance and seek redress. In contrast, while HIPAA was acknowledged for setting essential standards, American participants showed relatively lower confidence in its enforcement and practical application. This suggests that users value legal frameworks more when they are backed by demonstrable enforcement mechanisms and transparent rights protections.

The Role of Audits in Reinforcing Trust: External audits were highlighted as a crucial organizational safeguard complementing legal compliance. Participants emphasized that while privacy-enhancing technologies like encryption and anonymization are important, their trust increases when these measures are validated through transparent third-party audits. Audits conducted by reputable firms enhance users' perception of provider accountability, particularly because users often lack the expertise to evaluate technical safeguards themselves. Together, legal constraints and professional audits offer layered protection that aligns with the UTAUT framework's notions of performance expectancy and facilitating conditions, reinforcing users' belief that their privacy is both respected and technically safeguarded.

Multi-layer Protection and Technical Confidence Participants expressed strong support for multi-layer privacy protection, noting that the combination of various techniques—such as encryption, anonymization, and multi-factor authentication—enhanced their trust in smart healthcare systems. While many users lacked technical expertise, they believed that layering different methods could reduce single points of failure and increase reliability. Features like two-factor authentication were especially appreciated, as they offered visible, user-facing indicators of security. This sense of reassurance directly influenced users' willingness to engage with smart healthcare services, aligning with the UTAUT construct of performance expectancy. **Proactive Provider Measures and Breach Response** Users also valued internal organizational practices, such as timely updates to privacy policies and responsive actions following data breaches, as signs of a provider's commitment to privacy protection. Regular policy updates, when clearly communicated, reassured participants that providers were keeping pace with technological and legal changes. After a breach, participants expected prompt notifications, transparency about affected data, and evidence of corrective action—such as improved security systems or audits. These proactive and reflective efforts serve as key facilitating conditions that influence continued user trust, even after a privacy incident. Providers who effectively communicate updates and breach responses are more likely to retain user confidence in the long term.

Cognitive Barriers to Understanding Privacy Policies: Participants widely reported cognitive challenges when engaging with privacy policies, citing long, text-heavy documents and complex legal jargon as key deterrents to reading or understanding them. These barriers were especially burdensome for older users, who also faced physical and digital literacy limitations. The confusing presentation and obscure terminology led to user frustration and mistrust, with some perceiving the complexity as an intentional obfuscation by providers. Participants suggested clearer formats like visual checklists, interactive summaries, and plain language versions to improve comprehension and enhance trust. Offering two parallel policy versions—one simplified and one legally detailed—was proposed to balance accessibility with compliance requirements.

Operational Barriers and Their Contextual Impact: Operational hurdles, particularly around authentication processes, were another major concern. Users found complex password requirements and recovery procedures burdensome, especially when compounded by poor connectivity or urgent health needs. While users accepted stricter authentication for high-risk services like mental health or prescriptions, they preferred minimal friction for lower-risk tasks like symptom checking or step tracking. Participants also noted difficulty locating privacy policies within app interfaces, which undermined their perceived importance. Although this didn't always affect service use directly, it shaped negative impressions of provider transparency. Users emphasized the need for adaptive privacy measures and intuitive design that aligns security requirements with task sensitivity and user context.

IV. Discussion

This study reveals that users generally view privacy protection measures in smart healthcare positively, particularly when multi-layer safeguards—such as encryption, anonymization, and multi-factor authentication—are employed, reinforcing their sense of security and aligning with UTAUT's performance expectancy construct. However, users also expressed concerns about limited transparency and control, especially when faced with complex or opaque privacy policies. Legal frameworks like the GDPR and HIPAA, along with third-party audits, were seen as crucial external supports that help balance the power disparity between users and providers [29][38]. Despite recognizing these safeguards, users often felt disempowered due to their lack of technical or legal literacy, particularly in urgent health situations where privacy is traded for immediate care needs [9][21][42]. These tensions echo the privacy calculus theory, where perceived privacy risks reduce trust and adoption willingness [44], though this is sometimes overridden by brand trust or social influence [19]. Users' perceptions of privacy risk vary based on the type of smart healthcare service and the sensitivity of data involved. Telehealth platforms were seen as higher risk due to their handling of sensitive medical histories, while wearable devices and mobile health apps were perceived as lower risk depending on context [9][40][41]. Unique concerns were also raised about medicine delivery services, particularly involving the disclosure of home addresses in offline interactions. These findings emphasize that privacy protections must be contextually adaptive. The study contributes to the literature by highlighting the often-overlooked user perspective, suggesting refinements to existing models like UTAUT and the privacy calculus theory, and offering actionable recommendations to enhance transparency, control, and user empowerment in smart healthcare design.

V. Conclusions and Future Work

This study investigates users' perceptions of privacy protection measures in smart healthcare through interviews with diverse participants, uncovering both negative and positive views. Negative perceptions largely stem from users' lack of transparency and control—such as not knowing who accesses their data, limited ability to manage or delete it, and being compelled to accept unclear privacy policies. Participants also faced cognitive and operational challenges, including overly complex policies and cumbersome authentication. In contrast, users responded positively to multi-layer technical safeguards, legal and audit oversight, and providers' proactive actions like transparent updates and breach responses. These findings emphasize the need for privacy strategies that are more user-centric, accessible, and empowering. Despite using established theoretical frameworks and rigorous qualitative methods, the study's small, purposive sample limits the generalizability of findings, particularly to minors and older populations. It also lacks analysis of how demographic factors or specific service contexts influence perceptions. Future research should incorporate mixed-method approaches to enable cross-cultural and service-specific comparisons. Additionally, a deeper theoretical integration of models such as TAM, UTAUT, and privacy calculus theory is recommended to refine concepts such as perceived transparency and risk. Practically, future work should develop tailored privacy design guidelines aligned with real-world healthcare applications, such as embedding user-focused encryption in telehealth platforms.

REFERENCES

[1] V. Garcia-Font, "SocialBlock: An architecture for decentralized user-centric data management applications for communications in smart cities," *Journal of Parallel and Distributed Computing*, vol. 145, pp. 13–23, Nov. 2020. doi: 10.1016/j.jpdc.2020.06.004

[2] V. Zimmermann, "Smart cities as a testbed for experimenting with humans? - Applying psychological ethical guidelines to smart city interventions," *Ethics and Information Technology*, vol. 25, no. 4, p. 54, Oct. 2023. doi: 10.1007/s10676-023-09729-3

[3] D. Eckhoff and I. Wagner, "Privacy in the Smart City—Applications, Technologies, Challenges, and Solutions," *IEEE Communications Surveys & Tutorials*, vol. 20, no. 1, pp. 489–516, 2018. doi: 10.1109/COMST.2017.2748998

[4] J. Sanghavi, "Review of Smart Healthcare Systems and Applications for Smart Cities," in *ICCCE 2019*, A. Kumar and S. Mozar, Eds. Singapore: Springer Singapore, 2020, pp. 325–331.

[5] European Union, "General Data Protection Regulation (GDPR)," 2016. [Online]. Available: https://eur-lex.europa.eu/legal-content/EN/TXT/?uri=CELEX%3A32016R0679

[6] D. El Majdoubi, H. El Bakkali, S. Sadki, Z. Maqour, and A. Leghmid, "The Systematic Literature Review of Privacy-Preserving Solutions in Smart Healthcare Environment," *Security and Communication Networks*, vol. 2022, no. 1, p. 5642026, 2022. doi: 10.1155/2022/5642026

[7] Y. Li, "Empirical Studies on Online Information Privacy Concerns: Literature Review and an Integrative Framework," *Communications of the Association for Information Systems*, vol. 28, pp. 453–496, Jan. 2011. doi: 10.17705/1CAIS.02828

[8] S. R. Simon, J. S. Evans, A. Benjamin, D. Delano, and D. W. Bates, "Patients' Attitudes Toward Electronic Health Information Exchange: Qualitative Study," *Journal of Medical Internet Research*, vol. 11, no. 3, p. e30, 2009. doi: 10.2196/jmir.1164

[9] X. Deng, D. Wang, and L. Yang, "The Impact of Perceived Risk on Online Medical Users' Privacy Protection Behavior," in *Proc. 27th Int. Conf. on Computer Supported Cooperative Work in Design (CSCWD)*, May 2024, pp. 1238–1243. doi: 10.1109/CSCWD61410.2024.10580280

[10] A. Odeh, A. Eman, and S. Walid, "Privacy-Preserving Data Sharing in Telehealth Services," *Applied Sciences*, 2024. doi: 10.3390/app142310808

[11] M. A. Sahi *et al.*, "Privacy Preservation in e-Healthcare Environments: State of the Art and Future Directions," *IEEE Access*, vol. 6, pp. 464–478, 2018. doi: 10.1109/ACCESS.2017.2767561

[12] D. E. Majdoubi, H. E. Bakkali, S. Sadki, A. Leghmid, and Z. Maqour, "HOPPy: Holistic Ontology for Privacy-Preserving in Smart Healthcare environment," in *Proc. 2021 Fifth World Conf. on Smart Trends in Systems Security and Sustainability (WorldS4)*, 29–30 July 2021, pp. 248–253. doi: 10.1109/WorldS451998.2021.9514051

[13] F. Tazi, A. Nandakumar, J. Dykstra, P. Rajivan, and S. Das, "SoK: Analyzing Privacy and Security of Healthcare Data from the User Perspective," *ACM Trans. Comput. Healthcare*, vol. 5, no. 2, p. Article 11, 2024. doi: 10.1145/3650116

[14] C.-L. Hsu and M.-R. Lee, "User acceptance of a community-based healthcare information system preserving user privacy," in *Universal Access in Human-Computer Interaction. Applications and Services for Quality of Life: Proc. 7th Int. Conf. UAHCI 2013, Part III*, Las Vegas, USA, July 21–26, 2013. Springer, pp. 453–462.

[15] S. M. E. Sepasgozar, S. Hawken, S. Sargolzaei, and M. Foroozanfa, "Implementing citizen centric technology in developing smart cities: A model for predicting the acceptance of urban technologies," *Technological Forecasting and Social Change*, vol. 142, pp. 105–116, 2019. doi: 10.1016/j.techfore.2018.09.012

[16] E. M. Schomakers, C. Lidynia, and M. Ziefle, "Listen to My Heart? How Privacy Concerns Shape Users' Acceptance of e-Health Technologies," in *2019 Int. Conf. on Wireless and Mobile Computing, Networking and Communications (WiMob)*, 21–23 Oct. 2019, pp. 306–311. doi: 10.1109/WiMOB.2019.8923448

[17] A. Kharlamov, R. Hohmann, and G. Parry, "Data sharing decisions: Perceptions and intentions in healthcare," *Strategic Change*, vol. 32, no. 6, pp. 223–237, 2023.

[18] E. Princi and N. C. Krämer, "Out of control – privacy calculus and the effect of perceived control and moral considerations on the usage of IoT healthcare devices," *Frontiers in Psychology*, vol. 11, p. 582054, 2020.

[19] Y.-J. Moon and Y.-H. Hwang, "A Study of Effects of UTAUT-Based Factors on Acceptance of Smart Health Care Services," in *Advanced Multimedia and Ubiquitous Engineering*, J. J. Park, H.-C. Chao, H. Arabnia, and N. Y. Yen, Eds. Berlin, Heidelberg: Springer, 2016, pp. 317–324.

[20] E. Pouyan, "The Impacts of the Perceived Transparency of Privacy Policies and Trust in Providers for Building Trust in Health Information Exchange: Empirical Study," *JMIR Medical Informatics*, vol. 7, 2019. doi: 10.2196/preprints.14050

[21] K. Halvorsen *et al.*, "Empowerment in healthcare: A thematic synthesis and critical discussion of concept analyses of empowerment," *Patient Education and Counseling*, vol. 103, no. 7, pp. 1263–1271, Jul. 2020. doi: 10.1016/j.pec.2020.02.017

[22] M. Duckert and L. Barkhuus, "Protecting Personal Health Data through Privacy Awareness: A study of perceived data privacy among people with chronic or long-term illness," *Proc. ACM Hum.-Comput. Interact.*, vol. 6, no. GROUP, p. Article 11, 2022. doi: 10.1145/3492830

[23] M. N. Alraja, H. Barhamgi, A. Rattrout, and M. Barhamgi, "An integrated framework for privacy protection in IoT — Applied to smart healthcare," *Computers & Electrical Engineering*, vol. 91, p. 107060, May 2021. doi: 10.1016/j.compeleceng.2021.107060

[24] S. M. Williamson and V. Prybutok, "Balancing Privacy and Progress: A Review of Privacy Challenges, Systemic Oversight, and Patient Perceptions in AI-Driven Healthcare," *Applied Sciences*, vol. 14, no. 2, p. 675, 2024. [Online]. Available: https://www.mdpi.com/2076-3417/14/2/675

[25] S. S. Raoof and M. A. S. Durai, "A Comprehensive Review on Smart Health Care: Applications, Paradigms, and Challenges with Case Studies," *Contrast Media & Molecular Imaging*, vol. 2022, no. 1, p. 4822235, 2022. doi: 10.1155/2022/4822235

[26] M. A. Jabbar, K. M. V. V. Prasad, and R. Aluvalu, "Reimagining the Indian Healthcare Ecosystem with AI for a Healthy Smart City," in *Emerging Technologies in Data Mining and Information Security*, A. E. Hassanien, S. Bhattacharyya, S. Chakrabati, A. Bhattacharya, and S. Dutta, Eds. Singapore: Springer, 2021, pp. 543–551.

[27] H. Kwon *et al.*, "Review of smart hospital services in real healthcare environments," *Healthcare Informatics Research*, vol. 28, no. 1, pp. 3–15, 2022.

[28] A. Algarni, "A Survey and Classification of Security and Privacy Research in Smart Healthcare Systems," *IEEE Access*, vol. 7, pp. 101879–101894, 2019. doi: 10.1109/ACCESS.2019.2930962

[29] H. Liu, X. Yao, T. Yang, and H. Ning, "Cooperative Privacy Preservation for Wearable Devices in Hybrid Computing-Based Smart Health," *IEEE Internet of Things Journal*, vol. 6, no. 2, pp. 1352–1362, 2019. doi: 10.1109/JIOT.2018.2843561

[30] S. Spiekermann and L. F. Cranor, "Engineering Privacy," *IEEE Transactions on Software Engineering*, vol. 35, no. 1, pp. 67–82, 2009. doi: 10.1109/tse.2008.88

[31] A. A. Alghanim, S. M. M. Rahman, and M. A. Hossain, "Privacy Analysis of Smart City Healthcare Services," in *Proc. 2017 IEEE Int. Symp. on*

Multimedia (ISM), 11–13 Dec. 2017, pp. 394–398. doi: 10.1109/ISM.2017.79

[32] C. Montes *et al.*, "A flexible, privacy enhanced and secured ICT architecture for a smart grid project with active consumers in the city of Zwolle—NL," in *22nd Int. Conf. and Exhibition on Electricity Distribution (CIRED 2013)*, IET, 2013, pp. 1–4.

[33] B. R. Louassef and N. Chikouche, "Privacy preservation in healthcare systems," in *Proc. 2021 Int. Conf. on Artificial Intelligence for Cyber Security Systems and Privacy (AI-CSP)*, 20–21 Nov. 2021, pp. 1–6. doi: 10.1109/AI-CSP52968.2021.9671083

[34] A. Dangi and R. Mogili, "Privacy Preservation Measure using t-closeness with combined l-diversity and k-anonymity," *Int. J. of Advanced Research in Computer Science and Electronics Engineering*, vol. 1, pp. 28–33, 2012.

[35] A. A. AlQudah, M. Al-Emran, and K. Shaalan, "Technology Acceptance in Healthcare: A Systematic Review," *Applied Sciences*, vol. 11, no. 22, p. 10537, 2021. [Online]. Available: https://www.mdpi.com/2076-3417/11/22/10537

[36] S. Attuquayefio and H. Addo, "Review of studies with UTAUT as conceptual framework," *European Scientific Journal*, vol. 10, no. 8, 2014.

[37] E.-M. Schomakers, C. Lidynia, and M. Ziefle, "The Role of Privacy in the Acceptance of Smart Technologies: Applying the Privacy Calculus to Technology Acceptance," *Int. J. of Human–Computer Interaction*, vol. 38, no. 13, pp. 1276–1289, 2022. doi: 10.1080/10447318.2021.1994211

[38] S. Li *et al.*, "Research on user's highly sensitive privacy disclosure intention in home intelligent health service system: A perspective from trust enhancement mechanism," *DIGITAL HEALTH*, vol. 9, p. 20552076231219444, 2023. doi: 10.1177/20552076231219444

[39] D. Grande, N. Mitra, A. Shah, F. Wan, and D. A. Asch, "Public preferences about secondary uses of electronic health information," *JAMA Intern Med*, vol. 173, no. 19, pp. 1798–1806, Oct. 2013. doi: 10.1001/jamainternmed.2013.9166

[40] M. S. Rahman, "Does Privacy Matter When We are Sick? An Extended Privacy Calculus Model for Healthcare Technology Adoption Behavior," in *Proc. 2019 10th Int. Conf. on Information and Communication Systems (ICICS)*, 11–13 June 2019, pp. 41–46. doi: 10.1109/IACS.2019.8809175

[41] D. Kim, K. Park, Y. Park, and J.-H. Ahn, "Willingness to provide personal information: Perspective of privacy calculus in IoT services," *Computers in Human Behavior*, vol. 92, pp. 273–281, Mar. 2019. doi: https://doi.org/10.1016/j.chb.2018.11.022

[42] G. Fox, ""To protect my health or to protect my health privacy?" A mixed-methods investigation of the privacy paradox," *Journal of the Association for Information Science and Technology*, vol. 71, no. 9, pp. 1015–1029, 2020.

[43] T. Schroeder, M. Haug, and H. Gewald, "Data Privacy Concerns Using mHealth Apps and Smart Speakers: Comparative Interview Study Among Mature Adults," *JMIR Formative Research*, vol. 6, no. 6, 2022. doi: 10.2196/28025

[44] H. Li, J. Wu, Y. Gao, and Y. Shi, "Examining individuals' adoption of healthcare wearable devices: An empirical study from privacy calculus perspective," *Int. J. of Medical Informatics*, vol. 88, pp. 8–17, Apr. 2016. doi: https://doi.org/10.1016/j.ijmedinf.2015.12.010

[45] A. Acquisti *et al.*, "Nudges for Privacy and Security: Understanding and Assisting Users' Choices Online," *ACM Comput. Surv.*, vol. 50, no. 3, p. Article 44, 2017. doi: 10.1145/3054926

[46] F. Schaub, R. Balebako, and L. F. Cranor, "Designing Effective Privacy Notices and Controls," *IEEE Internet Computing*, vol. 21, no. 3, pp. 70–77, 2017. doi: 10.1109/MIC.2017.75

[47] M. W. Vail, J. B. Earp, and A. I. Antón, "An Empirical Study of Consumer Perceptions and Comprehension of Web Site Privacy Policies," *IEEE Trans. on Engineering Management*, vol. 55, pp. 442–454, 2008.

[48] K. Liu and D. Tao, "The roles of trust, personalization, loss of privacy, and anthropomorphism in public acceptance of smart healthcare services," *Computers in Human Behavior*, vol. 127, p. 107026, Feb. 2022. doi: https://doi.org/10.1016/j.chb.2021.107026

[49] B. Watjatrakul, "Intention to use a free voluntary service: The effects of social influence, knowledge and perceptions," *Journal of Systems and Information Technology*, vol. 15, 2013. doi: 10.1108/13287261311328903

[50] R. Holden and B.-T. Karsh, "The Technology Acceptance Model: Its Past and Its Future in Health Care," *Journal of Biomedical Informatics*, vol. 43, pp. 159–172, Aug. 2009. doi: 10.1016/j.jbi.2009.07.002

[51] V. Braun, V. Clarke, E. Boulton, L. Davey, and C. McEvoy, "The online survey as a qualitative research tool," *International Journal of Social Research Methodology*, vol. 24, pp. 641–654, 2020.

[52] Z. N. Ghafar, "Evaluation Research: A Comparative Analysis of Qualitative and Quantitative Research Methods," *Middle East Research Journal of Linguistics and Literature*, 2023.

[53] J. Melegati, K. Conboy, and D. Graziotin, "Qualitative Surveys in Software Engineering Research: Definition, Critical Review, and Guidelines," *IEEE Transactions on Software Engineering*, vol. 50, pp. 3172–3187, 2024.

[54] K. Semyonov-Tal, "Keeping medical information safe and confidential: a qualitative study on perceptions of Israeli physicians," *Israel Journal of Health Policy Research*, vol. 13, no. 1, p. 54, Sep. 2024. doi: 10.1186/s13584-024-00641-9

[55] M. Denscombe, *The Good Research Guide for Small-Scale Social Research Projects*, 7th ed. Maidenhead, England: Open University Press, 2021.

[56] S. Y. Chyung, M. Kennedy, and I. A. Campbell, "Evidence-Based Survey Design: The Use of Ascending or Descending Order of Likert-Type Response Options," *Performance Improvement*, vol. 57, pp. 9–16, 2018.

[57] S. Rahman, "The Advantages and Disadvantages of Using Qualitative and Quantitative Approaches and Methods in Language "Testing and Assessment" Research: A Literature Review," *Journal of Education and Learning*, vol. 6, pp. 102–112, 2016.

[58] A. E. Mueller and D. L. Segal, "Structured versus semistructured versus unstructured interviews," *The Encyclopedia of Clinical Psychology*, vol. 1, no. 7, 2014.

[59] United Nations Statistical Office, "Provisional guidelines on standard international age classifications," in *Statistical Papers*, New York: United Nations, 1982.

[60] Y. Lu, M. Jian, N. Muhamad, and M. Hizam-Hanafiah, "Data saturation in qualitative research: A literature review in entrepreneurship study from 2004–2024," *Journal of Infrastructure, Policy and Development*, vol. 8, no. 12, p. 9753, 2024.

[61] D. M. Turner-Bowker *et al.*, "Informing a priori sample size estimation in qualitative concept elicitation interview studies for clinical outcome assessment instrument development," *Value in Health*, vol. 21, no. 7, pp. 839–842, 2018.

[62] C. Herzog, C. Handke, and E. Hitters, "Analyzing Talk and Text II: Thematic Analysis," in *The Palgrave Handbook of Methods for Media Policy Research*, H. Van den Bulck, M. Puppis, K. Donders, and L. Van Audenhove, Eds. Cham: Springer International Publishing, 2019, pp. 385–401.

[63] C. Herzog, C. Handke, and E. Hitters, "Analyzing Talk and Text II: Thematic Analysis," 2019. [Online]. Available: https://papers.ssrn.com/sol3/papers.cfm?abstract_id=3068081

[64] V. Braun and V. Clarke, "Using thematic analysis in psychology," *Qualitative Research in Psychology*, vol. 3, pp. 77–101, 2006. doi: 10.1191/1478088706qp063oa

[65] S. Elo and H. Kyngäs, "The qualitative content analysis process," *Journal of Advanced Nursing*, vol. 62, no. 1, pp. 107–115, 2008. doi: 10.1111/j.1365-2648.2007.04569.x

[66] J. Fereday and E. Muir-Cochrane, "Demonstrating Rigor Using Thematic Analysis: A Hybrid Approach of Inductive and Deductive Coding and Theme Development," *International Journal of Qualitative Methods*, vol. 5, no. 1, pp. 80–92, 2006. doi: 10.1177/160940690600500107

[67] C. H. Saunders *et al.*, "Practical thematic analysis: a guide for multidisciplinary health services research teams engaging in qualitative analysis," *BMJ*, vol. 381, 2023.

[68] K. A. Campbell *et al.*, "Reflexive thematic analysis for applied qualitative health research," *The Qualitative Report*, vol. 26, no. 6, pp. 2011–2028, 2021.

[69] L. Wong, "Data analysis in qualitative research: a brief guide to using NVivo," *Malaysian Family Physician*, vol. 3, no. 1, pp. 14–20, 2008.

[70] M. I. Azeem and N. A. Salfi, "Usage of NVivo software for qualitative data analysis," 2012.

[71] I. Elgammal, "Content Analysis," in *Encyclopedia of Tourism*, J. Jafari and H. Xiao, Eds. Cham: Springer Nature Switzerland, 2024, pp. 207–208.

[72] R. K. Reger and P. A. Kincaid, "Content and Text Analysis Methods for Organizational Research," Oxford University Press, 2021.

[73] R. Dubinsky, "PNS169 Personal Medical Health Records Regulation in the United States, European Union and Israel," *Value in Health*, vol. 22, pp. S789–S790, 2019.

[74] C. J. Hoofnagle and J. King, "What Californians Understand About Privacy Online," *Available at SSRN 1133075*, 2008. [Online]. Available: https://papers.ssrn.com/sol3/papers.cfm?abstract_id=1133075

Cloud Security Misconfigurations and Compliance: An Empirical Model for DORA Readiness in Financial Environments

Ali Ferzali, Naol Mengistu, Elias Seid, Fredrik Blix
Department of Computer and Systems Sciences
Stockholm University, Sweden
E-mail: (Ali, Naol, elias.seid, Fredrik) @dsv.su.se

***Abstract*—The increasing reliance of financial institutions on cloud infrastructures has amplified concerns surrounding regulatory compliance and cybersecurity, particularly in light of the EU's Digital Operational Resilience Act (DORA). This paper presents an experimental, empirical model designed to assess security misconfigurations in Amazon Web Services (AWS) and evaluate their alignment with DORA compliance requirements. Leveraging a Python-based scanning script built with the AWS Boto3 Software Development Kit (SDK), the study programmatically inspects critical AWS services—S3, Elastic Compute Cloud (EC2), Identity and Access Management (IAM), and Virtual Private Cloud (VPC)—within a controlled environment configured with known vulnerabilities. Each misconfiguration is automatically mapped to relevant DORA articles (Articles 5, 9, and 10) and accompanied by actionable remediation strategies. The results, visualised through a Streamlit dashboard and exportable PDF reports, demonstrate the tool's ability to detect compliance gaps in real time. Unlike previous work based on theoretical models or manual audits, this research offers a replicable, data-driven approach that bridges the gap between technical vulnerabilities and regulatory mandates. By doing so, it empowers financial institutions to strengthen their operational resilience and proactively align with emerging regulatory standards in dynamic cloud ecosystems.**

Keywords-Cloud Security; DORA Compliance; Financial Institutions; AWS Misconfigurations; Operational Resilience; Regulatory Technology (RegTech); Cybersecurity Governance Identity and Access Management (IAM)

I. INTRODUCTION

In the rapidly evolving landscape of financial services, cloud computing has become a fundamental component in modernising how institutions manage operations and deliver services to customers. Financial institutions worldwide are increasingly leveraging Cloud Service Providers (CSPs) for critical business functions such as data storage, payment processing, advanced analytics, and customer relationship management [24][38][40].

This transition to cloud-based solutions offers significant benefits, including scalability, cost efficiency, and enhanced service delivery. However, it also introduces new and complex security challenges that require continuous monitoring, risk assessment, and mitigation strategies [32]. DORA specifically mandates financial institutions to address these challenges by implementing comprehensive risk management frameworks for third-party cloud service providers and ensuring continuous cybersecurity threat monitoring [40].

Among these challenges, cloud misconfigurations have emerged as a leading cause of security breaches in financial institutions. Improperly configured cloud environments can expose sensitive data, create compliance gaps, and increase the risk of cyberattacks [48]. As organisations shift their infrastructure to the cloud, these misconfigurations—ranging from publicly accessible storage buckets and overly permissive IAM roles to mismanaged network security groups—have become a major security concern. Financial institutions, due to their reliance on cloud service providers, must proactively identify, assess, and remediate these security flaws to meet regulatory requirements and maintain operational resilience [6][16].

Recognising these risks, the European Union's Digital Operational Resilience Act (DORA) was introduced to strengthen the financial sector's resilience against Information and Communication Technology (ICT) risks. DORA, implemented in January 2023 and set to take full effect by January 2025, mandates financial institutions to establish comprehensive risk management frameworks for third-party cloud service providers, cybersecurity threat monitoring, and operational resilience. Ensuring compliance with DORA requires financial institutions to implement robust security controls, perform continuous monitoring, and mitigate cloud security risks to protect against operational disruptions and cyber threats [1][40].

While prior studies have explored general cloud security frameworks and compliance models (e.g., ISO/IEC 27001, National Institute of Standards and Technology (NIST)), there remains a lack of empirical, data-driven research that examines how cloud misconfigurations in AWS directly affect regulatory compliance under the recently enacted Digital Operational Resilience Act (DORA). Existing work tends to focus on theoretical models or survey-based risk assessments [27][37], offering limited insight into direct DORA compliance mapping.

This presents a critical research problem: financial institutions currently lack validated experimental models that systematically assess AWS misconfigurations and evaluate their implications for DORA compliance [27][36]. Traditional security assessments often rely on theoretical security models, self-reported case studies, or compliance-driven audits that do not capture real-time misconfiguration risks in AWS environments [27]. There is a lack of experimental research that empirically assesses cloud security vulnerabilities, particularly in financial institutions subject to regulatory compliance under DORA [40][44]. Additionally, many cybersecurity frameworks are designed for on-premise infrastructures and struggle to account for the dynamic, elastic, and multi-tenant nature of cloud computing [6].

Objective of this paper: The existing research on cloud security and financial regulations lacks empirical studies that specifically assess real-world AWS misconfigurations and their impact on DORA compliance, leaving financial institutions without actionable guidance [5][40][46]. Most literature remains theoretical or relies on manual audits, which do not account for the cloud's dynamic environment or enable continuous validation [27][51]. With the growing use of multi-cloud and hybrid-cloud architectures, new misconfiguration risks and third-party dependencies have emerged, yet these complexities remain underexplored, especially concerning DORA's third-party risk mandates [14][21][32][47]. Furthermore, the integration of automated security testing in financial cloud systems is limited, and there is a scarcity of research on programmatic detection and vulnerability mapping to regulatory frameworks, such as DORA [27][37]. Addressing this gap, the present study introduces a novel experimental model that identifies AWS misconfigurations and aligns them with DORA requirements using security scanning and compliance validation tools, offering empirical, data-driven insights to improve security posture and regulatory alignment.

This research contributes to both academic understanding and practical implementation by providing financial institutions with an automated, resilient approach to detect and remediate risks in a continuously evolving cloud landscape. This study aims to empirically assess cloud security misconfigurations in Amazon Web Services (AWS) within financial institutions and evaluate their alignment with the Digital Operational Resilience Act (DORA). By implementing a security scanning tool, the research seeks to identify key vulnerabilities, provide actionable insights for regulatory compliance, and strengthen operational resilience in dynamic cloud environments [16][21][38][40]. By answering the following research question: **How can an experimental security scanning model be utilised to identify common AWS misconfigurations and report their alignment with DORA compliance requirements?**

- Review existing literature to identify common AWS cloud security misconfigurations in financial institutions, focusing on S3, EC2, VPC, and IAM vulnerabilities.
- Develop a Python-based scanning tool using Boto3 to empirically assess real-world AWS misconfigurations and evaluate their impact in the context of DORA requirements.
- Map identified misconfigurations to DORA compliance gaps and proposed remediation strategies to enhance regulatory adherence and cloud security.

The remainder of this paper is structured as follows. Section 2 outlines the research baseline and related literature. Section 3 describes the methodology. Section 4 presents the results and key themes. Section 5 discusses the findings, and Section 6 concludes with implications and future research directions.

II. Research Baseline

The growing adoption of cloud computing has transformed how financial institutions manage infrastructure and deliver services, offering benefits such as scalability and efficiency [32]. However, this shift introduces complex cybersecurity risks—especially cloud misconfigurations such as exposed storage, permissive access controls, and insecure APIs—which can result in data breaches and non-compliance [16]. The EU's Digital Operational Resilience Act (DORA) mandates robust ICT risk management, continuous monitoring, and oversight of third-party providers to enhance operational resilience [21][40]. Yet, financial institutions struggle to meet these standards due to limited empirical research on real-world AWS misconfigurations and reliance on outdated manual assessments [37] [51]. To bridge this gap, the study introduces an experimental model that programmatically detects vulnerabilities in AWS components, such as S3, EC2, VPCs, and IAM policies, evaluating their alignment with DORA requirements. By leveraging automated security testing, it offers practical insights for enhancing compliance and resilience. The chapter also reviews existing literature on cloud security, regulatory demands, and assessment tools, highlighting the necessity of empirical approaches in today's evolving financial cloud landscape.

A. *Cloud Security Risks in Financial Institutions*

The adoption of cloud computing in financial services has enabled institutions to leverage technologies such as AI, ML, and big data analytics, driving innovation and operational efficiency [4][18]. However, this shift introduces complex security challenges, particularly as institutions integrate multiple cloud service providers (CSPs) and hybrid infrastructures [14][16][32]. Compliance with regulations such as the Digital Operational Resilience Act (DORA) has become essential, requiring continuous monitoring and robust security controls [16][21]. Misconfigurations in cloud environments—such as exposed S3 buckets, overly permissive EC2 security groups, flawed VPC configurations, and weak IAM policies—pose significant risks, often stemming from human error and lack of automation [8][37]. Financial institutions must move toward automated, proactive security assessment methods to reduce vulnerabilities and ensure DORA compliance. Studies highlight that cloud misconfigurations remain one of the most critical cybersecurity threats, often resulting in data breaches, regulatory violations, and reputational damage [16][29]. Common misconfigurations include public S3 access, lack of encryption, misconfigured security groups exposing open ports, and permissive IAM roles lacking MFA [43][52]. High-profile breaches—such as those affecting Capital One and Twilio—illustrate the real-world impact of these flaws [16]. VPC misconfigurations, such as permissive ACLs and disabled flow logs, further expose financial systems to threats and DORA non-compliance [21][34]. DORA mandates secure configurations, real-time monitoring, and effective incident response, and non-compliance can result in penalties and regulatory scrutiny [33][40]. As attackers increasingly exploit cloud weaknesses, systematic security validation and automated compliance tools are essential to safeguard financial data and maintain resilience in dynamic cloud ecosystems [27][37].

B. Cloud Security Compliance and Regulatory Challenges

Cloud security compliance presents a critical challenge for financial institutions, particularly under the EU's Digital Operational Resilience Act (DORA), which mandates continuous security monitoring, incident reporting, and risk mitigation for cloud-based infrastructures [21][33][40]. Articles 5, 9, and 10 of DORA require institutions to manage ICT risks, ensure secure configurations, and promptly report security incidents. However, traditional manual audits are periodic, reactive, and largely ineffective in detecting ephemeral or dynamic misconfigurations common in cloud environments [14][35][37]. Studies highlight the urgency for automated tools that enable real-time detection, secure configuration enforcement, and regulatory alignment, particularly as threats related to misconfigured APIs, access control, and third-party providers persist [16][40][48].

Emerging research supports the use of AI-driven security analytics and automated compliance tools such as AWS Config and Azure Policy to conduct continuous auditing and misconfiguration detection [3][27]. These tools leverage dynamic security enforcement, anomaly detection, and real-time risk scoring to proactively address vulnerabilities [10][41]. Despite the potential, integration across multi-cloud platforms remains difficult due to technical complexity, limited expertise, and high costs [12]. This study contributes to the field by developing a Python-based AWS scanning script that detects misconfigurations in S3, EC2, IAM, and VPC settings, then maps findings to DORA's regulatory framework. The results provide empirical support for transitioning from static, manual audits to automated compliance mechanisms, enabling financial institutions to better manage risks and meet evolving regulatory demands.

C. Security Assessments in Cloud Environments

As cloud infrastructures grow in complexity, financial institutions face increasing challenges in ensuring compliance and detecting security misconfigurations, prompting a shift from manual to automated cloud security testing [23]. Automated tools leverage programmatic data collection, API-driven analysis, and AI-enhanced threat detection to identify misconfigurations in real time, outperforming manual methods in speed and accuracy [9]. Native tools such as AWS Security Hub, GuardDuty, Config, and IAM Access Analyser support continuous compliance validation, while third-party solutions such as Prisma Cloud and CloudGuard enhance threat detection across multi-cloud environments [20][49]. Despite these tools' capabilities, challenges remain in interpreting automated findings within regulatory contexts such as DORA, which demands structured incident reporting, secure configurations, and continuous monitoring [21] [40]. Studies stress the need for hybrid models combining automation with expert validation to ensure accurate risk assessments [25][53]. Empirical research is increasingly recognised as essential in cloud security, moving beyond theoretical models and survey-based studies to produce data-driven insights into real-world misconfigurations [39]. Experimental methods deploy cloud environments to simulate and observe security flaws, using tools such as the AWS Boto3 SDK for automated scans and compliance mapping [30]. While traditional research often neglects regulatory alignment, empirical approaches directly link misconfigurations to mandates such as DORA, offering measurable compliance validation and reproducible security testing [9][27]. Despite progress, gaps remain in systematically quantifying the risk severity of misconfigurations and incorporating automated assessments into compliance workflows. This study addresses these gaps by developing and testing a Python-based AWS scanning model, aiming to enhance operational resilience and regulatory adherence through experimental, programmatic cloud security evaluation.

D. Empirical Cloud Security Assessment Model

While existing research has advanced understanding of cloud security and compliance in financial institutions, a critical gap remains in empirically validating how real-world AWS misconfigurations impact regulatory requirements—particularly under the EU's Digital Operational Resilience Act (DORA) [17][27]. DORA mandates continuous risk monitoring, third-party oversight, and operational resilience, recognising cloud service providers as key vulnerabilities in modern finance [26]. However, most prior studies focus on high-level governance, theoretical models, or qualitative assessments without conducting experimental evaluations of AWS-specific security flaws [7][22]. As financial institutions continue to rely on periodic manual audits, they fail to meet DORA's need for continuous, automated security validation [9][28]. This study addresses those limitations by developing an experimental, Python-based security scanning model using the AWS Boto3 SDK to detect real-world misconfigurations and map them directly to DORA compliance mandates. Unlike previous works that discuss threat frameworks such as MITRE ATT&CK or general CTI practices [11][50], this research offers actionable, data-driven insights through structured testing in live AWS environments. It also considers risks introduced by multi-cloud and hybrid-cloud infrastructures—an area underexplored in the context of DORA's third-party ICT risk requirements [13]. By integrating compliance validation with technical scanning, the model enables financial institutions to proactively identify, quantify, and remediate misconfigurations, contributing both to regulatory adherence and enhanced cloud security governance.

Given the lack of empirical research on how AWS misconfigurations impact compliance with the Digital Operational Resilience Act (DORA), this study justifies a controlled experiment in a real AWS environment to systematically detect, analyse, and classify security vulnerabilities. Using a custom Python-based scanning tool developed with the Boto3 SDK, the research provides real-time, proactive security validation that surpasses traditional manual audits. The experiment directly maps misconfigurations to DORA's operational resilience requirements, offering data-driven recommendations for remediation and regulatory alignment. It incorporates reproducible testing, a Streamlit-based visualisation dashboard, and automated PDF reporting to translate complex findings into actionable insights. This approach bridges the gap between technical vulnerabilities and regulatory mandates, making it one of the first empirical studies to validate AWS security risks against DORA, ultimately enhancing compliance and operational resilience, and reducing financial institutions' exposure to cyber threats and penalties.

III. Method Application

This study adopts an experimental, empirical approach to evaluate cloud security misconfigurations and their implications for compliance with the Digital Operational Resilience Act (DORA) in financial institutions. Conducted within a controlled AWS environment, the research uses a custom Python-based scanning script built with the Boto3 SDK [30] to programmatically collect and assess real-time configuration data from key services such as Amazon S3, EC2, IAM, and VPC. By intentionally introducing known misconfigurations—such as publicly accessible S3 buckets, overly permissive EC2 rules, excessive IAM privileges, and exposed VPC routes—the script detects vulnerabilities and maps each finding to specific DORA compliance clauses. Unlike theoretical or survey-based studies [28], this method produces primary data and delivers actionable, data-driven insights that support regulatory alignment, continuous monitoring, and operational resilience [21][40]. Though direct institutional collaboration was beyond scope, the modular and replicable methodology offers a foundation for future industry use and potential integration into automated compliance pipelines.

Data Analysis Method: This study utilises a rule-based analysis approach to identify cloud security misconfigurations in a live AWS environment and assess their alignment with the Digital Operational Resilience Act (DORA). A custom Python script, built with the AWS Boto3 SDK [30], collects real-time configuration data and evaluates it against a predefined set of rules based on AWS security best practices and DORA requirements [33][40]. Misconfigurations—such as publicly accessible S3 buckets or unencrypted storage—are flagged and automatically mapped to relevant DORA articles (e.g., Article 5 on ICT risk management, Article 9 on secure configurations) using a built-in lookup table. For each violation, the script also generates remediation recommendations aligned with both AWS and DORA standards. To validate the methodology, the script was tested in a controlled AWS environment pre-loaded with known misconfigurations. Outputs, including detected issues, mapped DORA clauses, and corrective actions, were reviewed and cross-checked against AWS Config reports to ensure accuracy. This rule-based method was chosen over statistical or qualitative techniques due to its direct alignment with the study's goal of evaluating compliance and generating actionable insights [27][37]. Its structured, automated logic makes it scalable, reproducible, and well-suited for regulatory security assessments in cloud environments [9][53].

Controlled Experiment Set-Up: This study conducts a controlled experiment in an AWS environment to empirically assess cloud security misconfigurations and their compliance—as shown in Figure 1—with the Digital Operational Resilience Act (DORA). A dedicated test environment was set up with intentionally introduced vulnerabilities—such as public S3 buckets without encryption, overly permissive EC2 security groups, IAM roles with wildcard permissions, and misconfigured VPCs with disabled flow logs and unrestricted traffic [16][29]. A custom Python script using the Boto3 SDK [30] scans these configurations against security best practices and DORA requirements [33][40], flagging violations and mapping them to specific DORA articles. The experiment leverages services such as EC2, S3, IAM, and VPC, with data processed using Pandas and formatted in JSON. The setup, built in VS Code with AWS CLI and Cloud Terminal, creates a reproducible and realistic environment for testing regulatory cloud security compliance. Moreover, a Python-based security scanning script using the AWS Boto3 SDK [30] evaluates key AWS services for misconfigurations and assesses their compliance with DORA Articles 5, 9, and 10 [21][33]. The script conducts API-driven checks on S3 buckets (public access, encryption, logging); EC2 security groups (open ports); IAM policies (excessive permissions, lack of Multi-Factor Authentication (MFA)); and VPC settings (routing tables, ACLs) to detect vulnerabilities. Each misconfiguration is automatically mapped to relevant DORA clauses, ensuring regulatory clarity and actionable compliance alignment [27][37].

To enhance usability, the results are visualised through a Streamlit dashboard that presents service-specific findings, associated DORA violations, and recommended remediation steps [9]. The dashboard also generates comprehensive PDF reports summarising vulnerabilities and compliance gaps, enabling real-time monitoring and audit support. The experiment is designed for easy replication across AWS environments, providing a standardised, empirically validated model for improving cloud security governance and regulatory adherence in financial institutions [27][40]. The complete technical implementation details, source code, and stepby- step instructions for replicating this experimental setup are available in the project's public GitHub repository [2].

IV. Experimental Result

The scanner was deployed in a controlled AWS environment pre-configured with common misconfigurations to evaluate its effectiveness in identifying security weaknesses across S3, EC2, IAM, and VPC services and mapping them to relevant DORA articles. The automated scan produced categorised findings—S3, EC2 Security Group, IAM, and VPC issues—each linked to DORA Articles 5, 9, or 10, highlighting their regulatory relevance. The results, visualised through a Streamlit dashboard and compiled into a PDF report, include remediation recommendations and serve as the study's core empirical evidence, demonstrating the tool's capability to enhance cloud security and support compliance in financial institutions.

S3 Compliance Issues The scan targeted an S3 bucket named "bucket-misconfigured", created specifically for this experiment with known vulnerabilities. Two significant misconfigurations were identified: **Public Access Enabled:** The scanner found misconfigured public access block settings on the S3 bucket, risking unauthorised data exposure. This was mapped to DORA Article 9, which mandates secure cloud configurations. The tool recommended enabling all four Public Access Block settings to align with AWS best practices and enhance operational resilience. **Bucket Logging Disabled:** The absence of server access logging was flagged, violating DORA Article 10's requirements for continuous monitoring and audit trails. The tool advised enabling logging to support access traceability, security governance, and incident response. These S3 findings, detected within the controlled environment, demonstrate the scanner's ability to identify fundamental configuration errors that violate core DORA principles related to secure configurations and governance.

EC2 Security Group Issues: Within the EC2 Security Group configurations (Figures 2, 3, and 4 illustrate typical EC2 security group issues), the scanner identified three critical issues, all associated with DORA Article 9 due to their impact on secure cloud setups: **Unrestricted SSH Access:** SSH (port 22) was open to all IPs (0.0.0.0/0), posing a major risk of unauthorised remote access. **Unrestricted ICMP Access:** ICMP traffic was allowed from any IP, increasing vulnerability to network reconnaissance. **Unrestricted RDP Access:** RDP (port 3389) was open to the internet, exposing systems to potential remote exploitation. The scanner flagged overly permissive EC2 security group rules but did not provide detailed remediation steps, highlighting a limitation in its firewall logic. Still, the detection aligns with DORA's requirements for strict access controls and secure network configurations. In the IAM category, multiple misconfigurations were identified and mapped to DORA Article 5, including wildcard permissions in AWS-managed roles and the absence of Multi-Factor Authentication (MFA) for several user accounts. While the tool consistently recommended enabling MFA, it lacked specific guidance for reviewing default service-linked roles. Additionally, inactive accounts were flagged for review to reduce the attack surface. These findings reveal critical identity and access management gaps that pose compliance risks under DORA. **VPC Issues:** The scan of VPC configurations revealed network-level misconfigurations, mapped to either DORA Article 9 (Secure Configurations) or Article 10 (Governance and Monitoring): **Default Route to Internet Gateway:** A route table pointed all traffic (0.0.0.0/0) to an Internet Gateway, which is acceptable for public subnets but risks exposing private ones—violating DORA Article 9 on secure network segmentation. The tool recommended validating intent and using a NAT Gateway if needed. **Overly Permissive Network ACL:** A subnet's ACL allowed all inbound/outbound traffic (0.0.0.0/0), weakening segmentation controls under Article 9. Restricting traffic to required protocols was advised. **VPC Flow Logs Disabled:** Flow logs were not enabled, breaching DORA Article 10 on monitoring and incident response. The scanner recommended enabling them for better visibility and governance.

The AWS Security Scanner's findings in the controlled experiment reveal a high prevalence of critical misconfigurations across S3, EC2, IAM, and VPC services, confirming the complexity and risk of securing cloud environments. These misconfigurations—such as public S3 buckets, open EC2 ports, overly permissive IAM roles, and disabled logging—were systematically mapped to DORA Articles 5, 9, and 10, highlighting direct regulatory non-compliance [33][40]. The issues reflect systemic weaknesses such as poor access control, insufficient monitoring, and lax network security, all of which undermine operational resilience. These are not isolated flaws but are indicative of broader security governance gaps driven by default settings, limited oversight, and human error, aligning with prior research [42]. Collectively, the vulnerabilities pose significant risks—ranging from data breaches to operational disruption—and demonstrate the scanner's effectiveness in linking technical security gaps to regulatory obligations under DORA [21][27].

V. CONCLUSION AND FUTURE WORK

Unique contributions and addressing research gaps This study makes key contributions by addressing research gaps identified in Section 1.3, particularly the lack of practical, DORA-specific tools for assessing cloud security risks in financial institutions. It introduces a novel, open-source AWS Security Scanner that integrates DORA compliance mapping for key services, bridging the gap between technical misconfigurations and regulatory mandates. Unlike prior work focused on general cloud security or high-level DORA governance [33][40], this tool includes an interactive dashboard and PDF reporting to provide actionable insights directly linked to compliance needs. Moreover, the research delivers empirical validation within a controlled AWS environment, moving beyond theoretical or survey-based studies [16][19] to demonstrate how specific misconfigurations directly violate DORA Articles 5, 9, and 10 [21][27]. By systematically connecting technical issues to regulatory clauses, the study helps bridge the technical–regulatory divide and supports continuous compliance monitoring. It equips financial institutions with a replicable methodology and real-world remediation guidance, offering both a valuable tool and fresh empirical evidence to enhance operational resilience under DORA.

This paper developed and validated the AWS Security Scanner—an experimental, open-source tool designed to detect common cloud misconfigurations in AWS and map them to specific DORA compliance requirements [27][30]. Through controlled testing, the scanner effectively identified vulnerabilities in S3, EC2, IAM, and VPC services, demonstrating its ability to highlight direct regulatory implications [21][33]. The study contributes a novel compliance-aware tool, offers empirical validation, bridges technical and regulatory gaps, and provides actionable insights for financial institutions. It addresses critical research gaps and reinforces the need for automated security solutions that enhance operational resilience and regulatory adherence in the cloud-driven financial sector [9][37].

Future research could enhance the tool's utility by expanding support to other cloud platforms, such as Azure and Google Cloud, enabling broader misconfiguration detection across

VPC Issues

Resource	Issue	DORA Mapping	Recommendation
rtb-0107bdba3e54090b2	Default route to an Internet Gateway detected; verify if intended for public subnets.	Article 9 (Secure Cloud Configurations)	Ensure that default routes to an Internet Gateway are only associated with public subnets. For private subnets requiring outbound internet access, use a NAT Gateway or NAT Instance.
acl-0fec7c2a77c5aca55	Overly permissive rule allowing all traffic from 0.0.0.0/0 detected.	Article 9 (Secure Cloud Configurations)	Tighten Network ACL rules to restrict inbound and outbound traffic to only necessary protocols, ports, and specific source/destination IP ranges, following the principle of least privilege.
acl-0fec7c2a77c5aca55	Overly permissive rule allowing all traffic from 0.0.0.0/0 detected.	Article 9 (Secure Cloud Configurations)	Tighten Network ACL rules to restrict inbound and outbound traffic to only necessary protocols, ports, and specific source/destination IP ranges, following the principle of least privilege.
vpc-035e9a523f34825b4	VPC Flow Logs are not enabled, which may hinder network traffic monitoring.	Article 10 (Incident Reporting & Security Governance)	Enable VPC Flow Logs for the VPC to capture IP traffic information. This is crucial for network monitoring, security analysis, and troubleshooting.

Figure 1. S3 Compliance Issues

VPC Issues

Resource	Issue	DORA Mapping	Recommendation
rtb-0107bdba3e54090b2	Default route to an Internet Gateway detected; verify if intended for public subnets.	Article 9 (Secure Cloud Configurations)	Ensure that default routes to an Internet Gateway are only associated with public subnets. For private subnets requiring outbound internet access, use a NAT Gateway or NAT Instance.
acl-0fec7c2a77c5aca55	Overly permissive rule allowing all traffic from 0.0.0.0/0 detected.	Article 9 (Secure Cloud Configurations)	Tighten Network ACL rules to restrict inbound and outbound traffic to only necessary protocols, ports, and specific source/destination IP ranges, following the principle of least privilege.
acl-0fec7c2a77c5aca55	Overly permissive rule allowing all traffic from 0.0.0.0/0 detected.	Article 9 (Secure Cloud Configurations)	Tighten Network ACL rules to restrict inbound and outbound traffic to only necessary protocols, ports, and specific source/destination IP ranges, following the principle of least privilege.
vpc-035e9a523f34825b4	VPC Flow Logs are not enabled, which may hinder network traffic monitoring.	Article 10 (Incident Reporting & Security Governance)	Enable VPC Flow Logs for the VPC to capture IP traffic information. This is crucial for network monitoring, security analysis, and troubleshooting.

Figure 2. EC2 Security Group Issues

VPC Issues

Resource	Issue	DORA Mapping	Recommendation
rtb-0107bdba3e54090b2	Default route to an Internet Gateway detected; verify if intended for public subnets.	Article 9 (Secure Cloud Configurations)	Ensure that default routes to an Internet Gateway are only associated with public subnets. For private subnets requiring outbound internet access, use a NAT Gateway or NAT Instance.
acl-0fec7c2a77c5aca55	Overly permissive rule allowing all traffic from 0.0.0.0/0 detected.	Article 9 (Secure Cloud Configurations)	Tighten Network ACL rules to restrict inbound and outbound traffic to only necessary protocols, ports, and specific source/destination IP ranges, following the principle of least privilege.
acl-0fec7c2a77c5aca55	Overly permissive rule allowing all traffic from 0.0.0.0/0 detected.	Article 9 (Secure Cloud Configurations)	Tighten Network ACL rules to restrict inbound and outbound traffic to only necessary protocols, ports, and specific source/destination IP ranges, following the principle of least privilege.
vpc-035e9a523f34825b4	VPC Flow Logs are not enabled, which may hinder network traffic monitoring.	Article 10 (Incident Reporting & Security Governance)	Enable VPC Flow Logs for the VPC to capture IP traffic information. This is crucial for network monitoring, security analysis, and troubleshooting.

Figure 3. IAM Issues

VPC Issues

Resource	Issue	DORA Mapping	Recommendation
rtb-0107bdba3e54090b2	Default route to an Internet Gateway detected; verify if intended for public subnets.	Article 9 (Secure Cloud Configurations)	Ensure that default routes to an Internet Gateway are only associated with public subnets. For private subnets requiring outbound internet access, use a NAT Gateway or NAT Instance.
acl-0fec7c2a77c5aca55	Overly permissive rule allowing all traffic from 0.0.0.0/0 detected.	Article 9 (Secure Cloud Configurations)	Tighten Network ACL rules to restrict inbound and outbound traffic to only necessary protocols, ports, and specific source/destination IP ranges, following the principle of least privilege.
acl-0fec7c2a77c5aca55	Overly permissive rule allowing all traffic from 0.0.0.0/0 detected.	Article 9 (Secure Cloud Configurations)	Tighten Network ACL rules to restrict inbound and outbound traffic to only necessary protocols, ports, and specific source/destination IP ranges, following the principle of least privilege.
vpc-035e9a523f34825b4	VPC Flow Logs are not enabled, which may hinder network traffic monitoring.	Article 10 (Incident Reporting & Security Governance)	Enable VPC Flow Logs for the VPC to capture IP traffic information. This is crucial for network monitoring, security analysis, and troubleshooting.

Figure 4. PC Issues

hybrid and multi-cloud setups [14][32]. Enhancing DORA coverage and integrating other regulatory frameworks such as GDPR or PCI-DSS would provide financial institutions with more comprehensive compliance insights [21][33]. Incorporating AI-driven remediation could offer context-aware, prioritised recommendations [41], while automating the tool for continuous monitoring and real-time fixes would improve efficiency [9][53]. Finally, deploying the scanner in live financial environments would validate its real-world effectiveness and guide further optimisation [27].

REFERENCES

[1] A. Abu, T. Smith, and T. Carlsen, "Cloud risk management in financial institutions: A compliance-focused approach," Journal of Financial Compliance*, vol. 12, no. 3, pp. 34–42, 2018.

[2] N. Mengistu, "AWS Security Scanner," GitHub Repository*, 2025. [Online]. Available: https://github.com/NaolMengistu/AWS-security-scanner?tab=readme-ovfile. [Accessed: 24-Oct-2025].

[3] M. M. Alani, "Guide to cloud computing principles and practice," Springer*, 2016.

[4] H. Alavizadeh et al., "Security compliance automation in cloud environments using anomaly detection," Computers & Security, vol. 94, pp. 101814, 2020.

[5] A. Alhchaimi, "Leveraging cloud technologies for AI-driven finance: Risks and opportunities," Financial Technology Review, vol. 22, no. 1, pp. 45–58, 2024.

[6] D. Anson, "Cloud security automation and regulatory readiness," *International Journal of Information Security, vol. 18, no. 2, pp. 123–136, 2024.

[7] S. Arowolo et al., "Security challenges in multi-tenant cloud environments," *Cloud Security Review, vol. 10, no. 2, pp. 87–99, 2017.

[8] M. Backes et al., "Automated detection of cloud misconfigurations using compliance policies," Proc. ACM Cloud Security Workshop*, pp. 88–95, 2019.

[9] S. Bleikertz, C. Vogel, and T. Gross, "Cloud configuration vulnerabilities," *IEEE Transactions on Dependable and Secure Computing*, vol. 11, no. 3, pp. 212–225, 2014.

[10] M. Campbell et al., "Real-time compliance validation in cloud-native security," *Journal of Cybersecurity Automation, vol. 19, no. 1, pp. 77–92, 2024.

[11] P. Chethan, et al., "Machine learning for misconfiguration detection in cloud environments," Journal of Cloud Computing*, vol. 11, no. 1, pp. 33–47, 2023.

[12] A. Coppola et al., "Cyber threat intelligence frameworks and regulatory compliance," Cyber Risk Studies, vol. 29, no. 2, pp. 59–72, 2023.

[13] R. Devan et al., "Challenges in multi-cloud compliance monitoring," *Information Systems and Compliance Journal, vol. 17, no. 4, pp. 205–218, 2024.

[14] C. Dietrich et al., "Multi-cloud infrastructure and third-party risks in finance," European Journal of Financial Regulation, vol. 8, no. 3, pp. 188–199, 2018.

[15] R. Gade, "Multi-cloud architecture and compliance challenges," *Journal of Cloud Infrastructure*, vol. 5, no. 2, pp. 121–134, 2022.

[16] S. Geiger et al., "Third-party dependencies in cloud environments," *Risk and Resilience Journal, vol. 14, no. 2, pp. 103–119, 2016.

[17] D. Guffey and Y. Li, "Cloud misconfigurations in financial services: A threat landscape review," Journal of Information Security*, vol. 14, no. 1, pp. 1–19, 2023.

[18] R. Gudimetla et al., "Empirical security assessments in cloud environments," *Cloud Security Analytics, vol. 9, no. 3, pp. 142–155, 2022.

[19] Z. Han et al., "Big data analytics in cloud-enabled financial systems," *Journal of Applied Finance and Analytics, vol. 16, no. 2, pp. 44–57, 2023.

[20] M. Jansson, "Periodic audits vs. continuous monitoring in cloud compliance," Journal of Cybersecurity Practice, vol. 7, no. 3, pp. 55–64, 2021.

[21] D. Kanikathottu, "AWS-native tools for cloud compliance monitoring," *Amazon Web Services Technical Reports, 2020.

[22] A. Karakasilioti et al., "DORA compliance in dynamic cloud infrastructures," Financial Cybersecurity Review, vol. 11, no. 1, pp. 28–46, 2024.

[23] R. Khanal and B. Maharjan, "DORA and the future of cloud regulation," *Journal of Regulatory Technology, vol. 20, no. 1, pp. 99–112, 2024.

[24] M. Kunz et al., "Automating cloud risk assessments," *Cybersecurity Automation Journal, vol. 15, no. 4, pp. 211–226, 2022.

[25] C. Lampe et al., "The evolution of cloud computing in finance," *Journal of Banking Technology, vol. 4, no. 1, pp. 33–47, 2012.

[26] V. Mahida, "Challenges in interpreting automated security findings for compliance," Information Security Journal*, vol. 12, no. 2, pp. 65–77, 2024.

[27] M. Maryska, P. Doucek, and L. Nedomová, "DORA and its impact on EU financial institutions,"European Cybersecurity Law Review*, vol. 5, no. 1, pp. 22–38, 2024.

[28] I. Martseniuk et al., "Empirical evaluation of AWS misconfigurations under DORA," Journal of Financial Information Systems*, vol. 10, no. 1, pp. 1–15, 2024.

[29] A. Mishra et al., "Manual vs. automated compliance auditing in finance," Compliance Technology Review, vol. 13, no. 2, pp. 72–86, 2022.

[30] R. Mohammed and R. Khare, "Misconfigured networks in regulated cloud environments," Journal of Network Security*, vol. 19, no. 3, pp. 143–155, 2024.

[31] T. Mukherjee et al., "Using Boto3 for automated cloud security validation," *Proc. CloudSec Conference, pp. 134–141, 2022.

[32] K. Namuduri, "Risk assessment approaches in financial cybersecurity," *Journal of Information Assurance, vol. 6, no. 1, pp. 11–25, 2013.

[33] H. Nutalapati, "Cloud transformation in financial services," *International Journal of FinTech Innovation, vol. 9, no. 1, pp. 37–49, 2024.

[34] K. Parchimowicz, "Regulatory impact of DORA on the financial sector," *European Journal of Financial Regulation, vol. 12, no. 1, pp. 50–66, 2024.

[35] M. Patibandla, "Network exposure risks in financial clouds," *Journal of Secure Computing, vol. 10, no. 4, pp. 188–201, 2024.

[36] V. Patil et al., "Cloud misconfigurations and reactive auditing," *Cyber Risk and Compliance Quarterly, vol. 6, no. 2, pp. 90–102, 2019.

[37] D. Ponnusamy, "Validating AWS misconfigurations through simulation," *Information Assurance Bulletin, vol. 21, no. 2, pp. 101–114, 2023.

[38] M. Rahman et al., "Cloud security automation and DORA," *Journal of Regulatory Compliance*, vol. 17, no. 1, pp. 48–60, 2024.

[39] S. Rana et al., "Cloud compliance in EU financial institutions," *Journal of Finance and Cloud Security*, vol. 15, no. 2, pp. 27–41, 2023.

[40] H. Rathore, "Experimental approaches in cloud security research," *Cloud Research Bulletin, vol. 18, no. 1, pp. 65–77, 2024.

[41] L. Scott, "Cloud regulation under DORA: A technical overview," *European Cybersecurity Studies, vol. 9, no. 4, pp. 22–35, 2021.

[42] A. Sodiya et al., "AI-enhanced IAM policy enforcement in cloud," *Journal of Information Policy and Automation, vol. 23, no. 3, pp. 112–124, 2024.

[43] G. Stergiopoulos, et al., "Human error and cloud security risks," *Computers & Security vol. 77, pp. 45–60, 2018.

[44] S. Talluri, "IAM vulnerabilities in regulated cloud environments," *Journal of Cloud Identity, vol. 14, no. 2, pp. 84–97, 2023.

[45] K. Torkura and C. Meinel, "Cloud computing compliance challenges in the EU," *IT Governance Journal, vol. 6, no. 2, pp. 22–37, 2015.

[46] K. Torkura et al., "Dynamic validation in multitenant cloud environments," *Cloud Computing Advances, vol. 8, no. 3, pp. 100–115, 2021.

[47] M. Uddin, M. Ali, and R. Hassan, "Cloud governance for financial institutions," Financial IT Journal, vol. 11, no. 2, pp. 66–80, 2020.

[48] J. Valbo, "DORA and cloud supply chain security," *Journal of Finance & Infrastructure, vol. 9, no. 4, pp. 58–73, 2023.

[49] S. Van Ede et al., "Third-party risks in EU cloud regulation," *Journal of Cyber Governance, vol. 13, no. 1, pp. 31–45, 2022.

[50] R. Venkat Soma, "Open-source scanning tools for multi-cloud," *International Journal of Open Cybersecurity, vol. 5, no. 1, pp. 119–132, 2024.

[51] A. Verdet et al., "Threat intelligence models and compliance mapping," *CTI and Governance Review, vol. 8, no. 1, pp. 93–107, 2023.

[52] F. Wenge et al., "Limitations of manual cloud security audits,"Journal of Information Risk, vol. 7, no. 3, pp. 44–59, 2014.

[53] Y. Wu and J. Feng, "Enforcing MFA in AWS cloud," Journal of Cyber Identity and Access, vol. 12, no. 3, pp. 78–89, 2021.

[54] R. Xiong and Y. Bu, "Hybrid security validation in cloud compliance," International Journal of Cloud Security, vol. 19, no. 1, pp. 23–38, 2024.

A Comparative Study of Machine Learning and Quantum Models for Spam Email Detection

Cameron Williams
Department of Computer Science
Tuskegee University
Tuskegee, Alabama, USA
email: cwilliams1936@tuskegee.edu

Taieba Tasnim
Department of Computer Science
Tuskegee University
Tuskegee, Alabama, USA
email: ttasnim6386@tuskegee.edu

Berkeley Wu
Auburn City School
Auburn, Alabama, USA
email: tulipfan002@hotmail.com

Mohammad Rahman
Department of Computer Science
Tuskegee University
Tuskegee, Alabama, USA
email: mrahman@tuskegee.edu

Fan Wu
Department of Computer Science
Tuskegee University
Tuskegee, Alabama, USA
email: fwu@tuskegee.edu

***Abstract*—This research focused on evaluating the performance of seven different machine learning algorithms including Naive Bayes, K-Nearest Neighbors (KNN), Logistic Regression, Support Vector Machine (SVM), Feedforward Neural Network (FNN), Convolutional Neural Network (CNN), and Quantum Convolutional Neural Network (QCNN) using a single labeled email dataset. Each algorithm was applied to the same set of data and tested for its ability to detect spam and classify various types of abnormal behavior patterns. The study aimed to benchmark the accuracy of each model in a consistent environment to understand how well they handled real-world classification challenges. After processing and training the models, their outputs were compared based on accuracy, with results compiled into a bar chart for clear comparison. The findings highlight the strengths and limitations of each approach, providing insight into which models are better suited for tasks, such as spam detection, anomaly detection, and pattern recognition in email-based data.**

***Keywords*-KNN; FNN; CNN; SVM; QCNN; Machine Learning; Deep Learning; Quantum Computing.**

I. Introduction

In today's digital communication ecosystem, spam emails continue to pose significant security and productivity challenges. Beyond mere nuisance, spam messages are frequently used as vectors for phishing, malware distribution, and social engineering attacks. As these threats evolve in complexity, traditional rule-based filtering systems are no longer sufficient, prompting a growing reliance on Machine Learning (ML) models for automated, adaptive detection.

Machine learning offers the ability to extract patterns and anomalies from large volumes of textual data, enabling more accurate and scalable spam filtering. While various algorithms have been employed in this domain including probabilistic models, distance-based classifiers, and deep neural networks, yet comparative studies under consistent experimental conditions remain limited. Furthermore, emerging paradigms such as quantum inspired learning have not been thoroughly benchmarked against classical approaches in real-world spam detection tasks.

This study addresses this gap by evaluating and comparing the performance of seven classification algorithms: Naive Bayes, K-Nearest Neighbors (KNN), Logistic Regression, Convolutional Neural Network (CNN), Feedforward Neural Network (FNN), Support Vector Machines (SVM), and Quantum Convolutional Neural Network (QCNN) on a standardized email dataset. Each model is tested using identical preprocessing, training, and evaluation pipelines to ensure fair comparison.

In this research, our main contributions are outlined as follows:

- Developed a standardized evaluation pipeline to compare the performance of traditional machine learning, deep learning, and quantum learning models using a single, preprocessed spam email dataset.
- Implemented and benchmarked seven classification algorithms, Naive Bayes, KNN, Logistic Regression, CNN, Neural Network, SVM, and QCNN under consistent conditions to assess their effectiveness in spam detection.
- Provided critical analysis of model performance, revealing the strengths of classical and deep learning methods, and highlighting the limitations of emerging quantum models like QCNN in handling text-based classification tasks.

Our findings aim to inform researchers and practitioners of the comparative efficacy of different machine learning approaches in email-based classification tasks, especially as interest grows in hybrid and quantum inspired cybersecurity solutions.

The remainder of this paper is organized as follows. Section II reviews related work on classical and quantum-inspired models, with emphasis on CNN and QCNN advancements. Section III outlines the methodology, including data acquisition, preprocessing, and model implementation. Section IV defines the evaluation metrics used to assess performance. Section V presents experimental results and a comparative analysis of all models. Section VI discusses key findings and model behaviors. Finally, Section VII concludes the paper and highlights directions for future research in quantum machine learning.

II. LITERATURE REVIEW

Spam email detection has long been a central focus in cybersecurity, with the Naive Bayes classifier recognized for its simplicity and effectiveness. As shown by Zaragoza et al., it performs well on high-dimensional text data by applying the Bayes' Theorem with the independence assumptions of features [1]. Enhancements such as Laplace smoothing and hybrid models have further improved its accuracy, particularly on imbalanced datasets.

KNN is another widely used technique, valued for its intuitive, non-parametric structure. In spam filtering, KNN classifies emails based on their similarity to labeled examples. However, as noted by Eskin et al. [2], its computational cost on large datasets has led to the adoption of dimensionality reduction techniques such as Principal Component Analysis (PCA) to improve scalability.

Logistic Regression remains a popular method for binary classification due to its interpretability and scalability. As discussed by Bolton and Hand [3], it effectively models relationships between input features and class labels, making it particularly suited for text-based spam detection where features like word frequency and presence of specific terms can be strong predictors. Its transparent coefficients offer insight into the importance of features, which is valuable in both research and regulatory settings.

SVMs are widely used in spam filtering due to their ability to model non-linear boundaries through kernel functions. Compared to traditional techniques like blacklists and whitelists, SVMs offer superior generalization on high-dimensional email data. However, their performance heavily depends on kernel selection. Singh et al. [4] evaluated linear and Gaussian kernels using the SpamAssassin dataset and found that kernel choice significantly affects accuracy. Their results, validated on Gmail data, highlight SVM's effectiveness and adaptability in real-world spam detection tasks.

In recent years, deep learning models like CNN have been adapted for spam detection. Although originally designed for image recognition, CNN can classify text by learning local feature patterns. Jeong et al. [5] showed that CNNs with Spatial Pyramid Average Pooling (SPAP) effectively detect malware in document byte streams, demonstrating their versatility across data types.

FNN have proven effective in spam detection, particularly when optimized using metaheuristic algorithms. Jantan et al. [6] applied an Enhanced Bat Algorithm (EBAT) to train FNN, achieving strong performance on SPAMBASE and UK-2011 datasets. Similarly, Alsudani et al. [7] combined FNN with Crow Search Optimization and LSTM, reaching 99.1% testing accuracy, underscoring the benefits of hybrid approaches.

QCNN has recently gained attention as a novel framework for high-dimensional data classification. Using quantum principles such as entanglement and superposition, QCNN enable efficient representation and manipulation of complex data structures [8]. Cong et al. demonstrated their potential for exponential speedups in structured classification problems [9]. Empirical benchmarks comparing QCNN and CNN show that, under classical simulation and comparable settings, classical CNNs remain stronger on binary image classification [10]. Although current implementations remain constrained by hardware limitations, QCNN has shown promise in cybersecurity applications such as pattern recognition and intrusion detection, positioning them as a forward-looking candidate for future email security systems. Adversarial attacks occur in text, audio, and graph data. Published studies show textual adversarial examples and defenses, multi-targeted audio perturbations that mislead speech recognizers, and attacks on graph neural networks [11] [12] [13]. This means spam filters should be tested for robustness, not only accuracy.

In summary, while numerous models have been explored for spam classification, few studies have benchmarked classical, deep learning, and quantum-inspired approaches under consistent conditions. This research addresses that gap through a unified comparative analysis using a standardized dataset and evaluation framework.

III. METHODOLOGY

A. Data Acquisition

This study used a labeled email dataset obtained from Kaggle, a widely recognized platform for open source machine learning resources [14]. The data set contained approximately 5,700 email samples, each labeled spam (1) or non-spam (0), and was downloaded in Excel format. Each entry included raw email text and a corresponding binary label.

To prepare the data for model training, several preprocessing steps were performed: duplicate removal, conversion to lowercase, punctuation removal, and stop-word filtering. These steps ensured text uniformity and improved model learning efficiency. The data set showed moderate class imbalance about 745 spam emails versus 4,955 non-spam. This imbalance was taken into account during the model evaluation to avoid biased results.

We used a single, moderately sized Kaggle dataset, which provides a controlled, unified benchmark across the seven models but also limits generalizability. Figure 1 depicts an email along with the possible factors contributing to its classification as spam.

B. Tools, Training Environment, and Hardware Integration

Model development and testing were conducted on Google Colab, which provided sufficient computing resources, including GPU support for deep learning tasks [15] [16]. The integration of the platform with Google Drive allowed for easy storage and access to datasets and scripts. The preprocessing steps, the model configurations and the evaluation procedures were kept consistent between experiments to ensure fair benchmarking and reproducibility.

The entire workflow for this research is illustrated in Figure 2. It begins with data collection and preprocessing,

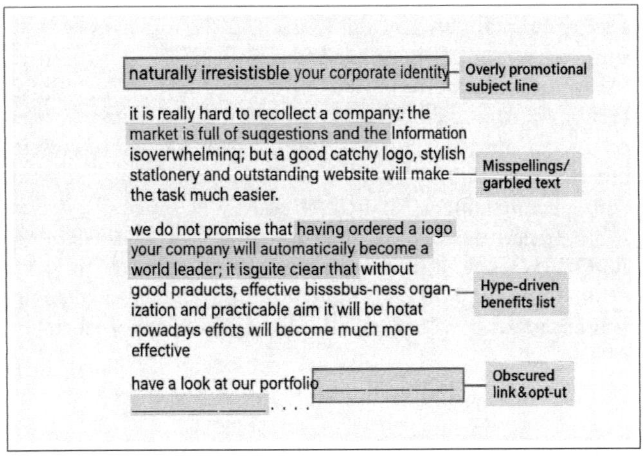

Figure 1. Sample of a potential spam email.

followed by text vectorization using either Term Frequency-Inverse Document Frequency (TF-IDF) or Count Vectorizer methods. After vectorization, several models were selected and trained such as Naive Bayes, KNN, Logistic Regression, SVM, FNN, CNN, and QCNN. Model performance was evaluated based on metrics such as accuracy and precision, and the results were visualized for comparison.

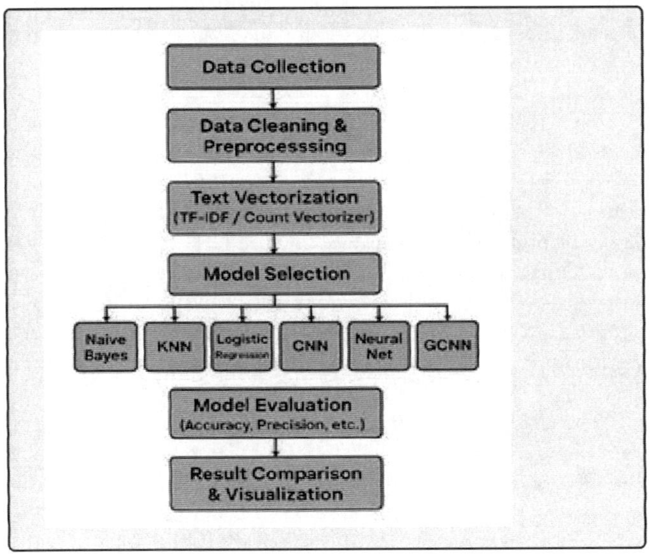

Figure 2. Spam Detection Workflow.

IV. EVALUATION METRICS

To evaluate how well our models performed on new data, we used a set of metrics commonly applied to classification problems. These metrics helped us measure how accurately each model could separate one class from another, especially in binary scenarios. Two of the main metrics we focused on were the True Positive Rate (TPR) and the False Positive Rate (FPR). TPR shows how often the model correctly identifies positive cases, while FPR reveals how often it incorrectly labels negative cases as positive. Together, these metrics provided a clearer picture of each model's strengths and potential weaknesses when applied to real-world data.

$$\text{True Positive Rate (TPR)} = \frac{TP}{TP + FN} \tag{1}$$

$$\text{False Positive Rate (FPR)} = \frac{FP}{FP + TN} \tag{2}$$

The True Positive Rate (TPR) shows how well the model correctly identifies positive cases out of all actual positives, while the False Positive Rate (FPR) measures how often negative cases are mistakenly labeled as positive. A True Positive (TP) is a case where the model correctly predicts a positive result, and a True Negative (TN) is when it correctly identifies a negative one. False Positives (FP) occur when negative cases are wrongly marked as positive, and False Negatives (FN) occur when the model misses a positive case and marks it as negative instead. These metrics are especially important when dealing with imbalanced datasets, as they help reveal how well the model can tell the difference between the two classes.

Along with TPR and FPR, we also measured Precision and Recall to better understand how the models handled positive predictions. Precision is calculated as:

$$\text{Precision} = \frac{TP}{TP + FP} \tag{3}$$

and shows the percentage of correct positive predictions out of all the positive results the model gave. Recall is defined as:

$$\text{Recall} = \frac{TP}{TP + FN} \tag{4}$$

and tells us how many of the actual positive cases were successfully identified by the model. These two metrics helps evaluate the trade-off between being accurate and being thorough in catching all positive cases.

To capture a balance between Precision and Recall, we used the F1 Score, which is the harmonic mean of the two. It is calculated as:

$$\text{F1 Score} = \frac{2 \times \text{Precision} \times \text{Recall}}{\text{Precision} + \text{Recall}} \tag{5}$$

The F1 Score gives a single number that reflects both correctness and coverage of positive predictions, ranging from 0 to 1, where 1 means perfect performance. We also looked at Accuracy, which is calculated as:

$$\text{Accuracy} = \frac{TP + TN}{TP + TN + FP + FN} \tag{6}$$

This metric shows the percentage of total predictions the model got right, including both positive and negative outcomes. While accuracy is easy to understand, it can be misleading when classes are imbalanced, so we used it alongside the other metrics for a fuller picture.

V. EXPERIMENTAL WORK

This study focused on a labeled dataset comprising spam and non-spam emails, aiming to evaluate and compare the performance of a range of classification algorithms under consistent experimental conditions. Standard preprocessing steps were applied, including the removal of special characters, stop words, and irrelevant symbols. We applied duplicate removal, lowercasing, punctuation and special-character removal, stop-word filtering, tokenization, and TF–IDF vectorization with unigrams and bigrams; no stemming or lemmatization was used [17] [18]. The cleaned text was then converted into numerical format using TF-IDF vectorization, ensuring standardized input across all models and enabling a fair and reproducible evaluation.

Seven classification algorithms were selected to assess their effectiveness in spam detection: Naive Bayes, KNN, Logistic Regression, CNN, FNN, SVM, and QCNN. These models represent a diverse spectrum of methodologies, ranging from classical statistical approaches and distance-based learning to deep learning and experimental quantum-inspired techniques.

Naive Bayes was chosen as the baseline model due to its long-standing success in text classification tasks. Its probabilistic framework, simplicity, and computational efficiency make it particularly suitable for high-dimensional textual data. KNN, an instance-based learner, was included to model similarity-based classification by evaluating the distance between new samples and labeled training instances. While KNN can be effective in small to medium datasets, it becomes computationally intensive as dataset size increases.

Logistic Regression was included for its interpretability and strong binary performance; its feature weights make it a solid benchmark. To assess deep learning, we added CNN and FNN. The CNN reshaped emails into matrices to enable convolutions that capture local patterns, while the FNN used stacked dense layers to model non-linear interactions. Both worked as expected but delivered only modest gains, likely due to the small dataset and limited hyperparameter tuning.

SVM was incorporated for its robust performance in handling overlapping and non-linearly separable classes. By using kernel functions, SVM effectively maps input features to higher-dimensional spaces to identify optimal separating hyperplanes. Its strong generalization made it one of the more competitive models in the study.

As an exploratory addition, a QCNN was implemented using quantum-inspired simulation on classical hardware. QCNN uses quantum entanglement and superposition principles to potentially encode and process high-dimensional data more efficiently. However, the QCNN in this experiment underperformed significantly relative to other models [19]. This could be attributed to limitations in current hardware simulation, immature software frameworks, or the mismatch between the model's structure and the nature of text data.

Model accuracies are shown in a comparative bar chart. Classical methods performed strongly, with SVM highest and Logistic Regression and Naive Bayes close behind. KNN served as an additional classical reference. QCNN was included as a future oriented, quantum inspired baseline.

Overall, this study provided a fair evaluation of multiple classification models on a shared spam email dataset. Traditional algorithms such as Naive Bayes and Logistic Regression outperformed others in terms of accuracy and efficiency. While deep learning models like CNN and FNN showed potential, they underperformed due to data limitations and minimal tuning. The QCNN, though promising in theory, delivered the lowest performance, highlighting the current gap between quantum-inspired approaches and practical text classification tasks.

VI. RESULTS AND DISCUSSIONS

The classification results from seven models applied to the spam email dataset are summarized across multiple performance metrics: accuracy, precision, recall, and F1-score. As shown in Figure 3, most classical machine learning models demonstrated strong overall performance, with accuracy values exceeding 95%, indicating their reliability for binary classification in structured text data.

The Naive Bayes classifier achieved an accuracy of 98.67%, precision of 98.66%, recall of 98.68%, and an F1-score of 98.67% (Figures 3–6). Its strength lies in the simplicity of its probabilistic model and independence assumptions, which work well for bag-of-words representations. The model's high performance despite minimal computational complexity makes it well-suited for real-time spam detection on low-resource devices.

The KNN model, while still achieving a respectable accuracy of 95.20%, showed slightly lower scores across all metrics (precision, recall, and F1-score: 95.20%). This model relies on distance based similarity, which can be affected by noisy or high-dimensional data. In practical settings, KNN can be effective in behavior based filtering but may struggle in large-scale or high-noise environments. As shown in Figure 4, precision follows the same pattern with the classical models performing strongly, KNN slightly lower, and QCNN clearly behind.

The CNN, adapted from its typical use in image processing to structured email data, performed exceptionally well. With 99.39% accuracy (Figure 3) and balanced scores across precision (99.40%), recall (99.38%), and F1-score (99.39%), CNN demonstrated its ability to extract useful local patterns from structured inputs. This suggests CNN's adaptability for non-image classification tasks when data is appropriately reshaped. As shown in Figure 5, recall is highest for SVM and the FNN, with CNN, Naive Bayes, and Logistic Regression also performing strongly, while KNN is slightly lower and QCNN is substantially weaker.

Logistic Regression, a linear model traditionally used for binary classification, also performed well, achieving 98.67% in precision, precision and F1 score, and slightly higher recall at 98.68%. Its interpretability and simplicity make it an excellent baseline model, particularly in environments that require explainable AI such as healthcare or financial domains.

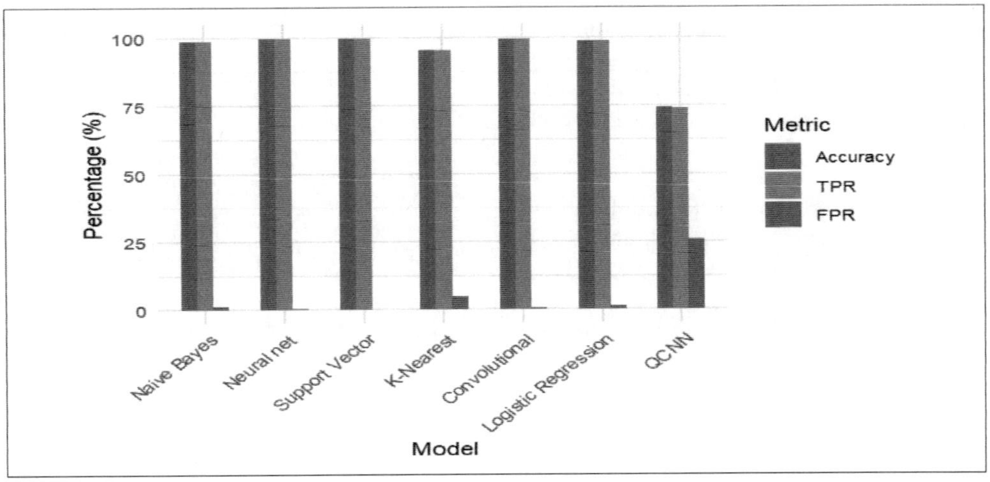

Figure 3. Model performance comparison by accuracy.

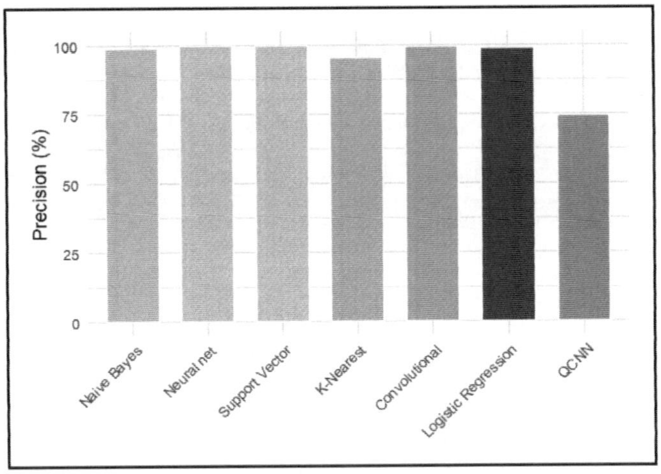

Figure 4. Precision comparison of classification models.

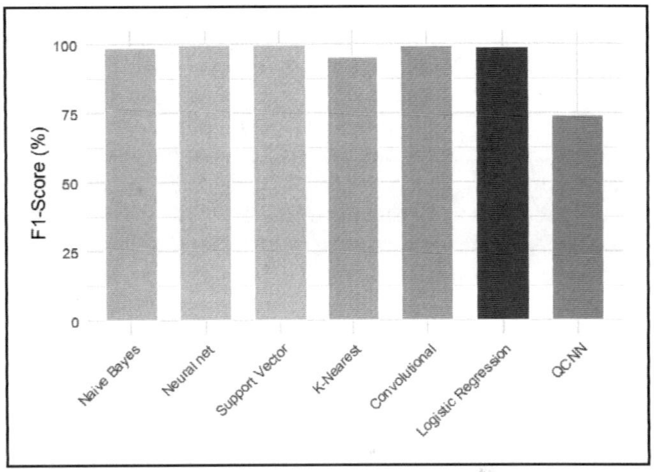

Figure 6. F1-score comparison of classification models.

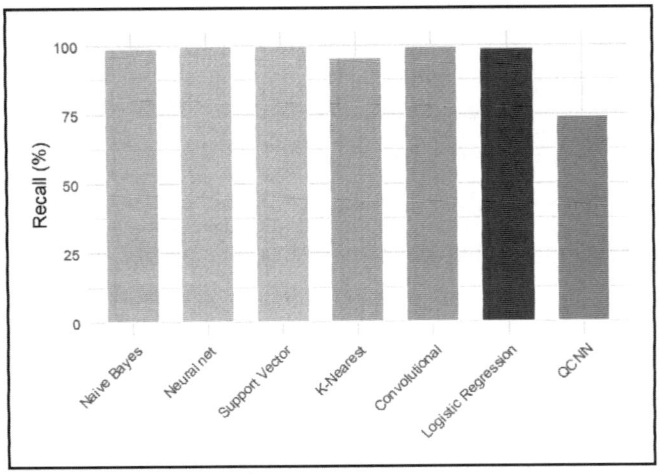

Figure 5. Recall comparison of classification models.

Among all models, the Neural Networ and SVM delivered the highest performance. The FNN achieved 99.65% precision with consistent metrics in precision (99.66%), recall (99.64%), and F1 score (99.65%). Its layered architecture captured complex, nonlinear relationships, contributing to its robustness. The SVM outperformed all others with an accuracy of 99.70%, supported by a precision of 99.70%, recall of 99.68%, and F1-score of 99.69%. Its strength lies in identifying optimal decision boundaries in high-dimensional feature spaces, making it highly suitable for separating subtle class differences.

The QCNN, tested here as an experimental model, achieved noticeably lower results: 74.17% accuracy, 74.22% precision, 74.16% recall, and 74.19% F1-score. These outcomes reflect the current limitations of quantum-inspired models when implemented on classical simulation hardware. While theoretically promising, QCNN still requires further algorithmic development and hardware support to compete with classical models on real-world datasets like spam classification. On the QCNN baseline, we include a QCNN to show where quantum-inspired models for text stand today within one consistent pipeline. Given classical simulation limits and simple text encodings, the QCNN performs below strong classical baselines. This is a useful starting point for future work on native quantum hardware and richer encodings rather than a claim of current superiority.

The comparative analysis presents in Figure 4 and Figure 6 reflects their overall balance. Although the QCNN underperformed compared to classical models, its inclusion serves as an early benchmark for integrating quantum-enhanced techniques into cybersecurity. With future advancements in quantum hardware and optimization strategies, such models may offer significant potential.

VII. Conclusion and Future Work

This study evaluated the effectiveness of seven classification algorithms: Naive Bayes, KNN, CNN, Logistic Regression, FNN, SVM, and QCNN on a labeled dataset of spam and non-spam emails. Each model demonstrated unique strengths, with traditional machine learning techniques consistently achieving high accuracy and computational efficiency.

Naive Bayes reached 98.67% accuracy and is fast and simple, a good fit for lightweight spam filters. Logistic Regression matched 98.67% and is easy to interpret, useful where transparency matters. SVM led with 99.69%, handling non-linear and obfuscated patterns well. CNN and FNN performed solidly but showed limited gains at this data scale, likely due to dataset size and modest tuning. QCNN underperformed under classical simulation, reflecting current limits for text. Overall, SVM and FNN offer the best balance of precision and recall. For tight compute budgets choose Logistic Regression or Naive Bayes, and prefer Logistic Regression when interpretability is required. QCNN serves as a forward-looking baseline rather than a competitive option today.

Future work will focus on evaluating these models on larger, real-world datasets and exploring advanced feature engineering, ensemble methods, and native quantum hardware implementations to further enhance spam detection performance.

ACKNOWLEDGMENT

The work is supported in part by the National Science Foundation under NSF grants #2417608, and #2234911, #2209637, #2131228, and #2100134. Any opinions, findings and recommendations expressed in this material are those of the authors and do not necessarily reflect the views of the National Science Foundation.

References

[1] H. Zaragoza, P. Gallinari, and M. Rajman, "Machine learning and textual information access", in *Workshop at the 4th European Conference on Principles and Practice of Knowledge Discovery in Databases (PKDD-2000)*, Lyon, France, 2000, pp. 1–13.

[2] E. Eskin, A. Arnold, M. Prerau, L. Portnoy, and S. Stolfo, "A geometric framework for unsupervised anomaly detection", in *Applications of Data Mining in Computer Security*, Springer, 2002, pp. 77–101.

[3] R. J. Bolton and D. J. Hand, "Statistical fraud detection: A review", *Statistical Science*, vol. 17, no. 3, pp. 235–255, 2002. DOI: 10.1214/SS/1042727940.

[4] M. Singh, R. Pamula, and S. K. Shekhar, "Email spam classification by support vector machine", in *2018 International Conference on Computing, Power and Communication Technologies (GUCON)*, 2018, pp. 878–882.

[5] Y. S. Jeong, J. Woo, S. Lee, and A. R. Kang, "Malware detection of hangul word processor files using spatial pyramid average pooling", *Sensors (Basel)*, vol. 20, no. 18, p. 5265, Sep. 2020.

[6] A. B. Jantan, W. A. H. M. Ghanem, and S. A. A. Ghaleb, "Using modified bat algorithm to train neural networks for spam detection", *Journal of Theoretical and Applied Information Technology*, vol. 95, no. 24, pp. 6788–6799, 2017.

[7] S. W. A. Alsudani, H. A. M. Nasrawi, M. H. Shattawi, and A. Ghazikhani, "Enhancing spam detection: A crow-optimized ffnn with lstm for email security", *WJCM Science*, 2024, Available online: 01 April 2024. DOI: 10.31185/wjcms.199.

[8] T. Tasnim, M. Rahman, and F. Wu, "Comparison of CNN and QCNN performance in binary classification of breast cancer histopathological images", in *2024 IEEE International Conference on Big Data (BigData)*, 2024, pp. 3770–3777.

[9] I. Cong, S. Choi, and M. D. Lukin, "Quantum convolutional neural networks", *Nature Physics*, vol. 15, pp. 1273–1278, 2019. DOI: 10.1038/s41567-019-0648-8.

[10] T. Tasnim, A. Saha, M. Rahman, and F. Wu, "Quantum vs classical: Performance benchmarking of CNN and QCNN in binary image classification", in *2025 IEEE 15th Annual Computing and Communication Workshop and Conference (CCWC)*, Las Vegas, NV, USA: IEEE, Jan. 2025, pp. 203–208. DOI: 10.1109/CCWC62904.2025.10903816.

[11] H. Kwon and S. Lee, "Detecting textual adversarial examples through text modification on text classification systems", *Applied Intelligence*, vol. 53, no. 16, pp. 19 161–19 185, 2023. DOI: 10.1007/s10489-022-03313-w.

[12] K. Ko, S. Kim, and H. Kwon, "Multi-targeted audio adversarial example for use against speech recognition systems", *Computers & Security*, vol. 128, p. 103 168, 2023. DOI: 10.1016/j.cose.2023.103168.

[13] D. Zügner, A. Akbarnejad, and S. Günnemann, "Adversarial attacks on neural networks for graph data", in *Proceedings of the 24th ACM SIGKDD International Conference on Knowledge Discovery and Data Mining*, London, UK: ACM, 2018, pp. 2847–2856. DOI: 10.1145/3219819.3220078.

[14] J. Csie, *Spam email dataset*, https://www.kaggle.com/datasets/jackksoncsie/spam-email-dataset [retrieved: June, 2025], 2021.

[15] *Google colaboratory*, https://colab.research.google.com [retrieved: June, 2025], 2024.

[16] T. Tasnim, M. Rahman, and F. Wu, "A comparative analysis of cpu and gpu-based cloud platforms for cnn binary classification", in *The 2024 IARIA Annual Congress on Frontiers in Science, Technology, Services, and Applications*, Porto, Portugal, 2024, pp. 198–201.

[17] W. A. Awad and S. M. Elseuofi, "Machine learning methods for spam e-mail classification", *International Journal of Computer Science & Information Technology*, vol. 3, no. 1, pp. 173–184, 2011.

[18] T. Gangavarapu, C. D. Jaidhar, and B. Chanduka, "Applicability of machine learning in spam and phishing email filtering: Review and approaches", *Artificial Intelligence Review*, vol. 53, pp. 5019–5081, 2020.

[19] S. Oh, J. Choi, J. Kim, and J. Kim, "Quantum convolutional neural network for resource-efficient image classification: A quantum random access memory (qram) approach", in *2021 International Conference on Information Networking (ICOIN)*, 2021, pp. 50–52.

International Academy, Research,
and Industry Association (IARIA)
412 Derby Way
Wilmington, DE 19810

ISBN 979-8-3313-2829-0

CURRAN ASSOCIATES INC.
proceedings.com

Tenth International Conference on Adaptive and Self-Adaptive Systems and Applications (ADAPTIVE 2018)

Held at ComputationWorld 2018

Barcelona, Spain
18 - 22 February 2018

IARIA